Children's Difficulties in Reading, Spelling and Writing

Date Due

Children's Difficulties in Reading, Spelling and Writing

Challenges and Responses

Edited by

Peter D. Pumfrey

and

Colin D. Elliott

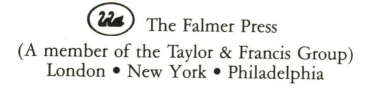 The Falmer Press

(A member of the Taylor & Francis Group)
London • New York • Philadelphia

UK   The Falmer Press, Rankine Road, Basingstoke, Hants RG24 0PR

USA   The Falmer Press, Taylor & Francis Inc., 1900 Frost Road,
        Suite 101, Bristol, PA 19007

First published 1990

British Library Cataloguing in Publication Data
Children's difficulties in reading, spelling and writing:
    challenges and responses.
    1. Primary schools: Curriculum subjects: Reading. Teaching
    2. Primary schools: Writing skills. Teaching
    I. Pumfrey, Peter D. (Peter David), *1930–*
    II. Elliott, Colin D.
    372.4

    ISBN 1–85000–690–3
    ISBN 1–85000–691–1   Pbk

Library of Congress Cataloging-in-Publiction Data
Children's difficulties in reading, spelling, and writing: challenges
    and responses/edited by Peter D. Pumfrey and
    Colin D. Elliott. p.   cm.
    ISBN 1–85000–690–3
    ISBN 1–85000–691–1 (pbk.)
    1. Learning disabled children – Education – Language arts
    2. Language arts (Elementary) – Great Britain. 3. Reading
        disability. 4. Reading – Great Britain – Remedial teaching.
        5. Literacy programs – Great Britain. I. Pumfrey, Peter D.
        (Peter David) II. Elliott, Colin D.
    LC4704.85.C487   1990
    372.4′3′0941–dc20

Jacket design by Caroline Archer

Typeset in 10½/12 Garamond by
Chapterhouse, The Cloisters, Formby L37 3PX

Printed in Great Britain by
Redwood Burn Limited, Trowbridge, Wiltshire

Contents

Acknowledgments

The editors have been greatly helped in the preparation of this book by many colleagues in various capacities. The contributors' considerable efforts in producing their respective chapters represent our major indebtedness. The authors' co-operation in meeting deadlines went well beyond the bounds of duty and contract. For their endeavours, we thank them most sincerely.

In addition, we were supported by colleagues in the Centre for Educational Guidance and Special Needs of the University of Manchester School of Education. These colleagues, together with the very considerable number of former and current students, teachers, educational psychologists, advisers, research workers and colleagues in other educational institutions who attended the series of lectures from which the book was developed, encouraged us in the venture. It was heartening that parents of children with difficulties in reading, spelling and writing also found certain parts of the programme of interest and value.

The editors, on behalf of the contributors, the audiences, and in their own editorial capacities, gratefully acknowledge the invaluable services of the staff of the In-service Education of Teachers (INSET) Unit in the University of Manchester Department of Education. The work done by Edward and Marjorie Burton, Deborah Cash and Marjorie Hendrickson contributed significantly to an enjoyable, stimulating and challenging programme.

We are also indebted to the following publishers: NFER-Nelson Publishing Company for permission to use Table 2.2 which originally appeared in the *British Ability Scales Introductory Handbook*; the British Psychological Society for permission to use Figures 3.1, 3.2 and 3.2 from a recent article in the *British Journal of Psychology* and Hodder and Stoughton Ltd. for permission to adapt Tables 12.2, 12.3 and Figure 12.4 from a book by one of the authors.

Finally, we wish to acknowledge the help and advice of the publisher's editor, Christine Cox, in bringing this book to press so quickly and efficiently. Any limitations that remain are acknowledged to be our responsibility.

Peter D. Pumfrey and Colin D. Elliott
Centre for Educational Guidance and Special Needs,
School of Education,
University of Manchester,
MANCHESTER, M13 9PL.

November, 1989.

Introduction

Peter Pumfrey and Colin Elliott

If you could not read English, it is unlikely that you would have bothered to get as far as this.

'Language expresses identity, enables co-operation, and confers freedom. In language we create a symbolic model of the world, in which past and present are carried forward into the future. Language is the naming of experience, and what we name we have power over' (Department of Education and Science, 1988: The Kingman Report, p. 7).

Most children have well-developed speaking and listening skills prior to the start of formal education. Learning to read, spell and write are among the most critically important and empowering skills that children will learn at school. The history of education testifies to the importance of literacy. In modern industrialized societies, literacy is the bedrock of education. Access to the core and foundation subjects in the National Curriculum requires that pupils become literate. The problems faced by children who have difficulty in acquiring literacy skills are matters of continuing concern, not only to their parents and teachers, but to the whole of the education service, various helping professions and to society itself.

The current estimates of adult illiteracy in the United Kingdom, the United States and elsewhere, indicate that their respective educational systems have many important lessons to learn in the interests of the pupils, their parents and the societies whom the systems are designed to serve. The prevention of later literacy difficulties has much to commend it educationally and economically. This indicates that increased attention to the efficacy of school literacy programmes is essential.

The editors have, for many years, been involved in trying to understand, identify and alleviate children's literacy difficulties. Currently contributions are made to a variety of taught courses and research programmes in this area. The former include a two-year part-time course for qualified and experienced teachers in the study of Specific Learning Difficulties (Literacy), courses on Children's Reading Difficulties in other Advanced Diploma and Master of

Education programmes, and the training of Educational Psychologists. In the research field, the editors are currently involved in a national survey of LEA policies and provision concerning specific learning difficulties and dyslexia. They are also engaged in the development of diagnostic and attainment tests and assessment techniques. In connection with this teaching and research, a series of evening lectures was given by visiting specialists at the University of Manchester during the 1988–1989 session. Their contributions have been edited and comprise the present book.

The book reflects a wide range of issues regarding children's literacy problems, mainly at the primary school level. Some of the authors are principally interested in how young children normally learn to read and spell, and also in how later reading and spelling difficulties can be *prevented* or *reduced*. Other contributors have devoted themselves to helping *alleviate* the problems of the many pupils in mainstream schools who have been identified as having difficulties in learning to read, spell and write. A sub-set of authors consider the rarer phenomena of children who have proved unusually resistant to good mainstream teaching methods and who have specific learning difficulties (literacy), or specific developmental dyslexia.

The purposes of this book are twofold: first, in Part 1, to identify some challenges in the field of literacy and, second, in Part 2, to give an account of various responses to these challenges.

Part 1 starts with a consideration of a major challenge facing the teaching profession: the importance of literacy in the National Curriculum. Then follow two chapters on the definition and identification of various types of specific learning difficulties. These are highly controversial issues with important implications for policy, resources, theory and practice. Part 1 concludes with another equally complex and controversial area, that of how to reconcile different approaches to helping children with literacy difficulties. This crucial concern is reviewed in Chapter 4.

Part 2 is focused on responses to the challenges of children's literacy difficulties — with understanding their nature and with proposals for the prevention and alleviation of difficulties in the fields of reading, spelling and writing. It is divided into two distinct yet related sections. The first of these concentrates on the growing corpus of work supporting the hypothesis that phonological awareness is a fundamental, often neglected, underlying ability necessary for children learning to read and spell.

Chapters 5, 6 and 7 present evidence indicating the crucial importance of phonological awareness in understanding the development of children's reading and spelling. They include descriptions of methods of early intervention that reduce later literacy difficulties. Chapter 8 applies this perspective to a consideration of developmental dyslexia. Two school-based teaching progammes then follow. The first, an interesting pilot study, introduces metacognitive notions; the second describes teaching programmes for children with specific learning difficulties attending a school for dyslexic children. Chapter 11 concludes this section with a description of some long-term effects of an intervention carried out in an independent centre where the programmes used have a strong phonic emphasis.

The second section presents a variety of relatively independent but promising educational strategies and techniques likely to be of particular interest to the practising teacher. A consideration of assessment issues in Chapter 12 is followed by two chapters presenting accounts of various classroom strategies for improving the teaching of children with reading and spelling difficulties in mainstream schools. A novel application of the use of a specially adapted tape-recorder system, suitable for use in both classroom and clinic, that capitalizes on the motivational value of the learner's own voice, is presented in Chapter 15. Chapter 16 gives an account of the use of other sophisticated applications of information technology for helping children with spelling problems. The special problems of children with specific learning difficulties are then considered, together with suggestions for improving areas of cognitive deficit and low attainments in literacy. The book concludes with an alternative, but possibly complementary, approach to improving the spelling and writing attainments of dyslexic children.

Each of the Parts, and the two sections within Part 2, starts with chapters dealing with the assessment, identification and characteristics of children with literacy difficulties. In Part 1 this is followed by more specialized challenges concerning current and impending literacy difficulties. In Part 2, sections 1 and 2, chapters dealing with teaching methods follow.

Both Parts 1 and 2 begin with important general issues relating to literacy in mainstream schools. Chapters concerning literacy difficulties in general are followed by specialized ones focusing on specific learning difficulties or dyslexia.

The contributors include teachers, advisers, psychologists and research workers. They address a range of policy, research and classroom concerns. As a consequence, the chapters vary in their technical complexities. The editors consider that the classroom and the literacy clinic are two crucibles in which theories and innovative practices are eventually tested. Knowing what to do and how to do it in both classroom and clinic are, without doubt, important. Knowing WHY one is doing what one is doing is far more important. There is nothing as practical as good theory. One of the major purposes of this book is to reflect and disseminate the dual development of both theory and practice.

Not all contributions will be equally readable or accessible to all readers. The professional responsibilities of the reader will determine the perceived relevance of the various chapters. For example, the technical detail of certain of the research oriented papers will have greater appeal to research workers and to teachers contemplating empirical dissertations or school-based research, than to other readers. An informed appreciation that there is research backing up teaching methods and also that there are practitioners putting ideas and developments into action, are important.

In short, we consider that the contributions that follow will be of interest and value to classroom teachers, specialist teachers, psychologists, special education advisers and policy makers, and researchers. Most important of all, the applications of some of the ideas contained therein could benefit many students currently experiencing difficulties in reading, spelling and writing.

Peter D. Pumfrey and Colin D. Elliott

Part One
Challenges

1
Literacy and the National Curriculum: the Challenge of the 1990s

Peter D. Pumfrey

How can standards of literacy be raised? How can national standards be assessed? How can individuals with special educational needs in the areas of literacy be identified and helped?

In all countries with state educational systems, literacy is seen as a key objective. The abilities of reading and writing (including spelling) are acknowledged as amplifiers of human capabilities. Via the medium of text, the skills of reading and writing give access to a high proportion of the accumulated thoughts, ideas and feelings of the culture. They also facilitate reflections concerning them. In most societies, not to be able to read is to be impoverished because of the effects both on career opportunities and on access to much of a country's (and the world's) cultural heritage. It is seen as a prime responsibility of schools to help all their pupils to read and write. Democratic societies require a literate and informed population.

The understanding of how literacy abilities are, or are not, learned is both complex and controversial. Contrasting opinions exist concerning how such developments can be conceptualized and how they can be assessed and encouraged. Theory, research and practice make their complementary and, at times, contradictory contributions in this continuing quest.

If it is believed that standards of literacy are falling, considerable public concern is typically expressed. Action is demanded to ensure that standards of literacy rise and that children learn to read and write adequately. In most countries, including Britain, the evidence for changes in primary school children's standards of literacy is often fragmentary. Characteristically, there is no systematic and comprehensive means of assessing standards of literacy. The absence of such information allows speculation and conjecture free rein. Even if all 7 year old children in Britain could accurately, fluently and with comprehension read Shakespeare, some would do so more accurately, fluently and with greater comprehension than others. It is quite possible that those performing at the lower levels would be deemed to have reading difficulties. The relative nature of the concept of literacy must never be forgotten. If we were collectively more aware, and more tolerant of inter- and intra-individual differences in children's standards of literacy, we might be able more effectively to improve standards (See Chapter 12).

The challenges to teachers and research workers generated by such a situation are many and varied. So are the responses in theory development, research and practice. The contributions contained in Parts 1, 2a and 2b of the present book testify to the range of challenges and the variety of responses.

At this stage, attention is drawn to three concerns. The first derives from the fact that each child is unique. Long before they attend school, there are marked differences in children's physical, mental and social/emotional characteristics. These are reflected in the ways and the rates at which children become literate. Are some of these characteristics important causes of success or failure in subsequent literacy? What does research tell us? Are differences between children in such pre-literacy abilities only quantitative, or are there qualitative differences characterizing some groups? Such issues have important implications for developing interventions that will prevent or alleviate children's reading, spelling and writing difficulties.

Accepted standards of literacy are usually based on what is typical of groups at particular times during their school careers. It has been shown that, for example, mean reading test scores for particular year groups can increase over a period of years. With this increase, it is also possible that there can be an increase in the proportion of children who fail. The increase in mean reading test scores over time was due to some able children doing much better, rather than all children doing better. Reading test scores became more widely dispersed over time. Intra-individual differences also differentiate: the individual's strengths and weaknesses in various aspects of literacy emerge.

The second point follows from the first. Many schoolchildren do not become literate. The estimate by the Adult Literacy Basic Skills Unit that some four hundred thousand adults in Britain are illiterate and that over five millions need help in basic skills, underlines the seriousness of the issue.

The third point is that children with a variety of learning difficulties, emotional and behavioural difficulties and other disadvantages, frequently show low standards of literacy for different reasons. The Education Act 1944 required that LEAs (Local Education Authorities) provide sufficient schools offering such variety that children could be educated according to their age, ability and aptitude. The provision of special educational treatment was based largely on a 'defect' model. LEAs were responsible for providing special educational treatment for pupils suffering any disability of mind or body. Ten different categories of handicap were officially recognized in England and Wales, and nine in Scotland. Approximately 2 per cent of children were identified as handicapped and were educated mainly in special schools, units or classes.

The Education Act 1981, (effective from 1st April 1983), changed the law on special education in the light of the Warnock Report and the consultations and discussions that ensued (Department of Education and Science, 1978).

Under Section 1 of the Education Act 1981, a child is deemed to

have special educational needs if they have a learning difficulty which calls for special educational provision to be made for them. Learning difficulty is defined in terms of children who have a significantly greater difficulty in learning than the majority of children of their age: and/or have a disability which either prevents or hinders them from making use of educational facilities of a kind generally provided in schools in their LEA area for children of their age.

How great must a child's reading, spelling or writing difficulty be to meet the requirements of Section 1? Nine years later we are still faced with the same question. Until the term 'significantly greater' is operationally defined, uncertainties will continue. Even if it is operationally defined, the arguments will not stop, but they would probably be somewhat different in nature. Special educational provision means educational provision that is additional to, or otherwise different from, that made generally for children of the same age in schools maintained by the LEA concerned. It is expensive.

LEAs must ensure that special educational provision is made for pupils who have special educational needs. It was accepted that most children with special educational needs would attend ordinary schools and that up to one in five pupils would, at some time during their school career, have such needs. Under the Act, children with identified special educational needs could be given the protection of a Statement. The status of such a document meant that the LEA was required to provide what was stipulated. The working of the Act is far from satisfactory. The great variation in the proportions of statemented pupils in LEAs emphasizes the ambiguity of the term special educational needs (Select Committee on Education, Science and the Arts, 1987). This situation has not been improved by the latest official advice on the identification and assessment of special educational needs (Department of Education and Science and the Welsh Office, 1988b).

Various voluntary organizations concerned with dyslexia were assured that the condition was recognized under the provisions of the Act. The *British Dyslexia Association*, *The Dyslexia Institute*, *The Foundation for the Underachieving and Dyslexic* and *Dyslexia Defined*, are but four of these. The problem of translating the terms of the Act into means of assessing and providing for children's special educational needs has led to a number of important legal actions being brought by parents whose children were experiencing severe literacy difficulties (see further discussion of this issue in Chapter 2).

Money to purchase the time and expertise required to assess and alleviate literacy difficulties is severely limited. The imprecise nature of the legal definition of special educational needs is an open invitation to legal action. Markedly different professional opinions exist concerning the nature and incidence of literacy difficulties and the means of alleviating such difficulties (Cornwall, Hedderley and Pumfrey, 1984). The Education Act 1981 widened the scope of special education by abolishing former categories and subsuming them under the superordinate category of special educational needs. The current consensus of professional opinion is that the former categories of handicap are undesirable. Not all workers agree with this viewpoint. Currently we now have two different and much larger categories. Either a child has, or does not have, special educational needs. When the incidence rises from about 2 per cent to about 20 per cent of the population, the numbers of children at the inevitable borderlines have increased dramatically. In such a situation, the incidence of parental dissatisfaction is bound to increase.

The causes of severe and prolonged difficulties in learning to read and write, are many and varied. They are likely to require different interventions if children are to be helped. If a pedagogic panacea to children's difficulties in reading, spelling and writing existed, it would probably have been identified by now. It has not.

The implementation of the Education Reform Act 1988 is intended to provide a framework wherein these three (and many other) challenges can be met. Making the Act effective will be a challenge for the next decade to all involved: pupils, parents and professionals.

The National Curriculum

The establishment of a National Curriculum applicable to all pupils aged from 5 to 16 years of age in all maintained schools, is now a legal requirement. The curriculum of every maintained school must include religious education for all pupils. In addition, the curriculum must incorporate specified 'core' and 'foundation' subjects. English, Mathematics and Science are designated core subjects. In Wales, Welsh is also a core subject in Welsh-speaking schools. The core subjects are seen as encompassing essential concepts, knowledge and skills without which other learning cannot take place effectively. The foundation subjects at all ages are History, Geography, Design and Technology, Music, Art and Physical Education. During the secondary school period, a modern foreign language is to be included (Department of Education and Science, 1989a).

In each area of the curriculum, attainment targets will be specified at up to ten levels of attainment, covering the age range 5 to 16 years. Attainment targets are defined in the Act as: ' . . . the knowledge, skills and understanding which pupils of different abilities and maturities are expected to have by the end of each key stage' (Education Reform Act, 1988, para. 2).

In the same Act, programmes of study are defined as: ' . . . the matters, skills and processes which are required to be taught to pupils of different abilities and maturities during each key stage' in each subject area (*ibid.*, para. 2).

A national assessment system will monitor what children ' . . . should normally be expected to know, understand and be able to do at the ages of 7, 11, 14 and 16. This will enable the progress of each child to be measured against national standards' (Department of Education and Science, 1989a, para. 6.4). Standard Assessment Tasks (SATs) are being developed for assessing whether pupils have attained the achievement targets at each of the key stages.

The assessment system is intended to serve the following purposes. The information elicited will be:

- *formative*. It will help the teacher in deciding how the pupil's learning should be furthered, provide both teachers and pupils with clear and understandable targets and feedback on progress towards these. It will also indicate whether further diagnostic testing is required.
- *summative*. The cumulative achievements of the pupil will be appraised: this will include what the individual knows, understands and can do.
- *evaluative*. Used comparatively it will identify where further resources may be required or where curricular changes are needed.
- *helpful to teachers' professional development*.
- *informative*. Communication between parents, professionals and pupils will be facilitated.

Whilst it will be many years before the full requirements of the Education Reform Act 1988 are in operation, fundamental changes in the ways in which teachers and schools organize and assess the work that is done are already well in train (Department of Education and Science and the Welsh Office, 1987, 1988a). In December 1988 the Department of Education and Science issued contracts to three consortia to develop Standard Assessment Tasks. These were piloted in some primary schools in the Autumn of 1989. The first full-scale national assessments should be carried out in 1991 and the first results published in 1992.

Focusing on Primary schools, in June, 1988, the Secretary of State for Education stated that 'Primary schools will be centre stage when attainment targets and programmes of study are introduced'. Attainment targets and programmes of study are being introduced according to the following timetable.

September, 1989: 5 year old pupils in English, Mathematics and Science.

September, 1989: 12 year old pupils in Mathematics and Science, with the introduction of English, plus Design and Technology, one year later; and

September, 1990: 7 year old pupils in English, Mathematics, Science, Design and Technology.

(Department of Education and Science, 1989, Annex C1).

It is absolutely clear that primary school children's progress and attainments in all aspects of English are of the essence. The effective delivery of the National Curriculum is virtually dependent upon pupils' ability to listen, talk, read and write satisfactorily. But what is meant by 'satisfactory'? How can those involved know what to do and whether they have been successful?

To assist the Secretary of State in his work, the National Curriculum Council, plus the Curriculum Council for Wales, were established. In addition, the Schools Examinations and Assessment Council was set up (Education Reform Act, 1988).

Somewhat earlier, a Committee of Inquiry into the Teaching of English Language, under the Chairmanship of Sir John Kingman, reported in March, 1988 (Department of Education and Science, 1988a). Their Report contained 18 recommendations. Probably the most important one was that a model (inevitably controversial) of the forms and patterns of written and spoken English language should provide a basis for teacher education. The model has four distinct yet related components: forms of language; communication and comprehension; development and acquisition; and historical and geographical variations. Examples of each aspect are provided in the report. Within these four categories, over 80 basic skills must be acquired by teachers if they are to be adequately prepared to teach all pupils. It is recommended that all intending primary school teachers undertake a language course based on the model.

The Kingman Report provided the foundation on which the National Curriculum Working Party on English, Chaired by Professor B. Cox, subsequently built. In November, 1988, the Report of the Cox Committee was published. It was entitled *'English for Ages 5 to 11'* (Department of Education and Science and the Welsh Office, 1988b). The Cox Report covers the first two key stages for the primary years of education, as defined in the Education Reform Act 1988. It is concerned with attainment targets and with programmes of study. The Cox Report presented six broad attainment targets in English for pupils aged 7 to 11 years. The subject of English was divided into three components: I. Speaking and Listening (one attainment target); II. Reading (two attainment targets); and III. Writing (three attainment targets) (Department of Education and Science and the Welsh Office, 1988b).

A consultation concerning the recommendations of the Cox Report was carried out very rapidly by the National Curriculum Council (NCC). Their subsequent report reduced the number of attainment targets to five by amalgamating Reading 1 and Reading 2, plus other changes (National Curriculum Council, 1989a). Cox and his working group, who were preparing the attainment targets and programmes of study for the secondary stages at the time, were reported as being ready to resign unless the NCC report recommendations were modified (Nash, 1989).

The saga was, in part, resolved when the Secretary of State published a draft order in respect of attainment targets and programmes of study for Key Stage 1 (5 to 7 year olds) only. After a further consultation, the final version was laid before Parliament in May, 1989 (Statutory Instruments, 1989). These took effect as from August, 1989. The requirements relating to Key Stage 2 (7 to 11 year olds) will not be introduced until the autumn of 1990.

The Secretary of State has accepted the NCC's advice that there should be five attainment targets for English, rather than six as recommended in the Cox Report. Reading 1 and 2 have been combined. However, he has decided to modify in some respects the NCC's advice on statements of attainment and programmes of study. The aim was to clarify intentions and remove inconsistencies. The profile components reflect the complex relationships between the various aspects of language. These five attainment targets are intended to be appropriate, at different levels, for children of different ages and abilities within the primary school. Levels of attainment within the targets and the statements of attainment at the various levels are intended to specify what each pupil 'SHOULD' know, understand and be able to do at the reporting age of 7 years. For anyone sensitive to the vast range of inter-individual differences between the attainments of children aged from 5 to 7 years, the normative moral imperative rings a number of warning bells.

The programmes of study are sufficiently broad to accommodate a variety of curricular paths leading towards the common objectives. The effects of curricular differences on achievement test data at item and objectives levels will be of considerable importance. This topic has been extensively studied in the USA. These curricular effects do not appear to be as great as advocates of the National Curriculum apparently anticipate (Phillips and Mehrens, 1988).

Implications of the National Curriculum for children with literacy difficulties

The implications and effects of the Act for pupils experiencing difficulties in learning to read, spell and write will have to be carefully monitored. The preparation of a Statement for such pupils, under the provisions of the Education Act 1981, is largely dependent on the results of observations, tests and consultations between the parents and a range of professionals with medical, social, psychological and educational qualifications. The perspectives of these groups vary, as do the types of tests that they use. An awareness of these contrasting viewpoints may reduce the likelihood of professional ego-centricism. No single professional group can claim children's literacy difficulties as its sole prerogative.

Chapter 13 of the Cox Report gives a brief consideration of special educational needs. All of the attainment targets in the Report can be assessed at various levels of attainment. It follows that children with special needs should be able to participate in the attainment targets, programmes of study and assessment arrangements. The point is made in the Report that Level 1 assessments are designed to identify children who may require special help in some form. From the available evidence, we know that children with reading difficulties will figure prominently.

The Cox Report anticipates that, in addition to the record of continuous and structured observation of their skills in English, children's reading comprehension will be tested via the Standard Assessment Tasks that have been developed. These are seen potentially as having advantages over existing normative and criterion-referenced tests. It is suggested that, for example, the work of the Assessment of Performance Unit in the field of language development should be capitalized upon (Gorman *et al.*, 1988).

> First, they should be designed to arise naturally out of good primary practice. The choice of texts should draw on reading materials of the kind that children will encounter in school through the programmes of study that we have recommended. . . . The test questions should be what experienced teachers would be likely to ask, taking into account the character of the reading material, its context and the purposes for which it would normally be encountered. The tests should be practicable to administer in the classroom context, and to mark and moderate. The marking should give credit for children's grasp of meaning and allow "positive" errors to be distinguished from "negative". The results should be capable of being used formatively and to indicate any particular need for support for the child, or for more specific, diagnostic assessment (Department of Education and Science and the Welsh Office, 1988b, paras. 9.23–9.24).

It is also required that the SATs be reliable and valid. In view of the wide and possibly incompatible demands being made of SATs, it is unlikely that their reliabilities and validities will be very high. The concept that appears dominant in the current thinking is that of 'ecological validity'. It is a concept worth remembering and questioning. 'In many cases this (further testing) will merely confirm what teachers already knew, and will strengthen their hands in taking appropriate action, for example is seeking a statement under the 1981 Act' (*ibid.*, para. 13.6).

The Cox Report continues

> In others, it will come as something of a surprise, and there may then be a need for the child to undergo further diagnostic tests to establish the extent of the problem. A level 1 performance should always be a signal for further investigation. This might, for example, reveal that a child who appeared to be a slow learner, or inattentive, was in fact showing symptoms of specific learning difficulties (dyslexia) or a hearing impairment, possibly an intermittent one such as otitis media (*ibid.*, para. 13.7).

How, one asks, can this be done unless the requisite material and professional resources are readily available? At present, they are not. Children with statements may have the requirements of the National Curriculum modified. However, this will not be the case for the majority of children with special educational needs

> ... either because the degree of special need is not considered severe enough to warrant it, or because their LEA's policy is to write statements only for children in special schools. Our suggestions will also be relevant to some of the unstatemented children with special educational needs, and hence to consideration of possible modifications, which the 1988 Act allows in respect of children falling within certain cases and circumstances, to Orders for attainment targets, programmes of study and assessment arrangements for English (*ibid.*, para. 13.9).

It is stated that children with learning difficulties are likely to make only slow progress in reading and writing. In such cases, it is suggested that initially greater emphasis should be given to oral work, though the skills of reading and writing must not be neglected. Despite its value, this is hardly a dazzling insight.

Enabling children with special educational needs to communicate their achievements, is recognized as a major challenge. Additional help may be required from professionals such as speech therapists, occupational therapists or psychologists. 'We recognize the resource implications, but feel the involvement of such experts to be essential if pupils with special educational needs are to be enabled to perform in English to their full potential' (*ibid.*, para. 13.15). It is interesting to see the word 'potential' being used in this report. If 'potential' is to be a criterion against which attainments in, for example, reading, spelling and writing will be appraised, how will potential be assessed?

Subsequently, the NCC has produced general guidance on children with special needs. This covers the modifications and disapplications procedures, revising Statements of Special Educational Needs and Temporary Exceptions from the National Curriculum (National Curriculum Council, 1989b). The NCC has also published guidance in helping pupils with special educational needs obtain access to the National Curriculum (National Curriculum Council, 1989c). Arrangements for carrying out multidisciplinary assessments, and making, or not making, statements of individual pupil's special educational needs under the Education Act 1981, were originally detailed in Circular 1/83 (Department of Education and Science, 1983). The Department is currently reviewing that Circular to take into account changes in both practice and the law that have taken place in the interim. To this end Draft Circular (/89) was widely distributed on 21st December 1988. (Department of Education and Science, 1988b). In it the concept of ' ... the child's TRUE LEARNING POTENTIAL' is also used (*ibid.*, para. 88) (Author's capitalization). This remains the case in the final document (Circular 22/89; DES, 1989b).

As with the Cox Report, its very use in an official document raises important issues concerning the relationships between 'potential' and 'attainments'.

- Why should significant discrepancies exist?
- Why should such discrepancies cause concern?
- How can each be validly and reliably assessed?
- Can the approach be used to identify children with specific learning difficulties in various aspects of literacy?
- Can such information help in deciding which individual pupils should receive additional resources such as extra small group and/or individual work?
- Do different groups of pupils require different types of help?
- Can we validly and reliably chart both inter- and intra-individual literacy related abilities?
- Of what utility is such information?
- Who has the required expertise?
- How much will this cost?
- From where will the money come?
- Is the additional investment in individual pupils with reading, spelling and writing difficulties worthwhile?
- How does a school establish priorities in the allocation of its income under Local Management of Schools?

These are weighty issues that will have to be addressed more explicitly than hithertofore as a consequence of the Education Reform Act 1988.

To improve the help we can give to children with reading, spelling and writing difficulties, we must learn to ask the pertinent questions concerning the nature of children's abilities and the conditions that foster their development. Meeting this initial challenge will sharpen and improve the responses of research workers and practitioners in extending understanding and control of children's language developments (Wolfendale, 1987; Pumfrey and Reason, 1989). Then the National Curriculum might be better implemented for more pupils and the problem of both child and adult literacy wither.

We have a long way to go, but some directions hold considerable promise.

References

Cornwall, K., Hedderley, R. and Pumfrey, P.D. (1984) 'Specific learning difficulties: the "specific reading difficulties" versus "dyslexia" controversy resolved?', *Division of Educational and Child Psychology Occasional Papers*, 7, 3, December, (all).

Department of Education and Science (1978) *Special Educational Needs*, (The Warnock Report), London, HMSO.

Department of Education and Science (1983) *Assessments and Statements of Special Educational Needs (Circular 1/83)*, London, Department of Education and Science.

Department of Education and Science (1988a) *Report of the Committee of Inquiry into the Teaching of English Language,* (The Kingman Report), London, HMSO.
Department of Education and Science (1988b) *Draft Circular /89. Revision of Circular 1/83 Assessments and Statements of Special Educational Needs: Procedures within the Education, Health and Social Services,* London, Department of Education and Science.
Department of Education and Science (1989a) *National Curriculum: From Policy to Practice,* London, Department of Education and Science.
Department of Education and Science (1989b) *Assessments and Statements of Special Educational Needs*: *Procedures within the Education, Health and Social Services,* (Circular 22/89) London, DES.
Department of Education and Science and the Welsh Office (1987) *National Curriculum Task Group on Assessment and Testing: A Report,* (The Black Report), London, Department of Education and Science and the Welsh Office.
Department of Education and Science and The Welsh Office (1988a) *National Curriculum Task Group on Assessment and Testing Report: A Digest for Schools,* London, HMSO.
Department of Education and Science and the Welsh Office (1988b) *English for Ages 5 to 11,* (The Cox Report), London, Department of Education and Science and the Welsh Office.
Education Reform Act (1988) Chapter 40, London, HMSO.
Gorman, T.P., White, J., Brooks, G., Maclure, M. and Kispal, A. (1988) *Language Performance in Schools: Review of APU Language Monitoring 1979–1983,* London, HMSO.
Nash, I. (1989) 'Cox "threatened to resign" ', *Times Educational Supplement,* no. 3799, p. 1.
National Curriculum Council (1989a) *National Curriculum Council Consultation Report,* March, York, National Curriculum Council.
National Curriculum Council (1989b) *Implementing the National Curriculum — Participation by Pupils with Special Educational Needs,* Circular number 5, York, National Curriculum Council.
National Curriculum Council (1989c) *A Curriculum for All,* York, National Curriculum Council.
Phillips, S.E. and Mehrens, W.A. (1988) 'Effects of curricular differences on achievement test data at item and objective levels', *Applied Measurement in Education,* 1, 1, pp. 33–52.
Pumfrey, P.D. and Reason, R. (1989) 'A national enquiry. Specific learning difficulties (dyslexia): challenges, responses and recommendations', *Division of Educational and Child Psychology Newsletter,* 23, pp. 14–16.
Secretary of State for Education (1987) *Special Educational Needs: Implementation of the Education Act, 1981. Observations by the Government on the Third Report of the Committee in Session 1986–1987,* December 15th, London, HMSO.
Select Committee on Education, Science and the Arts (1987) *Special Educational Needs: Implementation of the Education Act 1981,* London, House of Commons.
Statutory Instruments (1989) *The Education (National Curriculum) (Attainment Targets and Programmes of Study in English) Order 1989,* London, HMSO.
Wolfendale, S. (1987) *Primary Schools and Special Needs: Policy, Planning and Provision,* London, Cassell.

2
The Definition and Identification of Specific Learning Difficulties

Colin D. Elliott

The problems facing the LD field

Bertrand Russell defined mathematics as 'the subject in which we never know what we are talking about, nor whether what we are talking about is true'. Without being impolite to co-authors, or wishing to suggest that the present author has an answer to the problem, the reader of this volume may well agree with Kavale and Forness (1985) that Russell's comments are even more applicable and appropriate to the field of learning disabilities (LD).

Huge amounts of time, effort and manpower have been devoted during this century to the unravelling of people's learning difficulties. There are thousands of empirical results in search of a theory. There have, indeed, been plenty of theories on the way, all of which have been found wanting. Whereas in the physical sciences, theory is based upon broad conceptions of causality, in the LD field it is much more shallow-rooted as the means of pulling together various empirical observations. The theories about learning disabilities are often not in a form which leads to testable and refutable hypotheses. If you cannot properly test or refute a theory, then one theory can be taken to be just as good as another. Hence many competing theories have sprung up, each with its devotees who have typically adopted polarized positions. Great indeed has been the noise of battle on occasion, but the protagonists have never really been able to find common ground on which to fight (or, more sedately, on which to compare and test their theories).

One of the major difficulties in the LD field has been that of defining exactly what it is we are arguing about. Definitions of learning difficulties abound and are well reviewed by Kavale and Forness (1985, Chapter 3) from an American perspective, and by Cornwall, Hedderly and Pumfrey (1983, Chapter 2) from a British one. The theories have produced a welter of terminology, such as strephosymbolia, dyssymbolia, word-blindness, minimal brain dysfunction, dyslexia, developmental dyslexia, specific developmental dyslexia, learning disorder, specific learning disability, and specific learning difficulty. With so many theories, so many terms, and so many definitions of learning problems, it is not surprising that there are very considerable variations in the criteria used to select samples of children for research. One of the reasons why it is so difficult to obtain consistent research results in the LD field is the heterogeneity of criteria for selecting and defining the children who are the subjects of study. Unless the samples used in research reports are very carefully described, it is difficult to judge whether we are comparing like with like. These, and some other sources of variation and disagreement between workers in LD research, are shown in Table 2.1.

Table 2.1 Some sources of differences commonly found between learning disability research studies

- Different theories of the nature of learning disability (e.g., cognitive, neuropsychological, educational), leading to:
- Different definitions of learning disability, leading to:
- Different criteria for sample selection.
- Different measuring instruments used (e.g., which tests, methods of making observations, etc.), with different reliability and validity.
- Variations in quality and rigour of research design.
- Different methods of data analysis.
- Different definitions of treatments and interventions (similar labels, e.g., multisensory teaching, may not necessarily mean identical teaching procedures).
- Presence of context-dependent factors (e.g, personal characteristics of teachers and researchers, where and when intervention took place).

In the US Congressional testimony relating to the proposed Public Law 94–142 *The Education for All Handicapped Children Act* (1975), a Congressman who was no doubt feeling some despair over the diversity of evidence on learning disabilities, observed that, since there are 53 basic learning disabilities and 99 minimal brain dysfunctions, 'no one knows what a learning disability is' (Congressional Record, 1975, reported by Kavale and Forness, 1985). The one thing that characterizes people with learning disabilities is that they have difficulties with learning in schools and other institutional settings where most others manage to get by. There seems to be no common agreement on anything else.

The LD field is thus characterized by such major difficulties as lack of theory, different criteria for defining those who have specific learning difficulties, heterogeneity of population, lack of agreement on assessment, and lack of agreement on intervention. Despite the large amount of work which has been undertaken over the years, Kavale and Forness (1985) have concluded that this quantity of data has not resulted in scientific knowledge. The field is characterized by empiricism without proper theory: it has not integrated its knowledge into a conceptual whole, a system of laws useful for explanation and prediction. It is, therefore, a pseudoscience. This conclusion is largely supported in a thoughtful and constructive article by Swanson (1988), which is accompanied by commentary from a number of workers in the LD field.

The views of Kavale and Forness and of Swanson were developed after major reviews of American literature in the LD field. Their conclusions apply equally well to the work which has gone on in the UK. It is interesting to observe how little attention is given by workers on one side of the Atlantic to work going on on the other side, although perhaps because of the relatively small size of the UK this fault is possibly more noticeable in US work. We all are trying to grapple with essentially the same sorts of problems, and have much to learn from each others' approaches. One of the stumbling blocks to a free interchange and acceptance of each others' findings is perhaps the somewhat different legislative systems in which we try to develop appropriate provision for LD children.

The major aim of this paper is to consider issues relating to the definition and identification of specific learning difficulties. In doing this, it is instructive to compare and contrast the legislative approaches to the problem which have been implemented in Britain and the USA. The two major pieces of legislation which govern special educational practice are the British Education Act, 1981, and the US Public Law 94–142 (The Education for All Handicapped Children Act), 1975.

The two education acts

The American Act (which we shall designate as 'PL 94–142'), passed in 1975 and implemented in 1978, had the fundamental purpose of bringing to an end what Abeson and Ballard (1976) described as 'the unconstitutional exclusion of handicapped children from the public education system'. The law stated that a free and appropriate public education must be provided for every handicapped child in the US. The law defined basic rights for children and parents and it prescribed administrative procedures (called 'due process procedures') for the identification and placement of handicapped children in various categories which have to be observed if a particular State is to qualify for and receive Federal funding assistance for its handicapped children.

The British 1981 Education Act (which we shall designate as 'the 1981 Act'), implemented in 1983, also represents an attempt to improve both assessment and provision for children with special educational needs.

There are a number of important similarities between the two Acts. Like PL 94–142, the 1981 Act provided enhanced definitions of rights and duties for professionals and for parents, although perhaps in a less thoroughgoing way. Both sets of laws emphasize the importance of the integration of handicapped children with the non-handicapped. Thus, under the 1981 Act, it is the duty of Local Educational Authorities (LEAs) to educate a child with special educational needs in an ordinary school, provided that this is compatible with giving both that child and others in the school an efficient education. As far as reasonably practicable, the child should engage in the activities of the school together with children who do not have special educational needs. Similarly, PL 94–142 contains a similar principle of a 'least restrictive environment', whereby, to the maximum extent appropriate, handicapped children are educated with children who are not handicapped. A third major similarity is in the purpose and outcome of formal assessment under the two Acts. In the British case, the end result of assessment is a 'statement of special educational needs', and in the American case the end result is an 'individualized education program'. Both provide a description of the child's functioning, aims or goals of provision, and a specification of the facilities and resources required.

Although there are a number of similarities of purpose and practice in the two sets of laws, the 1981 Act has been called 'a pale reflection of similar legislation already in force in other countries (for instance the Education for All Handicapped Children Act in the US)' (Newell, 1985, p. 1).

There are a number of major differences between the two Acts. One is that, in contrast to PL 94–142, the 1981 Act does not provide for extra Government funding to be made available to Local Educational Authorities for children identified as having special educational needs. One of the purposes of PL 94–142, on the other hand, is to channel Federal funding to school districts for all children identified as handicapped. A major task for individual States and school districts is to determine whether a child is eligible to receive these resources: extra funds are not provided until eligibility is established.

Other than this question of additional Government funding, the two major differences between the Acts which are particularly relevant to children with specific learning difficulties, and which will be outlined and discussed in more detail, are (a) contrasts between the Acts in their use of statutory categories of handicap; and (b) questions of definition of such terms as 'learning disability', 'learning difficulty' and 'special educational needs'.

The use of statutory categories of handicap

The 1981 Act got rid of classification labels which had previously been in use in special education in Britain. Some of these were archaic (such as 'educationally subnormal') and were considered offensive. Also the definitions of some of the handicaps had on occasion caused some difficulty, particularly where a child had more than one handicap. In some cases it became difficult to decide which handicap was primary, and where the child should be placed. The Act replaced the previous definitions of handicap with the concept of special educational needs.

Since all labels for categories of handicap or disability have been abandoned by the 1981 Act, there is no reference in the Act to Specific Learning Difficulties. Hence LEAs have had to work out their own individual policies on whether such difficulties can be recognized under the Act (some LEAs at least initially refused to make any distinction between these and any other learning difficulties) and also on whether special provision needs to be made for such children, and of what type.

By way of contrast, PL 94–142 uses and defines no fewer than eleven categories of handicap: deaf, deaf-blind, hard-of-hearing, mentally retarded, multihandicapped, orthopedically impaired, other health impaired, seriously emotionally disturbed, specific learning disability, speech impaired, and visually handicapped. Each of these categories is fairly carefully defined (even though there is sometimes keen debate about the adequacy and interpretation of the definitions).

Before moving on to examine the question of various definitions of specific learning difficulty, a number of important points need to be made which will perhaps help to clarify the issue of definitions.

Are the categories homogeneous?

Each of the categories of handicap listed in the section above relates to a group of individuals with a broadly common configuration of problems. We must not assume from this that all children within a group have precisely the same difficulties, or the same strengths, and neither should we assume that the causes of their handicaps are the same. In other words, each category is *not* homogeneous. A moment's reflection upon the categories of visual or orthopaedic impairment reveals that within each of these categories there is a wide range of distinctively different problems. For example, a person with one or more limbs missing has a different aetiology, has different teaching needs and requires different resources than a person with athetoid cerebral palsy. Similarly, it is unreasonable as well as undesirable to make the assumption that children categorized as having a specific learning difficulty in literacy are homogeneous with regard to the causes of their difficulties, their patterns of difficulties, or their teaching needs.

What is required is the development of a taxonomy which will describe and define groupings *within* each category. Classification research, outlined for example in a seminal article by Morris, Blashfield and Satz (1986), has much to offer the LD field. There is already substantial evidence that categories of children variously labelled 'LD', 'Specific Learning Difficulty'. 'Reading Disabled', 'Dyslexic', and so on, are fairly heterogeneous and can be subdivided into more homogeneous subgroups. Tyler reviews this evidence in Chapter 3 in this book. In the meantime, nothing in this chapter should be taken to imply that LD children are homogeneous or that they have a uniform pattern of problems (see also Elliott, 1989).

The purpose of the definitions which we shall now consider is to identify children who, even though they have a variety of patterns of difficulty, can still be considered to have a specific learning difficulty.

Definitions

Under the 1981 Act, the various category labels which were previously used have been replaced by the generic concept of 'special educational needs' which in its turn defines two further related concepts. These definitions are as follows, directly quoted from Section 1 of the Act:

(a) 'A child has *"special educational needs"* if he or she has a learning difficulty which calls for special educational provision to be made for him.'

(b) 'A child has a *"learning difficulty"* if he has a significantly greater difficulty in learning than the majority of children of his age, or he has a disability which either prevents or hinders him from making use of educational facilities of a kind generally provided in schools.'

(c) *'Special educational provision'* means 'provision which is additional to, or otherwise different from, the educational provision made generally for children of his age'.

The Local Education Authorities charged with implementing the Act have understandably interpreted these definitions in a variety of ways. Some have taken the view that if a child is attending an ordinary, mainstream school, he or she does not have 'special educational needs' under the Act, since they are able to make use of facilities generally provided in schools for children with learning or other problems. Other LEAs have taken a more liberal view of the wording of the Act, and hence a wide variation in practices has developed between LEAs.

In an effort to enquire into this variety of practices, the Division of Educational and Child Psychology of the British Psychological Society sponsored a survey of all LEAs and of most educational psychologists in England in early 1989. The survey work is being co-ordinated on behalf of the Society by two contributors to this book, Peter Pumfrey and Rea Reason. By early May 1989, 72 out of a total of 104 LEAs had replied to a questionnaire about their policies and practices in relation to specific learning difficulties. Forty out of the 72 LEAs (56 per cent) said that they had formulated a policy on specific learning difficulties, leaving 44 per cent who had not formulated a policy. It seems reasonable to conclude that the variety of LEA policies or non-policies in Britain is directly due to the absence of any definition or specification of specific learning difficulties in the 1981 Act.

PL 94–142, on the other hand, provides a definition of specific learning disability as follows:

'Specific learning disability' means a disorder in one or more of the basic psychological processes involved in understanding or in using language, spoken or written, which may manifest itself in an imperfect ability to listen, think, speak, read, write, spell, or to do mathematical calculations. The term includes such conditions as perceptual handicaps, brain injury, minimal brain dysfunction, dyslexia, and developmental aphasia. The term does not include children who have learning problems which are primarily the result of visual, hearing, or motor handicaps, of mental retardation, of emotional disturbance, or of environmental, cultural or economic disadvantage.

This definition is virtually the same as one developed by the National Advisory Committee on Handicapped Children in 1968 and incorporated into 1969 legislation on specific learning disability. Although taken on its own, without further elaboration, the definition is general and open to interpretation, the US Office of Education (1977) provided procedural guidelines for interpretation. The criteria for determining the existence of a specific learning disability states that a child has such a disability if:

1. the child does not achieve commensurate with his or her age and ability levels in one or more of the areas listed in paragraph (2), when provided with learning experiences appropriate for the child's age and ability levels; and
2. the team finds that a child has a severe discrepancy between achievement and intellectual ability in one or more of the following areas: (i) oral expression; (ii) listening comprehension; (iii) written expression; (iv) basic reading skill; (v) reading comprehension; (vi) mathematics calculation; or (vii) mathematic reasoning.

The regulation repeated the exclusion clause contained in the final sentence of the original definition.

An example of state regulations

Even the attempt, which has just been outlined, to define criteria for the detection of learning disability has resulted in a wide range of interpretations by individual States. Although the Federal Government determines the legislative framework under which the States must operate, it is up to each individual State to formulate its own regulations and interpretations of the law. The wide range of regulations and interpretations of the law has been recently reviewed by Frankenberger and Harper (1987).

According to this study, 57 per cent of States do include achievement discrepancy criteria in their guidelines. These will typically involve a comparison of achievement test scores with scores from an intelligence test or some other tests of generalized cognitive abilities, such as reasoning, memory, perceptual or spatial abilities, and so on. In order to illustrate these procedures, the regulations from the State of Texas will be described.

The Texas Education Code (Texas, 1986) defines learning disabled students in a very similar way to the definition in the Federal regulations. There are, however, a few differences. *Spelling* is added to the list of seven areas of achievement. *Motor handicap* is dropped from the list of exclusion conditions. And finally, the learning disability has to exist 'to a degree such that [the child] cannot be adequately served in the regular classes of the public schools without the provision of special services other than those provided under compensatory education programs'.

The child must receive a comprehensive individual assessment from a multidisciplinary team who must report on (a) language dominance (i.e., the child's first language); (b) a formal or informal assessment of expressive and receptive language proficiency; (c) physical factors; (d) a formal or informal assessment of emotional/behavioural factors; (e) an assessment of sociological variables which *must* consist of identifying the child's family and community situation influencing learning and behavioural patterns; (f) an assessment of intellectual functioning which *must* include a standardized intelligence test, in the case of students who may be learning disabled. Intellectual functioning should be the last factor assessed, since the student's performance in this area should be analyzed and interpreted in the light of all the other data; (g) an assessment of educational performance levels and competences which shall include criterion-referenced or curriculum-referenced measures, and which shall also include norm-referenced measures, in the case of students who may be learning disabled.

The regulations specify that the standardized intelligence and achievement test scores shall be compared. *A severe discrepancy exists* when the student's intellectual ability is above the mentally retarded range, and when the student's assessed educational achievement in the specified areas is *more than one standard deviation below the student's intellectual ability*.

This is, of course, an extremely simple definition of a severe discrepancy between ability and achievement, and we would expect on statistical grounds that, with a correlation of, say, 0.7 between intelligence and school achievement, there would be about 8 per cent of children who would meet this criterion. Other States have adopted more stringent and more statistically complex severe discrepancy criteria. Some States have taken regression to the mean into account in specifying their criteria (this phenomenon relates to the tendency for the school achievement scores of children of *above average* intelligence to be lower than their intelligence scores, and for the school achievement scores of children of *below average* intelligence to be somewhat higher than their intelligence scores). Also, some States specify a bigger discrepancy than Texas for a child to meet their criteria; for example, while the State of Alabama has essentially the same criteria as Texas for children between 7 and 10 years, for children 11 years of age or older a discrepancy of 1.5 standard deviations must be found, whilst in Kansas the discrepancy must be 1.96

standard deviations. Many States also specify lists of approved tests which may be used for this purpose.

The effect of the US legislation

The US Department of Education has reported a dramatic rise in the numbers of children classified as learning disabled since PL 94–142 came into force. In 1976–77 the number of children counted as learning disabled in the USA was 797,213. In 1980–81, the number had risen to 1,468,014 and in 1981–82 it stood at 1,627,344. It rose again to 1,811,489 by 1983–84, and this at a time of falling school rolls. It has risen slightly in more recent years, being 1,897,043 in 1986–87 (US Department of Education, 1988). With a total school population of about 41 million, about 4.6 per cent of students are therefore classified as LD. In 1986–87, 47 per cent of all handicapped children (across all eleven categories of handicap) were classified as LD.

It is notable that the number of children classified as Educable Mentally Retarded has shown a considerable drop over this period, probably indicating that, because of the relatively loose definition of specific learning disability, more professionals and more parents prefer to use this classification than the less socially desirable one of EMR.

Algozzine and Ysseldyke (1981), at an early stage in the development of procedures for implementing PL 94–142, suggested that schools frequently misclassify LD students. In a later article they analyzed the classification decisions that would result if seventeen eligibility criteria were applied to a number of LD and other low achieving students. They concluded, not surprisingly, that the number of children classified as having a specific learning disability depends on which definition is used (Algozzine and Ysseldyke, 1983). Dawson (1984) has called this a 'diagnostic scandal' for the profession of school psychology.

Such a condemnation of school psychology is perhaps somewhat harsh. It is not so much a diagnostic scandal as an inevitable consequence of variations in classification criteria. There are variations between States, some of whom employ remarkably lenient criteria of 'severe discrepancy'. There are variations in the tests which are used with children, both within and between States. And if seven or eight deficit areas are allowable for an LD classification, this again makes the LD population more heterogeneous. The situation is scandalous only if we look on specific learning difficulty as something akin to measles: you either have it or you don't. And if doctors were unable to identify those who had it as against those who hadn't, that would be a diagnostic scandal. However, such a view of specific learning difficulties is clearly unsupportable. Even with the tightest, most rigorous definition, it is evident that learning difficulties fall along a continuum of severity. Essentially, the problem of setting criteria for LD classification depends upon how many students we want to identify as learning disabled (see also Braden and Algina, 1989). It depends upon the resources society is willing to devote to their education. The question thus becomes a political or social one, once psychologists and educators have persuaded society that an identifiable problem exists. In principle, once we know how many people with learning difficulties we want to identify and provide for, we can set the criteria accordingly.

But wherever the cut-off point is set, we will find that people around that borderline will be located above or below it according to which tests or other assessment devices are used: the problem is in essence due to human variability rather than to the inherent weaknesses of tests. No tests, whether norm-referenced or criterion-referenced, no ratings, no judgments, no assessment devices of any sort will *ever* be perfectly reliable. We have to learn how to live with unreliability, or 'error', in our assessments of people, and not to make our selection decisions too rigid and inflexible.

Further developments and implications for practice in Britain

The US National Joint Committee for Learning Disabilities has subsequently further considered the PL 94–192 definition, believing that it contains weaknesses and ambiguities which limit its usefulness. These have been outlined by Hammill, Leigh, McNutt and Larsen (1987), together with a new definition proposed by the NJCLD. Although recently adopted by the National Association of School Psychologists (NASP, 1989, p. 1), together with a small clarifying amendment, the NJCLD definition has, however, been critically reviewed by Kavale and Forness (1985). They express the opinion that future definitions of learning disability should be simplified by emphasising the major criteria of high ability together with low achievement, deleting any reference to aetiology or to conditions which are included in the definition. Exclusion conditions, such as gross physical or neurological handicaps, uncorrected impairments in visual or auditory acuity, serious emotional disturbance, or lack of environmental or instructional opportunity, should be retained. 'The definition of LD would thus stress significantly sub-average academic impairment, IQ in the normal range, and exclusion of the conditions named above' (Kavale and Forness, 1985, p. 84).

It should be noted here that even though PL 94–142 has been subject to some criticism, largely on the grounds of misclassification, over-classification or inconsistent classification of LD children, its US critics have not suggested the British system as a possible alternative: better definitions, rather than looser definitions or no definitions at all, seem to be the objective.

Thus the question of definition of specific learning disability remains a very live issue in the USA. The debate and the concern in Britain have probably been at a lower level, although there now seems to be a growing awareness of the need to have a distinctive definition and to have distinctive educational provision for children with specific learning difficulties. This awareness has undoubtedly been fostered by voluntary organisations such as the British

Dyslexia Association and the Dyslexia Institute and by recent litigation. As is the way with British law, it is the courts who so often define the precise meaning of statutory wording, so gradually we may perhaps expect to see greater uniformity of practice arising from appeal cases. In the recent British Psychological Society survey of LEAs, referred to earlier in this article, 6 per cent of the 72 LEAs reported that they had been involved in court cases, in 1988 alone, with reference to children with specific learning difficulties. Also in 1988, 39 per cent had been involved in local appeals and 4 per cent in appeals to the Secretary of State for Education and Science.

One of the effects of having a loose definition of learning difficulties, as in the 1981 Act, is that not only does it produce a tendency for the British to be even more diverse than the US in definitions, but it also encourages considerable diversity in assessment practices. If we do not know quite what we are looking for, or why, it is not surprising that the methods we use to achieve this nebulous end-result are both ill-defined and diverse. They are likely to be subject to professional fashions, and, without a clear rationale underpinning them, likely to be subject to marked fluctuations in usage and popularity.

So it is with the assessment practices of British educational psychologists (EPs). Differences between EPs in terms of assessment practices are now so great that one may be forgiven for wondering if they are all working in the same profession. Some EPs have continued in what has often been characterized as the traditional role of the profession in using psychometric tests, particularly intelligence and other ability tests. Others seem to make a virtue of never using psychometric tests: if they see individual children at all they will use criterion-referenced or curriculum-based assessments.

Trends in the assessment practices of EPs have been recently documented by Farrell, Dunning and Foley (1989). One of their findings was that, while 77 per cent of a sample of EPs in 1981 said that they would use an IQ test as part of their assessment of 9-year-old children, only 25 per cent said they would do so in 1986. This seems to be a remarkably low figure: whether what psychologists do is quite the same as what they *say* they would do is, perhaps, a moot point, but nevertheless their attitudes seem to have changed markedly. Another problem of this investigation was that the expression 'IQ test' appears to have been used as a blanket term to cover all cognitive ability tests, even those whose primary aim is to yield differential profiles of various abilities. Some EPs may, of course, have interpreted the question literally, to include tests which only yield an IQ score and little else. In such a case one might have a great deal of sympathy with the view that an IQ is of little utility. However, it does seem likely that Farrell *et al.*'s use of the term is commonly understood as a more general label in the profession. The suggestion is made by Farrell *et al.* that 'the giving of IQ tests is still central to the professional identity of many educational psychologists...If they (i.e., the tests) are rejected, some educational psychologists may feel insecure because they can no longer claim to perform a function which is exclusive to their profession' (p. 53). Whether or not the full implications of this were fully intended by Farrell *et al.*, this comment is consistent with the 'party line' of the critics of psychometrics: there is no good reason to use psychometric tests, and therefore if you do use them, it must be that you feel insecure, and that you have nothing else to offer.

The charge needs to be answered in the context of a consideration of the overall purpose of assessment. This in turn is dependent upon our view of the nature of children (or, indeed, people in general) and the causes of their difficulties in learning. The argument in essence is as follows. We are all born with amazingly complex sensory and neurological systems which develop, and respond to and process information coming in from the world around us. Our first assumption is that there is a wide range of individual differences in this physical equipment which is evidenced in differences in behaviour, temperament and the ways and the speed with which we learn things and process information. We shall call these 'within-person' factors.

In addition, we are subject to a huge variety of environmental experiences. Initially, these are mainly centred in the home and family, but broaden out as we get older to include our peer group, our schools, and also, from a very early age for many of us, media influences. Our second assumption is that virtually all of our repertoire of behaviours is learned from these environmental sources. We shall call these 'external' factors.

If a child develops in an average or above average way in skills which society values, we can be fairly certain that the within-person sensory and neurological equipment is functioning satisfactorily and that the child's environmental experiences have been at least adequate. In the case of sub-average skill development we are often concerned to try to identify the source of the difficulty so that the child might be helped appropriately. In doing this, we need information which enables us to evaluate the relative contributions of within-person and external factors.

The pre-eminent function of psychometric tests of ability is that they enable some assessment to be made of within-person factors. Aside from their known technical qualities of reliability and validity (which are often lacking in other assessment procedures), they provide evidence of effective *generalized* cognitive strengths in certain areas as well as weaknesses in others. It is one of the major assumptions of neuropsychological assessment that there are individual differences in the style and quality of information processing, and that these have some link (even though the precise mechanisms are not identified) with neural functioning (Swanson, 1988; Taylor, 1988; Torgesen, 1986). The author has also argued that cognitive ability tests are of considerable value in the identification of within-person factors when learning difficulties are being investigated (Elliott, 1983). The abandonment of such tests makes the identification of specific learning difficulties problematic, if we define such difficulties in terms of within-person factors as discussed earlier in this paper. Norm-referenced cognitive ability tests are distinctively different from criterion-referenced or curriculum-based behavioural assessments in a number of ways, as shown in Table 2.2 (from Elliott, 1983, page 106)[1]. Because each of the approaches to assessment has its own strengths and limitations, what is needed is a mixture of the two in order to provide a balanced view of a child and his or her strengths and difficulties in learning. This is, indeed, exactly what is specified in the Texas Education Code, outlined earlier.

Table 2.2 *A Framework For Assessment*

	Cognitive Approaches	*Behavioural Approaches*
Focus	Generalized skills and abilities.	Specific skills and abilities.
Question	What are the child's cognitive weaknesses and/or strengths?	What has the child failed to learn?
Implication	The problem may be within-child.	The problem may be contextual/environmental.
Methods	Psychometric tests of various cognitive abilities – IQ, group factors, specific cognitive functions (e.g. memory) or scholastic abilities. Experimental or observational assessments of specific cognitive abilities.	Criterion-referenced tests or observations, linked to curriculum hierarchies. These are generally developed as an outcome of applied behaviour analysis, task analysis or precision teaching methods.
Outcomes	(a) Reports contain an analysis of the child's problem in terms of the question above. (b) Reports contain recommendations for teaching *method* based upon a consideration of the child's cognitive strengths and/or weaknesses.	(a) Reports are written giving an analysis of the problem in terms of the question above. (b) Reports contain recommendations for teaching *content* based upon task and curriculum analyses.
Limitations	(a) Usually they do not cover specific curriculum content. (b) Implications of cognitive weaknesses and/or strengths for teaching methods are not always clear.	(a) Usually they do not cover generalized problems which the child may have in various cognitive areas. (b) The approaches deal best with basic skill hierarchies and are difficult to apply to complex skills.

The use of a definition of specific learning difficulty which (a) points to a discrepancy between ability and achievement, and (b) emphasizes the need to demonstrate that this is probably due to within-child factors, would not only bring much needed order into a somewhat chaotic practice in Britain. It would also provide a rationale for balanced assessment practices which would include psychometric assessment as a component. It is not being argued here that we should return to the days of IQ testing as such, nor that ability assessment should be absolutely pre-eminent in the procedures that are used. No doubt this may actually still be the case in certain areas of the USA, but it is certainly not called for in the formal procedures for diagnosing specific learning disability in that country. The fact that some professionals or LEAs may use a procedure undesirably does not invalidate that procedure when used properly.

What is needed in Britain is an agreed definition of specific learning difficulties which carries some legal force, together with an agreed balanced general system of assessment of such difficulties. Although the American system has many problems, largely to do with ill-defined concepts (Algozzine and Ysseldyke, 1986, 1987), much can be learned from US definitions and practices. Unless a major attempt is made to resolve the situation in the UK, the present debates and even conflicts between professionals seem set to continue, with those parents who are more articulate, more determined and more wealthy continuing to obtain the lion's share of available resources for their children.

Notes

1. Note that this table is similar to those of Pumfrey in Chapter 12 in this book. He makes similar points with regard to reading tests and assessment devices.

References

Abeson, A. and Ballard, J. (1976) 'State and federal policy for exceptional children', in Weintraub, F. (Ed.) *Public Policy and the Education of Exceptional Children*, Reston, Virginia, Council for Exceptional Children.

Algozzine, B. and Ysseldyke, J. E. (1981) 'Special education services for normal children: better safe than sorry?', *Exceptional Children*, 48, pp. 283–243.

Algozzine, B. and Ysseldyke, J. E. (1983) 'Learning disabilities as a subset of school failure: the oversophistication of a concept', *Exceptional Children*, 50, pp. 242–246.

Algozzine, B. and Ysseldyke, J. E. (1986) 'The future of the LD field: screening and diagnosis', *Journal of Learning Disabilities*, 19, pp. 394–398.

Algozzine, B. and Ysseldyke, J. E. (1987) 'Questioning discrepancies: retaking the first step 20 years later', *Learning Disability Quarterly*, 10, pp. 301–312.

Braden, J. P. and Algina, J. (1989) 'A method of determining the probability of special education eligibility', *Journal of School Psychology*, 27, pp. 5–13.

Cornwall, K., Hedderly, R. and Pumfrey, P. D. (1983) 'Specific learning difficulties: the "specific reading difficulties" versus "dyslexia" controversy resolved?', *Occasional Papers of the Division of Educational and Child Psychology of the British Psychological Society*, 7, 3, pp. 1–121.

Dawson, M. M. (1984) 'LD: professional dilemma or diagnostic scandal?', *Paper Presented to the Annual Convention of the National Association of School Psychologists*.

Elliott, C. D. (1983) *The British Ability Scales. Manual 1: Introductory Handbook*, Windsor, NFER-Nelson.

Elliott, C. D. (1989) 'Cognitive profiles of learning disabled children', *British Journal of Developmental Psychology*, 7, pp. 171–178.

Farrell, P., Dunning, T., and Foley, J. (1989) 'Methods used by educational psychologists to assess children with learning difficulties', *School Psychology International*, 10, pp. 47–55.

Frankenberger, W. and Harper, J. (1987) 'States' criteria and procedures for identifying learning disabled children: a comparison of 1981/82 and 1985/86 guidelines', *Journal of Learning Disabilities*, 20, pp. 118–121.

Hamill, D. D., Leigh, J. E., McNutt, G. and Larsen, S. C. (1987) 'A new definition of learning disabilities', *Journal of Learning Disabilities*, 20, pp 109–113.

Kavale, K. A. and Forness, S. R. (1985) *The Science of Learning Disabilities*, Windsor, NFER-Nelson.

Morris, R., Blashfield, R., and Satz, P., (1986) 'Developmental classification of reading-disabled children', *Journal of Clinical and Experimental Neuropsychology*, 8, pp. 371–392.

NASP (1989) 'NJCLD LD definition adopted', *Communiqué, National Association of School Psychologists*, 17, 7, p. 1.

Newell, P. (1985) *ACE Special Education Handbook: The New Law On Children With Special Needs*, 2nd ed., London, Advisory Centre for Education.

Swanson, H. L. (1988) 'Toward a metatheory of learning disabilities', *Journal of Learning Disabilities*, 21, pp. 196–209.

Taylor, H. G. (1988) 'Neuropsychological testing: relevance for assessing children's learning disabilities', *Journal of Consulting and Clinical Psychology*, 56, pp. 795–800.

Texas (1986) *State Board of Education Rules for Handicapped Students*, Austin, Texas, Texas State Board of Education.

Torgesen, J. K. (1986) 'Learning disabilities theory: its current state and future prospects', *Journal of Learning Disabilities*, 19, pp. 399–407.

US Department of Education (1988) *To Assure the Free Appropriate Public Education of All Handicapped Children: Tenth Annual Report to Congress on the Implementation of Public Law 94-142: The Education For All Handicapped Children Act*, Washington, D. C., US Department of Education.

US Office of Education (1977) Education of the handicapped regulations: assistance to states for education of handicapped children: procedures for evaluating specific learning disabilites, *Federal Register*, 42, 65082–65085.

3
Subtypes of Specific Learning Difficulty: A Review

Stephen Tyler

Introduction

In much of the literature on specific learning difficulties (or learning disability or dyslexia) there appears to remain an assumption that what is being discussed, irrespective of nomenclature, represents a unitary condition. At the least it is often presented as if the similarities shared by the children identified as learning disabled are more significant than any differences that may be found between children within the group. Morris (1988) argues, however, that the term 'learning disabled' rarely describes more than academic learning difficulties and seldom provides any information regarding aetiology, treatment requirements or prognosis. Usage of such a nonspecific term it is suggested, has created significant confusion for parents, teachers and researchers. A similar point may be made for the term dyslexia. Thus, in most descriptions of dyslexia the reader is provided with a list of symptoms, none of which are sufficient and few even necessary for the diagnosis of the condition. Consequently, persons identified as dyslexic may display an individually varying number of symptoms. Yet it is clear that children may experience educational failure for a number of reasons and it is important to be able to differentiate which features are most salient both for individuals and for groups.

As John *et al.*, (1977) and more recently Elliott and Tyler (1986, 1987) have pointed out, the treatment of a heterogeneous population as if it were homogeneous may serve to obscure rather than clarify diagnostic features and the effectiveness of educational programmes. Recently, therefore, increased attention has been paid to the issues surrounding the classification of children with learning difficulties (Rourke, 1985; Morris, 1988; Hulme and Snowling, 1988). It may be suggested that the development of a good classificatory system is important in order to enhance communication and to improve prediction (Blashfield and Draguns, 1976). In research it may allow for the selection of more homogeneous samples of subjects, thereby reducing 'noise' in the data and diminishing tendencies for complementary patterns of strengths and weaknesses to cancel each other out (Tyler and Elliott, 1988). At a practical level, it may be seen that if different cases of learning disability arise from different underlying cognitive impairments it is probable that different programmes of tuition will be indicated. The question of classification of learning difficulty, therefore, transcends the purely theoretical and has important implications for classroom practice.

It seems probable that learning disabilities may take several forms in terms of achievement patterns and/or associated cognitive information processing abilities which may additionally vary as a function of aetiology or age (Satz and Morris, 1981). In recent years considerable efforts have been made to identify more specific subtypes of learning disabled children who share common attributes which distinguish them from other subtypes, and to clarify the learning processes by which a skill such as reading may be acquired.

As Rutter (1978) points out, several distinctions have to be made in considering differential diagnosis in a case of low academic achievement. In the *first* instance, a failure to acquire educational skills must be distinguished from a later apparent loss of skills. Children who fail to achieve having previously mastered a basic set of skills almost certainly have a different set of underlying problems (e.g. primary emotional difficulties) from those children who have experienced difficulty in acquiring reading and number skills from the beginning. A *second* distinction may be made in terms of the particular area of academic failure observed. For the most part, attention in the literature has been focused upon reading and spelling skills, whilst problems encountered by children in other areas, e.g. mathematics, have received more limited consideration, and surprisingly little regard has yet been paid to the similarities and differences between underachievement in different subjects. However, there remains the possibility of a valid distinction between reading retardation associated with failure in mathematics and reading failure which occurs as an isolated disability. A *third* basic distinction within groups of retarded readers may be made between general backwardness and specific reading retardation.

Specific reading retardation and general reading backwardness

The differentiation of children with reading problems into two groups according to the relationship between the difficulty and their measured level of intelligence stems from the work of Rutter and Yule (Rutter and Yule, 1975). General reading backwardness (GRB) is defined in terms of low achievement in reading regardless of intelligence while specific reading retardation (SRR) refers to achievement which is low for the child's age and with respect to measured IQ. Thus SRR refers to a difficulty in learning to read that is not explicable by reference to general intelligence, while in GRB the reading problem is consistent with relatively poor performance in other areas of ability and attainment.

Rutter and Yule argue for the validity of the distinction between SRR and GRB on the basis of population studies which appear to show that specific reading retardation is more common than would be predicted in the samples upon statistical grounds alone. Subsequently, this finding has been challenged by further studies which have sought to eliminate any artefacts introduced into the data by ceiling effects or other peculiarities in the tests utilized in data collection (Rodgers, 1983; Share *et al.*, 1987). Van der Wissel and Zegers (1985) propose on statistical grounds that the distinction between the two groups is spurious and recommend abandoning its use. However, other authors have argued that the distinction may still have validity and practical utility (e.g. Frith, 1985; Hulme and Snowling, 1988).

It may be argued that there is educational value in the differentiation of the two groups of poor readers on the grounds that the children within them have characteristics that are significantly different. Thus, for example, in Rutter and Yule's original work there was a greater preponderance of boys in the SRR group than in the GRB group (Rutter and Yule, 1975). This difference beween the groups has been confirmed in recent studies (Share *et al.*, 1987; Tyler and Elliott, 1988) and the general finding that as the mean IQ of children with reading difficulties increases so does the ratio of boys to girls is often reported in the literature (e.g. Lovell *et al.*, 1964; Miles, 1983; Silva *et al.*, 1985). Van der Wissel and Zegers (1985) suggest that this finding may be explained by the general difference in the reading score distributions of boys and girls and ceiling effects in the tests administered, but this position is not substantiated by other studies where such effects are excluded (Tyler and Elliott, 1988).

Rutter and Yule (*ibid.*) argue also for differences between SRR and GRB on other factors such as motor difficulties and global language deficits and more recent studies have replicated these findings. As Hulme and Snowling (1988) argue, the pattern of a child's reading and spelling performance and the way that this changes during development depends upon the interplay of the child's cognitive strengths and weaknesses and the methods of tuition. It remains conceivable that paths towards literacy differ in the two groups, although whether educational outcomes are affected is unclear. A recent study by Fredman and Stevenson found that retarded readers do not necessarily use different reading strategies from backward readers and that reading level explains most of the difference in reading between retarded and backward children (Fredman and Stevenson, 1988). However, the children studied were aged 13 and differences may by this stage have been disguised by attempts at remediation. In addition, although the implications for differential remediation of the reading difficulty itself are uncertain it may be the case that more general teaching strategies may be affected by the distinction of SRR and GRB (Tyler, 1989). Thus, whereas SRR children may benefit from the normal curriculum if consideration is given to the manner in which it is delivered, it is probable that GRB children may require some alteration in curriculum content as well. The concept of SRR may, therefore, have practical consequences. Although the process of distinguishing between reading retarded and reading backward children on the basis of regression equations remains esoteric, attempts have been made to make the process more accessible to teachers (Dobbins, 1986) and it remains to be seen whether this has practical benefits.

Dyslexia, specific reading retardation and the reading process

Similarities between the characteristics of children with specific reading retardation and those described as dyslexic raise the possibility of the two conditions being one and the same thing (Tansley and Panckhurst, 1981). Speech and language difficulties and problems in sequencing are the behaviours most strongly associated with specific reading retardation and yet these are also the areas that are said to be most problematic in the dyslexic child (Miles, 1983). Similarities in the cognitive profiles of children diagnosed as dyslexic and others identified as having specific reading retardation have also been found (Tyler and Elliott, 1988). Yet, the possibility remains that both these groups contain further subtypes. Ellis (1985) distinguishes between typologies based on extrinsic factors, where children are classified into groups on the basis of features which accompany but are not part of the literacy problem, and those based on intrinsic factors focusing on the analysis of the reading performance *per se*. Typologies based on extrinsic factors will be discussed in the next section of this chapter, but we turn our attention first to typologies based on factors intrinsic to the reading process itself.

In the literature various attempts have been made to classify retarded readers in accordance with the principal deficiencies within the reading process that they exhibit. Thus, for example, Vernon (1979) suggests that different degrees of severity of reading retardation may correspond to specific types of deficiency which impede acquisition of successive skills essential for reading competence. She goes on to identify five groups. The typology proposed by Aaron (1982) is rather different in that it is based upon the proposition of an imbalance hypothesis linking skills necessary to the reading process with underlying psychological mechanisms. It is argued that normal reading requires the deployment of both simultaneous and sequential processing of stimuli and that underutilization or overdependence upon one of the systems leads to inefficient reading. Consequently, Aaron proposes that there are two principal types of reading disorder depending upon which of the two processing methods is unduly dominant. It is also observed that since some children demonstrate fluent oral reading skills but fail to comprehend what they have read, a third subtype, comprehension dyslexia, may be identified.

Three subgroups of dyslexic children have also been differentiated by Boder, in a highly influential model which emphasizes that reading/spelling/writing patterns have diagnostic, prognostic and therapeutic implications (Boder, 1973). The first group identified (termed 'dysphonetic') is the largest and manifests deficits in the integration of symbols with their sounds with a resulting deficit in the development of phonic word analysis skills. Children within this group tend to rely on sight vocabularies and have difficulty decomposing words auditorily. The second group ('dyseidetic') have deficits in visual perception and memory for letters and whole-word configurations, with a resulting failure to develop a sight vocabulary. Children within this group retain however, the ability to develop phonic attack skills. The third group ('alexic') constitute a mixed dysphonetic/dyseidetic group with deficiencies in both simultaneous and sequential processing. The clear similarity between Boder and Aaron who each made a distinction between subgroups with apparent auditory (or sequential) processing deficits as opposed to visual (or simultaneous/holistic) processing problems is also well supported in the literature (Satz and Morris, 1981). However, the attempt to validate subtypes by comparison between studies is fraught with difficulty for methodological reasons. Moreover, the terms used to identify subtypes represent abstractions from the data and may be subject to observer bias.

Statistical classification approaches

A relatively large number of studies have now approached the problem of identifying subtypes of children with learning disabilities by recourse to multi-variate statistical techniques, including Q-technique factor analysis and cluster analysis (Rourke, 1985). In many instances a tripartite division of the overall sample again seems to be most successful, although in some studies investigators have favoured the delineation of larger numbers of subgroups with varying degrees of confidence (Malatesha and Dougan, 1982). While some researchers have continued to utilize diagnostic criteria to identify a target group of learning disabled children prior to subtyping, others have avoided this potential problem and have utilized statistical methods to discriminate the groups of disabled children in the first place. The clusters of children that are obtained are defined in terms of correlates associated with the reading problems. The basic assumption of this work is that there are children who show patterns of similarities and differences on a range of attributes and that the identification of these relationships both within and between groups will bring about a better understanding of their aetiological basis and educational needs (Morris, 1988). However, such studies have been criticized since correlational factors are not necessarily linked causally to reading difficulties and many of the measures used in the initial analysis are apparently remote from the reading/spelling process (Hulme and Snowling, 1988). Yet this criticism does not apply in all cases, especially where putative links between the cognitive profiles and theories of reading can be made as in the studies cited below.

A number of investigations have described the use of the Wechsler Intelligence Scales for Children (WISC) with learning disabled children to point out the possible areas of related cognitive deficit and to suggest diagnostic use of the profiles obtained (Thomson and Grant, 1979). A similar exercise has also been conducted with the British Ability Scales (BAS) (Thomson, 1982). Meta-analyses of a large number of such studies have continued to emphasize the presence of verbal as opposed to visual deficits in the learning disabled group, with particular emphasis on problems with short-term memory processing (Kavale and Forness, 1984; Lawson and Inglis, 1985). Attention has been given in a number of reports (Bradley and Bryant, 1978; Bryant and Bradley, 1985; Ellis and Large, 1987) to the question of the causality of such cognitive profiles. In particular it has been argued that where studies compare both good and poor readers who are matched for mental age, the differences in profiles obtained may be caused by different reading experiences. In a recent study using the BAS (Tyler and Elliott, 1988), the effect of chronological age was excluded through the use of standardized scores and the effect of variations in reading ability was controlled through the identification of groups with very similar, below average reading levels. In part of this study the BAS scores of a sample of children identified as dyslexic on clinical grounds were entered into a cluster analysis from which a three cluster solution emerged as being most satisfactory statistically. Examination of the profiles obtained suggested the identification of the first group as having deficits in mixed visual-spatial and linguistic processing, the second as having sequential processing problems and

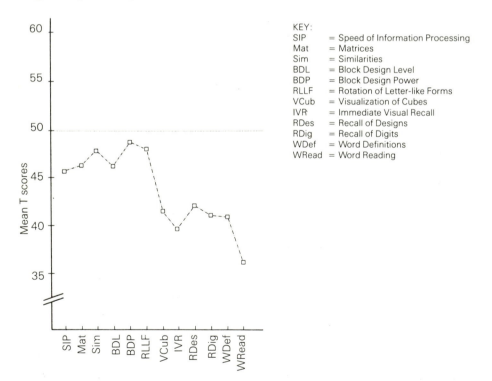

Figure 3.1 Profile of dyslexic children — Cluster 1: mixed visual spatial and linguistic problems

the third as having difficulties with the holistic retrieval of information (Figures 3.1–3.3). Each group was then analysed for fit to a proposed statistical model of learning disability (the model assuming that learning disability is a unitary phenomenon). While the fit to this model for the whole sample had been good (Elliott and Tyler, 1986, 1987), the fit for the subgroups was poor. It was concluded that a model implicating a single aetiology for dyslexic children is inadequate. It is interesting that while this study still does not demonstrate causal connections between the identified cognitive deficits and the problems encountered by the children it is possible to hypothesize how the cognitive processing problems could contribute to difficulties in learning to read. Moreover, the subtyping bears a distinct resemblance to that adopted by others (e.g. Boder, 1973) from examination of difficulties encountered by children within the reading process itself.

A second study recently reported also goes some way towards meeting potential criticisms of typologies based on multi-variate analyses. Morris *et al.*, (1986) describe the findings of a longitudinal cluster analysis to classify a sample of normal and reading disabled males based on their performances on a battery of test items at kindergarten and at second and fifth grades. Using a validation framework, five developmental subtypes of children were found. While three

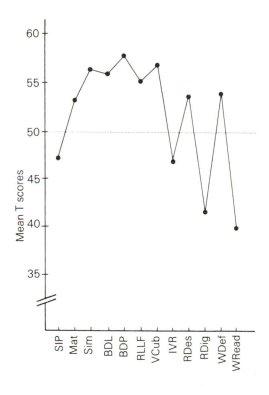

Figure 3.2 Profile of dyslexic children — Cluster 2: sequential processing problems

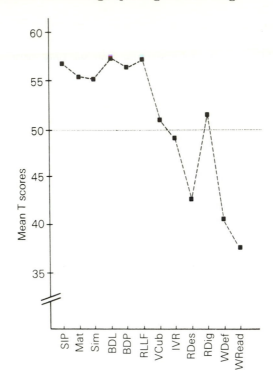

Figure 3.3 Profile of dyslexic children — Cluster 3: problems of holistic retrieval of information

of these five groups could best be described as partitions of a multi-variate normal distribution the other two contained children with reading difficulties with different covariance structures suggesting different developmental patterns. One subtype showed a rapid development of visual-spatial abilities over time from below to above average levels, whereas language abilities developed at slower than average rates. By contrast the second subtype showed a consistently slow rate of visual-spatial development, whereas language skills fell from average to below average levels. These findings raise questions about the use of cross-sectional samples for subtyping and are consistent with other research which suggests that subtype characteristics may change with age and with stages of learning to read. Thus, Bakker (1979, 1984) proposes that a child who is learning to read must first utilize the visual-spatial perceptual processes of the right hemisphere but must then switch to the linguistic processing strategy of the left hemisphere in order to become a fluent reader. Within Bakker's classification, which contains both extrinsic and intrinsic elements, one may distinguish between children who do not switch from the first strategy to the second ('P-type children') and those who do not begin with the first strategy ('L-type children'). These two subtypes of poor readers seem to have a striking similarity with other classificatory systems described above.

Conclusions

A variety of ways of breaking down groups of children with learning disabilities is described in the literature. Most recently, attempts have also been made to link patterns of acquired and developmental dyslexia (Ellis, 1985; Hulme and Snowling, 1988), although the exact nature of the relationships remains unclear, and to employ information processing models of the reading process (Seymour, 1986). As yet no agreement has been reached as to the most successful way of subtyping children with reading difficulties but it is possible to conclude that *treatment of children with reading difficulties as members of a global category of learning disability is unlikely to prove profitable in the longer term*. Rather, it is probable that a multi-variate approach linking cognitive attributes to observations of the child's reading and spelling skills will prove most profitable. While ultimately each child may have a unique pattern of strengths and weaknesses if sufficient numbers of variables are taken into account, it may be possible to generalize on the basis of a reduced number of items to inform remediation. At the present time it remains to be seen what level of subdivision of learning disabled children will have the greatest pragmatic and theoretical value.

Nevertheless, inspection of the literature shows a large number of studies employing a variety of methodologies which have differentiated between groups where there is either a sequential processing (language) problem or a holistic processing (visual-spatial) problem or a more severe mixed processing deficit. It seems likely, on the evidence obtained so far, that this form of subtyping may prove most successful both theoretically and practically.

There remains, however, a need (1) to clarify the relationships of these groups with other groups of children with language or visual-perceptual difficulties, (2) to link tuition strategies to proposed typologies, (3) to make processes of allocation of children to different groups available to teachers, and above all (4) to reduce terminological confusion.

References

Aaron, P. G. (1982) 'The neuropsychology of developmental dyslexia', in: Malatesha, R. N., and Aaron, P.G. (Eds) *Reading Disorders: Varieties and Treatments*, New York, Academic Press.

Bakker, D.J. (1979) 'Hemispheric differences and reading strategies: Two dyslexias?' *Bulletin of the Orton Society*, 29, pp. 84–100.

Bakker, D.J. (1984) 'The brain as dependent variable', *Journal of Clinical Neuropsychology*, 6, pp. 1–18.

Blashfield, R. K and Draguns, J. (1976) 'Evaluative criteria for psychiatric classification', *Journal of Abnormal Psychology*, 85, pp. 140–150.

Boder, E. (1973) 'Developmental dyslexia: a diagnostic approach based on three atypical reading-spelling patterns', *Developmental Medicine and Child Neurology*, 15, pp. 663–687.

Bradley, L. and Bryant, P.E. (1978) 'Difficulties in auditory organisation as a possible source of reading backwardness', *Nature*, 271, pp. 746–747.

Bryant, P.E. and Bradley, L. (1985) *Children's Reading Problems*, Oxford, Basil Blackwell.

Dobbins, A. (1986) 'An empirical classification of children with reading difficulties', *Educational and Child Psychology*, 3, 2, pp. 70–79.

Elliott, C.D. and Tyler, S. (1986) 'British Ability Scales profiles of children with reading difficulties', *Educational and Child Psychology*, 3, 2, pp. 80–89.

Elliott, C.D. and Tyler, S. (1987) 'Learning disabilities and intelligence test results: a principal components analysis of the British Ability Scales', *British Journal of Psychology*, 78, pp. 325–333.

Ellis, A.W. (1985) 'The cognitive neuropsychology of developmental (and acquired) dyslexia: a critical survey', *Cognitive Neuropsychology*, 2, 2, pp. 169–205.

Ellis, N. and Large, B. (1987) 'The development of reading: as you seek so shall you find', *British Journal of Psychology*, 78, pp. 1–28.

Fredman, G. and Stevenson, J. (1988) 'Reading processes in specific reading retarded and reading backward 13-year-olds', *British Journal of Developmental Psychology*, 6, 1, pp. 97–108.

Frith, U. (1985) 'The usefulness of the concept of unexpected reading failure: comments on reading retardation revisited', *British Journal of Developmental Psychology*, 3, pp. 15–17.

Hulme, C. and Snowling, M. (1988) 'The classification of children with reading difficulties', *Developmental Medicine and Child Neurology*, 30, pp. 391–406.

John, E.R., Karmel, B.Z. and Corning, W.C. (1977) 'Neurometrics', *Science*, 196, pp. 1393–1410.

Kavale, K.A. and Forness, S.R. (1984) 'A meta-analysis of the validity of Wechsler scale profiles and recategorizations: patterns or parodies?', *Learning Disability Quarterly*, 7, pp. 136–156.

Lawson, J.S. and Inglis, J. (1985) 'Learning disabilities and intelligence test results: a model based on a principal components analysis of the WISC-R', *British Journal of Psychology*, 76, pp. 35–48.

Lovell, K., Shapton, D. and Warren, N.S. (1964) 'A study of some cognitive and other disabilities in backward readers of average intelligence as assessed by a non-verbal test', *British Journal of Educational Psychology*, 34, pp. 58–64.

Malatesha, R.N. and Dougan, D.R. (1982) 'Clinical subtypes of developmental dyslexia: resolution of an irresolute problem', in Malatesha, R.N. and Aaron, P.G. (Eds) *Reading Disorders: Varieties and Treatments*, New York, Academic Press.

Miles, T. (1983) *Dyslexia: The Pattern of Difficulties*, London, Granada.

Morris, R.D. (1988) 'Classification of learning disabilities: old problems and new approaches', *Journal of Consulting and Clinical Psychology*, 56, 6, pp. 789–794.

Morris, R., Blashfield, R. and Satz, P. (1986) 'Developmental classification of reading-disabled children', *Journal of Clinical and Experimental Neuropsychology*, 8, 4, pp. 371–392.

Rodgers, B. (1983) 'The identification and prevalence of specific reading retardation', *British Journal of Educational Psychology*, 53, pp. 369–373.

Rourke, B.P. (Ed.) (1985) *Neuropsychology of Learning Disabilities: Essentials of Subtype Analysis*', New York, Guilford Press.

Rutter, M. (1978) 'Prevalence and types of dyslexia', in Benton, A. L. and Pearl, D. (Eds) *Dyslexia: An Appraisal of Current Knowledge*, New York, Oxford University Press.

Rutter, M. and Yule, W. (1975) 'The concept of specific reading retardation', *Journal of Child Psychology and Psychiatry*, 16, pp. 181–197.

Satz, P. and Morris, R. (1981) 'Learning disability subtypes: a review', in Pirozzolo, F. J. and Wittrock, M. C. (Eds) *Neuropsychological and Cognitive Processes in Reading*, New York, Academic Press.

Seymour, P. H. K. (1986) *Cognitive Analysis of Dyslexia*, London, Routledge & Kegan Paul.

Share, D., McGee, R., McKenzie, D., Williams, S. and Silva, P. (1987) 'Further evidence relating to the distinction between specific reading retardation and reading backwardness', *British Journal of Developmental Psychology*, 5, pp. 35–44.

Silva, P., McGee, R. and Williams, S. (1985) 'Some characteristics of 9-year-old boys with general reading backwardness or specific reading retardation', *Journal of Child Psychology and Psychiatry*, 26, pp. 407–421.

Tansley, P. and Panckhurst, J. (1981) *Children with Specific Learning Difficulties*, Windsor, Berks., NFER-Nelson.

Thomson, M. E. (1982) 'The assessment of children with specific reading difficulties (dyslexia) using the British Ability Scales', *British Journal of Psychology*, 73, pp. 461–478.

Thomson, M. E. and Grant, S. E. (1979) 'The WISC subtest profile of the dyslexic child', in Newton, M. J., Thomson, M. E. and Richards, I. L. (Eds) *Readings in Dyslexia*, Wisbech, England, LDA.

Tyler, S. (1989) 'Patterns in the Assessment of Specific Learning Difficulty', *Paper presented at the First International Conference of the British Dyslexia Society, City of Bath College, March 1989*.

Tyler, S. and Elliott, C. D. (1988) 'Cognitive profiles of groups of poor readers and dyslexic children on the British Ability Scales', *British Journal of Psychology*, 79, pp. 493–508.

Van der Wissel, A. and Zegers, F. C. (1985) 'Reading retardation revisited', *British Journal of Developmental, Psychology*, 3, 1, pp. 3–9.

Vernon, M. D. (1979) 'Variability in reading retardation', *British Journal of Psychology*, 70, pp. 7–16.

4
Reconciling Different Approaches to Intervention

Rea Reason

The right to read

It is now nearly twenty years since James E. Allen, then Commissioner of Education in the United States, coined the phrase 'the right to read' as part of his oft-quoted statement ' . . . there is no higher nationwide priority than the provision of the right to read for all . . . ' (Allen, 1970). Commissioner Allen provided public recognition of the fact that one cannot live a full individual and social life without adequate competence in literacy.

Life in Britain in the 1990s will seem even tougher and more dependent on reading and writing. As the attitudes and services associated with a freely available welfare system recede, there may be less patience for those who struggle with basic literacy or numeracy. Employers will want school leavers who can ensure cost effective production. Schools will want pupils who can ensure that their published test results are high. So school life itself may become harder for those who experience educational difficulties.

If pupils have trouble with written tasks appropriate for their age levels, access to all subject areas, including Science and Mathematics, becomes reduced. At the time of writing, the report of the National Curriculum Council Working Group in English has just been published. It argues that the 'secretarial' aspects of English, good spelling and handwriting, should not be taught at the expense of the quality of writing, i.e. of conveying meaning, structure and interest. But it does also recognize indirectly the existence of some pupils for whom the acquisition of these 'secretarial' skills does not come so easily (Department of Education and Science and the Welsh Office, 1988, Chapter 13).

A central assumption in this chapter is that all pupils with difficulties in basic literacy have the right, regardless of labels, to receive as much help as will be necessary. This help encompasses two interdependent aspects. First, the provision of 'support' in the form of information and resources to develop a range of adaptations which maximize access to the National Curriculum.

Second, the provision of 'remediation' consisting of relevant and meaningful help with the acquisition of literacy.

The devolved control introduced by the 1988 Education Reform Act makes schools even more accountable for ensuring that pupils receive both the support and the remediation that is required. Schools will have to explain to parents why some pupils may need modifications to the curriculum, what those modifications will be and what educational arrangements will be made. Whatever their socio-cultural standing, therefore, parents and governors will be looking for convincing plans and adequate provision for their children.

The purpose of this chapter is to link the theoretical underpinnings of different teaching methods in a way which provides teachers and other applied practitioners with a coherent framework for intervention. This framework comprises both support and remediation in the context of mainstream education. The first part of the chapter introduces theoretical considerations which form the basis for teaching approaches concerned with word recognition skills. The second deals with the theory underlying those approaches which promote the whole language and reading experience from the very start. The third part is concerned with a synthesis of the two orientations. The rest of the chapter applies that framework to the concept of specific learning difficulties and to a range of methods of intervention.

This chapter draws heavily on two previous publications: first, Reason *et al.* (1988), an article reflecting the consensus of an interest group consisting of support teachers and educational psychologists from nine local education authorities in the North-West; and secondly, Reason (1988), a brief account of a seminar and workshop given at the annual conference of the Division of Educational and Child Psychology of the British Psychological Society.

Theoretical debate

The theoretical position taken here is that understanding of the complex interaction between the various causal factors of literacy remains imperfect. Our thinking, therefore, has to be probabilistic, i.e. we can only say that an explanation *may* be appropriate or a plan of action is *likely* to work but we cannot know before the plan is tried out with particular individuals in a particular context. There can be no one certain recipe, whether 'psycholinguistic' or 'multisensory', while theoretical understanding of the processes involved in reading and writing is incomplete. What there can be, however, is comprehensive knowledge of different theoretical viewpoints and practical approaches to enable informed choices to be made.

Because reading and writing are so essential to modern life, it is only natural that feelings should run high. Strong feelings can result, however, in unnecessary polarization of opinion about different approaches to intervention. Furthermore, psychological research can contribute to this 'binary' thinking by setting up studies to support or refute particular theoretical stances (cf. Bryant and Impey, 1986, versus Coltheart, 1987, described below). Consequently, some traditions of scientific research call for debate rather than an appraisal of common elements. Meanwhile applied practitioners, such as teachers and educational psychologists, have to respond to particular situations. Their task is to synthesize that which is useful into workable plans of action. This chapter is an attempt to do that.

The enquiry into Specific Learning Difficulties by the Division of Educational and Child Psychology of the British Psychological Society (Cornwall, Hedderly and Pumfrey, 1983) recognized that the conceptual bases and constraints of various professional disciplines could lead to differing interpretations of the same issues. The report reproduced Saxe's poem of the Indian parable about 'truth': an elephant touched from different sides by blind men, each touching part of that truth but none perceiving the whole.

The analogy has seemed so apt that this author has drawn an overhead slide of a large elephant with many of the different professional and theoretical orientations mapped on to it. These include Neurophysiology, Biochemistry, Orthoptics, the consideration of dyslexia as a syndrome/disability, the study of that disability through neurologically damaged adults, the theory of specific language disability, cognitive models of underlying processes, attempts to relate ability profiles to reading attainments, the study of phonological delay, and the psycholinguistic orientations which reject the focus on deciphering individual words.

How can teachers make sense of this diversity? Seymour (1986) suggests that different approaches should be considered in terms of the expertise of those involved in the investigation: for example, educationalists, research psychologists or neurophysiologists. Teachers will be concerned with instructional matters, i.e. the description of children's competencies directly related to reading. Cognitive researchers, however, will be interested in examining the underlying processes which may be different in cases of learning difficulties. Neurophysiologists on their part will want to understand these processes in relation to brain structure and neural functions.

It seems that confusion in the educational context can arise from insufficient differentiation of the purposes of those involved in the study of learning difficulties. There is a danger of indulging in a 'cocktail' of descriptions which refer simultaneously, for example, to reading ages, short-term memory and cerebral dominance. With no unifying rationale, such practices can then label the individual with a selection of 'deficits' which have no clear educational purpose. Then the collection of labels, culled from tentatively phrased research findings, can detract attention from instructional issues.

The focus here is on educational practice. The chapter is concerned with only those aspects which relate to teaching methods. Two major stances are singled out: first, the cognitive basis for supporting systematic practice of subskills and, second, those viewpoints which stress the centrality of meaningful language experiences in natural contexts. The purpose will be to show that these two orientations are complementary, not conflicting.

Cognitive models

The primary interest of cognitive research into reading has not been with education but with the modelling of human information processing. The study of the way people read or how individuals considered to have impairments or deficits do not read has been undertaken to illustrate or test these models. Intervention has rarely been mentioned and, when it has, these researchers have tended to favour structured cumulative approaches, i.e. the systematic practice of subskills of reading and writing.

The research has mainly centred on the single word and the elements within it. Researchers have by no means been unaware of the wider linguistic aspects but, for them, the number of variables in the single word has been quite sufficient. So reading has become defined as the translation of sequential visual symbols into sounds with the meaning of the word extracted through that process. Clearly this focus on the automatic processing of letter strings has provided a much narrower conception of reading and writing than that in the broader educational context. It has resulted in models of reading which share the principle of dual access, i.e. written words can be processed through a phonological route and/or through a more direct (visual) route to the semantic system concerned with meaning.

The concept of 'working memory' features in the discussion of constitutional reasons to explain why some children struggle with the processes of learning to read written words (Shankweiler and Crain, 1986). Working memory, a broader and more complex notion than short-term memory, accounts reasonably for most of the basic findings of earlier short-term memory research. In essence working memory refers to the immediate mental workspace which shares its limited resources between processing and storage. It is then argued that children with reading difficulties place a greater strain on the limited capacity of working memory or, alternatively, that working memory does not process information as efficiently in these cases.

The phrase 'architecture of the apparatus' was used by Bertelson (1986) to denote the development of models of the reading process (see Ellis, 1984; Morton, 1979; Seymour, 1986; Singleton, 1987). These models, consisting of diagrammatic representations of cognitive processes, can make one wonder how anyone ever learns to read (Reason, 1988). Singleton's working model, for example, illustrates the many different components which may not develop normally or which may be damaged. It is as if a model of the processes involved in running down the stairs had been constructed so that we can marvel at the way most of us achieve this feat quite effortlessly.

For the educationalist, these models emphasize the many different ways in which children may or may not learn to read. The uniqueness of individual patterns is illustrated by Seymour's detailed case studies which point convincingly to the danger of assuming the existence of a small number of dyslexic sub-types (Seymour, *op.cit.*). Such theoretical viewpoints, while unable to provide direct prescriptions, give support to educational approaches which attempt to work out a combination of methods to help an individual learn most effectively.

Word recognition

Studies of children learning to read single words lead to discussion of the fundamental differences between the skills involved in dealing with print and in dealing with speech. It then follows that reading and writing are not seen as natural extensions of primary linguistic activity but as complex skills which must be taught deliberately and carefully.

Of note, for example, is the developmental view of reading as a sequence ranging from the early 'logographic' stage to an intermediate 'alphabetic' stage to the final 'orthographic' stage (Frith, 1985; Seymour and McGregor, 1984). While the child at the 'logographic' stage makes use of visual recognition of overall word patterns, the child at the 'alphabetic' stage has learnt to utilize sound/symbol correspondence and the fluent 'orthographic' reader is characterized by context-dependent use of pronunciation rules and analogies.

Other researchers, for example Treiman (1984), consider individuals to have characteristically different strategies for deciphering the printed word. They hypothesize that children can be classified as 'Phoenicians', relying primarily on phonological codes, or as 'Chinese', relying on the visual appearance of words. This work links neatly with the dual route models, i.e. that written words can be processed through a phonological and/or more direct (visual) route to the semantic system (see Chapter 8).

Particular mention needs to be made of the work of Bradley and Bryant, described in other chapters of this book, which has attempted to demonstrate a relationship between the ability to categorize words on the basis of sound similarity at pre-school or reception infant level and performance on standarized reading tests some three years later.

Bryant and Bradley (1985) have concentrated on the notion of phonological awareness as the key to literacy. They argue that it can be taught and that explanations in terms of cognitive defects are not necessary. Bryant and Impey (1986) then challenge the work of those concerned with drawing parallels between adults who, due to injury, have lost some aspect of their ability to read (acquired dyslexics) and children who experience marked difficulties in learning to read (developmental dyslexics). Their view is that these adult typologies of defect are not relevant to children whom they regard as being delayed, particularly in the development of phonology. Coltheart (1987) responds forcibly to Bryant and Impey. According to him some children acquire visual or phonological word recognition skills *abnormally* slowly, i.e. there is a defect.

Bryant and Impey's article and Coltheart's response illustrate the kind of binary debate, mentioned earlier in this chapter, which is indeed important and relevant to cognitive research. But what are the implications in the

Table 4.1   The influence of that branch of cognitive psychology concerned with word recognition

1. Difficulties with learning to read and write occur at the word processing level involving automatic recognition of letter strings.

2. Deficient word recognition results in poor comprehension. Learners cannot attend to the content if they are laboriously deciphering print.

3. Models of cognitive processing illustrate the many different components which may be involved in the process of learning to recognize written words.

4. Written words can be processed through a phonological route and/or through a direct (visual) route to the semantic system concerned with meaning.

5. Manipulation of phonetic units requires activities which enhance phonological awareness and training through conversion rules and analogies.

6. Reading is not necessarily a natural extension of spoken language communication but a complex skill. Learning to read can be difficult and can require structured cumulative methods of instruction.

educational context? In the author's opinion none currently, except that the term 'delay' sounds more optimistic than the term 'defect'. As described later, we do not seem to use any particular educational methods which differentiate between the two terms. What we have is a process of interactive assessment and teaching methods through which we try to determine what the individual needs to learn and the way in which that person learns best.

It is now time to summarize the influences which that branch of cognitive psychology concerned with written words can have in an educational context. Table 4.1 lists, in a rather over-simplified form, the main points derived from that body of work. As we move on to consider more general theories of cognition and learning, those sections will also end with a list of points (Table 4.2). It will then be possible to discuss the extent to which views based on research about word recognition can be regarded as a subset of the broader context of psychological theory.

Communicating for a purpose

Psycholinguistic orientations promote the whole language and reading experience from the very start. The focus is on the purpose for communication and the enjoyment derived from the content of the text. Consequently, many authors hold the view that reading in its fullest sense cannot be taught in a formal sequenced way (Goodman, 1967; Meek, 1982; Smith, 1978). They see the acquisition of written language as being comparable to that of spoken language. Children learn to speak by being surrounded by speech, gradually joining in that which is meaningful, being supported in what little they can do until they are able to do more. Similarly it is argued that, in learning to read, children learn through having the opportunity to listen to, read with assistance and talk about books and information which hold meaning and enjoyment for them (Arnold, 1982; Holdaway, 1980; Waterland, 1986).

Smith (*op.cit.*) writes that learning to read does not require the memorization of phonic rules or lists of words; such subskills are taken care of in the course of reading with assistance as long as children have the opportunity to generate and test their own hypotheses about reading and get feedback in the process of so doing. The pre-requisites for learning to read are then an adequate prior understanding of the purposes of language, plenty of opportunity to use that language and to predict the way it is represented in a visual form as a written text. It needs to be noted, however, that Smith does not reject direct teaching but places it very much in a secondary role:

> I am not saying that nothing should be taught, that children should not learn the alphabet or build up sight vocabularies ... But all of these are by-products of reading that make more sense as reading itself is mastered and understood (p.190).

Psycholinguistic views are supported by research about the way children acquire language. Wells and his co-workers, for example, emphasize the interactional perspective of language acquisition (Wells, 1985). The essence of their work can be conveyed by paraphrasing the saying 'How do I know what I mean until I hear what I say?' with 'How do I know what I mean until I hear what my parent says in response to what I have said?' So Wells and his co-workers place the pragmatic aspects of conversation, i.e. the uses to which it is put, at the source of all other language development. For them, the consideration of syntax and semantics becomes only relevant in the context of a purpose for communication. Similarly, then, it is the purpose of communication in the written form which psycholinguists see as the source of all other learning associated with reading.

In learning to communicate through speech, young children are not subjected by their parents, siblings or other children to a structured sequence of instruction. Language is learnt untidily in real situations (Wiles, 1985). The parallel can then be extended to reading, also learnt untidily in real situations with 'real books'. Indeed the follow-up study by Wells and his co-workers (*op.cit.*) shows that reading proficiency at age 7 is related to the child's knowledge of and interest in books before starting school, i.e., a knowledge associated with the understanding of the abstractions involved in story telling not embedded in the immediate context. This means that the child has learnt about the purpose of print incidentally through hearing stories and other information read and not through deliberate instruction.

Effort after meaning

In case it be thought that psycholinguistic orientations hold a monopoly of the emphasis on meaningful learning, it is essential to make a brief detour into more general psychological theory. A few paragraphs cannot do justice to this task; yet lack of mention would deny the importance of eminent psychologists such as Bartlett and Bruner, fathers of current work concerning the interactive nature of learning.

Frederick Bartlett's enduring phrase, 'effort after meaning', encapsulated his views (Bartlett, 1932). He introduced the notion of 'schema' to explain the systematic errors that were apparent in the recall of pictorial or textual material. The errors occurred because his subjects were unconsciously attempting to relate the new material to established knowledge structures or 'schemata'. A 'schema' was defined by Bartlett as 'an active organization of past reactions, or of past experiences' which then leads to ' . . . the tendency to interpret present material in accordance with the general character of earlier experience'.

We can see clear parallels between the way psycholinguists describe the process of learning to read and Bartlett's notions. Learners bring to the reading task their expectations based on previous experience and the 'schema' they have developed about the nature of language and communication. They then predict what reading is likely to be about, in terms of content, interest and language structures and, furthermore, their predictions and expectations extend to knowledge about words and the letter strings of which the words are made.

With regard to content, the reader tries to make sense of the purposes and thoughts conveyed by an author. As described by Rumelhart (1975), if a reader arrives at the 'schema' intended by the author, then the text has been comprehended. If the reader can find no 'schema' to accept the textual information, the text is not understood. And if the reader finds 'schema' other than the one intended by the author, the text is misinterpreted.

The current view of 'schema' is of higher order, generic cognitive structures which underlie all aspects of human knowledge and skill (see Reason, 1990, for further references). Although their processing lies beyond the direct reach of awareness, their products — words, images, feelings and actions — are available to consciousness. These are the products children bring to the reading task which determine whether they become readers with a lifelong interest in books and other written information or whether they see reading as a job to be done through deciphering the text.

Shared meaning

Bruner has recently re-considered his life's work about the nature of human knowledge and children's learning (Bruner, 1986). He comments on the way his own thinking has changed: 'I have come increasingly to recognise that most learning in most settings is a communal activity, a sharing of the culture' (p. 127).

Bruner uses the notion of culture as an educational 'forum' in which teachers and pupils become involved in the negotiation of shared meanings,

Table 4.2 *The social and interactive learning of visually guided thinking*

1. 'Effort after meaning' underlies all aspects of learning. Children learn to read and develop a lifelong interest in reading and writing only when they can see the purpose for such communication.

2. Learning is in essence social and interactive. Learning to read requires shared interest, gentle assistance and plenty of opportunity. It does not have to be taught in a formal sequenced way.

3. Language is learnt untidily in real situations. Reading is learnt untidily with 'real books' written for the purpose of conveying shared meaning rather than the practice of a restricted reading vocabulary.

4. As reading is a natural extension of spoken language, difficulties are associated with limited interest, enjoyment, comprehension and opportunity. Poor readers may not be using higher order knowledge about language to guide the learning of lower level word processing skills.

the teacher interacting with the pupils in a way that supports a participatory and future-orientated process of education. This can lead to a discussion of the rationales adopted about the nature of learning. If it is assumed that learning can be 'poured' into the brain, then didactic teaching follows. If, as Bruner argues, learning is in essence social and interactive, then collaborative teaching methods move to the centre stage of education.

The recognition that knowledge, learning and thought are not just to do with how an individual thinks or learns, but are intrinsically social and interactive has influenced much of psychological research today. The development of common shared knowledge, between teacher and pupil and between the pupils themselves, has been investigated, for example, by Edwards and Mercer (1987). They introduce the term 'scaffolding' to describe the teacher's task of creating through joint action and talk a contextual framework for educational activities which develop common knowledge.

To link back to the topic of reading and writing, we can make reference to another eminent cognitive psychologist, Neisser, who defined reading as 'visually guided thinking' (Neisser, 1967). For him context provided the focus from which efficient recognition of individual words was developed. This led to the practical conclusion that teachers should stress the importance of relevance, content and interest rather than word recognition.

When pupils read and write together with their teachers, parents or friends, and they spend much time discussing the content which they find relevant and enjoyable, these shared activities can be described as *'the social and interactive learning of visually guided thinking'*. This, in essence, provides the theoretical rationale for global language-based approaches to the teaching of literacy. Their major features and assumptions are summarized in Table 4.2.

A synthesis

Two theoretical orientations have now been outlined which, on initial examination, would appear diametrically opposed with regard to their practical implications. Table 4.1 has summarized the influences of that branch of cognitive psychology concerned with word recognition. The implicit assumption here is that word recognition skills are learnt through structured cumulative methods of teaching, i.e. complex skills become built up from their elements, the letter strings within words. Table 4.2 has, in turn, summarized the influences of psychological theories which emphasize the social and interactive nature of learning. Learning to read now requires shared interest, gentle assistance and plenty of opportunity rather than a formal sequence of targets. This approach assumes that children can learn to recognize printed words as a natural extension of higher order knowledge about language and life in general.

The up-turned triangle in Figure 4.1 provides a framework for accommodating both these approaches. The first and largest segment of the triangle refers to the overall context of learning. Listed in that segment are phrases taken from the work of Bartlett and Bruner, described earlier in this chapter. Previous and current experiences of 'life' and Bartlett's 'effort after meaning' determine whether the purposes and thoughts conveyed by the author can make sense to the reader. Then the interactive nature of learning is emphasized, i.e. Bruner's communal activity resulting in shared knowledge. Learners also need to bring to the task an expectation that they will be able to achieve competence and a sense of enjoyment or satisfaction from it. Here we are referring to aspects such as confidence in one's own ability to learn, determined by the way the learner has been treated on previous occasions.

The second segment of the triangle is concerned with all the above aspects in relation to language learning and its purpose of communication either through speech or the printed text. It links with the psycholinguistic views which promote the whole language and reading experience from the very start, i.e. children learn to speak and read by being involved in these activities and, assisted by parents and teachers, gradually joining in with that which is meaningful to them.

The nature of print now becomes a small, but essential, third segment of the triangle. While dependent on the major areas of learning covered by the larger segments, there are additional features, studied by those cognitive psychologists concerned with word recognition processes and described in previous sections of this chapter summarized in Table 4.1. Some pupils, for example Clarke's young fluent readers, will have learnt all they need about print incidentally through shared interest and gentle assistance (Clarke, 1976). Others will, in addition, require at least some direct and systematic teaching of aspects such as phonological awareness, letter sounds and sight words.

Proponents of psycholinguistic orientations have objected to an over-precipitate narrowing of the teaching of reading and writing to only this last

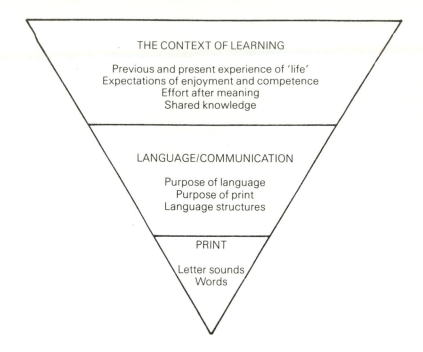

Figure 4. 1   Ingredients of Literacy

small part of the triangle. Apparently reading has been taught by some teachers only as a right/wrong word by word activity involving the deciphering of words or 'pages' in the context of carefully controlled vocabularies, i.e. reading schemes. In these cases the overall approach and atmosphere in the classroom has not facilitated the interaction and enthusiasm about content pre-requisite for the other large and important segments of the triangle in Figure 4.1.

The emphasis on 'real books', written by authors for children because they have something which they want to communicate to children has, in principle, rejected the use of reading schemes. Meanwhile some publishers have attempted to make the content of these schemes more meaningful for learners while, of necessity, retaining the restricted reading vocabularies required by a structured repetitive approach. However, the use of reading schemes does not necessarily deprive children from access to stories, poems and information available in books outside the schemes (Root, 1986). What matters is that these schemes are used flexibly and imaginatively as a supplement to a wide range of children's literature and that teachers themselves have an interest in and knowledge of that literature.

Specific learning difficulties

Figure 4.1 also provides a starting point for conceptualizing specific learning difficulties. Traditional definitions tend to concentrate on the inverted apex of the triangle, i.e. on deficiencies in the recognition and reproduction of print. They assume that the experiences associated with the other broader aspects of the triangle have taken place, hence the references to conventional instruction and adequate socio-cultural opportunity, for example, in the 1968 World Federation of Neurology definition of dyslexia.

But if conventional instruction has only been concerned with the deciphering of print rather than the wider experiences pre-requisite for the purposes of that activity, there may be large gaps in the pupils' learning. To exaggerate the point, children may find that the activity bears no relation to their previous life experiences and that the sterile practice pays no attention to the sharing of knowledge and interaction between the learner, teacher and author. Furthermore, the learner may approach the task with little expectation of enjoyment and competence, possibly reinforced by the teacher's own low expectations of the pupil. We now arrive at something resembling Smith's nine 'rules of reading instruction' for ensuring that the business of learning to read becomes cumbersome and meaningless (Smith, 1985, p.139).

There are, however, cases in which children may need to learn in a very precise way about print. This applies to children from all socio-cultural backgrounds. Defining specific learning difficulties 'by default', as something evoked only when explanations in terms of other factors cannot account for the difficulties, runs the danger of excluding all those pupils whose home backgrounds are not traditionally middle-class. We know, for example, that 'avid readers' tend to come from homes where there are books and parents belong to public libraries (Pumfrey, 1988). Furthermore, culture-specific knowledge can determine how we interpret the functions of the text (cf. Bartlett's 'schema' earlier in this chapter).

Wallace (1986) has provided illustrations of the way in which texts are comprehended according to our cultural 'scripts' for social situations. She uses the following extract from 'Auntie Pat in Hospital' (Link-Up reading scheme) to make her point with regard to young children:

Sally's daddy said we are going to see Auntie Pat in hospital.
Sally and her daddy went to a shop to get some . . .

Predicting that the word 'flowers' follows will not be obvious to those children for whom flower buying is not part of the 'script' for visiting people in hospital. Consequently, if the purpose is to learn about the nature of print in a meaningful context, this text may not make that task easy.

The promotion of equal opportunities supports those approaches to the teaching of reading and writing which emphasize reciprocity and the validity of black experience, perspectives and culture. Some children, regardless of background, will also need to learn about phonology and word recognition in a structured way. It would be very wrong if social circumstances differentiated between the teaching methods offered to children so that some were seen to need 'structured multisensory approaches' (see below) and others 'language experience'. What is needed, therefore, is an assessment of the most suitable combination of methods required by the individual pupil.

Reading together

What should that 'most suitable combination' of teaching methods be? Obviously it will take account of all the elements in Figure 4.1. It has also been assumed that pupils who have difficulty with the deciphering of print will require a cumulative and repetitive approach to this area of learning such as that described in the teachers' manual written by Reason and Boote (1986).

There is, however, an alternative viewpoint presented by Stanovich (1986). He agrees that recent evidence supports the notion that small cognitive differences such as phonological awareness, predictive of reading success, predate the onset of schooling. But, according to Stanovich, these differences may not in themselves be significant. What makes them significant is the way in which they become exaggerated through insufficient opportunity to develop as a consequence of the language experiences associated with learning to read. The implications are then that children not only learn to read by reading but that many underlying competencies also develop through the reading.

It may well be that pupils with specific learning difficulties in the area of print recognition also require much more opportunity for meaningful assisted reading. In other words, the amount of productive and enjoyable time spent in activities to do with the appreciation of nursery rhymes, poetry and literature, combined with plenty of supported reading, becomes the most significant determinant of success.

The various forms of 'shared' (Branston and Provis, 1986; Greening and Spenceley, 1987), 'paired' (Miller, 1987; Morgan and Gavin, 1988) or 'relaxed' (Lindsay, Evans and Jones, 1985) reading are ideal for this purpose. They also draw on behavioural learning theory because parents or other helpers are shown how to model the reading to the child and provide frequent low key praise. But there are no complicated instructions. There is no protracted struggle with deciphering individual words. The sense of warmth, intimacy and shared interest, combined with a reduction of stress associated with a fear of failure, have probably accounted for the short-term positive outcomes reported by many studies. Judging by the current popularity of these approaches, they represent a most promising area of growth.

An interactive-compensatory approach

An interactive-compensatory model of learning to read can account for the way in which children with some difficulties learn (Presland, 1982; Stanovich, 1980). It is based on the assumption that readers simultaneously synthesize information from several sources: previous experience, knowledge of meaning and grammar, information about print i.e. all three segments of the triangle in Figure 4.1. When there is difficulty about one source of information, another may compensate for it. It is, for example, possible to deduce the meaning of a word from its context or, using Wallace's example above, to learn from reading that 'some people bring flowers when they visit patients in hospital'. The context can also to some extent make up for problems with the recognition of print.

The interactive-compensatory model provides the rationale for the methods suggested in the Reason and Boote manual (*op.cit.*). It implies that the acquisition of reading can proceed in different ways according to the learning opportunities, cognitive make-up and particular strategies of the individual. Assessment and intervention are therefore planned on a broad front so that the learner also has the opportunity to compensate for weaknesses with strengths. Some children, for example, are very good at making guesses on the basis of context. That is a strength which can be built on. Others may not have discovered the strategies of intelligent guesswork, relying on only one or two aspects such as initial letters or a limited number of words they can recognize by sight. They are described by Arnold in this book as thinking that the only way into reading is through phonics and sight words (see Chapter 30). These children, in turn, need to be shown how they can take advantage of word meanings, context and content.

Word recognition should, in time, become automatic and not reliant on guesswork. There are, however, some pupils who have developed excellent strategies for using context but who continue to have difficulties with the details of print. Their guesswork has become so efficient that it actually hinders attention to their weaker areas of learning. It may result in an inaccurate but fluent reading style which, through strategies of self-correction, makes good sense of the content. Lack of print-related skills then shows up in poor spelling which does not allow for inaccuracies. These pupils illustrate a need to learn about the elements within words in a systematic way as part of an instructional framework which also encompasses the other aspects.

The 'multisensory' approach

The term 'a structured multisensory approach' refers to a technique in which pupils read and write individual letters or words in the context of a cumulative and repetitive programme of instruction (Hickey, 1977; Hornsby and Shear, 1980). It is said to involve simultaneous input from visual, auditory and kinaesthetic modalities. In order to learn to recognize the sound of a letter, the child will trace round the outline of the letter while looking at its shape and vocalizing its sound. The child does this several times on several occasions until she or he can write it automatically from dictation. This is also done for individual words: first practised in isolation until the learner can write them fast and automatically as part of a dictated short sentence.

The learning of the letter sounds and phonologically regular words is usually undertaken in a pre-determined sequence which does note take account of the child's own language or interests. Cotterel (1985) has, however, combined skillfully this structure with language experience through shared story writing and topic work. She recommends that children write 'guided sentences' about matters which are of interest to them. The words in these sentences then form the starting point for learning about phonics. This method does require much individual attention from the teacher but might be adapted for group work in the classroom.

Recent research has shown that young children benefit from this 'multisensory' technique because they become better at recognizing visual forms, i.e. the shapes of letters (Hulme, 1981; Hulme, Monk and Ives, 1987). A study by Bradley (1981) has also demonstrated that it is effective in teaching retarded readers to spell. The medical flavour of the term 'multisensory' is, however, unfortunate because it can result in misunderstandings by implying some exceptional form of instruction provided in clinics. Many teachers would regard it as 'common sense' with a long pedigree (cf. Montessori, 1915).

Recording individual progress

The three previous sections have outlined intervention strategies ranging from the most natural language-based approaches to supported reading and ending with the 'multisensory' repetitive practice of words in print. Whatever the emphasis, however, the experience of reading for meaning and enjoyment has continued to be central. In this way children, unable to read for themselves, have not been deprived of reading with assistance and expanding their experiences and knowledge through it.

In assessing the needs of the individual, the starting point is now the child's previous opportunities to learn. The evaluation of literacy difficulties should be informed by the extent and quality of teaching methods and approaches that have already been tried. The following kinds of questions might be asked:

1. What is the school's overall language policy? What is the emphasis in relation to the three sections of the triangle in Figure 4.1? Do approaches based on language experience predominate? Or is the teaching mainly focused on print? What is the balance of approaches in the particular school or class?
2. Is there an ethos of enthusiasm about literacy? Are story times exciting or routine? Are pupils reading to and writing for each other? Is a wide range of literature available? Is the purpose of print emphasized through all kinds of media?

3. Is collaborative work actively planned and encouraged? How is the class organized to ensure participation? Are children taught how to help each other? Are methods developed which enable pupils to record their own progress and views?
4. To what extent are parents involved in school? Are they supportive of the school's language policy? Are methods of reading together with their children used widely?
5. What additional provision is made for pupils who do not seem to be learning easily? What methods are used? How do these methods link with the approaches generally used in the school? If structured multisensory approaches have been introduced, what has been the effect?

By getting a history of previous learning opportunites we can clarify the needs of the individual. If, for example, there has already been much emphasis on language experience through 'real books', then there might be a need to introduce, in addition, a more structured and repetitive plan of action. Conversely, if the pupil already concentrates on phonics and sight words, then plenty of assisted reading might correct the balance. But, before making such decisions, there is a need to take account of the child's current strategies when faced with print.

A framework for assessing the child's approaches to reading and writing is provided in the manual by Reason and Boote (*op.cit.*) under the following three headings:

(a) Concepts, approaches, enjoyment.
(b) Immediate word recognition.
(c) Use of phonics.

It now seems that the framework does not take sufficient account of the assisted mode of reading, i.e. the 'apprenticeship approach' which looks at children's behaviour when adults read the text and their approaches to known and unknown words when someone is available to read or write for them immediately (e.g. Waterland, *op.cit.*). The Reason and Boote format concentrates on examining the child's strategies when reading and writing with minimum assistance. Assessment and record keeping needs to take account of both modes, that is:

1. The learner's approaches to reading and writing when plenty of immediate assistance is available (e.g through 'shared', 'paired' or 'relaxed' reading and 'process writing');
2. The learner's attainments when required to read and write more independently (possibly backed by reading schemes and structured cumulative methods of instruction).

By encompassing both modes, we can observe reading and writing behaviours with specified objectives in mind as has been suggested by Clay (1979) and, more recently, by Tann (1987) who uses flow charts to map the actions teachers can take on the basis of informal observations.

There is currently much emphasis on giving pupils a chance to show what they can do in terms of the two large top segments of the triangle in Figure 4.1. That is, pupils are given credit for the way they can convey information or express themselves in writing, when allowances are made or assistance is provided for the 'secretarial aspects' of spelling and handwriting. It seems indeed likely that at least some of the standard assessment tasks for the National Curriculum in English will follow this format. For pupils with specific learning difficulties in the area of print recognition and reproduction, these developments will be very welcome as they enable them to show what they can do rather than only concentrating on what they cannot do. It will, however, also be important to ensure additional help with those aspects which are causing difficulty. In other words, the pupils will need both support and remediation.

Summing up

The purpose of this chapter has been to provide a rationale for reconciling those teaching approaches which emphasize global language experience and those which are concerned with structured cumulative methods of instruction. Descriptions of the theoretical bases of both approaches have led to Figure 4.1, a synthesis giving the aspects concerned with print a small but essential role in the diagram. The rest of the chapter has then applied this rationale to the concept of specific learning difficulties and to a range of methods of intervention. The main points made are summarized below:

- There can be no certain recipe, whether 'psycholinguistic' or 'multisensory', while theoretical understanding of the processes involved in reading and writing remains incomplete. Consequently, polarized viewpoints are of little use.
- That branch of cognitive psychology concerned with word recognition has emphasized the many possible constitutional factors which can result in difficulties with automatic recognition of letter strings. For some pupils, learning to read and write can be difficult and require structured cumulative methods of instruction.
- Psycholinguistic orientations promote the whole language and reading experience from the very start. Literacy in its fullest sense is learnt untidily in real situations and difficulties are associated with limited interest, enjoyment and comprehension. Learning to read requires gentle assistance and plenty of opportunity.
- The contributions of eminent psychologists such as Bartlett and Bruner have emphasized the social and interactive nature of all learning. The individual makes sense of present experiences on the basis of expectations formed by previous ones.

● The up-turned triangle in figure 4.1 provides a framework for accommodating both psycholinguistic and structured cumulative methods of instruction. The first and largest section of the triangle refers to the overall context of learning. The second is concerned with language learning and its purpose of communication through speech and the printed text. The nature of print now becomes a small but essential third section of the triangle which can require direct and systematic teaching.

● Traditional definitions of specific learning difficulties tend to concentrate on the apex of the triangle i.e. on deficiencies in the recognition and reproduction of print. It is argued that all the other aspects of Figure 4.1 need to be considered.

● Some children will need to learn in a very precise way about print. This applies to children from all socio-cultural backgrounds. We must ensure that social circumstances do not become the basis for determining the teaching methods offered.

● A range of teaching methods reflecting the emphasis of the different sections in Figure 4.1 have been outlined. In assessing the needs of the individual, the starting point can be the nature of the child's previous opportunities to learn. The severity of learning difficulties then becomes a function of the extent and quality of methods that have already been followed.

● Finally, mention is made of the need for assessment and record keeping which takes account of both assisted reading and writing and attainments based on more independent work. It seems likely that the National Curriculum in English will enable pupils to demonstrate what they can achieve in the broader context of 'language' when assistance is provided with those aspects concerned with print recognition or reproduction.

References

Allen, J.E. (1970) 'The right to read — Targets for the 70's', in Melnik, A. and Merritt, J. (Eds) *Reading Today and Tomorrow*, London, Hodder and Stoughton.

Arnold, H. (1982) *Listening to Children Reading*, London, Hodder and Stoughton.

Bartlett, F.C. (1932) *Remembering: A Study in Experimental and Social Psychology*, Cambridge, Cambridge University Press.

Bertelson, P. (1986) 'The onset of literacy: Liminal remarks', *Cognition*, 24, pp. 1–30.

Bradley, L. (1981) 'The organisation of spelling patterns for spelling: an effective remedial strategy for backward readers', *Developmental Medicine and Child Neurology*, 23, pp. 83–91.

Branston, P. and Provis, M. (1986) *Children and Parents Enjoying Reading*, London, Hodder and Stoughton.

Bruner, J.S. (1986) *Actual Minds, Possible Worlds*, London, Harvard University Press.

Bryant, P. and Bradley, L. (1985) *Children's Reading Problems*, Oxford, Blackwell.

Bryant, P. and Impey, L. (1986) 'The similarities between normal readers and developmental and acquired dyslexics', *Cognition*, 24, pp. 121–137.

Clarke, M.M. (1976) *Young Fluent Readers*, London, Heinemann.

Clay, M. (1979) *Reading: The Patterning of Complex Behaviour*, London, Heinemann.

Coltheart, M. (1987) 'Varieties of developmental dyslexia: a comment on Bryant and Impey', *Cognition*, 27, pp. 97–101.

Cornwall, K., Hedderly, R. and Pumfrey, P.D. (1983) 'Specific Learning Difficulties: the "specific reading difficulties" versus "dyslexia" controversy resolved?', Division of Educational and Child Psychology of the British Psychological Society, *Occasional Papers*, 7, 3.

Cotterell, G. (1985) *Teaching the Non-Reading Dyslexic Child*, Wisbech, Learning Development Aids.

Department of Education and Science and the Welsh Office (1988) *English for Ages 5 to 11*. Proposals of the Secretary of State for Education and Science and the Secretary of State for Wales. DES and WO.

Edwards, D. and Mercer, N. (1987) *Common Knowledge: the Development of Understanding in the Classroom*, London, Methuen.

Ellis, A.W. (1984) *Reading, Writing and Dyslexia: A Cognitive Analysis*, Hillsdale, Lawrence Erlbaum.

Frith, U. (1985) 'Beneath the surface of Surface Dyslexia', in Patterson, K., Marshall, J.R. and Coltheart, M. (Eds) *Surface Dyslexia*, Hillsdale, Lawrence Erlbaum.

Greening, M. and Spenceley, J. (1987) 'Shared reading: support for inexperienced readers', *Educational Psychology in Practice*, 3, 1, pp. 31–37.

Goodman, K. (1967) 'Reading: a psycholinguistic guessing game', *Journal of the Reading Specialist*, 6, pp. 126–135.

Hickey, K. (1977) *Dyslexia — a Language Training Course for Teachers and Learners*, Kathleen Hickey Publications.

Holdaway, D. (1989) *Independence in Reading*, 2nd ed., Sydney, Ashton Scholastic.

Hornsby, B. and Shear, F. (1980) *Alpha to Omega*, 3rd ed., London, Heinemann.

Hulme, C. (1981) *Reading Retardation and Multi-Sensory Teaching*, London, Routledge and Kegan Paul.

Hulme, C., Monk, A. and Ives, S. (1987) 'Some experimental studies of multi-sensory teaching: the effects of manual tracing on children's paired-associate learning', *British Journal of Developmental Psychology*, 5, pp. 299–307.

Lindsay, G., Evans, A. and Jones, B. (1985) 'Paired reading versus relaxed reading: a comparison', *British Journal of Educational Psychology*, 55, pp. 304–09.

Meek, M. (1982) *Learning to Read*, London, Bodley Head.

Miller, A. (1987) 'Is there still a place for paired reading?', *Educational Psychology in Practice*, 3, 1, pp. 38–43.

Montessori, M. (1915) *The Montessori Method*, London, Heinemann.

Morgan, R. and Gavin, P. (1988) 'Paired reading: evaluation and progress', *Support for Learning*, 3, 4, pp. 201–206.

Morton, J. (1979) 'Facilitation on word recognition: experiments causing change in the logogen model', in Kolers, P.A., Wolstad, M. and Bouma, H. (Eds) *Processing of Visible Language, 1*, New York, Plenum.

Neisser, U. (1967) *Cognitive Psychology*, New York, Prentice Hall.

Presland, J.L. (1982) 'Applying psychology to teaching the three Rs, reading and written English'. Division of Educational and Child Psychology of the British Psychological Society, *Occasional Papers*, 6, 1, pp. 3–38.

Pumfrey, P.D. (1988) 'A three-year longitudinal study of children's reading behaviours: what has been learned?' *Educational Research*, 30, 3, pp. 163–176.

Reason, J. (1990) *Human Error*, New York, Cambridge University Press.

Reason, R. (1988) 'Can the "specific" in specific learning difficulties determine teaching methods?', *Educational and Child Psychology*, 5, 4, pp. 59–65.

Reason R. and Boote, R. (1986) *Learning Difficulties in Reading and Writing: A Teacher's Manual*, Windsor, NFER-Nelson.

Reason, R., Brown, B., Cole, M. and Gregory, M. (1988) 'Does the "specific" in specific learning difficulties make a difference to the way we teach?', *Support for Learning*, 3, 4, pp. 230–236.

Root, B. (1986) *In Defence of Reading Schemes*, Reading, Reading and Language Information Centre, University of Reading.

Rumelhart, D.E. (1975) 'Notes on a schema for stories', in Bobrow, D. and Collins, A. (Eds) *Representation and Understanding: Studies in Cognitive Science*, New York, Academic Press.

Seymour, P.H.K. (1986) *Cognitive Analysis of Dyslexia*, London, Routledge and Kegan Paul.

Seymour, P.H.K. and MacGregor, C.J. (1984) 'Developmental dyslexia: a cognitive experimental analysis of phonological, morphemic and visual impairments', *Cognitive Neuropsychology*, 1, pp. 43–82.

Shankweiler, D. and Crain, S. (1986) 'Language mechanism and reading disorder: a modular approach', *Cognition*, 24, pp. 139–168.

Singleton, C.H. (1987) 'Dyslexia and cognitive models of reading', *Support for Learning*, 2, 2, pp. 47–56.

Smith, F. (1978) *Understanding Reading*, London, Holt, Rinehart and Winston.

Smith, F. (1985) *Reading*, 2nd ed., Cambridge, Cambridge University Press.

Stanovich, K.E. (1980) 'Toward an interactive-compensatory model of individual differences in the development of reading fluency', *Reading Research Quarterly*, 16, pp. 32–71.

Stanovich, K.E. (1986) 'Matthew effects in reading: some consequences of individual differences in the acquisition of literacy', *Reading Research Quarterly*, 21, 4, pp. 360–407.

Tann, S. (1987) *Using Miscue Analysis to Develop Diagnostic Reading Strategies — a Flow Chart*, Reading, Reading and Language Information Centre, University of Reading.

Treiman, R. (1984) 'Individual differences among children in reading and spelling styles', *Journal of Experimental Child Psychology*, 37, pp. 463–477.

Wallace, C. (1986) *Learning to Read in a Multicultural Society*, Oxford, Pergamon Press.

Waterland, L. (1986) *Read with me: An Apprenticeship Approach to Reading*, Stroud, Gloucestershire, The Thimble Press.

Wells, G. (Ed.) (1985) *Language, Learning and Education*, Windsor, NFER-Nelson.

Wiles, S. (1985) 'Language and learning in multi-ethnic classrooms: strategies for supporting bilingual students', in Wells, G. and Nicholls, J. (Eds) *Language and Learning: An Interactional Perspective*, London, Falmer Press.

Part Two: Responses
(A) Phonological Approaches: Theory and Research

5
Phonological Development and Reading

Peter E. Bryant

Two approaches to pre-school education

The debate on the significance of the young child's pre-school experiences has gone this way and that, but it seems reasonably clear now that they do play a considerable part in the progress that he makes when he arrives at school. At any rate we know now that children whose experiences are enriched during the pre-school period eventually do better at school as a result (Lazar and Darlington, 1982; Osborn and Millbank, 1987). Evidence of this sort must mean that the skills which children bring with them when they first go to school — skills which they have acquired in the preceding years — are going to be a significant factor in their success or lack of it when they get there. Such research provides us with an answer, but it is an answer which poses another equally important question. What sort of experiences should be encouraged, which skills enhanced, in the pre-school period? Broadly speaking there are two possible ways to answer this question, and they are radically different from each other. One concentrates on the skills which children normally acquire informally in their pre-school years, the other on the new skills which children have to learn when they get to school.

The first approach is to turn to the experiences which children normally have before reaching school. It seems likely that during the preschool years children, quite naturally and for reasons which at the time have no obvious bearing on education, acquire skills which are going to play a considerable role in their progress when they eventually get to school. If this is the case it is also possible that some children have better luck than others as far as these informal skills are concerned, and are thus better prepared when they get to school. But whatever the differences between children, all should be helped by being given better opportunities to acquire the skills in question.

The other approach, in complete contrast, is simply to bring education forward by a year or so. Children have to learn to recognize the alphabet, to recognize words, to count, to add if they are to make any progress in school: so why not prepare them for these hurdles by introducing them to these basic requirements, in a suitably gentle way, in the pre-school years? Notice that the emphasis here is entirely on the new skills that a child has to acquire at school: the underlying idea is that children learn these skills by being taught them.

It is easy to see that the two answers lead to quite different approaches to the problem of what to do with pre-school children. If the first is the correct answer we should do our best to discover the skills which children acquire informally out of school but which affect their success in the classroom, and then we should strengthen them. If the second is right we should start teaching children formal skills earlier than we do now. The difference between these two approaches takes us directly to children's reading, for over the last ten years or so some psychologists concerned with reading have argued for the first and others for the second way of looking at pre-school education. The controversy between them concerns the relationship between 'phonological awareness' and learning to read.

Phonological awareness and learning to read

By 'phonological awareness' the author means the understanding that words can be broken down into constituent sounds ('cat' into 'c' 'a' and 't') and the ability to work out what those sounds are. It seems quite possible that there is a direct connection between this kind of awareness of sounds on the one hand and learning to read on the other. After all, children have to learn about the alphabet in order to read and write, and the alphabetic letters in a written word, by and large, signify the phonemes in the spoken version of that word. No one could possibly understand the way in which the alphabet works without a considerable degree of phonological awareness. In fact we now have a great deal of evidence for a strong connection between this form of awareness and children's progress in learning to read. The more sensitive a child is to the constituent sounds in words the more successful he is likely to be in reading and in spelling (Stanovich, Cunningham and Cramer, 1984). This relationship holds even when possible extraneous factors such as differences in the children's intelligence, in their social background and in the extent of their vocabulary are held constant (Bradley and Bryant, 1983; Bryant and Bradley, 1985; Lundberg, Oloffson and Wall, 1980). Some studies have also shown that children who are given extra tuition about the way in which words can be divided into smaller phonological segments make more rapid progress in reading than others who do not receive this extra teaching. This evidence for the importance of phonological awareness is now so compelling that it is hardly ever disputed (Bryant and Bradley, 1985; Stanovich, 1987). Nonetheless there is an argument here. It is between people who have radically different opinions about what is cause and what is effect in the relations between children's phonological awareness and their success in reading.

Two views about the nature of the connection

The connection between phonological awareness and reading poses an obvious causal question. Which of the two skills is the cause, and which the effect? Do the children's phonological skills determine how well they learn to read? Or does their success in reading determine how sensitive they are to phonological segments? Both views have been advanced, and it is easy to see how one view leads to one of the two approaches to pre-school education which were described earlier and one to the other.

Let us take two (fictitious) psychologists, both of whom accept the proposition that it is possible to give children extra experiences before they go to school which will enhance their chances of success when they get there. One of these psychologists believes that children's phonological awareness has a direct causal influence on their progress in reading. If this form of awareness is a cause of reading, then it must precede reading, and that means that phonological skills which children build up some time before knowing how to read play a significant role when they are taught how to read and write. So this particular psychologist would argue that one should look at the way children acquire these pre-school phonological skills informally in the pre-school period and that one should find ways of enhancing these skills. The second psychologist believes that children only become aware of phonological segments, in a way that is relevant to written words, as a direct result of being formally taught about reading and spelling. In that case children's awareness of phonological segments should come after the experience of learning to read. Thus the psychologist in question would take the view either that children of nursery school age have no phonological awareness or that any phonological skills that they do acquire during the pre-school period play no part when it comes to learning to read.

Both views have been advanced, the first by Lynette Bradley, Morag Maclean and the author (Bryant and Bradley, 1985; Maclean, Bryant and Bradley, 1987; Bryant, Bradley, Maclean and Crossland, 1989), and the second by a group of psychologists who work in Brussels (Morais, Alegria and Content, 1987).

The first position: the importance of rhyme and alliteration

The original reasons for our own position can be described fairly briefly. Some time ago we became interested in rhyme and alliteration. From our own informal observations it seemed quite clear that long before they go to school many children are well aware that words rhyme. Young children enjoy rhymes, and often produce poems with rhyming or alliterative words (Chukovsky, 1963; Dowker, 1989). There is now considerable evidence that 3 and 4 year old children can judge (though with varying degrees of success) when words rhyme with each other and also when they start with the same sound (Lenel and

Cantor, 1981; Knafle, 1973, 1974; Maclean, Bryant and Bradley, 1987). The apparent importance of rhyme to young children is extremely interesting for a number of reasons. One is that we can now be sure of at least one identifiable instance of a phonological skill in relatively young children. To know that 'cat' and 'hat' rhyme is to make a judgment that the two words have a phonological segment 'at' in common. The fact that many 3 and 4 year olds can make that judgment is conclusive evidence that they are sensitive not just to the sound of a word, but also to some of the phonological units within the word. Whether this particular skill will have an effect on the progress that children make when they begin to learn to read is another matter. Rhyming sounds, the phonological units which children have to detect in order to be able to judge that words rhyme, lie somewhere between a phoneme and a syllable. The 'at' sound which 'mat' and 'cat' share is only a segment of those one syllable words, but it contains two phonemes. However alphabetic letters, on the whole, represent single phonemes. So rhyme involves speech units which are grosser and more global than the phoneme; that means that we cannot be sure that an awareness of rhyming sounds will be relevant to reading.

Our doubts about a connection between rhyme and reading were swept away by a flood of evidence. To begin with Lynette Bradley and the author found that many, though not all, of a large group of dyslexic children were insensitive to rhyme (Bradley and Bryant, 1978). Their performance in a rhyme detection task was even worse than that of a group of much younger children who read at a normal level for their age and whose reading levels were the same as that of the dyslexic group. Our conclusion, that the dyslexic children's insensitivity to rhyme might be one of the causes of their difficulties with reading, led to a new hypothesis about the normal development of reading. We suggested that rhyme might play a causal role in all children's reading. Our hypothesis at the time was that their early experiences with rhyme might prepare children for the phonological demands involved in learning to read. We tested this hypothesis in a large scale piece of research which was in part a longitudinal study and in part a training experiment (Bradley and Bryant, 1983). The study began when we gave over 400 children of 4 and 5 years a number of tasks which included a test of rhyme and alliteration detection, and ended four years later when we measured how well the same children (whose number by then had dwindled to 365) could read and spell and do sums. Our aim was to discover if there was a definite relationship between the children's scores in the rhyme task and their success in reading three or four years later. In between these two times we gave a few children some extensive training. They were 6 years old when this training began and, since the training stretched over a two-year period, 7 years old when it ended. Some were taught just about rhyme, others about rhyme and about alphabetic letters, and a third group, a control group, was given exactly the same material and seen for the same amount of time but learned about conceptual categories rather than about rhyming categories.

We believe that this combination of longitudinal prediction and training is the best way to test a causal hypothesis. A successful longitudinal prediction would establish the existence of a genuine connection between children's early rhyming skills and their progress in reading later on. The training study should show us whether this connection is a causal one (Bryant and Bradley, 1985). Both parts of the study produced positive results. There was a strong and consistent relationship between the children's scores in the initial rhyme and alliteration tasks and their reading and spelling, though not their mathematical performance, several years later on. This relationship held even after stringent controls were made for the effects of differences in the children's I.Q. and in their vocabulary. We concluded that we now had considerable empirical support for our hypothesis that rhyme affects reading.

This is a clear instance of the first of the two approaches that were described earlier. Children learn about rhyme quite informally and for reasons which at the time have nothing to do with reading. Yet this informal phonological skill seems to play a considerable role in helping children to read. The implications for pre-school education are clear. Enhance this informal skill. Make sure that young children become expert in rhyme: that should help them when they begin to learn to read. There were, however, some loose ends to see to before we could take that step. One was the question of the size of the speech unit involved in rhyme. As we have seen these units typically contain two or more phonemes, and yet alphabetic units usually represent one phoneme only. So what is the connection between rhyme and reading? Another serious problem for us was that at exactly the same time as we were developing our hypothesis about rhyme and reading, another group of researchers (Morais, Cary, Alegria and Bertelson, 1979) was working on a radically different idea. While our work was a clear example of the first approach to pre-school experiences, theirs was an equally clear instance of the second. While we argued that early informally acquired skills affect reading, they claimed that the phonological skills that are relevant to reading are acquired as a direct result of learning to read. While we pointed to the importance of rhyme, they suggested that rhyme is a 'global' skill which has little relevance to reading (Morais, Alegria and Content, 1987).

The second approach: evidence that reading leads to phonological awareness

In 1979 Morais, Cary, Alegria and Bertelson published a striking paper about the effects of literacy. They studied a group of illiterate adults in Portugal and compared them to another comparable group who had been illiterate but had taken literacy classes and could now read. Morais *et al.* gave these people two phonological tasks. One involved working out what a word would sound like if the first sound (in effect the first phoneme) were removed: thus the people being tested were given 'purso' and the question was whether they realized that the word would become 'urso' without its first sound. The other task involved reversing the order of phonemes in a word: the people in the experiment were asked to say single words like 'os' backwards — 'so'. The main result of the experiment was that the people in the illiterate group fared a great deal worse than the others in both these phonological tasks. Morais *et al.* concluded that the experience of learning to read is responsible for awareness of phonemes. The literate group, they claimed, managed the two tasks better because the training that they were given in reading had made them aware of phonemes. The illiterate group were relatively insensitive to phonemes because they had not learned to read.

Subsequent research seemed to support this conclusion. In a later study the same research group confirmed the difficulties of the illiterate group in tasks which involved the detection of phonemes. They also found that the two groups, illiterate and literate, were not so different in tasks in which they did not have to make judgments about phonemes — tasks involving rhyme or musical sequences. This and the earlier study could always be dismissed on the the grounds that, despite the disclaimers of the people doing the research, the illiterate group were less intelligent or less motivated than the people in the literate control group. However some work with people who are literate and yet have had no experience with an alphabet provided convincing support for the position adopted by the Brussels group.

In China the traditional script is ideographic: each symbol in the script represents a word. However in the late 1940s an additional alphabetic script, called pinyin, was introduced. Charles Read noticed on a visit to China that some people had learned this script, while others, mostly those who were educated before its introduction, had not. He and some Chinese colleagues gave people who knew the new pinyin script and others who did not versions of the Morais *et al.* tasks (Read, Zhang, Nie and Ding, 1986). (Both sets of people knew the traditional ideographic script, and thus no illiterate people took part in this experiment.) So this was a comparison between two literate sets of people, one of which had had the experience of learning to read an alphabetic script and the other not. Once again the non-alphabetic group, this time the group that had not learned pinyin, did a great deal worse on the phoneme manipulation tasks than the group that had learned pinyin.

At about the same time Mann (1986) carried out another study with a similar rationale which led to much the same conclusions. She compared Japanese and American school children. The Japanese learn two kinds of script. One is called kanji and is ideographic: in the other type of script, which is called kana, each symbol represents a syllable. Thus the syllabaries (there are in fact two Japanese syllabaries) are phonological but not alphabetic, because the symbols in them do not represent phonemes. This meant that the comparison that Virginia Mann made was between two groups of children, both of which were literate, but only one of which (the American group) had had experience with an alphabet while the other (the Japanese) had not. She gave them tasks in which they had to make judgments about phonemes and others in which the judgments were about syllables. For example, one of the tasks was a tapping task: and the children had sometimes to tap out the number of phonemes in a word spoken to them and sometimes the number of syllables. She found not much difference between the American and Japanese children in any of the syllable tasks but a vast difference in the phoneme tasks. The Americans — the alphabetic group — were much better at these than the Japanese children were, and the difference was particularly pronounced among the youngest children in the experiment who were 7 years old. Once again the experience of having learned to read an alphabetic script seemed to have made children more aware of phonemes.

These experiments make a convincing case for the formidable effects of learning to read on phonological awareness. Morais *et al*. nowadays adopt an 'interactive' hypothesis. They argue that cause and effect go both ways. The experience of learning to read makes children aware of phonemes, and that awareness then helps them to amke further progress in reading. There is one causal link, however, which they do not accept. They believe that any phonological awareness that is present in the pre-school years is unimportant. It does not, in their view, affect reading. Their interactive hypothesis is only about events after reading has begun. Morais *et al*. accept the fact that children are aware of rhymes long before they can read, but argue that rhyme cannot be relevant to reading because it is too 'global'. It involves phonological units which are not as precise as phonemes and therefore cannot be relevant to learning an alphabetic script. As far as the Brussels group is concerned the only kind of phonological skill worth considering is phoneme detection.

The importance of the size of the phonological unit

Our dispute with the Brussels group turns almost entirely on the size of the phonological unit. On the one side we have shown that awareness of rhyme and alliteration in the pre-school years is an excellent predictor of reading and spelling many years later, and a specific one at that since it predicts reading but not mathematics. Our training study also provides sufficient evidence that the connection between early rhyme and success in reading is a causal one. But the work on rhyme that has been described so far does not provide a pathway. It demonstrates a causal connection, but it does not show how the connection works. On the other side Morais *et al*. have a cogent model about a pathway which is based on the quite plausible assumption that phoneme detection is the only phonological skill with any relevance to reading. This skill, they point out, comes relatively late in a child's life and, given the impressive data about Portuguese illiterates and Chinese and Japanese readers, largely as a result of learning to read an alphabet.

Thus at this stage (we are roughly now at 1983) we were in the position of having demonstrated an empirical connection but not being able to say how it worked. At the same time the Brussels group were able to argue that this connection was quite unfeasible because it involved phonological units which are not relevant to reading.

How rhyme could be related to reading

How true is it that a causal connection between rhyming and reading is unfeasible? In the author's view it need not be true at all. There are two ways in which rhyme might play a significant part in learning to read, and they are represented by the first and the second model in Figure 5.1. (model 3 represents the position adopted by Morais *et al.* that rhyme plays no part in reading.)

Model 1 shows how there could be an indirect effect. Awareness of rhyme might develop into awareness of phonemes and this second form of awareness influences the speed with which the child learns about letter-sound relationships. The experience of learning to read might spark off the child's awareness of phonemes, as some of the evidence that was reviewed earlier suggests, but the child's success in segmenting words into phonemes might rest on his earlier experience with cruder phonological units such as rhymes. This suggestion is only a small modification of the Brussels hypothesis, because it is based on the idea that phoneme detection is the only relevant phonological skill and that rhyme influences reading only because it plays a part in the child's eventual ability to learn about phonemes.

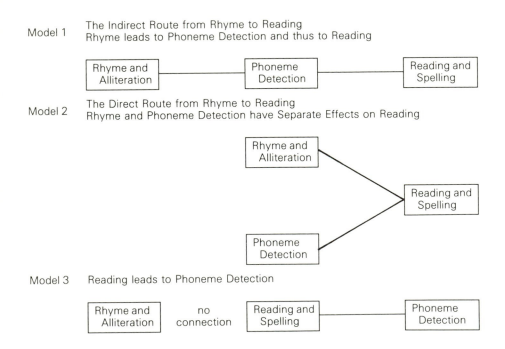

Model 1   The Indirect Route from Rhyme to Reading
           Rhyme leads to Phoneme Detection and thus to Reading

Rhyme and Alliteration ———— Phoneme Detection ———— Reading and Spelling

Model 2   The Direct Route from Rhyme to Reading
           Rhyme and Phoneme Detection have Separate Effects on Reading

Rhyme and Alliteration
Phoneme Detection
Reading and Spelling

Model 3   Reading leads to Phoneme Detection

Rhyme and Alliteration   no connection   Reading and Spelling ———— Phoneme Detection

Figure 5.1   Three models of the relation between rhyme and reading

Model 2 involves a more radical step. It is based on a suggestion that rhyme has a direct effect on reading. In other words rhyme is not too global: it deals with phonological units which are appropriate for reading. How could this be? Written words are not just collections of single letters each representing a single sound. Words often contain sequences of letters, and different words which have letter sequences in common often share common sounds as well. Consider 'light', 'fight', and 'might'. These three words, when written, also have the letter sequence 'ight' in common, and this sequence represents the rhyming sound. This means that awareness of rhyme could play a direct part in learning to read. Rhyme could help a child to realize that words have sounds in common and that these sounds are represented by common letter sequences. Through rhyme the child could learn to form spelling categories.

Models 1 and 2 provide two possible pathways between rhyme and reading, and thus the argument that rhyme is necessarily too global loses its force. Since we already know that there is a connection and since we now have two possible explanations for it, the next step must be to see which holds water.

The direct and the indirect route from rhyme to reading

One needs a further study, preferably a longitudinal one, in which measures are taken both of children's awareness of rhyme and of their eventual ability to break words up into phonemes, as well as of their progress in learning to read. There are clear differences in the predictions that would be made about such a study by supporters of the different routes from rhyme to reading. Those who hold that rhyming skills develop into phoneme detection which in turn affects reading (Model 1 — the indirect route) would expect two things: (1) that their early rhyme scores would be related to their later performance in tests of phoneme detection; and (2) that the connection between rhyme and reading should be completely explicable in terms of the children's ability to detect phonemes. In contrast, the idea of a direct path between rhyme and reading (Model 2 — the direct route) suggests a different set of relationships: if the idea is right (1) there should be no particular connection beween rhyme and the development of the ability to detect phonemes; and (2) the relationship between rhyme and reading should be independent of the connection between phoneme detection and reading.

We carried out a second longitudinal study in order to look at these relationships (Bryant, Maclean, Bradley and Crossland, 1989). It involved sixty-five children whom we started seeing when they were 3 years 4 months and continued doing so until they were 6 years 7 months. From the start we measured their ability to judge whether words rhyme and, in other tests, whether different words start with the same sound. Later, from the age of 5 years, we began to give them phoneme detection tests as well. At the end of the project (as well as before) we gave them tests of reading, spelling and arithmetic. Our test of rhyme was an oddity task. It consisted of a series of trials in each of which we showed the child three pictures and said the names of each picture. Two of the words rhymed while the other one did not (e.g. 'peg', 'cot', 'leg'). Our main tests of phoneme detection were versions of tasks used by other people. One was a tapping task (Liberman *et al.*, 1978; Mann, 1986): the children heard single words and then had to tap out the number of phonemes in that word (e.g. four taps for 'sand'). The other was a phoneme deletion task (Content *et al.*, 1986): in our version the children were shown a puppet which never said the first sound of any word ('if I say "Hello, Ben"', he says "Ello En"') and had to judge how the puppet would say a series of different words.

The connection between rhyme and phoneme detection (Model 1)

In studies of this sort simple correlations mean very little. For example a correlation between rhyme and phoneme detection may have nothing to do with phonological ability *per se* and may simply be a matter of differences in intelligence: the children who do better both in rhyme and phoneme detection tests may be doing so well simply because they are also more intelligent and thus the correlation may simply reflect the effects of differences in intelligence. The solution is to control for the effects of extraneous variables like intelligence statistically. The simplest way to do this is in a multiple regression in which variables are entered in a fixed order. An example is the multiple regression that we ran when we wanted to see if the children's early rhyme scores predicted how good they became later on at detecting phonemes. The dependent variable was their performance in a phoneme detection test. We first entered into the multiple regression all the extraneous variables that we considered pertinent — their age, their social background (as indicated by their mothers' educational level), a measure of their vocabulary, and their I.Q. As the final step in the multiple regression we entered the variable that interested us — the children's early rhyme scores. We had controlled for the effects of differences in the four extraneous variables by entering them earlier: thus we knew that any significant relationship between rhyme and phoneme detection would be independent of differences in I.Q., social class and so on.

In fact this particular analysis did produce a significant relationship between the two things that interested us: the children's scores in a rhyme test given when they were 4 years 7 months did predict their performance in both tests of phoneme detection which they had to do more than a year later when they were 5 years 11 months. Figure 5.2 gives a graphic version of these two multiple regressions.

This result supports the idea of the indirect route from rhyme to reading via phoneme detection. Rhyming skills probably do lay the basis for children's eventual success at detecting phonemes.

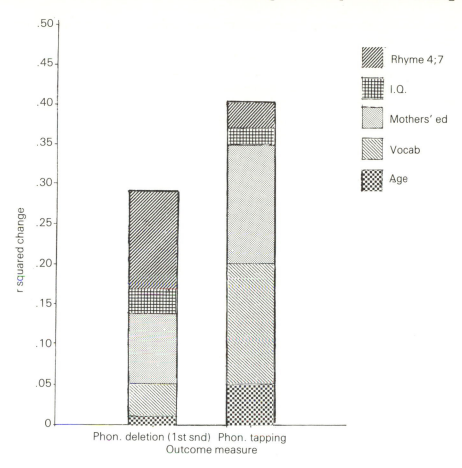

Figure 5.2 Rhyme at 4;7 predicts phoneme detection at 5;11 (N = 65)

The direct connection between rhyme and reading (Model 2)

However another, slightly more complex, multiple regression provided support for the direct route from rhyme to reading. Its purpose was to see whether children's rhyme scores predict their success in reading later on, even when the effects of differences in phoneme detection were controlled by entering phoneme detection scores as an earlier step in the regression. So the dependent variable was success in reading, and the final step entered into the regression was the children's early rhyme scores. The step entered just before this was their performance in phoneme detection. If there is only an indirect route via phoneme detection between rhyme and reading, the effect of entering the phoneme detection scores as an earlier step in the analysis should be to demolish the relationship between rhyme and reading. If, on the other hand, rhyme makes a direct, distinctive and independent contribution to reading there should be a significant relationship between rhyme and reading despite the entry of phoneme detection as an earlier step.

The analysis provided good support for the idea of a direct route from rhyme to reading. The relationship between proficiency at rhyme and reading later on was still significant even after the effects of differences in phoneme detection had been controlled. Figure 5.3 presents the multiple regressions which show this.

Thus we now have evidence for both routes. Rhyme, to some extent at least, lays the basis for the children's eventual proficiency at isolating phonemes, and thus contributes to the child's success at picking up single letter-sound relationships. Quite apart from this, rhyme makes its own

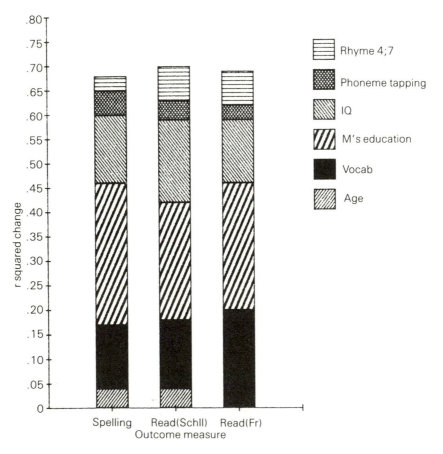

Figure 5.3 Rhyme at 4;7 predicts reading at 6;7 even after controls for phoneme detection (tapping) (N = 64)

distinctive contribution to reading, and this probably takes the form of helping the child to form spelling categories — categories of words that share common sounds and, in their written form, common letter sequences as well. That seems the most likely explanation for the direct route that we demonstrated in our multiple regressions. Fortunately we now have clear empirical evidence that this is the right explanation. As we shall see, children are aware of letter sequences as well as of single letter-sound correspondences when they learn to read, and they easily grasp the fact that rhyming words often share letter sequences as well.

Analogies about letter sequences — the work of Usha Goswami

Suppose that we are faced with a child who has begun to learn to read, but cannot yet decipher the words 'peak', 'beak' or 'leak'. These are words which rhyme and share a common letter sequence. So a child who realizes the (albeit imperfect) connection between rhyme and spelling sequences should, if she is told what the written word 'peak' signifies, be able then to have a reasonable shot at working out what the other two writen words 'beak' and 'leak' mean.

Goswami (1986, 1988: see also Goswami and Bryant, 1989) designed a series of experiments to see if children who are learning to read do make this kind of inference, and showed convincingly that they do. She found that children who are told, for example, what a written word like 'peak' says are more likely as a result to read words with common sounds and letter sequences than words like 'bake' which have as many letters in common with the original word but in a different sequence. These inferences, or 'analogies' as Goswami calls them, are made even by many beginning readers and are very common in children who have been reading for a year or more. Goswami showed that children make them too when they are reading prose passages, and also when they are working out how to spell a word. Furthermore there is also a significant relationship in a fixed order multiple regression between children's rhyming skills and the number of analogies that they manage to make. Goswami's work shows that children understand the connection between rhyme and spelling sequences and use the connection to help them read. This is the stuff of the direct connection between rhyme and reading.

Speech units, onset and rime

So far we have accepted the simple distinction between phonemes and rhyming sounds and also the idea that children are aware of rhyme some years before they can detect a word's phonemes. It certainly is true that the sounds which rhyming words have in common usually contain more than one phoneme. But there is more to be said about the ways in which children can divide words into constituent sounds before they are fully aware of phonemes.

For some time now linguists have claimed that there is a natural way of dividing speech syllables into two parts (Halle and Vergnaud, 1980). These are usually called the 'onset' and the 'rime'. The onset is the syllable's opening consonant or consonants, and the rime the rest of the syllable. So 'c' is the onset and 'at' the rime of the spoken word 'cat', and 'str' the onset and 'ing' the rime in 'string'. One of the linguistic reasons for this distinction is that there are severe restrictions in any language on the sounds that can be combined within either the onset or the rime, but no such constraints when it comes to combining onset with rime. This is not simply a conceptual, linguistic distinction. There is also impressive evidence that the two speech units play a powerful role in adults' speech patterns. The mistakes that we make often reflect the onset-rime distinction: Mackay (1972) showed that when people mistakenly combine parts of two different words, they tend to divide these words at the onset-rime boundary: they say 'don't shell' (an unplanned combination of 'shout' and 'yell') and not 'don't shoull'. Furthermore Treiman (1983) found that adults are more successful in a game in which they have to transform words when the transformations do not cut across the onset-rime boundary.

Words which rhyme share a common rime, and thus young children's undoubted facility with rhyme suggests that they too may be affected by the onset-rime distinction. If they are, we can immediately see that the formula, that rhyme detection is a more primitive skill than phoneme detection, begins to look a little threadbare. The point here is that if young children are aware of onset and rime they should on occasion also be aware of single phonemes, because occasionally these speech units coincide with single phonemes. Take our original example of the word 'cat': here the onset is the single phoneme 'c'. If children can divide words into onset and rime they should be able to disentangle the 'c' sound in 'cat': but they should not be able to isolate the final consonant 't' because that is only part of the other speech unit, the word's rime.

Kirtley *et al.* (1989) have found exactly this pattern among 5 years 7 months old children. We gave them two oddity tests: in these the children simply heard four words at a time without having to look at pictures. In one task they had to judge which of four words began with a different sound from the rest ('man' 'mint' 'peck' 'mug'): in the other which word ended with a different phoneme from the rest ('pin' 'gun' 'hat' 'men'). The first of these tasks should be easy because the odd word has a different onset from the rest. The second task should be much more difficult; here all four words have different rimes (as well as different onsets), and the distinctive feature which tells the odd word apart from the rest, being only part of the rime, does not coincide with either speech unit. This prediction was emphatically confirmed in our study. The first of the two tasks, the task involving the opening consonant, was much easier than the second in which the judgments were about the phoneme at the end of the word. This difference was particularly marked among the thirty-one children in the group who at that time had made no progress in learning to read. The number of correct answers that they produced was well above chance level in the task involving the opening consonant, but fell to chance level in the task in which the distinctive feature was the final consonant. The rest of the children, the ones who had made some progress in learning to read also found the first task easier than the second, but their performance was above chance level in both cases. This last result raises the intriguing possibility that although the onset and rime were natural speech units for all the children, some of them had also begun to learn how to disentangle the rime as a direct result of learning to read.

The hypothesis that children easily divide syllables into onset and rime can be tested in other ways too. So far we have only considered oddity judgments that children make about consonants at the beginning or end of a word. We can now turn to the significance of the vowel sound. The vowel in a single syllable word like 'cat' is part of the rime. Therefore when children have to make judgments about the beginnings of words the presence or absence of the vowel sound as a distinguishing feature should make little difference. Suppose that a child is given two oddity tasks in which the odd word out begins with a different consonant from the other two. In one of these tasks the odd word has a different vowel from the other two as well ('doll' 'dog' 'can'). In the other only the opening sound tells the odd word apart ('doll' 'deaf' 'can'). Common sense suggests that the first of these tasks should be a great deal easier because in it there are two differences between the odd word and the other two. In the second task the odd word out only differs from the other two in one way (a different consonant). However the onset-rime distinction leads to a different suggestion. In both tasks the odd word can be identified by having a different onset and so both should be reasonably easy tasks. However the fact that the vowel also distinguishes the odd word from the other two in the first task should make no difference because that vowel has nothing to do with the onset and is only part of the rime.

In a second experiment (reported in the same paper), this time with 5, 6 and 7 year old children, we found exactly this pattern. The first task was slightly easier than the second but the difference was not impressive. It seems that children stick to the opening consonant — the onset — when they have to make oddity judgments about the opening sound and pay little heed to the vowel. The vowel, however, should be a great deal more important when it comes to judgments about the ends of words. If two words end in the same vowel and consonant while the third does not ('top' 'rail' 'hop') two of the three words share a common rime (they rhyme) while rime in the odd word is quite different: but, as we have already noted, if all three words have different vowels and the odd word is only odd because it has a different end consonant ('top' 'rail' 'whip'), then all three words have different rimes which means that it should be hard for the children to find the odd word.

Again the results confirmed our expectations. The task in which two of the three words ended with the same vowel and consonant (the same rime) was much easier than the one in which all three words had different vowel sounds.

Children can easily judge whether words end in the same rime: they find it much harder to see that they end in the same single consonant. These two experiments establish that the speech units, onset and rime, play an extremely powerful role in children's phonological awareness. The importance of these natural speech units fits well with young children's evident skills with rhyme, since rhyming words share rimes. We can also see that young children are aware of phonemes, and can disentangle them from the rest of the word, provided that the phoneme coincides with the word's onset.

The origins of children's awareness of rhyme

The discovery of the significance of natural speech units, which fit so neatly with the phenomenon of rhyme, suggests that the awareness of rhyme might be innate. But one needs to be cautious about accepting this conclusion at any rate in its strong form. In every study that we have done on pre-school children's sensitivity to rhyme we have found appreciable differences between different children. Of course these differences might also be innate: but one cannot dismiss the possibility that some of the variation in children's rhyming skills might be due to environmental differences as well. Young children hear rhymes frequently. Nursery rhymes are full of rhyming words and the words in them which rhyme tend to be heavily emphasized by adults who recite these rhymes to young children. The same is true of various action games (e.g. 'Round and round the garden'). The songs and even the television jingles which children listen to and eventually learn have their rhyming couplets too. So it is quite possible that a child who is exposed to nursery rhymes a great deal will as a result become particularly sensitive to rhyme.

We have gathered some, albeit indirect, evidence for this kind of environmental influence (Maclean, Bryant & Bradley, 1987; Bryant, Bradley, Maclean & Crossland, 1989). At the beginning of the longitudinal study of sixty-five children which was mentioned earlier on, we took measures of the children's knowledge of nursery rhymes. They were 3 years 4 months at the time, and we had not expected much acquaintance with nursery rhymes in children so young. In the event their knowledge surprised us. Our method was simple. We said the names of five of the commonest nursery rhymes ('Humpty Dumpty', 'Baa baa black sheep', 'Hickory dickory dock', 'Jack and Jill', 'Twinkle, twinkle'), and asked the children to recite each of them. There was a wide range of knowledge in this group of 3 year olds: some knew all five rhymes virtually perfectly: others hardly knew them at all. But only one child in the group did not manage to reproduce any part of the five nursery rhymes. So we established that nursery rhymes are still a living and effective tradition. We found a difference when we compared the knowledge of nursery rhymes in middle and working class children: the middle class children knew more. But this superiority disappeared when we controlled for I.Q. (Maclean, Bryant & Bradley, 1987). The social class difference therefore could be due to variations in the rate of intellectual development and not in the amount of contact that the children had had with nursery rhymes. Since we took this measure at the beginning of a longitudinal project, we could then go on to test a specific hypothesis about nursery rhymes. Knowledge of nursery rhymes, we argued, helps to introduce children to the phenomenon of rhyme, and affects their rhyming skills and hence their success in learning to read. Thus their performance in our early test of nursery rhyme knowledge should predict their scores in later tests of rhyme detection and in reading tests as well.

Our subsequent results provided strong support for this hypothesis. First we showed that the children's initial scores in our test of their knowledge of nursery rhymes predict their performance in subsequent tests of rhyming skills given over the following two years. This relationship stands even after the usual controls for differences in age, I.Q. and social background in fixed order multiple regressions (Bryant, Bradley, Mclean & Crossland, 1989). It cannot be claimed that children's knowledge of nursery rhymes only predicts their later performance in rhyme because the children who knew more nursery rhymes were better at rhyming in the first place. Nursery rhyme scores (taken at 3 years 4 months) continued to predict performance in a rhyme detection task at 4 years 7 months even when we also controlled for differences in the children's success in a rhyme test given to them in the same session in which we asked them to recite nursery rhymes. The nursery rhyme score definitely predicts the development of rhyming skills. In that case the same score should also predict the children's eventual success in reading. Further multiple regressions (which controlled the usual extraneous variables) showed a remarkable connection between the children's nursery rhyme scores at 3 years 4 months and their success in tests of reading and spelling three years later on (6 years 3 months). Significant predictions over such a long period of time which stand up to the most stringent statistical controls are extremely impressive. We can be sure that nursery rhymes are connected in some way to reading.

Once again we must ask about the pathway. How could the child's knowledge of 'Baa baa black sheep' at 3 years play a part in the way that she manages to learn to read when she is 6? Our hypothesis is simple and testable. It is that the knowledge of nursery rhymes affects children's rhyming skills which in turn, for reasons discussed earlier, influence children's reading. The idea leads to a prediction: the children's nursery rhyme scores should no longer predict their success in reading and spelling after controls for differences in later rhyming skills. So we carried out another series of fixed order multiple regressions in which we entered as the first steps the children's age, their social background and their I.Q.: then we entered their scores in a rhyme oddity test given them at 4 years 7 months, and only then did we enter as the final step their initial nursery rhyme scores. Our prediction was upheld. The relationship between the children's knowledge of nursery rhymes and their later reading and spelling scores vanished. So it seems that the route from nursery rhyme knowledge to reading is via the children's rhyming skills.

These are important results, because they suggest that there are informal ways of influencing young children's phonological skills before they go to school and thus of preparing them for reading. It must be a very rare parent indeed who introduces her children to nursery rhymes with reading and spelling in mind. Yet our data demonstrate a strong and entirely comprehensible connection between these two apparently disparate parts of the child's life. We had always been sure that phonological skills develop informally and for reasons which at the time have nothing explicitly to do with reading. Now that we have identified some of the connections between factors that prompt phonological development on the one hand and success in reading on the other, we can begin to plan a more helpful, but equally enjoyable, environment for pre-school children.

Summary

This chapter began with a question about the connection, or lack of connection, between informal pre-school skills and formal education. It was argued that the research on phonological awareness and reading shows that, in this case at least, there is a definite connection. Children soon become aware of some phonological distinctions but not of others. Before they go to school they are not at all skilled at dividing words up into their constituent phonemes. However they do become quite proficient at dividing words and syllables into onsets and rimes, and it looks as though these natural, 'intra-syllabic', speech units play a momentous part in the child's early phonological development. For they make it possible for the child to see that words that are recognizably different from each other nevertheless have the same onset as each other in some cases and in other cases the same rime.

In the former case the different words are alliterative, and in the latter they rhyme. Once a child understands that words can be grouped by rhyme or by alliteration she can begin to categorize words by their sounds. These categories are occasionally based on single shared phonemes as, for example, when words beginning with a single consonant are grouped by their onset ('can' 'cup' 'cot'). More often, they are based on shared sounds which contain more than one phoneme: this is usually the case when words rhyme ('cat' 'mat' 'fat'). Words which have a sound in common often share a common spelling sequence as well ('light' 'fight' 'might'). Thus a child might prepare herself for learning about spelling patterns by making herself familiar with rhyming categories. Goswami's work shows that even beginning readers seem to grasp, and to take advantage of, the fact that words which rhyme often contain the same spelling sequence.

It is not surprising then that measures of children's rhyming skills taken before they go to school predict their later success in reading very well, or that training in rhyme leads to improvement in reading. Our data suggest that rhyme affects reading in two ways. One, the direct route, is by giving the child an extremely effective way of learning about spelling sequences. The other link, which has been referred to as the indirect route, comes about because, as our data show, the ability to detect rhymes also gradually develops into an ability to recognize and isolate single phonemes as well.

Now that we know the immense consequences of children's sensitivity to rhyme, we should begin to find out how to encourage this informal skill. Our recent longitudinal project suggests one way to do this. It is to foster children's informal experience with nursery rhymes, songs, and acting games which involve rhyming words. These traditional and enjoyable activities, it can now be seen, may have considerable educational importance as well.

It is extremely interesting and encouraging too find that informal skills, which are probably acquired for reasons that have much more to do with sheer enjoyment than with education, nevertheless have considerable educational significance. To know about links between the informal pre-school environment and formal education later on is to be able to recommend how to improve that environment. The first step is to be sure that such links do exist. Our work has established one such link.

References

Bradley, L. and Bryant, P. E. (1978) 'Difficulties in auditory organisation as a possible cause of reading difficulties', *Nature*, 271, pp. 746–747.

Bradley, L. and Bryant, P. E. (1983) 'Categorising sounds and learning to read — a causal connection', *Nature*, 301, pp. 419–421.

Bryant, P. E. and Bradley, L. (1985) *Children's Reading Problems*, Oxford, Blackwell.

Bryant, P. E., Bradley, L., Maclean, M. and Crossland, J. (1989) 'Nursery rhymes, phological skills and reading', *Journal of Child Language*, 16 (In Press).

Bryant, P. E., Maclean, M., Bradley, L. and Crossland, J. (1989) 'Rhyme and alliteration, phoneme detection and learning to read', *Developmental Psychology* (in press).

Chukovsky, K. (1963) *From Two to Five*, Berkeley, University of California Press.

Content, A., Kolinsky, R., Morais, J. and Bertelson, P. (1986) 'Phonetic segmentation in pre-readers: effect of corrective information', *Journal of Experimental Child Psychology*, 42, pp. 49–72.

Dowker, A. (1989) 'Rhyme and alliteration in poems elicited from young children', *Journal of Child Language*, 16, pp. 181–202.

Goswami, U. (1986) 'Children's use of analogy in learning to read: a developmental study', *Journal of Experimental Child Psychology*, 42, pp. 73–83.

Goswami, U. (1988) 'Children's use of analogy in learning to spell', *British Journal of Developmental Psychology*, 6, pp. 21–34.

Goswami, U. and Bryant, P. E. (1989) 'Rhyming, analogy and children's reading', in Gough, P. B. (Ed) *Reading Acquisition*, Hillsdale, N.J., Lawrence Erlbaum.

Halle, M. and Vergnaud, J. (1980) 'Three dimensional phonology', *Journal of Linguistic Research*, 1, pp. 83–105.

Kirtley, C., Bryant, P. E., Maclean, M. and Bradley, L. (1989) 'Rhyme, rime and the onset of reading', *Journal of Experimental Child Psychology*, (In Press).

Knafle, J. D. (1973) 'Auditory perception of rhyming in kindergarten children', *Journal of Speech and Hearing Research*, 16, pp. 482–487.

Knafle, J. D. (1974) 'Children's discrimination of rhyme', *Journal of Speech and Hearing Research*, 17, pp. 367–372.

Lazar, I. and Darlington, R. (1982) 'Lasting effects of early education: a report of the Consortium for longitudinal studies', *Monographs for the Society for Research in Child Development*, 47, 195 (whole issue).

Lenel, J. C. and Cantor, J. H. (1981) 'Rhyme recognition and phonemic perception in young children', *Journal of Psycholinguistic Research*, 10, pp. 57–68.

Liberman, I. Y., Shankweiler, D., Liberman, A. M., Fowler, C. and Fischer, F. W. (1978) 'Phonetic segmentation and recoding in the beginning reader', in Reber, A. S. and Scarborough, D. L. (Eds) *Toward a Psychology of Reading*, New York, Lawrence Erlbaum.

Lundberg, I., Oloffson, A. and Wall, S. (1980) 'Reading and spelling skills in the first school years predicted from phonemic awareness skills in kindergarten', *Scandinavian Journal of Psychology*, 21, pp. 159–173.

Mackay, D. G. (1972) 'The structure of words and syllables: evidence form errors in speech', *Cognitive Psychology*, 3, pp. 210–227.

Maclean, M., Bryant, P. E. and Bradley, L. (1987) 'Rhymes, nursery rhymes and reading in early childhood', *Merrill-Palmer Quarterly*, 33, pp. 255–282.

Mann, V. (1986) 'Phonological awareness: the role of reading experience', *Cognition*, 24, pp. 65–92.

Morais, J., Alegria, J. and Content, A. (1987) 'The relationships between segmental analysis and alphabetic literacy: an interactive approach', *Cahiers de Psychologie Cognitive*, 7, pp. 415–438.

Morais, J., Bertelson, P., Cary, L. and Alegria, J. (1986) 'Literacy training and speech segmentation', *Cognition*, 24, pp. 45–30.

Morais, J., Cary, L., Alegria, J. and Bertelson, P. (1979) 'Does awareness of speech as a sequence of phonemes arise spontaneously?', *Cognition*, pp. 323–331.

Osborn, A. F. and Millbank, J. E. (1987) *The Effects of Early Education: A Report From the Child Health and Education Study*, Oxford, Clarendon Press.

Read, C., Zhang, Y., Nie, H. and Ding, B. (1986) 'The ability to manipulate speech sounds depends on knowing alphabetic spelling', *Cognition*, 24, pp. 31–34.

Stanovich, K. E. (1987) 'Introduction: children's reading and the development of phonological awareness', *Merrill-Palmer Quarterly*, 33, pp. 251–254.

Stanovich, K. E., Cunningham, A. E., and Cramer, B. R. (1984) 'Assessing phonological awareness in kindergarten children: issues of task', *Journal of Experimental Child Psychology*, 38, pp. 175–190.

Treiman, R. (1983) 'The structure of spoken syllables: evidence from novel word games', *Cognition*, 15, pp. 49–74.

6
Rhyming Connections in Learning to Read and Spell

Lynette Bradley

Identifying children with reading and spelling difficulties

The form of the problem

There are two different ways we can approach the problem of children with reading and spelling difficulties. The first is to identify the nature of the difficulty so that we can try to discover what is causing it and develop appropriate teaching strategies to help overcome it. The second is to prevent children from ever becoming backward readers in the first place. If we have some idea what is causing the problem we can find ways of preparing children before they go to school so that they can cope with reading and writing when they get there.

In recent years there has been overwhelming evidence for one such possible cause of reading and spelling problems. Carefully designed and controlled studies from around the world have demonstrated a powerful connection between phonological awareness and learning to read (Lundberg, Olofsson and Wall, 1980; Bradley and Bryant, 1983, 1985; Wagner and Torgesen, 1987). Children who are tuned in to the sounds in the words of their language are more likely to be successful in learning to read and spell. This is not surprising as the number of letters in the printed word usually represent the same number of phonemes in the spoken word, and children who are alert to these phonemes are more likely to be able to make the connection with the alphabetic code.

Ingvar Lundberg and his colleagues carried out a large study in Denmark to see if children could be helped to develop this skill before they started school (Lundberg, Frost and Petersen, 1988). For 8 months they trained 235 6 year old children with daily sessions of games and metalinguistic exercises to help them attend to the phonological structure of their language, but they did not give them any reading (children in Denmark do not start school until 7). The children played rhyming games and games segmenting sentences into word units. They clapped hands to the syllables in their own names, and used iteration to identify phonemes in them e.g. TTTT–om. When these children went to school they were better at phonemic tests and in reading and spelling than children not given the pre-school training.

These results are encouraging, but we must treat the results with a little caution, as the study lacked some important controls. The children in the control groups were in different schools in different parts of the country, so they had different backgrounds and different teachers, and lacked this special attention. We cannot be certain that the differences were due to the training as the children's circumstances were different in so many respects.

Training in phonological awareness is not a new idea. It has been a traditional part of the curriculum in this country, particularly in remedial reading, though many children with learning difficulty have not been helped by it. This could be because the training is inappropriate: not all children have difficulty with phonological awareness; or because training is introduced too late; or sadly because much 'phonics' teaching has little to do with phonological awareness. In many cases it has become a mechanistic and meaningless ritual far removed from reading — the 'ker-arh-ter says cat' approach, a labyrinth of elaborate programmes and rules, which must only add to the children's difficulties. It is not surprising that in many areas it has fallen out of favour.

Two pioneers in the field of phonological awareness, Liberman and Mattingley, discuss the reader's situation in great depth (Liberman and Shankweiler, 1985; Mattingley, 1972, 1985). When we read or spell we use only twenty-six letters, in different combinations, to represent all the spoken words that there are in our language. We can do this because each spoken word has a phonological structure, a string of abstract phonological elements, and we represent the phonological elements or sounds of all the spoken words in our language with different combinations of these few alphabetic letters. It is a flexible system that can cope with an expanding language. We can introduce new technical terminology and slang words into our language and transcribe them without difficulty using the same alphabetic letters.

Readers can understand and use the alphabetic system when they are aware that the spoken word *stop* can be divided into four segments which are represented by four letters in the printed word. But to be able to use the system we must develop phonological awareness, awareness of and access to the phonology of the language. However we are not consciously aware of the phonological elements of words when we are speaking. Most children learn to read and write without thinking very much about the fact that they are picking up or *mapping* this phonological structure. Even pre-school children who have not been taught to read can use the system in their spontaneous spelling (Read, 1971).

But the system seems to present an insurmountable barrier for other children. Even children who come to school with some degree of phonological awareness and some knowledge of the alphabet have to learn to put the two together, and this is not altogether straightforward. Speech is continuous — although we leave a space between each written word we do not leave a space between each word when we talk. Then the smallest pronounceable speech unit is the syllable, but a one syllable unit can be represented by any number of letters from one to eight in print. There are three speech units or syllables in the spoken word 'understand', but the first unit, *un*, has two letters, the second, *der*, has three letters, and the third, *stand*, has five letters. How is the child to work out this relationship? Nor do we say words one sound after the other: *stop*, for example, as *s.t.o.p.*. The phonological units in each spoken word are not separable, but overlap; we cannot truly separate them in speech and when we try to 'sound out' the word *stop* it sounds more like *suhtuhohper*. And that is still not the end of the child's problem. The alphabetic side is also complex. At the level of the individual letter English orthography is highly variable as particular letters often signify different sounds in different words. This means that children who are taught that O says *o* will be quite perplexed if they have to read the words *coat, book, moon* or *brought*. We can simplify this problem if we think of a sequence of letters as one unit. So *o* considered as part of the stable sequence *ought* will always be the same (for example, in b/*ought*, br/*ought*, n/*ought*, f/*ought*, etc.). Obviously it will help children if they can recognize sequences like this as units rather than have to build them up letter by letter or phoneme by phoneme (Donaldson, 1978). Children with reading and spelling difficulties who are taught to understand the implications of rhyming units reduce the problem of mastering the alphabetic code to a manageable proposition.

Coincidentally, it is also easier for young children to hear the sound similarities in spoken words when they have a string of sounds in common. Words which are identical have most sounds in common, but words which rhyme are almost the same as each other — they usually only differ by one phoneme (e.g. h/*en* p/*en*, f/*ought* b/*ought*, h/*umpty* d/*umpty*). This means that the rhyming connection is a very easy one to hear, and it is widely reported in the literature on early language development (Vihman, 1981; Chukovsky, 1963). Chukovsky says that it is the most natural system of practice in phonetics, and gives many examples of the way pre-school children make up words to achieve rhyme in their word play. One 3 year old talked about a straw house as 'the red house, made of strouss'. The child changed str/aw to str/ouss so that it would rhyme with house, and to achieve this rhyme she changed the word within the syllabic unit. Treiman has designed several elegant studies to show that words divide naturally into these *onset* (or beginning) and *rime* (or rhyme) units (Treiman, 1988; see also Bryant's Chapter 5 for further coverage of onset and rime). The division places the vowel with the rime. This fits well with linguistic descriptions of rhyming words as identical from the stressed vowel to the end of the word. Thus, when children distort words to achieve rhyme in word play, the rhyme is achieved by changing the word within the syllable. In Chukovsky's example the child kept the same *onset* for both words. Treiman suggests that this natural division into onset and rime units forms an intermediate step between sensitivity to whole words and sensitivity to individual phonemes. Rhyming word play certainly leads naturally from play with large sound units to analysis into smaller units, at the level of the phoneme.

Do pupils with difficulty have anything in common?

The evidence for rhyming as part of the pre-school child's language experience shows that young children have a way to prepare for learning to read and to spell before they meet words in print. Practice in word play, and particularly rhyming, must help them to appreciate the phonology of their language as they attend to sounds in the words they hear and use. Little children make up their own words to achieve rhyme in word play, and so they analyze words into onset and rime units, within the syllabic unit, often at the level of the phoneme. But rhyming helps them practise another skill too; by attending to these units they learn to *generalize* from one spoken word to another. These spoken units that they recognize frequently coincide with stable sequences of letters in the written words (str/aw str/ouss; h/umpty d/umpty). If the child can grasp this series of connections he has a headstart. He can make the first connection, the onsets and rimes in spoken words, before he comes to school and before he meets printed words.

But children with reading and spelling difficulties appear to be particularly insensitive to these connections, which leads to what Stanovich (1986) terms the Matthew effect: one problem leads to another and this can happen in many different ways. If children do not hear the connections then every word they need to read or to spell is a unique word, and the task of learning to read and spell them must seem overwhelming. It must be like having to learn every word in a dictionary without any way of organizing the task, no way to begin except to choose a word and learn it, and then to take any other word, and learn that, and so on. On the other hand a child may use rhymes in word play but not be truly aware of them, and not be able to make judgments about them or use this information. Or he may appreciate the rhymes but not make the connection between the rimes and the letter pattterns. If this happens the child who learns to read and to write the word *and* cannot use this information to read or to spell words like *s/and, h/and, st/and, c/and/le*, or *h/and/some*. To find out whether insensitivity to onsets and rimes was a common difficulty among children with reading problems the author gave rhyme and alliteration judgment tasks (our terms for onset and rime) to three groups of children (Bradley, 1979).

The reading age design

A large group of children of normal intelligence but eighteen months or more behind the average reading skill for their age were compared with a group of younger children also of normal intelligence whose reading skills were normal for their age and were matched with those of the backward readers. The average age of the sixty-two children with reading problems (specific learning difficulty or dyslexia) was 10 years 4 months; they were all attending normal schools, had received reasonable schooling and remedial teaching, and had no primary organic or emotional problems. The reading level of the dyslexic group and of the younger children was 7 years 6 months. The reason for making this comparison was to distinguish between cause and effect. If the younger children were better at the rhyming tasks, the dyslexics' failure could not be due to lack of reading experience because both groups were reading at the same level. A second control group of children the same age as the dyslexics (10 years 4 months) were reading normally for their age. The trouble with this more usual comparison in reading studies is that if the normal readers are able to do the rhyme and alliteration tasks we will not know whether their skill at rhyming has helped them to learn to read, or whether their reading experience has helped them to be good at rhyme. As it happened this group could do all the tasks, but as this comparison does not tell us whether rhyming helps reading or vice-versa we will concentrate on the performance of the first two groups of children, the dyslexic children and the younger normal readers reading at the same level.

The rhyming test

In the sound categorization test, which has become known as the rhyming test, there were six trials in each of three conditions. In two conditions three of the words rhymed while the fourth did not; in one rhyming condition three of the words shared the same end phoneme (hen, pen, *bed*, men), and in the other the three rhyming words shared the same mid phoneme (*hug*, dig, pig, wig). In the third condition three of the words had the same opening phoneme while the odd one out did not (sun, see, sock, *rag*); in subsequent tests the vowel was kept constant from one word to another). The child's task was to listen to the four words and to spot the odd one out. Two dyslexics were excluded because they did not always remember the words, but although the remaining sixty dyslexic children could repeat the words perfectly well only nine of them were able to make rhyme judgments consistently. On the other hand hardly any of the younger children could remember the words but they could nearly always hear the odd word out. Only 26.6 per cent of the young normal readers made more than one error overall, while 85 per cent of the dyslexics made more than one error.

This difference was all the more remarkable given that the dyslexic children, being on average more than 3 years older, were actually of a considerably higher intellectual level than the normal reading group. These results suggested that insensitivity to rhymes was commonplace among children with reading problems, and that this difficulty with categorizing sounds might be one cause of their reading failure (Bradley, 1984; Bradley and Bryant, 1978).

Rhyming skill in non-readers

Our results also suggested that the experiences which children have with rhyme before they go to school might contribute to success later on in learning to read and write, as categorizing words by rhyme and alliteration involves attending to their constituent sounds, and so does learning to use the alphabet in reading and spelling. To discover how important rhyming is for young children learning to read Bryant and I carried out a large scale project in Oxford over the next five years (Bradley and Bryant, 1983, 1985). Our study combined two different methods. The first was longitudinal, to establish whether a relationship existed between early rhyming skill and later success in reading. The second was intervention, to determine whether any such relationship was a causal one or not. If rhyming really does affect reading, extra help with rhyming should improve reading skill.

Longitudinal evidence

We saw 403 children, 118 4-year-olds and 285 5-year-olds before they learned to read, and tested their skill on the rhyme and alliteration judgment tasks using the same method as before (Bradley, 1984). We increased the number of trials in each condition to ten, and we limited the number of words per trial to three for the youngest children, as a pilot study showed that four words might be too many for them to remember. We did ask the children to repeat the words in separate trials as a memory check, and tested their vocabulary (English Picture Vocabulary Test), and later in the study, their intelligence (WISC/R).

Our first discovery was that little children who have not begun to read are very good at sound categorization. Their scores of 6 or 7 correct out of 10 on the rhyme and alliteration judgment tasks were well above the chance level of 2.5 (see Table 6.1). We now had powerful evidence that young children develop this skill before they come to school.

To find out whether this skill affected their progress in reading and spelling we followed the children in school over the next three years. Some of them moved away during this time, but when they were 8 to 9 years old we gave the remaining 368 children standardized tests of reading, spelling and mathematics. We found that the children who were better at rhyming when they came to school were better at reading and spelling (but not mathematics) three years later, and our statistical tests showed that these relationships

Table 6.1 Examples of words given to pre-readers and their scores on the sound categorization tests

	4-yr group (N = 118)		5-yr group (N = 285)	
	Words given to children	Mean correct (out of 10)	Words given to children	Mean correct (out of 10)
Sounds in common				
First sound	*tap* hat ham cup cut *fun*	5.69	bus bud bun *rug* pip pin *hill* pig	5.36
Middle sound	pin tin *man* *mug* log dog	7.53	*hug* dig pig wig red *lid* fed bed	6.89
End sound	bun gun *hut* *pal* map cap	7.42	bun gun *hut* sun *pal* map cap gap	6.67

remained strong even when the influences of intellectual level, vocubulary, age and memory had been taken into account.

These longitudinal data showed that there was a definite relationship between the young child's skill at categorizing sounds and success in reading and spelling, and that the relationship was specific to written language tasks. But we could not be certain that this relationship was a causal one. Both the skill at rhyming and the success in reading and spelling may have been determined by some other unknown factor, such as especially caring parents or teachers. The way to resolve this question is through properly controlled training studies, which demonstrate cause-effect relationships. If we could show that children given extra help in sound categorization made more progress in reading than a control group given exactly the same treatment except for the help with sound categorization, this would confirm that the relationship was causal. For this reason we included a training study in our longitudinal project.

The training study

Design

When we had finished testing the 403 children on the sound categorization tasks as the end of the first year of our project we had selected the sixty-five children who had most difficulty on the rhyming test to take part in a training programme. They were matched on the rhyme test scores, and on age, sex, and vocabulary scores across four groups, two experimental (Group 1 and Group 2) and two control (Group 3 and Group 4). There were no differences between the groups in intellectual level (WISC/R). The children in our first experimental group were trained to categorize words by the sounds in them, and the children in our first control group were trained to categorize the same words by their meaning. Thus these two groups received exactly the same treatment as each other except that one categorized words by sounds, and the other semantically.

Training

The training began in the second year of the project when the children were beginning to turn 6 years old. Each child was seen for 40 ten minute individual sessions over the next two years which together amounted to less than seven hours training for each child. There were thirteen children in each of the two experimental groups and in the first year (twenty sessions) these children received exactly the same training as each other. They were taught to categorize words by their sounds using picture cards of familiar objects. They were taught that the same word shared common beginning (hen, hat), middle (hen, leg), and end (hen, man) sounds with other words. Thus the spoken word *hen* would eventually be categorized in three different ways, and we hoped that the children would come to realize that there were three different sounds in the word *hen* without ever seeing it written down. The middle and end sound categories were always introduced through rhyming groups: *man* would be introduced into the group (*cat hat bat rat man*) to draw attention to the last sound of the words, and, at a later stage, *net* to draw attention to the mid-sound (*cat hat net bat rat*).

In the second year of training, for the final twenty sessions, the second experimental group was taught to make the same words with plastic alphabetic letters. This was to test a teaching method which the author had developed for pupils with difficulty in sound categorization to help them understand the *connection* between the sound and visual patterns that rhyming words often share. Training in sound categorization alone will test our causal hypothesis, but children with great difficulty in this modality — which is why they had been selected for the training study — might not respond to teaching in that modality only. The children in the second experimental group did not have longer sessions. They categorized the words by their sounds as usual, and then made the words with the plastic letters in the same ten minute session. These children soon learned that they did not need to change all the letters when they changed the first word into a word that rhymed with it. They discovered that the sound segments which were the same from one word to the next were represented by the same letters.

There were twenty-six children in the first control group and these children were trained to categorize the same words as the twenty-six children in the two experimental groups, but they categorized them semantically, in terms of concept categories. They put the pictures for *hen* and *man* together because they were both living things; *hen fox* because they were both animals, and *hen pig* because they were both farm animals. The training for the experimental and control groups was controlled at every stage so that the only difference in treatment between them was the training in sound categorization. The second control group of thirteen children were tested but not trained.

Results

The children were 8 to 9 years old when they were tested after the training had finished. Children in both experimental groups had made more progress in reading and spelling, but not mathematics, than the children in the control groups. On two different reading tests there were no significant differences between the two experimental groups, or between the two control groups. The experimental group trained only on sounds were 3–4 months ahead of the concept-trained control group on both reading tests and in spelling. Even though this difference was not statistically significant, the consistent advantage for training in sound categorization over training in conceptual categorization, together with our powerful longitudinal data, was generally accepted as the most convincing demonstration of the importance of phonological awareness in learning to read and to spell (see Figure 6.1).

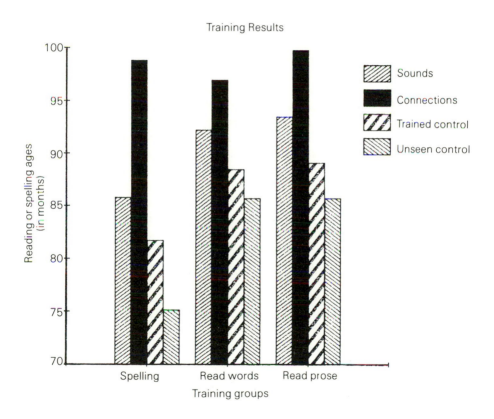

Figure 6.1 *Reading and spelling scores at age 8 to 9 years after early training*

91

As we have already pointed out, it would have been surprising if children who had such difficulty with sound categorization had responded very well to this training. On the other hand children in the second experimental group taught in a tangible way that alphabetic letters signified the phonology of the language made striking progress. The connection between the rime units and the letter strings is captured in such an obvious way using this approach that children cannot fail to appreciate it. They were 8–10 months ahead of the trained control group on the reading tests and 17 months ahead in spelling, and even further ahead of the untrained control group. To find such great differences in progress after only three years in school shows the importance of appropriate teaching for children with learning difficulties.

The follow-up study

Four years later we had the opportunity to find out how the children who had been involved in the training study were getting along. We were able to trace sixty-three of the original sixty-five children. They were now 13 years old and attending middle schools in the county. We had not seen the children for more than four years, so we checked up to see if they had received any special help over that time. We found that 46 per cent of the trained control group and 54 per cent of the untrained control children had been receiving remedial help because of their poor progress in reading, and many were still receiving special teaching. On the other hand only 23 per cent of the experimental group trained in sound categorization and 7.7 per cent of the second experimental group had received help. We thought that so many of the control children had received remediation over a long period that the differences that had existed between the groups when we last saw them must have disappeared, and that it would certainly eliminate the 3–4 month difference between the first experimental group trained in sound categorization and the trained control group. Any trace of a continuing effect for the difference in training between these two groups would be powerful confirmation of the causal relationship between early skill at sound categorization and later reading and spelling. A gap of six months would be a stringent test of the effectiveness of any intervention. But because five years had elapsed since our training ended we no longer expected to find any difference between any of the groups as a result of our early intervention.

The children were all tested by personnel who had not met them before, and who had no knowledge of the training or in which groups the children had been. They were given the original Schonell tests of reading and spelling and Neale reading, but because these reading tests have a ceiling of 12 years 6 months the children were also given the Boder and Jarico (1982) reading test, a graded word-reading test similar to the Schonell, which continues to adult level.

Table 6.2 Mean test scores for the different groups at age 13 (Percentage of children at ceiling on each test in brackets)

Groups	Experimental		Control	
	1 (*Sounds*) (N = 13)	2 (*Connections*) (N = 12)	3 (*Trained*) (N = 26)	4 (*Unseen*) (N = 12)
Boder words read	143 (8%)	161 (15%)	136 (8%)	120 (0%)
Schonell Reading (months)	122 (23%)	130 (46%)	120 (19%)	116 (15%)
Schonell Spelling (months)	121 (8%)	131 (25%)	117 (8%)	112 (0%)
Neale (months)	121 (61%)	123 (77%)	119 (46%)	114 (38%)
Arithmetic (WISC/R scale score)	8.46	9.33	9.04 (n = 25)	7.3 (n = 10)

Results

We were amazed to find that the differences between all the groups were still there. Our post-tests showed that the advantages gained by the experimental groups in their first three years in school as a result of less than seven hours of individual training when the children were 6 and 7 years old had been maintained. The experimental group who were trained in sound categorization alone were still ahead of the trained control group on all four reading and spelling tests, but not in mathematics (see Table 6.2) (Bradley, 1989). These extraordinary and powerful results give the strongest possible support to our causal hypothesis. Skill in sound categorization is vitally important in learning to read and to spell. A child's early rhyming skill will help determine success in reading; early help in sound categorization will help children without this skill to succeed in reading too.

However our results showed something else that was equally important. The children in the experimental group who were trained to connect the sound and letter patterns were ahead on every reading and spelling test by a large margin. The importance of early and appropriate intervention is obvious, and the prognosis for children not given this early help is poor, since children who had been given special help by the remedial services since our study ended had made progress, but were still two years and more behind their peers and were unlikely to be able to make up that difference in their remaining school years.

To summarize thus far, children need to be aware of the phonology of our language if they are to learn to read and to spell. We have shown that it is a relatively easy matter to identify children who have not mastered phonological awareness when they begin school. Stanovich points out that phonological measures often predict reading ability better than comprehensive standardized intelligence tests and usually take no longer than ten minutes to give (Stanovich, 1989). Children who were helped at this early stage made good progress. The type of help that we give makes a big difference to the progress that the children make. The time of intervention is also crucially important for, if we delay too long, children who have not grasped how the alphabetic system works will have fallen too far behind their peers to be able to make up that ground in the time available. This will, inevitably, affect their general progress in school.

The next step

The relationship between phonological awareness and success in reading has now been shown many times, and has been hailed as one of the great success stories in developmental psychology (Wagner and Torgeson, 1987; Stanovich, 1987). In a pre-school project subsequently carried out in Oxford, we showed that children as young as 3 years of age acquire a degree of phonological awareness before learning to read (Maclean, Bryant & Bradley, 1987), and that early linguistic routines like nursery rhymes help the child to develop this awareness (Bryant, Bradley, Maclean and Crossland, 1989). But we had another measure in this pre-school project which also proved to be an important and independent pre-cursor of reading and spelling ability. That was a measure of the four year old child's knowledge of letter names (Bradley, Maclean, Crossland and Bryant, 1989).

The importance of knowledge of letter names in learning to read and spell is not a new finding by any means. The earliest and perhaps most rigorous of these separate longitudinal studies were carried out in the United States by Jansky and her colleagues (de Hirsch, Jansky and Langord, 1966; Jansky and de Hirsch, 1972), but the same connection has been found in studies in Australia (Share *et al.*, 1984) and more recently in London (Tizard *et al.*, 1988). The important feature about our own study is that we were able to show that a combination of the measures of rhyming skill and knowledge of letter names provided a simple and powerful predictor of later progress in reading and in spelling.

To a large extent this explained the reason for the success of the method of teaching children the connection between rhymes in words and alphabetic letters. But some aspects of this connection were still puzzling. The children trained in this way made significantly more progress in spelling than all other groups, and this advantage was maintained. To do so well on the spelling tests they had to spell many irregular words. How did the training with congruent rhymes help this? For example, many rhyming words, like hair/pear, and feet/seat, do not have similar letter patterns, yet the rhyming training had produced striking results in spelling. We also needed to know if this kind of training would help all children, or whether it was only important for children with difficulty in sound categorization. To answer these questions we ran another longitudinal and training study.

Longitudinal and training study with young normal readers

The children in the new study were sixty young children in their first year at school. These children were 5 and 6 years old and they were just beginning to learn to read; most of them could recognize a few words, and were making normal progress and had no difficulty in sound categorization (Bradley, 1988, 1989). The study followed a cross-lag design. The children were tested on rhyming tests and for their skill at remembering letter strings and in reading and spelling at age 6, age 7, and again at age 9, and their performance on these measures was compared at each age, and from one age to another. We also tested their intelligence (WISC/R).

The two new tests devised for this study were the tests of incongruent rhyme and the test of memory for letter strings. These tests were included to try to find out why the training with rhymes and letters had such a powerful effect on spelling. The children were given the same rhyming tests as before (Bradley, 1980). In the two rhyme conditions in that test the children make judgments about congruent rhymes: the words we *say* to them both sound and look alike (e.g. pin win *sit* fin; lot cot pot *hat*) and the children have to say which word sounds different. The children were also given a new test of *incongruent* rhymes, in which the odd word had a similar letter pattern to the other words but sounded different (e.g. beak *steak* freak leak), or where words sounded alike but looked different (e.g. saw for *were* more). The children listened to this rhyme judgment task too and did just as well as on the congruent rhyme tasks.

The second new test was the memory for letter strings task, in which each child was shown ten highly frequent but irregularly spelled words one at a time for five seconds, after which the word was removed and the child asked to write the word down. The average number of words that these little children remembered was 2.4 words.

There was a short training study with stringent controls for the letters in the first year. Once again children taught the connection between sounds and letters made significantly more progress in reading than children given exactly the same training but taught about sounds in one session and letters in the next and not about the connection between them. They also made better progress than children taught only about sounds, or only about letter patterns. They made particularly good progress in reading comprehension, which is not surprising as it is the phonology of the language that carries the meaning. The difference between *bag* and *bat* is not that one ends in 'g' and the other in 't'; the difference is that the first is a container for carrying things, and the second can be a little creature that hangs upside down.

Although children trained only with letter patterns did not do as well as children trained to connect sound and letter patterns they made better progress than children trained only in sound connections. This was to be expected as these young children had no difficulty with phonological categorization. Children trained with letter patterns probably put the two together, but these young normal children given only sounds needed the experience with letters too. In contrast, later on we repeated this study with older backward readers, and the only children to make any progress at all in reading comprehension in one year were those trained in making these connections. The backward readers trained in letter patterns only actually regressed in reading comprehension. So training in the connection between rhymes and letter patterns is particularly important for children with learning problems, who do not appear to make these connections for themselves.

Our analysis of the test data for the young normal readers at ages 6, 7, and 9 years using multiple regression techniques showed us that there was again a relationship between the young child's skill on the rhyming tasks and progress in *reading*, and this applied to skill on the incongruent rhyme judgment task as well. These young children were listening to the words, and making judgments about what they heard, and at the first testing they had hardly begun to read, and would not have been affected by the incongruent letter patterns.

Even so the relationship between rhyming and *spelling* was confined to the congruent rhyme measure. There was no relationship between the children's skill at judging incongruent rhymes and progress in spelling, even though this was a listening task. We looked at the relationship between the congruent and incongruent rhyme measures, the memory for letter string scores and spelling and discovered that children got better on the memory for letter strings task as they got older if they were good at congruent rhymes when the study began, (but not incongruent rhymes), and if they were good at remembering letter strings they got better at spelling. We thus showed that it is making judgments about words that sound and look alike which helps children develop their memory for spelling.

This result suggests that children get better at remembering letter strings, or the spelling of words, if they have some way to organize the task. If children make the connection between rhyming words they hear in their early word play before they come to school they have a way to categorize words at their fingertips. If they realize very early on that rhyming words often have similar letter patterns they have found a way to reduce the number of words they have to learn. They only need to remember one word from each rhyming category. This will leave more working memory free to deal with words which must be remembered individually because of their unusual letter patterns (e.g. people), or because only the letter patterns convey enough information (e.g. homonyms: so, sow, sew), and which cannot be categorized in the same way. Now we can see why training in the connection between sound and letter patterns has such a beneficial effect on progress in spelling.

Reading and spelling difficulties and remedial teaching

At the beginning of this chapter the author suggested that one way to approach the problem of children with reading and spelling difficulties was to try to determine the nature of the difficulty so that we can try to prevent it. In the past few years we have been able to identify one such factor. Our research shows that young children begin to develop sensitivity to the phonological aspects of language before they come to school, and before they meet print (Bradley and Bryant, 1983, 1985; Maclean, Bryant and Bradley, 1987). Research also shows that phonological measures taken before children learn to read are related to their eventual success in reading even when other relevant variables such as IQ have been controlled (Bradley and Bryant, 1983, 1985; Lundberg, Olofsson and Wall, 1980), and are superior to IQ tests as predictors of future reading achievement (Stanovich, 1987). Because so many studies show this striking connection between phonological awareness and success in learning to read our research, showing that young children who are poor at making phonological judgments can be identified early on and helped before they fail, is particularly encouraging (Bradley and Bryant, 1985; Bradley, 1988).

A variety of measures of phonological awareness have been used by different researchers (Stanovich, 1986); some studies show different results to others with what appear to be similar measures. For example, in some of the Swedish studies the connection between rhyming skill and reading was not as strong as the connection between other phonological measures and reading. But we need to interpret these results with care. In that particular study the children were 7 years old, two years older than the children in our study, and they were only asked to detect the odd word out of three words, so the test would have been far too easy for children of that age, and would not have discriminated between them at all well. On the whole rhyming tests seem to give the most consistent results when testing younger children (Share *et al.*, 1984; Stanovich, 1986; Bradley and Bryant, 1983, 1985) and children with reading difficulties (Bradley and Bryant, 1978). If we want to think in terms of prevention, our training results (Bradley, 1989) show that we need to intervene as early as possible, and rhyming tests are particularly suitable measures for identifying young children who need help, as it is a task most young children manage very well.

Knowledge of alphabetic letters has also been shown to be an important precursor of reading and spelling skill. Several studies now have shown that the young child's skill at rhymes together with knowledge of letter names accounts for an appreciable amount of the variance in later reading skill (Share *et al.*, 1984; de Hirsch, Jansky and Langford, 1966; Bradley, Maclean, Crossland and Bryant, 1989). It would of course be impossible to learn to read and to spell without using the alphabet, so to that extent this skill must be causally related to progress in reading and spelling. However there is no evidence that knowledge of letter names *on its own* helps children learn to read, and since alphabetic letters convey the phonology of the language it is imprudent to suggest that we could divorce the two.

Identification of these factors as precursors of success in reading and spelling suggests that fostering these skills in pre-school children will help them once they come to school. While we still need rigorously controlled training studies to show us what form this training might take, the delightful examples given from studies of normally developing infants by Vihman (1981), Chukovsky (1963) and Dowker (1989) show us the kinds of rhyming games and linguistic routines that we might encourage.

On the other hand we now have rigorous evidence from our carefully controlled intervention studies to show that we can introduce training which will probably be successful in preventing reading failure once we have identified a difficulty with phonological awareness. We have however to take two factors into account.

The first factor is the time of intervention. We need to intervene as early as possible. This needs a general rethinking as regards current policy in many areas, where resources are allocated to children who have already failed. While we have a responsibility to children with reading problems, implementation of a preventive policy will be more effective in the long term. In our intervention study children given less then seven hours help at the ages of 6 and 7 were doing well in school at the age of 13, whereas children not given this early and appropriate help needed remedial teaching from the age of 8 till the end of their time in school. Clearly the policy of allocating resources after failure occurs needs changing.

The second important factor concerns the kind of intervention that is given. Children who were poor at sound categorization who were trained in phonological awareness alone did not make as much progress as children trained to connect sound and letter patterns. Even young children without difficulty in sound categorization made better progress when they were taught the connection between the two, and understanding this connection was crucial to understanding what they were reading. This was even more true for children with reading problems, and neither group were helped as much by training with letter patterns alone as they were by being taught that these represented the phonology of the language. Children with reading difficulties who are taught about the patterns words share by writing lists of words frequently fail to make the connection between the letter patterns that they see and the words that they hear. They do not understand the concept we are trying to teach. Using the plastic alphabetic letters, so that the unit the words shared stayed from one word to the next, made this connection explicit.

Children with reading problems trained with letters on their own made no progress in reading comprehension, and none in memory for letter strings for spelling. This is not as strange as it seems when we remember that children make more progress in spelling when they organize their approach to handling the alphabet by recognizing rhyming patterns.

There is now a body of rigorously controlled research which shows that the most effective training programmes are those which develop the child's ability to use *both* phonological and holistic processing rather than programmes which emphasize one approach to the exclusion of the other (Bradley, 1988; Vellutino and Scanlon, 1977), and another body of research which supports multisensory teaching for children with reading problems (Hulme, 1981; Bradley, 1981). A recent conference in Virginia was devoted to reporting research on intervention studies teaching children to understand the alphabetic system (Ellis, 1987). The extraordinary and long lasting effect we achieved in our eight year study when we trained children to appreciate the connection between rhyming and letter patterns suggested that this is a particularly effective way to help children grasp the relationship between phonological awareness and the alphabet (Bradley, 1988), and one that has not been captured in much of the traditional 'phonics' teaching.

References

Boder, E., and Jarrico, S. (1982) *The Boder Test of Reading-Spelling Patterns*, New York, Grune and Stratton.

Bradley, L. (1979) *Perceptual and Cognitive Difficulties Experienced by Able Backward Readers*, Unpublished Ph.D. thesis, University of Reading.

Bradley, L. (1981) 'The organisation of motor patterns for spelling: an effective remedial strategy for backward readers', *Developmental Medicine and Child Neurology*, 23, pp. 83–91.

Bradley, L. (1984) *Assessing Reading Difficulties: A Diagnostic and Remedial Approach*, 2nd ed., Basingstoke and London, Macmillan Education.

Bradley, L. (1988) 'Making connections in learning to read and to spell', *Applied Cognitive Psychology*, 2, pp. 3–18.

Bradley, L. (1988) 'Rhyme recognition and reading and spelling in young children', in Masland, R.L. and Masland, M.R. (Eds) *Pre-school Prevention of Reading Failure*, Parkton, Maryland, York Press.

Bradley, L. (1989) 'Predicting learning disabilities', in Dumont, J. and Nakken, J. (Eds) *Learning Disabilities: Cognitive, Social and Remedial Aspects*, Amsterdam, Swets and Zeitlinger.

Bradley, L. and Bryant, P. (1978) 'Difficulties in auditory organisation as a possible cause of reading backwardness', *Nature*, 271, pp. 746–747.

Bradley, L. and Bryant, P. (1983) 'Categorizing sounds and learning to read: a causal connexion', *Nature*, 301, pp. 419–421.

Bradley, L. and Bryant, P. (1985) *Rhyme and Reason in Reading and Spelling*, International Academy for Research in Learning Disabilities Series, Michigan, University of Michigan Press.

Bradley, L., Maclean, M., Crossland, J. and Bryant, P. (1989) 'Rhyme and knowledge of letters are powerful predictors of children's reading' (submitted).

Bryant, P., Bradley, L., Maclean, M. and Crossland, J. (1989) 'Nursery rhymes, phonological skills and reading', *Journal of Child Language*, 16 (In Press).

Chukovsky, K. (1963) *From Two to Five*, Berkeley and Los Angeles, University of California Press.

De Hirsch, K., Jansky, J. and Langford W. (1966) *Predicting Reading Failure*, New York, Harper and Row.

Donaldson, M. (1978) *Children's Minds*, Glasgow, Fontana.

Dowker, A. (1989) 'Rhyme and alliteration in poems elicited from young children', *Journal of Child Language*, 16, pp. 181–202.

Ellis, W. (1987) (Ed) *Intimacy with Language: Dyslexia and Evolving Educational Patterns*, Baltimore, Orton Dyslexia Society.

Hulme, C. (1981) *Reading Retardation and Multi-Sensory Teaching*, London, Routledge and Kegan Paul.

Jansky, J. and de Hirsch, K. (1972) *Preventing Reading Failure*, New York, Harper and Row.

Liberman, I. and Shankweiler, D. (1985) 'Phonology and the problems of learning to read and write', *Remedial and Special Education*, 6, 6, pp. 8–17.

Lundberg, I., Olofsson, A. and Wall, S. (1980) 'Reading and spelling skills in the first school years predicted from phonemic awareness skills in kindergarten', *Scandinavian Journal of Psychology*, 21, pp. 159–173.

Lundberg, I., Frost, J. and Petersen, O. (1988) 'Effects of an extensive program for stimulating phonological awareness in preschool children', *Reading Research Quarterly*, 23, 3, pp. 263–284.

Maclean, M., Bryant, P. and Bradley, L. (1987) 'Rhymes, nursery rhymes and reading in early childhood', *Merrill-Palmer Quarterly*, 33, pp. 255–282.

Mattingley, I. (1972) 'Reading, the linguistic process and linguistic awareness', in Kavanah, J. and Mattingley, I. (Eds) *Language by Ear and by Eye*, Cambridge, MA, MIT Press, pp. 133–147.

Mattingley, I. (1985) 'Did orthographies evolve?', *Remedial and Special Education*, 6, 6, pp. 18–23.

Read, C. (1971) 'Pre-school children's knowledge of English phonology', *Harvard Educational Review*, 41, pp. 1–34.

Share, D. L., Jorm, A. F. Maclean, R. and Matthews, R. (1984) 'Sources of individual differences in reading acquisition', *Journal of Educational Psychology*, 76, pp. 1309–1324.

Stanovich, K. (1986) 'Matthew effects in reading: some consequences of individual differences in the acquisition of literacy', *Reading Research Quarterly*, 21, pp. 360–407.

Stanovich, K. (1987) 'Introduction: children's reading and the development of phonological awareness', *Merrill-Palmer Quarterly*, 33, pp. 251–254.

Stanovich, K. (1989) 'Speculations on the causes and consequences of individual differences in early reading acquisition', in Gough, P. (Ed) *Reading Acquisition*, Hillsdale, N, Lawrence Erlbaum Associates.

Tizard, B., Blatchford, P., Burke, J., Farquhar, C. and Plewis, I. (1988) *Young Children at School in the Inner City*, Hove, Erlbaum Associates.

Treiman, R. (1988) 'The internal structure of the syllable', in Carlson, G., and Tanenhaus, M. (Eds) *Linguistic Structure in Language Processing*, Dordrecht, Reidel.

Vellutino, F. and Scanlon, D. (1987) 'Phonological coding, phonological awareness, and reading ability: evidence from a longitudinal and experimental study', *Merrill-Palmer Quarterly*, 33, pp. 321–363.

Vihman, M. (1981) 'Phonology and the development of the lexicon: evidence from children's errors', *Journal of Child Language*, 8, pp. 239–264.

Wagner, R. and Torgesen, J. (1987) 'The nature of phonological processing and its causal role in the acquisition of reading skills', *Psychological Bulletin*, 101, pp. 192–212.

7
Learning to Spell, Learning to Read

Suzanne Cataldo and Nick Ellis

In this chapter we will analyze the way that spelling facilitates growth in reading. There will be four approaches, (1) Introductory Review, (2) A Longitudinal Study of the Development of Spelling, Reading and Phonological Awareness, (3) Clinical Observations of Children's Spelling Attempts, (4) A Longitudinal Study of Pattern and Prediction of Spelling Errors.

Introductory review

Recent correlational and longitudinal studies identify spelling as an independent contributor to the emergence of reading (Morris and Perney, 1984; Tornéus, 1984; Mommers, 1987; Cataldo and Ellis, 1988). These studies support theoretical analyses that assign spelling the major role in promoting insight into the alphabetic nature of the written language (Smith, 1973; Marsh *et al.*, 1980; Bryant and Bradley, 1980; Frith, 1985; Juel, Griffith and Gough, 1986). Spelling is a necessary component in a complete theory of early literacy acquisition.

The use of phonological awareness in children's early efforts in spelling encourages them to approach the printed word as a sequence of phonetic cues to pronunciation (Liberman and Shankweiler, 1979; Frith, 1985). As children refine their ability to detect and isolate the sound content of spoken words through repeated practice in spelling, so they build a store of knowledge about the relationships among sounds, letters and pronunciations that can be applied to the task of reading (Chomsky, 1977; Ehri and Wilce, 1987a, 1987b; Juel, Griffith and Gough, 1986). Ehri and Wilce (1987a) explored the idea that spelling may help children to read. They taught kindergarten children to spell words by attending to constituent letter-sound sequences, and when necessary, to phonetic, phonemic and articulatory cues. These children learned to read words better than children who were taught isolated letter-sound relationships. Thus children trained in spelling were superior to the controls in their ability to use phonetic cues and letter-sound constituents when learning to read words. Ehri and Wilce propose that beginners approach spelling in a similar manner to reading: in both tasks they rely on a store of associations between letter-name knowledge and word pronunciations and thus spelling words helps children detect and utilize phonetic cues in the printed word. Support for this early use of phonetic cues in reading comes from the longitudinal study of Ellis and Large (1988). Using crossed-lagged correlational analyses of abilities at age 5 that contribute to reading ability at age 6, they found that a combination of phonological awareness, letter recognition and ability at visual digit span predicted reading development. This suggests that children's first-stage reading strategy is one which concentrates on the analysis of letters in words and that this analysis involves both visual and phonological processing. Phonetic-cue reading begins when the learner first makes associations between a salient letter (or letters) in the printed word and corresponding sounds in the spoken word. According to Ehri and Wilce, this nascent sound strategy of using partial phonetic cues is formed during early reading experience. At some later point the learner develops a highly systematic and efficient strategy of decoding the printed word. This new ability has been described as 'deciphering' (Gough and Hillinger, 1980), 'sequential decoding' (Marsh, Friedman, Welch and Desberg, 1981), 'alphabetic-stage' reading (Frith, 1985), and 'phonological-recoding' (Harris and Coltheart, 1986). Three alternative explanations for the shift from phonetic-cue reading to systematic deciphering include (1) a qualitative change from one type of processing to another, (2) a gradual expansion of knowledge, with increased reading experience, of the orthographic system in addition to a more complete set of phonetic cues, and (3) the acquisition of phonological awareness (Ehri and Wilce, 1987b). If we neglect to include spelling in the configuration of factors promoting alphabetic-stage reading, we fail to recognize an important source of knowledge that helps elucidate the relationship between printed words and their pronunciations. Spelling practice, as it occurs in various contexts, may enhance the knowledge base from which novice readers draw information in their attempts at phonetic-cue and cipher reading.

Frith (1985) provides a theoretical framework within which spelling and reading interact to advance the learner towards increased proficiency in each ability. In her model, spelling plays a fundamental role in the movement from a visual, or logographic reading strategy to alphabetic approach: alphabetic spelling is the pacemaker for the use of an alphabetic strategy in reading. If we consider phonetic-cue reading as a pre-alphabetic strategy, we see children moving from the use of visual features (Gough and Hillinger, 1980; Marsh, Friedman, Welch and Desberg, 1981; Seymour and Elder, 1985) and partial phonetic cues (Ehri and Wilce, 1987b) to the use of deciphering or 'cipher' reading (Gough and Hillinger, 1980).

It is conceivable that it is the orderly sequential production of letters when writing which might be 'copied', even unnecessarily, for word recognition. Thus, the piecemeal left-to-right decoding of a word might first make sense to a child as a deliberate reflection of the first-to-last writing process. This then would become the guiding principle of analysis that was missing before. When a child has learned to spell a word then he or she may realize that what is important is temporal order rather than salient graphic features. The first letter is both prominent in the spelling sequence and graphically salient. This may be an example of a merging of components of two strategies (Frith, 1985, p. 314).

As children learn to spell by decomposing spoken words into constituent phonemic units, they are learning to represent the temporal sequence of sounds in a left-to-right direction. Transfer of this knowledge by itself to the task of reading a word would result in a recital of individual sounds (k/a/t for cat) which does not produce the key to the word's pronunciation. Indeed, children who can 'sound out' in this manner but who have not gained insight into how the sounds map onto the pronunciation, may be confused as to why they observe other children sounding out successfully when the method does not work for them. Early spelling practice typically involves dividing spoken words into phonemes and representing these phonemes with letters. In this way experience in spelling words affords the opportunity for making comparisons between the phonetic information in individual letters and sounds as they are embedded in the spoken word. Spelling practice helps to establish this abstract concept through two very concrete means; articulatory and kinesthetic rehearsal. Through repeated practice in spelling, the child may come to appreciate the subtle relationship between a symbol in the written word and its corresponding sound in the context of the spoken word. The discovery of this relationship is the key to alphabetic insight. The stumbling block for our beginning reader who could sound out, but not read, words is in mapping individual sequences of letter-sound correspondences onto the overlapping sequences of sounds in the spoken word. The crux of the problem is 'knowing how to combine the letters into units appropriate for speech' (Liberman and Shankweiler, 1979, p. 141). Early efforts in spelling may provide the opportunity to experiment in a very concrete way with the properties of this abstract concept. As children struggle to decompose words into individual phonemic units, they commonly experiment with various articulatory rehearsals of word parts and they search for distinguishable articulatory units that correspond to letter-sound units. This process of their separating sounds in a word through consciously monitoring their own articulations may serve a dual purpose: it may both help the development of phonological awareness and enhance knowledge of the alphabetic principle.

The idea that explicit knowledge of the sound content of words comes to reading via spelling may account for the power of spelling to predict reading in recent studies (Shanahan and Lomax, 1986; Mommers, 1987; Ellis and Large, 1988; Cataldo and Ellis, 1988; Ellis and Large, 1987). These studies reveal the previously hidden role that spelling plays in the child's first steps towards literacy. But now we need a broader and more detailed description of the interactive development of all three components, reading, spelling, and phonological awareness, in order to clarify the details of precisely how spelling mediates the influence of phonological awareness on reading. In terms of educational practice it is vital to explore how the early development of spelling and phonological awareness helps children across the threshold to literacy.

A longitudinal study of the development of spelling, reading and phonological awareness

In our recent longitudinal study (Cataldo and Ellis, 1988) we examined the growth of reading, spelling, and phonological awareness (PA), from the formulative stage of each skill through the early stages of its development. We followed a group of children as they progressed through the earliest stages of literacy acquisition. By charting their development in spelling, reading and phonological awareness, we were able to analyze the factors which contribute to the early formation of these skills as well as the sequences of interaction which facilitate later strategy shifts in each ability.

Method

Subjects

Forty children were selected from three schools in North Wales. At the beginning of the study, the children were attending either reception or infant classes. The children were English speaking and were taught reading and spelling in English. Initial testing commenced in the autumn of 1985 when the children were between 4 and 5 years old. At this time most of the children did not demonstrate even rudimentary skill in reading or spelling. The children were assessed on three subsequent occasions; once when most were at the end of their first year in school, again in the autumn of their second year and finally at the beginning of their third school year. By the final testing time, twenty-eight subjects had taken the full complement of tests, and it is the performance of these children which is used in the following LISREL analyses (Jöreskog and Sörbom, 1984).

Procedure

Children between 4 and 5 years old were tested individually in reading, spelling, phoneme segmentation, auditory categorization, letter-sound knowledge, short term memory (STM) and full WPPSI IQ (Wechsler, 1967;

Saville, 1971). Tests of reading, spelling and phonological awareness were repeated when most of the children were finishing their first year at school. The full set of tests (excluding the WPPSI) was readministered the following autumn. One year later, when the majority of the children were beginning their third school year, a final administration of the reading and spelling tests was given. In order to compare performances in very different areas, test scores were converted to stanine scores; this standardizes the means and variances of each variable and normalizes the data in accord with the assumptions of LISREL causal modeling. Each of the tests, testing procedures and scoring methods is described below. For a more detailed description of procedures see Cataldo and Ellis, 1988.

Tests of Reading and Spelling

The reading and spelling tests consisted of phonemically regular, consonant-vowel-consonant (C-V-C) words. All words contained short vowels.

(C-V-C) Reading Test: This consisted of ninety-six C-V-C words; half of these were real words and half were nonsense words. Each word was presented individually to the child who was given one opportunity to read it. Two scores were taken for each subject; number of words read correctly and number of phonemes correct in each 'word' response. The second scoring method was used to measure reading at the first testing time, when the majority of the children were performing at floor level with the first measure.

(C-V-C) Spelling Test: Each child was asked to spell thirty-two of the words in the reading test. This subset consisted sixteen real words and sixteen nonsense words. The real words were presented first; once alone, again in the context of a sentence, and a final time in isolation. Nonsense words were presented three times in isolation. To reduce memory load an alphabet of lower case letters was placed in front of the child during testing. As in the reading test, two scores were taken for spelling: at the initial testing we used number of letters spelled correctly, thereafter, the measure was the number of words spelled correctly.

Tests of Phonological Awareness

Two different types of phonological tasks were chosen, a rhyme detection task and a phoneme segmentation task. Whereas early research into the relationship between reading and phonological awareness did not discriminate between different types of phonemic awareness tasks (Lewkowicz, 1980; Bradley and Bryant, 1985), more recent work suggests that the level of phonemic awareness demanded by the phonological tasks influences the strength of the relationship between reading and phoneme awareness (Backman, 1983). Stanovich, Cunningham and Cramer (1984) asked children to perform tasks involving the analysis of words for explicit sound content (nonrhyming tasks) and for overall similarity of sound content (rhyming tasks). They found that the nonrhyming, or analytic phonological tasks formed a cluster of related skills and that the rhyming tasks did not correlate strongly with the nonrhyming tasks. Snowling and Perin (1983) found that children's ability to perform a segmentation task was not significantly different from their ability in spelling, the close connection between these skills indicating the necessity of explicit PA in spelling. Thus there seem to be two, developmentally different, measurable levels of PA. Children's first awareness of the sound properties of speech is implicit. Spontaneous play with rhyming and nonsense words is thought to reflect an overall sensitivity to the sound content of words (Chukovsky, 1968; Slobin, 1978; Clark 1978). At this point they are not yet able to consciously reflect on language (Shankweiler, Liberman and Savin, 1972; Andresen in Valtin, 1984). Valtin (1984) describes a three-stage model for the development of phonological awareness. Initially the child is not aware of the sound value of speech; s/he senses when, but not why, speech acts fail to be communicative. During the next stage, 'children become increasingly able to abstract the language from the action and the meaning context and to think about some of the properties of the form of language. Their knowledge of language units is still implicit, however, and related to psycholinguistic units of speech' (Valtin, 1984, p. 214). Once the child achieves conscious awareness, s/he demonstrates explicit phonological awareness and can reflect upon and manipulate phonemic units within spoken words.

The knowledge that growth in phonological awareness follows a developmental continuum from implicit to explicit levels raises the question of how children utilize these different types of phonological awareness in their reading and spelling strategies. We used two different phonological tasks in order to examine this question. The minimal requirement for success in rhyme detection is a global awareness of the sound property in words, while successful performance of phoneme segmentation tasks requires an explicit awareness of individual sounds within words.

Implicit Awareness: Test of Auditory Organization (Bradley, 1980). The test of auditory organization is divided into three conditions: initial (comprised of words that begin with the same sound), final (with words that end with the same sound), and medial (containing words that share the same vowel sound). For each condition the child listens as a series of four words is spoken. S/he is asked to identify the 'odd one out' of the four words (the word that does not share a common sound component with the other three words). A warm-up procedure similar to that suggested by Bradley (1980) was used before testing each child.

Explicit Awareness: Phoneme segmentation test. A modification of the Elkonin procedure (Elkonin, 1973; Helfgott, 1976) was used to test ability in explicit phoneme segmentation. Each child was asked to perform three types of segmentation on eight real C-V-C words and eight nonsense C-V-C words given in spoken form. In the initial segmentation task subjects were asked to segment words into two parts; the initial consonant and the remaining vowel-consonant portion (C-VC). For the final segmentation task, the children were asked to segment the final sound from each word by producing the initial CV component followed by the final phoneme (CV-C). The complete segmentation task required each child to segment words into three distinct sound components (C-V-C). The children practised each type of segmentation task before testing on that task commenced. Words within each type of task were presented in random order: real words were presented first, followed by nonsense words. Scores represent the total number of test words correctly segmented. Descriptive data for the results of these phonological tests at each testing time are shown in Table 7.1.

Table 7.1 Per cent correct in auditory organization (implicit awareness) and phoneme segmentation (explicit awareness) for three testing times. (As different words were used in the tests of Implicit and Explicit Phonological Awareness, scores within tests are directly comparable, whereas scores across tests are not.) Mean (standard deviation).

Test	Beginning Yr. One		End Yr. One		Beginning Yr. Two	
Total Implicit	37.14	(15.94)	43.57	(17.45)	47.62	(19.20)
Total Explicit	12.13	(23.30)	31.55	(30.12)	51.26	(28.16)
Initial Implicit	28.93	(16.18)	39.29	(19.04)	47.86	(22.83)
Initial Explicit	14.51	(28.31)	46.65	(41.96)	74.11	(32.75)
Final Implicit	39.29	(21.93)	46.43	(19.29)	43.21	(20.56)
Final Explicit	8.93	(22.34)	12.50	(23.26)	22.10	(35.25)
Medial Implicit	43.21	(22.62)	45.00	(24.72)	51.79	(25.25)
Complete Explicit	12.95	(26.57)	35.49	(38.04)	57.59	(32.51)

Letter-sound associations

Knowledge of isolated letter-sound associations alone does not account for success in learning to read and spell. However, it does contribute to the development of reading (Ellis and Large, 1988) and use of letters helps children learn to segment words into constituent phonemes (Hohn and Ehri, 1983).

Test of Letter-Sound Knowledge: Each of the twenty-six lower case letters was presented individually on an 8.5 cm by 11 cm white card. The child was asked, 'What sound does this letter make?'. If the child responded with a letter name s/he was asked if s/he knew the sound it made; if the child gave the sound, the response was scored as correct.

Wechsler preschool and primary scale of intelligence

Five verbal and five performance tests were given to each child. Full scale scores on this test were used in the initial matching of groups for training and for purposes of partialling out the effect of IQ in the LISREL analyses.

Lisrel analysis methodology

In this study LISREL was used to formulate a descriptive model that identifies significant contributors to the early growth of literacy (Jöreskog and Sörbom, 1984; Saris and Stronkhorst, 1984). With small samples LISREL is appropriate only for exploratory purposes (Crano and Mendoza, 1987). The limited number of subjects in this study restricts us to a preliminary structural equation model which needs further validation with a larger number of subjects. We fitted exploratory low constraint time-interval type models where each ability could result from an effect of *any* ability measured at the previous time (Cataldo and Ellis, 1988; Ellis, 1989). This type of model allows us to compare the effects of two different abilities on a third ability. Table 7.2 gives the pathweight coefficients indicating the contribution of each ability to the development of later abilities. With standardized data, pathweights represent the amount of change in a variable (in standard deviation (sd) units) caused by one sd of change in another variable. In Table 7.2 the column headers represent the abilities measured at the prior time, the rows the effect variable measured at the later time; thus in Phase One we can see that an increase of one sd in spelling ability at the beginning of the first school year was associated with an increase of 0.31 sds in ability to read real words at the end of that year; in contrast, an increase of one sd of reading at the beginning of year one is only associated with an increase of 0.10 sds in later spelling ability.

Table 7.2 LISREL path coefficients indicating contributions of early ability to development of later abilities (Path coefficients in **medium** are significant at $p < 0.05$ *) (READ: Reading; SPELL: Spelling; EXPL.PA: Explicit Phonological Awareness; IMPL. PA: Implicit Phonological Awareness; LS: Letter Sound. See text for details.)

		Reading-Spelling Model			
	Phase One: Beginning first school year to end of first school year				
Gamma	Read	Spell	EXPL.PA	IMPL.PA	LS
READ (real)	**0.37**	**0.31**	0.08	**0.36**	0.06
READ (non)	0.18	0.23	0.17	**0.41**	0.08
SPELL (real)	0.10	0.35	0.32	0.38	0.07
SPELL (non)	0.06	0.24	0.31	0.31	0.21
EXPL.PA	−0.04	0.13	**0.42**	**0.36**	0.11
IMPL.PA	0.15	**0.53**	0.06	**0.49**	−0.20

Phase Two: End of first year to autumn of second year

BETA	READ REAL	READ NON	SPELL REAL	SPELL NON	EXPL. PA	IMPL. PA
READ (real)	0.66	− 0.34	0.64	− 0.10	0.21	− 0.25
READ (non)	0.31	0.07	**0.60**	− 0.09	0.18	− 0.09
SPELL (real)	0.14	− 0.33	**0.76**	− 0.02	**0.34**	0.07
SPELL (non)	0.00	− 0.04	**0.77**	− 0.22	**0.45**	0.05
EXPL.PA	0.34	− 0.10	− 0.02	0.20	**0.50**	0.03
IMPL.PA	0.27	0.37	− 0.22	− 0.19	0.35	0.12
LS	0.36	0.24	− 0.20	− 0.14	0.26	− 0.08

Phase Three: Beginning of second year to beginning of third year

BETA	READ REAL	READ NON	SPELL REAL	SPELL NON	EXPL. PA	IMPL. PA	LS
READ (real)	0.20	0.24	0.00	0.12	0.30	0.08	**0.38**
READ (non)	0.03	0.22	− 0.00	− 0.05	**0.53**	0.01	**0.30**
SPELL (real)	0.03	0.01	0.04	− 0.10	**0.63**	0.09	0.09
SPELL (non)	0.21	0.43	− 0.32	0.13	**0.49**	0.27	0.17

*The standard error of the path coefficients are computed individually. Unlike correlation coefficients, it is *not* the case that for a given sample size any coefficient above a critical magnitude will necessarily be statistically significant (Jöreskog and Sörbom, 1984).

Results and discussion

By broadening the phonological awareness-reading paradigm to include spelling, we are able to see a clearer picture of the early interaction among these abilities. Our model of reading and spelling development describes three measured phases of development. Phase One spans the children's first year in school. Phase Two charts the development from spring of the first school year to autumn of the second year. Phase Three looks at development from the beginning of the second year in school to the beginning of the third year. The Phase One pathweights from spelling to reading real words (0.31) and nonsense words (0.23) identify spelling as an important contributor to the early formation of reading. This pattern of influence is repeated in the second phase (spelling to reading real words 0.64 and nonsense words 0.60). The pronounced influence of spelling on reading contrasts with the contribution of reading to spelling (Phase One: 0.10 real words, 0.06 nonsense; Phase Two: 0.14 real, 0.00 nonsense). Implicit PA initially predicts early attempts to read (0.36, 0.41) as well as to spell (0.38, 0.31) but loses its influence on both reading and spelling in the following two phases. In contrast to the diminishing predictive power of implicit PA, explicit PA consistently predicts spelling in all three phases, this influence increasing with phase. Explicit PA only emerges as a strong predictor of reading in Phase Three.

To summarize, the early flow of information between reading and spelling appears to be unidirectional: knowledge gleaned from spelling is contributing to reading. Similarly, both implicit and explicit PA affect spelling development with explicit PA increasing its influence as the contribution of implicit PA diminishes. Later in the developmental sequence, explicit PA begins to contribute directly to reading. The pattern of interactions among abilities in Phase One clarifies the different roles of implicit and explicit PA in the early formation of reading skill. Implicit information about the sound properties of words directly affects early reading attempts: explicit knowledge of phonemic content influences reading via spelling experience. Beginners may be using implicit PA both to help them detect acoustic properties that define a word by its sound boundaries and to detect sounds with salient qualities. Their use of these rudimentary sound strategies allows them to form associations between sounds in spoken words and pronunciations and to call upon these associations to perform phonetic-cue reading (Ehri and Wilce, 1985). The use of implicit awareness of rhyming components in words may also help beginners to generalize from an unknown word to a word that contains a similar spelling (Bryant and Goswami, 1987), but this strategy is more likely to be employed at later stages of reading development when children have enough lexical entries from which to generalize. The first evidence of the direct influence of explicit PA on reading occurs in Phase Three, when explicit PA predicts ability to read nonwords. In earlier phases explicit PA does not influence reading directly but acts as the strongest predictor of spelling both real and nonsense words. In turn, spelling is the most consistent predictor of reading.

This early interactive sequence describes the pattern of growth from pre-alphabetic to alphabetic stage reading. While implicit knowledge of the sound properties of words helps children forge initial connections between the printed words and its pronunciation, spelling acts as a mediator for the use of explicit PA until the child begins alphabetic stage reading by directly applying explicit PA to reading. Out data suggest that as children practise spelling they develop proficiency in the use of the alphabetic principle and apply this knowledge to the task of reading. The emergence of explicit PA as a significant predictor of reading marks the entry into the alphabetic stage of reading. Examination of the Phase Three pathweights suggests that children apply a strategy reliant on letter-sound knowledge and to a lesser degree, explicit PA to read real words, but letter-sound knowledge and explicit PA jointly predict nonsense word reading. While learners appear to use a pre-alphabetic strategy with real words, they utilize a true alphabetic approach to nonsense words. This interpretation accords with children's introduction to reading during the first few years in school. They learn to rely on contextual clues and accompanying pictorial information in conjunction with distinctive graphic features in the printed word in order to arrive at a meaningful rendition of text. With increased reading experience, this early strategy is expanded to include reliance on partial phonetic cues accessed through constituent letters and on similarity of the component letters of the to-be-read-string to component letters of real words stored in the lexicon. In this way novice readers evolve a pre-alphabetic strategy that they associate with the quickest route to reading real words for meaning. But when children are confronted with nonsense or new words in the absence of meaningful context and analogous counterparts in the real word lexicon, they may switch to an alphabetic approach. Here we see evidence of the selective use of strategies for different purposes. Children are able to shift from one level of reading strategy to another, depending on the demands of the task. Beginners attempt to read unknown words via a strategy of combining context, visual and phonetic cues, and only when this fails, switch to deciphering. Initially, deciphering is used exclusively for reading unknown words when other strategies fail. But with practice children integrate this alphabetic approach into their repertoire set of strategies and eventually the beginner comes to appreciate the general usefulness of this deciphering strategy, perhaps temporarily reneguing other approaches to word recognition for the sake of practising this skill and gaining automaticity. Paradoxically, one way that a child could manifest movement into this new stage is by treating a word that was formerly mastered with a pre-alphabetic strategy as an unknown word and attempting to read it using a systematic sound strategy.

Clinical Observations of Children's Spelling Attempts

Precisely what do children practise in spelling that facilitates alphabetic stage reading? Transcriptions of their verbal responses during spelling testing indicate that the majority attempted to explicitly segment phonemic content by experimenting at the articulatory level; they were generating and reinforcing their knowledge about the way letters map onto sounds as they occur in the stream of speech. They would often attempt to segment sounds units and then compare these units with either a larger unit (/a/ with /ka/ or /at/) or with the spoken word (/a/ with /kat/ or /at/ with /kat/). This type of monitoring, back and forth between a segmented unit and the larger context, served as a concrete means for grasping an abstract concept. Some examples are described below (spoken responses are enclosed in //, written responses in ').

Two samples of subjects' articulatory rehearsal of /gun/:

(1) /g/ /g/ /g/ /u/ /u/ /u/ /g/ /u/ /gu/
(2) /gun/ /g/ /u/ /g/ /n/ /u/ /gun/ /n/ /r/

One subject's attempts to articulate the separate sounds in the nonsense word /san/:

/san/ /s/ /ar/ /s/ /ar/ /sar/ /ar/ /ar/ /ar/ /n/

Many children spelled each word by correctly segmenting the word into its phonemic units as they wrote the corresponding letters. This process was frequently finished by reading the word. It seems that it is through articulatory rehearsal that beginning spellers forge the link between letter-sound constituents and phonemic segments in the spoken word. Baddeley (1979) has suggested that a component of the short-term memory (STM), the articulatory loop, is used by beginning readers as a working storage system as they decipher unfamiliar words. Our evidence suggests that children use the articulatory loop in spelling. They may utilize articulation, vocally or subvocally, to hold parts of, or entire spoken words in memory for the purpose of comparison and monitoring. But such articulations may furthermore serve the secondary purpose of reinforcing partial or complete word spellings with phonological memory traces, and such practice may also explain why early literacy acquisition results in an improvement of STM abilities (Ellis, 1989).

The idea that children's misspellings reflect a developing sense of phonetic properties in words was pioneered by Read (1971, 1975, 1986). He found evidence that young inventive spellers used a system of grouping sounds together according to shared phonetic features. Thus they might represent a particular vowel sound in their spelling by substituting a letter whose *name* shared a salient phonetic feature with the sound. Read suggested that children use both production and perception of sound to group sounds together and that these categorizations may not coincide with the classification system used by adults. His exhaustive studies of invented spellings attuned further research to the analysis of misspellings in an attempt to uncover a developmental sequence for spelling that reflects a heightening awareness of the internal sound structure of words:

> We now value spellings for what they can tell us about psycholinguistic processes. Standard spellings are of less interest, not because they represent successful instruction, but because they do not indicate how a child arrived at them . . . Some non-standard spellings represent a more advanced conception of the task or the language than others. Occasionally, we can even discern that the same spelling occurs for different reasons, one more advanced than another (Read, 1986, p. 47).

The idea that spelling errors provide a gauge of how a child understands metalinguistic properties of language has led researchers to categorize developmental strategies in spelling. Henderson and Beers (1980) analyzed samples of children's creative writing and assigned each error to a category according to the completeness of phonetic information mapped by the misspelling. They charted movement from prephonetic to phonetic stages of spelling. As a result of their work and that of Gentry (1982), it is now generally agreed that children move through five distinct stages of spelling, viz. precommunicative, prephonetic, semiphonetic, phonetic, transitional and correct spelling. It is the first three of these developmental stages that are relevant to the question of how phonological awareness plays a role in children's early spelling. Precommunicative spellings are characterized by the strategy of randomly selecting letter strings to represent words. Although at this stage children can produce letters in writing, their spellings reflect a complete lack of letter-sound or letter-name knowledge. Semiphonetic spellings contain a partial mapping of phonetic content. Phonetic spellings contain a complete description of the sequence of sounds in pronunciations. Although precommunicative spellings are not regarded as reflecting the child's conscious attempts to map alphabet letters onto sounds in words, it is nevertheless plausible that some children who produce precommunicative spellings may possess the necessary segmentation ability but that their spelling efforts are blocked by their ignorance of letter-sound associations. These children either abandon their attempts or resort to the arbitrary selection of letters. If in beginning spelling the child segments sounds from a word and searches for a 'match' between phonetic information in the isolated sounds and information in letter-sound associates, a breakdown at the 'matching' stage could lead to precommunicative spellings. Our transcriptions of the children's verbal responses as they performed the spelling test demonstrated frequent examples of such children. After she was asked to spell /big/ on the first administration of the test, a 5-year-old subject responded, 'How do you write /b/ /g/?' On this and other items of the test she correctly segmented phonemes and demonstrated the knowledge that the next step in spelling required the selection of a letter to represent each segmented sound. Each time she was stopped in the spelling process by a lack of letter-sound knowledge she left the space for the word blank. Another subject, when asked to spell /pig/ during the second testing time, responded with 'Which one is /p/?' and produced the spelling 'qrt'. A third encountered the same block when asked to spell /gun/. Her verbal response, '/g/ /u/ /l/ /n/' showed that she could decompose the word properly but her written response, 'qmt', in the absence of knowledge of her articulations, would indicate a precommunicative understanding of spelling. Similarly, when asked to spell the nonsense word /gub/ she responsed '/gub/ /g/ /u/ /l/ /ub/' and spelled 'diz'. She also demonstrated a semiphonetic strategy by producing 'ht' for /hit/ and 'hd' for /hud/, and further used a phonetic strategy to produce the spelling 'bik' for /big/. (For the beginner, 'k' would be an appropriate spelling for /g/ in /big/ because the sound /k/ is articulated in the same place and manner as /g/.) A descriptive analysis of this child's spelling performance demonstrated that she correctly segmented 68 per cent of the initial consonant phonemes in the test words, 37 per cent of the medial vowel phonemes, and 25 per cent of the final consonant phonemes. In 46 per cent of the test words she successfully segmented at least two phonemes; in the majority of these items she segmented the initial consonant followed by the vowel. Her segmentation performance suggests that she should be starting to utilize a phonetic level strategy and that this strategy would be reflected in semiphonetic and phonetic spellings. Although she did produce phonetic spellings for some words ('rol' for /rul/, 'drt' for /dot/), she also produced precommunicative ('qmt' for /gun/) and semiphonetic ('ht' for /hit/) spellings. While lack of a sufficient store of letter-sound associates clearly accounted for some precommunicative spellings, it is possible that the relative difficulty in locating articulatory cues in particular pronunciations may determine whether the child produces a semiphonetic or phonetic spelling. It is more difficult to disentangle the /i/ from the /h/ in /hit/ as the word is articulated than it is to 'find' where the /b/ ends and the /i/ begins in /big/. This suggests that the complexity of the word in terms of the availability of articulatory cues to constituent sounds may determine the type of error produced by the young speller. This last subject appears to be utilizing three levels of strategy; precommunicative, semiphonetic and phonetic at the same testing point, with precommunicative spellings in some cases reflecting frustrated attempts to communicate the sound content of words. There thus seems to be considerable overlap of strategy during movement from one level of awareness of sound properties to one more advanced. Although it has been suggested that categories of spelling errors reflect the level of phonological awareness achieved (Morris and Perney, 1984) such patterns are not clear cut and when children are confronted with words that contain a sequence of phonemes that are not easily separable in an articulatory sense, they resort to use of an earlier spelling strategy.

The children in our study frequently used articulatory rehearsal while spelling to help them detect where one sound ended and the next sound began. They also used articulatory renditions of both their segmented pronunciations and their completed written spellings to check their answers for completeness. These uses of articulation during spelling give children insight into the alphabetic nature of written language and serve to strengthen their memory traces for spellings; children subsequently use this information to help them in reading.

A longitudinal study of pattern and prediction of spelling errors

Our results in Section 2 indicate that as spelling begins to take form, the beginner relies on a phonological strategy based on an overall impression of the sound content of words. In turn, these early endeavours in spelling contribute to an awareness of the general sound properties of words. In the next stage, as children begin to demonstrate proficiency in spelling with increasingly complete phonemic descriptions, the novice is more analytic in her approach to pronunciations. This progression from wholistic to analytic phonological strategy is analogous to the movement from semiphonetic to phonetic spelling proposed by Gentry (1982). In Section 2 we measured first-stage spelling by the number of phonemes correctly represented and second and third-stage spelling by number of words correctly spelled. Recognizing that children's misspellings provide valuable insight into the formation of spelling ability, we must now explore the relationships among different groupings of misspellings and different levels of PA. By including different types of error as well as correct spellings we can examine more closely the relative influence of each level of PA on the evolution of spelling strategy.

Method

Subjects

Only those subjects who produced at least five spelling errors were included in this analysis, since the amount of each type of error was measured in terms of per cent of total errors for each subject and the inclusion of data for children who produce only a few errors would thus create a misleading picture of the early development of spelling strategies. This criterion of at least five spelling errors resulted in thirty-eight subjects at the first testing point, thirty-five subjects at the second, thirty at the third, and seventeen children at the final testing time. Because of these small samples, the results obtained must be treated with caution.

Procedure

For the purpose of looking at the influence of PA on patterns of spelling development, we classified misspellings in five categories that reflect increasing insight into the phonetic structure of the word. Our hierarchical classification of spelling errors is based on work by Henderson (1980), Morris (1983), and Gentry (1982). The most rudimentary spelling skill, 1st letter strategy, preserves only the information for the initial letter. Closer approximations have both boundary sounds intact. The highest level of informed error are partial-sequential and sequential errors where only the middle phoneme is in doubt: the representation of consonant sounds is 'safer' than vowel sounds in that consonant sounds are more reliably 'matched' to letters on a one-to-one basis than are vowel sounds. Each spelling was handscored and assigned to a category of error based on the criteria described in Table 7.3. In Table 7.4 we show the mean number of such errors made at each testing time, the mean percentage of the child's total errors which this category of errors comprised, along with the mean performance on the explicit and implicit phonological awareness tests for each sound position.

Results and discussion

The following general patterns emerge:

1. When children in this age band make a spelling error which bears any phonetic resemblance to the target, it is more often the case that only information for the initial consonant is preserved. Responses which are not totally correct, yet which approximate more than this to the correct phonetic analysis are more rare. The next more typical responses are those where both boundary sounds are correct (either with or without an incorrect intervening vowel).

2. By the time the children are at the beginning of year three the total numbers of errors has, of course, declined. Errors which fall into this hierarchical classification system become predominant (54 per cent at the beginning of years two and three vs 23 per cent at the beginning of year one) — the children are indeed moving from being precommunicative to semiphonetic spellers. And this progression is also found within the semiphonetic stage: the lowest phonemic content errors (1st letter intact) decline with age, and, in percentage terms at least, higher order errors (sequential and partial sequential) which preserve more of the phonetic content come to the fore.

3. The patterns of ability on explicit segmentation are highly positionally determined: children are most accurate at segmenting the initial sound from the rest. This contrasts dramatically with performance on the implicit task where children seem to be roughly as accurate at identifying the 'odd one out' whatever the position, initial, medial or final, of its errant sound, but with a slight tendency for them to have most difficulty with the alliterative task of the implicit initial condition (the same pattern was found by Bradley and Bryant, 1985).

4. There is little measurable developmental improvement on the implicit segmentation task. In contrast there are large improvements in explicit segmentation skill during year one and the transition to year two.

In contrast to the pattern for implicit segmentation, that of explicit phoneme segmentation doubly mirrors that of spelling: it follows both its developmental surges and its positional sensitivity. This echoes the findings of Snowling and Perin (1983) that children's ability to perform an explicit segmentation task did not differ significantly from the ability in spelling, the close connection between these skills indicating the necessity of explicit PA in spelling.

In order to explore the patterns of development within each level of development, Spearman's rank correlations were computed between the subjects' percentage spelling errors of each type and their abilities on explicit segmentation (initial, final and complete) and implicit segmentation (initial, medial and final) within each testing time. The resultant correlations are shown in Table 7.5.

Table 7.3 Categories of spelling error. Description of each error type with examples from data. (Example spellings followed by pronunciation of target word in //.)

First letter strategy	Boundary sounds strategy	Partial-sequential strategy	Sequential strategy	Correct mapping
Initial cons	Initial-final consonants	CV Segment	CVC Unit Incor V	CVC Unit + Extra
C /KOD/	CD /KOD/	CO /KOD/	REF /RIF/	NOLME /NOL/ FISS /FIS/
Initial Cons plus Incor Letter(s)	Initial-Final Consonants + Extra Letters	CV Segment + Incor Final Cons	CVVC Unit One or Two Incor V	Correct Spelling
CGTZNY /KOD/ CAN /KOD/	GBC /GUB/ WDNGIST /WID/ BSI /BIS/	COT /KOD/	HIED /HID/	COD /KOD/
	Initial-Final Cons Embedded in String	CV Segment + Ext Let	CVC + Extra Let (V Incor)	
	MWDS /WID/ BERBO /RUB/	COWZO /KOD/	DELL /DAL/ BASUS /BIS/	
	Initial + Final Cons at Bounds of String	CV Segment Embedded in Letter String		
	FOATL /FUL/ SRRN /SAN/ WAESD /WID/	MNOP /NOL/		

Notes on scoring: When scoring children's early attempts to spell it was necessary to evaluate letter-forms that were either crudely formed or printed in the opposite direction. In the former case, we relied on notes taken for each child during testing. Letters printed in the reverse direction were scored correctly. Children frequently printed the letters s, h, r, a, c, and p in the opposite direction. In the case of the letters b and d, it was decided to score 'reversals' as correct responses due to the frequency with which children verbally segmented the proper sound (/b/ or /d/), pointed to the correct letter (b or d), and proceeded to produce the letter in the opposite direction.

Based on previous investigations and theories outlined in the text, we expected to see a strong association between both implicit and explicit PA and semiphonetic spelling. Semiphonetic spellings prove only a partial map of phonetic content: with implicit PA a child should be able to detect some of the sound content in a word and produce a partial spelling ('c' or 'ct' for /kat/). We also expected explicit PA to contribute to an analytic approach which should result in phonetic spellings that provide more complete mappings of words and that begin to show insight into the internal sound structure of words ('ca' or 'cet' for /kat/). Furthermore we expected that phonemic segmentation skill for a particular position of the spoken word would be associated with spelling skill for that particular position in the word.

Table 7.4 Descriptive Data

Mean raw scores for each category of SPELLING errors at the four testing times *				
	CATEGORIES OF ERROR * *			
	1st Letter Intact /CAT/ = 'C'	Boundary Intact /CAT/ = 'CT'	Partial- Sequential /CAT/ = 'CA'	Sequential (CVC Intact) /CAT/ = 'CET'
Beginning year one	5.7	.39	.55	.31	
	sd 8.4	sd .85	sd 1.1	sd .84	
n = 38	18%	1%	2%	2%	(Total 23%)
End year one	7.4	1.2	1.3	.71	
	sd 9.9	sd 2.1	sd 2.3	sd 1.6	
n = 35	23%	5%	5%	4%	(Total 37%)
Beginning year two	9.4	1.3	2.4	1.3	
	sd 8.4	sd .85	sd 1.1	sd .84	
n = 30	31%	7%	10%	6%	(Total 54%)
Beginning year three	4.0	1.9	1.8	2.3	
	sd 8.5	sd 3.8	sd 1.9	sd 2.5	
n = 17	15%	8%	12%	19%	(Total 54%)

Mean number of items correct on EXPLICIT SEGMENTATION at each testing time				
	Initial 'k-at'	Final 'ka-t'	Complete 'k-a-t'	Total
Beginning year one	2.6	.78	1.8	5.3
	sd 4.6	sd 2.8	sd 4.2	sd 8.9
End year one	7.0	1.4	5.0	13.6
	sd 6.7	sd 3.0	sd 6.1	sd 13.8
Beginning year two	11.3	3.3	9.0	23.7
	sd 5.7	sd 5.6	sd 5.5	sd 14.0

Mean number of items correct on IMPLICIT SEGMENTATION at each testing time				
	Initial	Final	Medial	Total
Beginning year one	3.0	3.8	4.4	11.10
	sd 1.6	sd 2.0	sd 2.0	sd 4.2
End year one	3.6	4.11	4.0	12.0
	sd 1.8	sd 1.5	sd 2.2	sd 4.0
Beginning year two	4.6	4.3	5.1	14.14
	sd 2.2	sd 2.1	sd 2.4	sd 5.6

*   This sample includes only those children with five or more spelling errors.
* *   For a complete description of each error category in terms of the early development of spelling see text.
* * * The percentage figure reflects the mean per cent of the child's total errors that were made in this category.

Table 7.5 Correlations between phonemic awareness and level of spelling development within each testing time (level of spelling development as reflected by category of error).

Beginning 1st year

CATEGORIES OF SPELLING ERROR

	1st Let /CAT/ = 'C'	Boun /CAT/ = 'CT'	Part-Seq /CAT/ = 'CA'	Sequen /CAT/ = 'CET'	Correct
Exp (In)	ns	41**	48**	54**	64**
Imp (In)	ns	ns	ns	ns	ns
Exp (Fn)	ns	31**	ns	ns	32*
Imp (Fn)	ns	ns	ns	ns	ns
Exp (Com)	ns	ns	40**	30*	40**
Imp (Med)	ns	ns	ns	27*	ns
Exp (Tot)	ns	35**	45**	48**	58**
Imp (Tot)	ns	ns	ns	27*	29*

End 1st year

	1st Let /CAT/ = 'C'	Bound /CAT/ = 'CT'	Part-Seq /CAT/ = 'CA'	Sequen /CAT/ = 'CET'	Correct
Exp (In)	ns	29*	52**	55**	70**
Imp (In)	ns	ns	ns	43**	38**
Exp (Fn)	ns	28**	ns	ns	ns
Imp (Fn)	ns	29**	ns	28*	28*
Exp (Com)	ns	37**	47**	50**	60**
Imp (Med)	ns	ns	ns	ns	30*
Exp (Tot)	ns	40**	54**	48**	65**
Imp (Tot)	ns	32*	ns	47*	48**

Beginning 2nd year

	1st Let /CAT/ = 'C'	Bound /CAT/ = 'CT'	Part-Seq /CAT/ = 'CA'	Sequen /CAT/ = 'CET'	Correct
Exp (In)	ns	ns	45**	ns	61**
Imp (In)	ns	ns	ns	42**	64**
Exp (Fn)	ns	35*	ns	29*	50**
Imp (Fn)	ns	ns	ns	ns	36*
Exp (Com)	ns	ns	31**	ns	68**
Imp (Med)	ns	ns	ns	ns	ns
Exp (Tot)	ns	ns	39**	ns	77**
Imp (Tot)	ns	ns	ns	39**	52**

* significant at $p < .05$
** significant at $p < .01$

The results showed:

1. As in the analyses of Section 2, both implicit and explicit phonemic awareness is associated with spelling skill (total correct), with explicit awareness showing the strongest relationship.
2. The magnitudes of these correlations with total correct spellings tend to increase with age, the associations between phonological skill and spelling increase with skill development in this range.
3. The magnitudes of these correlations increase as we go from left to right in the table, from the most rudimentary of semiphonetic spellings where phonemic knowledge for only the first letter is preserved, through more analysis (partial-sequential and sequential strategic errors), to completely correct spellings: these increasing associations validate the spelling error classification in terms of a hierarchy of increasing phonemic skill.
4. With regard to the expected association between phonemic analysis skill for a particular position in the spoken word and spelling ability on that position's letter, well, we won some, we lost some! There does seem to be a general significant association across the phases whereby explicit phoneme segmentation ability for the final sound is associated with correct spelling of that sound as indexed by boundary errors. Furthermore complete explicit segmentation is associated with sequential and partial-sequential errors. It does seem to be the case that the level of explicit phonemic awareness predicts the level of spelling mistake.

   However, a pronounced pattern in each phase of development is the absence of a significant relationship between first-letter strategy and either level of PA. We had expected that an immature form of phonological awareness would be linked with use of the first-letter strategy. However, the consistent pattern of nonsignificant correlations between each level of PA and first-letter strategy does not suggest a connection between the two skills. This lack of apparent relatedness between either level of PA and first-letter spellings may be due to failure of the measurement tools to detect the nascent level of PA used by the children. It is possible that neither the explicit (initial) test nor the implicit (initial) test tapped the incipient level of phonological awareness that helps children produce first-letter spellings. Beginners may use a simpler method of extracting relevant phonetic information from the beginning of a word than a complete segmentation of the initial phoneme from the rest ('cat' —⟩/k/—/at/) required in the explicit segmentation task, and perhaps, in retrospect, we should have tested for ability to segment just the initial sound from the word ('cat' —⟩/k/) in order to tap this most rudimentary of explicit segmentation abilities. In the same way the initial condition of the test of auditory categorization may be too demanding in terms of memory load and individual differences may be reflecting working memory capacity as much as ability to use alliteration. A version of this task that required comparison of the beginning sounds in two instead of three and four words may serve the purpose of measuring implicit PA as it first develops.

5. Although it is generally true that explicit segmentation ability is the stronger associate of spelling than implicit segmentation skill, it is nonetheless true that both skills are increasing in their relationship with spelling as it develops. It is tempting to conclude that the influence of explicit PA on the ability of children to produce correct spellings reflects an explicit phoneme segmentation strategy in spelling whilst the increasing association between implicit segmentation skill and spelling reflects them using ability to detect rhyme to help them arrive at spellings by analogy. By the beginning of the third year in school, when our subjects were last tested, the children's on-going reading and spelling experience would have helped them build up a store of lexical entries. It is plausible that the ability to detect rhyme, as measured on the final and medial conditions of the test of auditory categorization, could be used at this point to make the connection between a word to be spelled and a rhyming word in the child's collection of lexical entries. This method of using rhyme to spell by analogy is similar to reading by analogy as described by Bryant and Goswami (1987).

Enough of a sensible pattern has emerged from this analysis of the way explicit and implicit PA are associated with the development of early spelling strategies to reassure us that phonemic awareness is an essential prerequisite of spelling. But much remains to be done on the details of the associations: (1) Our categorization system for spelling errors serves, but it needs refinement (e.g. we used misspellings that contained letters present in the correct word spellings so that the misspelling 'ct' for /kat/ would be categorized as a phonetically relevant error, but the misspelling 'gt' would be classified as a precommunicative error that did not necessarily reflect a mapping of the sounds in /kat/. However, 'gt' may be a misspelling worth noting, as the letter 'g' represents a sound that is identical with the sound represented by 'c' in two different articulatory features, place and manner and different in only one, voicing). (2) We must in further analyses cumulate across positions (e.g. we have separately analyzed for initial letter skill, ignoring the fact that that ability is also demonstrated in all other categories of error, and even the correct response). (3) In future testing we must use simpler initial segmentation tasks which are more sensitive to ability on that sound alone. (4) As in our other work, we must analyze for longitudinal development, looking for predictions from prior abilities to later ones. These improvements, at least, are in hand.

Conclusions

Models of reading and spelling must describe *development*, the movement from one stage to the next. Our results describe the ways in which spelling acts as a mediator for the influence of explicit phonological awareness on reading. Children's very first efforts at reading are characterized by a visual or logographic strategy where letters are analyzed for salient graphic cues to rapid word recognition; this is the Pre-Alphabetic Stage. When a small number of pronunciations can be accessed in this manner, the child may embark upon a more advanced strategy of using associations between partial phonetic cues in the spoken word with letters in the printed version and subsequently utilize these associations to recognize the words. Children appear to use implicit PA to help them make these rudimentary sound analyses of pronunciation. In addition, spelling practice may contribute to the store of associations between the spoken words and letter-sound constituents in printed words. At first, spelling may encourage children to focus on the first letter of printed words and to begin to analyze this first letter, in the reading task, for phonetic cues to pronunciations. Thus, the practice of turning attention to the first letter-sound unit in spelling may influence children to discriminate between stored pronunciations on the basis of the first letter of the printed word. This method of early word recognition is described by Marsh *et al.* (1981) as 'discrimination net substitution'. As visual and phonetic cue strategies make increasing demands on the child's memory, the efficiency of this strategy descreases. Conversely, as the source of knowledge about letter-sound associates, and the relationships between letters in printed words and sounds in spoken words swells, the child is discovering that s/he can rely on the use of this knowledge for successful word recognition. Our studies support the idea that the transition from pre-alphabetic stage reading to alphabetic stage reading is facilitated by spelling. By employing explicit PA in spelling practice, the child gains familiarity with the alphabetic nature of writing and builds a reliable fund of information about letter-sound correspondences and explicit phonemic content in words. Spelling affords the opportunity to forge a meaningful link between phonological awareness and letter-sound knowledge. This connection is a prerequisite to the development of phonological strategies in reading. Furthermore, the data suggest that progress from the pre-alphabetic stage of literacy to the alphabetic stage involves an overlapping of strategies and in this sense there is no one 'reading' but rather a cascade of very different strategic blends of information processing skills being used at different points in the fast changing stream of the development of reading (Ellis and Large, 1988, Ellis, 1989).

References

Backman, J. (1983) 'The role of psycholinguistic skills in reading acquisition: a look at early readers', *Reading Research Quarterly*, 18, pp. 466–479.

Baddeley, A. D. (1979) 'Working memory and reading', in Kolers, P. A., Wrolstad, M. E. and Bouma, H. (Eds) *Processing of Visible Language*, Vol 1, New York, Plenum Press.

Bradley, L. (1980) *Assessing Reading Difficulties: A Diagnostic and Remedial Approach*, London, Macmillan Education.

Bradley, L. and Bryant, P. (1985) *Rhyme and Reason in Reading and Spelling*, (International Academy for Research in Learning Disabilities, No. 1), Ann Arbor, The University of Michigan Press.

Bryant, P. E. and Bradley, L. (1980) 'Why children sometimes write words which they do not read', in Frith, U. (Ed) *Cognitive Processes in Spelling*, London, Academic Press.

Bryant, P. E. and Goswami, U. (1987) 'Phonological awareness and learning to read', in Beech, J. R. and Colley, A. M. (Eds) *Cognitive Approaches to Reading*, Chichester, Wiley.

Cataldo, S. and Ellis, N. (1988) 'Interactions in the development of spelling, reading and phonological skills, *Journal of Research in Reading, 11, 2* pp. 86–109.

Chomsky, C. (1977) 'Approaching reading through invented spelling', in Resnick, L. B. and Weaver, P. A. (Eds) *The Theory and Practice of Early Reading*, Vol. 2, Hillsdale, N.J., Lawrence Erlbaum.

Chukovsky, K. (1968) *From Two to Five*. Berkeley, University of California Press.

Clark, E. V. (1978) 'Awareness of language: some evidence from what children say and do', in Sinclair, A., Jarvella, R. J. and Levelt, W. J. M. (Eds) *The Child's Conception of Language*, New York, Springer-Verlag.

Crano, W. D. and Mendoza, J. L. (1987) 'Maternal factors that influence children's positive behaviour: demonstration of a structural equation analysis of selected data from the Berkeley Growth Study', *Child Development* 58, pp. 38–48.

Ehri, L. C. (1979) 'Linguistic insight: threshold of reading acquisition', in Waller, T. G. and MacKinnon, G. E. (Eds) *Reading Research: Advances in Theory and Practice*, Vol. 1, New York, Academic Press.

Ehri, L. C. and Wilce, L. S. (1985) 'Movement into reading: is the first stage of printed word learning visual or phonetic?', *Reading Research Quarterly*, 20, pp. 163–179.

Ehri, L. C. and Wilce, L. S. (1987a) 'Does learning to spell help beginners learn to read words?', *Reading Research Quarterly*, 22, pp. 47–65.

Ehri, L. C. and Wilce, L. S. (1987b) 'Cipher versus cue reading: an experiment in decoding acquisition', *Journal of Educational Psychology*, 79, pp. 3–13.

Elkonin, D. B. (1973) 'U.S.S.R.' in Downing, J. (Ed) *Comparative Reading*, New York, Macmillan.

Ellis, N. C. (1989) 'Reading, phonological skills and short-term memory: interactive tributaries of development.' (Under submission.)

Ellis, N. C. and Large, B. (1987) 'The development of reading: as you seek so shall you find', *British Journal of Psychology*, 78, pp. 1–28.

Ellis, N. C. and Large, B. (1988) 'The early stages of reading: a longitudinal study' *Applied Cognitive Psychology, 2*, pp. 47–76.

Frith, U. (1985) 'Beneath the surface of developmental dyslexia', in Patterson, K., Coltheart, M. and Marshall, J. (Eds) *Surface Dyslexia*, London, Lawrence Erlbaum.

Gentry, J. R. (1982) 'Analysis of developmental spelling in GNYS AT WORK', *The Reading Teacher*, 36, pp. 192–200.

Gough, P. B. and Hillinger, M. L. (1980) 'Learning to read: an unnatural act', *Bulletin of the Orton Society*, 30, pp. 171–176.

Harris, M. and Coltheart, M. (1986) *Language Processing in Children and Adults*, London, Routledge and Kegan Paul.

Helfgott, J. A. (1976) 'Phonemic segmentation and blending skills of kindergarten children: implications for beginning reading acquisition', *Contemporary Educational Psychology*, 1, pp. 157–169.

Henderson, E. H. (1980) 'Developmental concepts of words', in Henderson, E. H. and Beers, J. W. (Eds) *Developmental and Cognitive Aspects of Learning to Spell: A Reflection of Word Knowledge*, Newark, Del., International Reading Association.

Henderson, E. H. and Beers, J. W. (1980) (Eds) *Developmental and Cognitive Aspects of Learning to Spell: A Reflection of Word Knowledge*, Newark, Del., International Reading Association.

Hohn, W. E. and Ehri, L. C. (1983) 'Do alphabet letters help prereaders acquire phonemic segmentation skill?', *Journal of Educational Psychology*, 75, pp. 752–762

Jöreskog, K. G. and Sörbom, D. (1984) *Lisrel VI User's Guide*, Uppsala, Department of Statistics.

Juel, C., Griffith, P. L. and Gough, P. B. (1986) 'The acquisition of literacy: a longitudinal study of children in first and second grade', *Journal of Educational Psychology*, 78, pp. 243–255.

Lewkowicz, N. K. (1980) 'Phonemic awareness training: what it is and how to teach it', *Journal of Educational Psychology*, 72, pp. 686–700.

Liberman, I. Y. and Shankweiler, D. (1979) 'Speech, the alphabet, and teaching to read', in Resnick, L. B. and Weaver, P. A. (Eds) *Theory and Practice of Early Reading*, Hillsdale, N.J., Lawrence Erlbaum.

Marsh, G., Friedman, M. P., Welch, V. and Desberg, P. (1980) 'The development of strategies in spelling', in Frith, U. (Ed) *Cognitive Processes in Spelling*, London, Academic Press.

Marsh, G., Friedman, M. P., Welch, V. and Desberg, P. (1981) 'A cognitive developmental theory of reading acquisition', in Waller, T. G. and MacKinnon, G. E. (Eds) *Reading Research: Advances in Theory and Practice*, Vol. 3, New York, Academic Press.

Mommers, M. J. C. (1987) 'An investigation into the relationship between word recognition, reading comprehension and spelling skills in the first two years of primary school', *Journal of Reading Research*, 10, pp. 122–143.

Morris, D. (1983) 'Concept of word and phoneme awareness in the beginning reader', *Research in the Teaching of English*, 17, 4, pp. 359–373.

Morris, D. and Perney, J. (1984) 'Developmental spelling as a predictor of first-grade reading achievement', *The Elementary School Journal*, 84, 4, pp. 441–457.

Read, C. (1971) 'Preschool children's knowledge of English phonology', *Harvard Educational Review, pp. 41*, 1–34.

Read, C. (1975) *Children's Categorizations of Speech Sounds in English*, Urbana, Ill., National Council of Teachers of English.

Read, C. (1986) *Children's Creative Spelling*, London, Routledge and Kegan Paul.

Saris, W. E. and Stronkhorst, H. L. (1984) *Causal Modelling in Nonexperimental Research*, Amsterdam, Sociometric Research Foundation.

Saville, P. (1971) *A British Supplement to the Manual of the Wechsler Preschool and Primary Scale of Intelligence*, Windsor, NFER-Nelson.

Seymour, P. H. K. and Elder, L. (1985) 'Beginning reading without phonology', *Cognitive Neuropsychology*, 1, pp. 43–82.

Shanahan, T. and Lomax, R. G. (1986) 'An analysis and comparison of theoretical models of the reading-writing relationship', *Journal of Educational Psychology*, 78, pp. 116–123.

Shankweiler, D., Liberman, I. Y. and Savin, H.B. (1972) 'General discussion of papers', in Kavanagh, J. F. and Mattingly, I. (Eds) *Language by Ear and by Eye*, Cambridge, Mass., MIT Press.

Slobin, D. J. (1978) 'A case study of early language awareness', in Sinclair, A., Jarvella, J. and Levelt, W. J. M. (Eds) *The Child's Conception of Language*, New York Springer-Verlag.

Smith, F. (1973) 'Alphabetic writing — a language compromise?', in Smith, F. (Ed), *Psycholinguistics and Reading*, New York, Holt, Rinehart and Winston.

Snowling, M. and Perin, D. (1983) 'The development of phoneme segmentation skills in young children', in Sloboda, J. (Ed) *The Acquisition of Symbolic Skills*, London, Plenum Press.

Stanovich, K. E., Cunningham, A. E. and Cramer, B. B. (1984) 'Assessing phonological awareness in kindergarten children: issues of task comparability', *Journal of Experimental Child Psychology*, 38, pp. 175–190.

Tornéus, M. (1984) 'Phonological awareness and reading: a chicken and egg problem?', *Journal of Educational Psychology*, 76, 6, pp. 1346–1358.

Valtin, R. (1984) 'The development of metalinguistic abilities in children learning to read and write', in Downing, J. and Valtin, R. (Eds) *Language Awareness and Learning to Read*, New York, Springer-Verlag.

Wechsler, D. (1967) *Manual for the Wechsler Preschool and Primary Scale of Intelligence*, New York, the Psychological Corporation.

Acknowledgments

We thank the headteachers, teachers and pupils of St. Gerards Convent School, Bangor, Our Ladies Roman Catholic School, Bangor, and Llandegfan Primary School, Anglesey for their constant help, encouragement and patience throughout the three years of this project.

8
Dyslexia in Childhood: a Cognitive-Developmental Perspective

Margaret J. Snowling

During the last decade, experimental psychologists have followed one of two lines when investigating 'childhood dyslexia'. Those in what has been called the 'deficit' tradition have compared groups of dyslexic and normally developing readers in search of differences between the groups which explain 'unexpected' reading failure. This approach has enjoyed considerable success and characteristic 'dyslexic' deficits in memory, segmentation and other primarily verbal processes have been unveiled (Vellutino, 1979; Bryant and Bradley, 1985). An alternative approach, at least partly inspired by the successful application of psycholinguistic models to the analysis of acquired dyslexia has been the investigation of dyslexic reading and spelling processes (Coltheart, Patterson and Marshall, 1980). Here group studies have found that dyslexic children have *specific* difficulty reading nonword stimuli (Snowling, 1981; Baddeley *et al.*, 1982). Individual case studies have corroborated this view to an extent but also have made clear that some dyslexics can decode novel stimuli with greater ease than others (Temple and Marshall, 1983; Seymour and McGregor, 1984). Thus, there is heterogeneity within the group of children described as dyslexic in so far as their written language skills are concerned.

Both of these approaches have greatly increased our understanding of dyslexia. However, because dyslexia is a disorder of *development*, what has to be explained is not just the nature of dyslexia but rather *why* dyslexic children fail to acquire reading skills at the expected rate and *how* their development proceeds after they have 'failed'. A third approach, the cognitive-developmental perspective examines the problems which children have in learning to read, taking a developmental model as a framework (Snowling, 1987). As the reading system evolves through time, this approach looks for the causes of reading failure in the cognitive system which underlies the reading system, and in the spoken language processes which predate literacy. The approach is ambitious in that it aims to elucidate not only the cause and the nature of dyslexia but also to describe how dyslexics compensate for deficiences in their reading over time.

A framework for literacy development

Before developing the argument further, it is important to outline a framework within which to understand the acquisition of reading. Having a clear idea of the ways in which normal children learn to read and spell is essential if the particular difficulties of dyslexic children are to be understood. Of course, long before a child learns to read, he or she normally has a fully functional system for the processing of spoken language. This is the foundation for literacy development.

The state of the child's processing system prior to reading acquisition is depicted in Figure 8.1. At this point, children can recognize, produce and understand a wide range of spoken words but cannot yet recognize their printed forms. According to the model, words in the spoken vocabulary are represented within an auditory lexicon containing auditory input logogens which are basically recognition units. This lexicon, responsible for word recognition, is linked with semantic memory where word meanings are stored. In addition there are nonlexical procedures (route B) which are used for processing novel or new words. These procedures include phoneme segmentation and phoneme synthesis or blending processes and are brought into play, for example, when new articulatory-motor programmes have to be compiled.

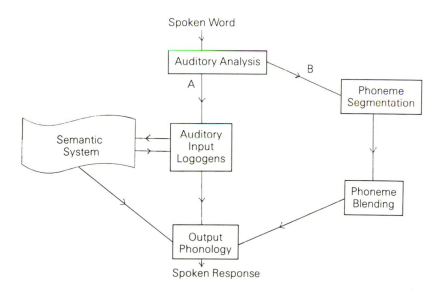

Figure 8.1 Child's language system prior to learning to read

It has long been realized that the developing child will exploit the underlying language system when learning to read (LaBerge and Samuels, 1974). For present purposes the important point is that the task of literacy acquisition is the integration of a system for processing written words with the one which already exists for processing spoken words. According to Frith (1985), this integration or acquisition process can be viewed as a series of phases, with written language skills only gradually becoming independent and automatic.

Initially children's attempts to read single words are visually based (the use of context will be discussed later); whilst a small sight vocabulary can be built using this approach, reading is inaccurate with a preponderance of visual errors. For instance, the child might read 'lorry' as 'yellow' because of the shared letters l,o,y, irrespective of serial position, or 'policeman' as 'children' because they are both 'long' words (Seymour and Elder, 1986). They also lean heavily on first letter information. Moreover, Frith (1985) has noted that the visual features which children use to memorize words are crude and may include peripheral information such as punctuation marks as in the rendering of 'Help'! as 'Bang!'. Thus, she calls this first phase of literacy acquisition the *logographic phase*: a small number of words can be recognized from partial information but spelling is, as yet, rudimentary. A second limitation is that new or unfamiliar words cannot be deciphered as they have no representation in visual memory. To get around these various limitation, children enter a new phase, the *alphabetic*, during which they begin to abstract and use the letter-sound relationships which are embodied in printed words. Hence, both reading and spelling become possible. Furthermore, the child gradually improves his or her ability to deal with unfamiliar words. These will be read via a grapheme-phoneme translation system and spelled by reference to a system of sound-to-letter correspondence rules. The written language system now approximates that which is characteristic of the fluent reader (see Figure 8.2). It can be seen that there are at least two ways in which printed words can be read. A direct visual or lexical route (route C) can be used for reading familiar words and a nonlexical phonological route for reading new words (route D).

Transition into the alphabetic phase is no small achievement. Before children can understand the relationship between graphemes (letter units) and phonemes (units of speech) they must have phonemic awareness (Gleitman and Rozin, 1977). They need to be able to segment the sound stream into phonemic units if they are to see how these map onto spelling patterns and to 'crack the alphabetic code'. There is much evidence to suggest that this is a stumbling block for many readers, especially dyslexics, and it is a point to which we shall return. However, by the close of the alphabetic phase children can spell with complete phonetic accuracy and are adept at handling new materials in both reading and writing. To this extent they are functionally literate but, in an irregular writing system such as English, being within the alphabetic phase brings with it problems. In particular, the alphabetic reader/speller will have no mechanism for dealing with irregular or inconsistent

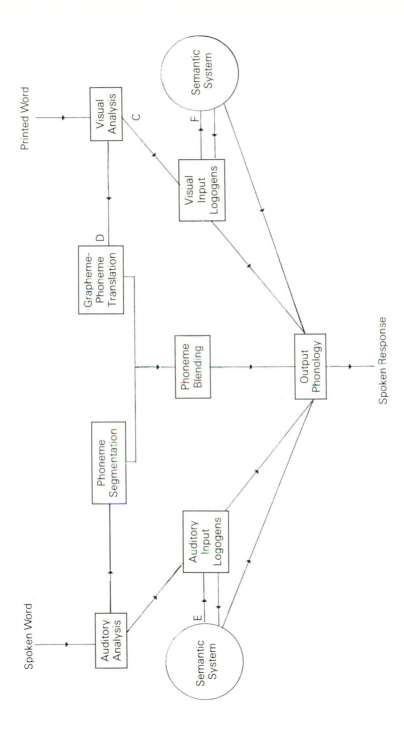

Figure 8.2 Model of the written language processing system which characterizes the fluent reader

orthographic patterns. 'Leaf' and 'deaf' would be pronounced as though rhyming, and there would be a tendency to 'regularize' irregular words such as 'island' and 'yacht'. These might be read as 'izland' and 'y-a-ch-t'. Moreover, they might be spelled 'iland' and 'yot'. So, for reading of English anyway, there is a final phase of literacy development, the *orthographic*, when reading and spelling are independent of sound.

The orthographic reader automatically recognizes spelling units during reading and, by this stage, graphemic clusters such as -tion, -cian, -ove and -ead have become totally familiar. According to Frith, children enter the orthographic phase first for reading and only later for spelling. Transition is brought about by the amalgamation of logographic and alphabetic strategies. The 'sketchy' word representations used during the logographic phase are now fully specified so that accurate reading and spelling can proceed accurately by reference to these. Furthermore, a fully furnished lexical system affords the reader a new strategy for deciphering unfamiliar words. This is the use of lexical analogies. Marsh *et al.*, (1980) noted that 'faugh' can be read either 'faw' by decoding or 'faff' (American or Northern English) by analogy with 'laugh'. In their study, it was college students who used analogy strategies. Goswami (1988) challenged this finding and has recently suggested that even beginning readers have the strategy at their disposal to some extent.

Nonetheless, the state of the reader's lexicon, its size and its current level of activation, remains an important determiner of the use of analogy strategies and, by the time the reader reaches the orthographic phase, it is probable that lexical strategies will override the use of grapheme-phoneme translation rules. It is important to note that, while sound is needed for the establishment of orthographic representations — indeed the application of alphabetic strategies directs the reader's attention to the letter-by-letter structures of words — processing within the orthographic phase is free of sound. This has implications for our understanding of dyslexia.

In the remainder of this chapter we shall pursue the cognitive-developmental theme. First, two experiments which examine the spoken language skills underpinning the written language system will be described. These reveal specific auditory processing deficits in dyslexic readers, most probably arising as the consequence of segmentation difficulties. The possible consequences of these deficits for the acquisition of reading will then be discussed with reference to a single case study and lastly, we shall consider how development proceeds following 'arrest'.

Auditory processing in dyslexic children

It is widely held that disabled readers are subject to phoneme segmentation problems (Liberman *et al.*, 1977; Bradley and Bryant, 1978). The possibility that these stem from difficulties with speech perception has been less popular and findings in the area are equivocal (Brandt and Rosen, 1980; Godfrey *et al.*,

1981). However, Brady, Shankweiler and Mann (1983) reported an experiment suggesting that poor readers require a higher quality of speech signal for accurate perception than normal readers. In a repetition task, these poor readers made more errors than good readers when high and low frequency words were presented in noise than if the stimuli were presented in clear surroundings. We decided to extend their experiment to elucidate the nature of the dyslexics' repetition deficit (Snowling, Goulandris, Bowlby and Howell, 1986). Referring back to Figure 8.1, their difficulty could have resided with auditory analysis, with output phonology or in auditory-lexical representation. Since Brady *et al.*, had not included nonwords amongst their stimuli, it was not possible for them to comment on the functioning of the nonlexical route (B). To investigate this we decided to include nonwords in our experiment.

Our subjects were nineteen dyslexic readers, all attending a specialist school for dyslexic children. Their mean age was 10 years 8 months but they were reading at the 8 year level. We compared them with nineteen normally developing 10-year-olds (chronological age controls) and, more importantly, with nineteen normal 8-year-olds who were readinga at the same level as the dyslexics. These were the Reading Age-matched controls (RA controls).

To examine input processing, we presented the experimental stimuli in clear surroundings or with noise masking. To avoid the possibility of ceiling effects we had three different presentation conditions: no noise, low noise and high noise. The rationale was that, if dyslexics have difficulty at an early stage of processing, they should be more affected by noise than normal readers. To throw light upon the functioning of the lexical system, we presented single syllable words of high and low frequency of occurence. In fact these were the same stimuli as Brady *et al.* had used with some modifications to allow for the fact that we were testing British children. If dyslexics have problems with lexical access or retrieval, then they should respond differently to these words than normal readers. Finally, to examine functioning of the nonlexical route we asked subjects to repeat nonwords which were compiled from the high frequency items by changing the initial phonemes. While we did not make a direct test of output phonology, we reasoned that, if the dyslexics had difficulty at this level, then their repetition would be poorer than that of controls throughout the experiment.

Altogether each subject repeated twenty-four high frequency words, such as cake and dog, twenty-four low frequency words like bale and dust, and twenty-four nonwords, for example, gake and tog. A third of the stimuli were presented with a noise mask at the same level as the signal — the high noise condition, one third were presented with a noise mask somewhat quieter than the signal — the low noise condition, and the remaining stimuli were presented without masking. Different subjects received different stimuli in each condition and the order of presentation of the three noise conditions was randomized.

Our results differed in a number of ways from those of Brady *et al.* (1983). First, we found no evidence of a differential effect of noise masking; the performance of all subjects deteriorated when there was noise and dyslexics did not differ from normal readers in this respect. Our conclusion was that dyslexics have no difficulty with input processing. Turning to the effect of word frequency, this was significant for all groups indicating that high frequency words were easier to procees than low frequency items. Moreover, there was an important group by word type interaction. All subjects were at ceiling on the high frequency words but on low frequency words, dyslexics made more errors than their chronological age controls although a similar number to Reading Age matched controls.

Leaving this result aside for the moment, the group differences for the repetition of nonwords were striking. Here dyslexics made significantly more errors than both CA and RA controls who in turn differed from one another (see Table 8.1). Furthermore, dyslexics were the only group for whom nonword repetition was significantly harder than the repetition of low frequency words.

Table 8.1 *Mean number of repetition errors made by dyslexic and normal readers according to word type (Max = 8).*

Subjects	N	High frequency (knife)	Low frequency (fig)	Nonwords (mife)
Dyslexics	19	1.84	4.58	7.53
CA-controls	19	0.64	2.58	3.57
RA-controls	19	1.41	4.14	5.04

In short, the dyslexics showed a 'nonword repetition deficit'. This could not be attributed to problems with acoustic analysis for they were not differentially affected by the addition of noise masking. A problem with output phonology could also be ruled out or else a more general articulation problem might have been anticipated. Hence, the most likely locus of their difficulty was within the nonlexical procedures involved in speech processing, namely phoneme segmentation and blending processes. Thus, this experiment adds to the evidence pointing to segmentation deficits in dyslexic readers. Of particular interest here are the developmental consequences of these deficits. First, it seems likely that a child who has difficulty in repeating unfamiliar words will be slow to learn 'new' vocabulary. So, even in the domain of spoken language it can be anticipated that dyslexics will show a 'delay' in development. This has a bearing on the previously noted finding for low frequency words. It will be recalled that dyslexics were no better than younger Reading Age-matched controls in repeating these items. Certainly they made more errors than the age-matched comparison group suggesting that, comparatively, they had access to fewer articulatory-motor programmes. Whether they also had access to fewer auditory-lexical representations remained an open question.

The stimuli in the second experiment were identical to those used in the previous experiment with the addition of nonwords derived from the low frequency items. Again, one third of the stimuli were presented without a noise mask, one third with a low noise mask and one third with a high noise mask, every third subject receiving different stimuli under different conditions. In contrast with the first experiment, subjects had to indicate (saying yes/no) on hearing a stimulus whether it was a word or a nonword.

The results are shown in Table 8.2. Again there was a significant effect of noise but each group was affected similarly. None of the groups had difficulty in detecting the high frequency items but there was a significant group difference for low frequency words. Here the dyslexics' performance was like that of younger Reading Age controls but not so good as their age-matched peers.

Table 8.2 *Mean number of correct YES responses in auditory lexical decision. A comparison of dyslexics, RA-controls and CA-controls under differing noise conditions (Max = 12).*

	No noise		Low noise	
	High frequency	Low frequency	High frequency	Low frequency
Subjects (N = 19 in each group)				
Dyslexics	11.42	6.47	11.68	5.42
RA-controls	11.37	5.73	11.47	5.21
CA-controls	11.63	7.84	11.63	7.15

In short, the results of this experiment were in line with the hypothesis that dyslexic readers are slower than their normally reading peers to set up auditory-lexical representations for spoken words. In its turn, a relative absence of lexical representations will have effects on other processing tasks involving words. For instance, naming deficits are to be anticipated (Katz, 1986; Snowling, vanWagtendonk and Stafford, 1988) and problems with verbal memory tasks (Vellutino and Scanlon, 1985).

A second direct consequence of the segmentation problems characteristic of dyslexic readers is an effect upon literacy development. Consideration of the acquisition process predicts that dyslexics who have problems with segmentation will fail to make the transition to the alphabetic phase (Frith, 1985). With this hypothesis in mind, we set out to examine the reading and spelling strategies available to seven dyslexics, all considered as individuals (Snowling, Stackhouse and Rack, 1986). Here just one of these cases is presented to illustrate the consequences of a segmentation problem for reading and spelling development.

Dyslexia and the acqusition of literacy

J. M. was referred for educational assessment when aged 8 years 5 months. In spite of his obvious intelligence, he was underachieving at school. He had a history of speech problems although his language skills had always been good. Psychometric testing established that J. M. had specific reading and spelling problems. His WISC-R I.Q. score was 123, placing him within the superior range of intelligence. On the basis of this score his predicted Reading Age was 9 years 4 months but he had only reached the 7 years 5 months level on the Schonell Graded Word Reading Test (Yule *et al.*, 1982). Similarly, his predicted Spelling Age was 8 years 11 months but achievement measured at the 6 years 7 months level. Since J. M.'s reading and spelling problems could not be accounted for by lack of educational opportunity and he did not have any primary emotional or behavioural difficulties, he was considered to be dyslexic. J. M. was also found to be subject to a range of verbal deficits and segmentation problems. He could segment by syllable but not reliably by phoneme, he performed below age level on rhyme detection tasks, had problems in verbal repetition and his verbal memory span was reduced. The hypothesis was therefore that he would surely have difficulty in moving from the logographic to the alphabetic phase of development. This hypothesis led to several predictions:

1. Single word reading should be visually based and reading errors should share visual features with their targets.
2. Nonword reading should not be possible.
3. Spelling should be rudimentary revealing a failure to apply alphabetic principles. Hence, spelling errors should be primarily nonphonetic.

We tested each of these predictions systematically and compared J. M.'s performance with that of normally developing readers who had reached a similar level of reading skill. These Reading Age controls were all 7-year-olds who were reading between the 7 years and the 7 years 3 months level on the SPAR reading test (Young, 1976). To examine J. M.'s reading of words and nonwords, he was asked to pronounce a mixed series of thirty-one regular (dance, cash) and thirty-one irregular (choir, vase) printed words matched for frequency. In each case, nineteen were of one syllable, twelve were of two syllables (market, litre). In addition, he attempted thirty-one nonwords which were compiled from the irregular items by changing the first phonene.

The results are shown in Table 8.3. Examination of the data from the normal readers suggested that already they were beginning to move into the alphabetic phase of development.

It can be seen that they read approximately 50 per cent of single syllable nonwords correctly and some 30 per cent of the two syllable items. While J. M.'s reading of real words was not significantly different from that of controls, unlike them, he had no success whatsoever with nonwords. Many of his attempts were 'lexicalizations' e.g. he read 'plood' as 'pool', 'hign' as

Table 8.3   Reading of real words and nonwords by J.M. (% correct) (No. of items = 31).

	One syllable		Two syllable	
	Real words cash	Nonwords fint*	Real words tutor	Nonwords bitre*
Normal 7 yr readers (N = 12)	45.5	49.9	34.2	29.8
range	(34–79)	(16–84)	(4–83)	(0–75)
J.M.	37.0	0	29	0

*Nonword responses were counted as correct if they were read either by letter-sound correspondence rules or by analogy with irregular real words.

'high', 'swad' as 'want' and 'wamp' as 'warm'. Thus, although J. M. had a sight vocabulary, he could not use a nonlexical route to phonology; it therefore seemed likely that he was still functioning within the logographic phase of literacy development. Further evidence for this hypothesis came from a demonstration that in other situations too, he avoided the use of phonological reading strategies.

One of the pieces of evidence which is frequently quoted as demonstration of the use of phonology in reading is the 'regularity' effect (Coltheart, 1978). The advantage of regular over irregular words (either in terms of speed of processing or error rate) is thought to reflect the fact that regular words can be read via one of two routes (lexical or nonlexical) whereas irregular words can only be pronounced via the direct route. To assess the extent to which J. M relied upon word-specific (lexical) information during reading, and how much he leant on phonological reading strategies, we examined his pronunciation of the regular and irregular words already described. Children who are within the logographic phase of development should have an equal chance of reading regular and irregular words correctly provided they are matched for frequency of occurrence, whereas children within the alphabetic phase should find regular words easier because they can be read phonologically.

Table 8.4   Reading of regular and irregular words by J.M. (Max = 31).

	N	Regular (dance)	Irregular (broad)
Normal 7 yr readers	12	17.3	9.75
range		(9–28)	(3–22)
J.M.	1	9.0	8.0

The performance of J. M. compared to that of Reading Age controls is shown in Table 8.4. These data corroborate the view that the normal readers have moved into the alphabetic phase for they show a significant regularity effect. In contrast, this was absent from J. M.'s data. While J. M. did as well as controls when reading irregular words, he did not reap the same advantage when attempting the regular words. It could be argued that he was still operating within the logographic phase. Moreover, his reading errors resembled their targets visually. Some 47 per cent were 'logographic' e.g. he read SIGN as 'sing', BOWL as 'blow', ORGAN as 'orange', and on 22 per cent of occasions, when he tried to use sound he ultimately made a guess e.g. he read FLOOD as 'fault', BLEAT as 'built'. One category of error which was present in the normal sample but absent from J. M.'s data was that of 'regularizations'. These occur when irregular words (e.g. BROAD) are read by grapheme-phoneme translation (e.g. to arrive at 'brode'). Nineteen per cent of normal readers' errors on single syllable words were regularizations but J. M. made none of these.

To assess J. M.'s alphabetic competence further, he was asked to spell a series of one, two and three syllable words which had already been given to a large sample of normally developing readers. We were interested to see firstly whether he spelled as well as Reading Age controls and secondly, whether his spelling errors were phonetic or dysphonetic. First, J. M. spelled fewer of the words correctly than normal children who were reading at the same level as him. It will be recalled that the spelling of children within the logographic phase is rudimentary and this probably accounts for J. M.'s problems. Importantly, however, examination of J. M.'s spelling errors showed that they were primarily dysphonetic. Normal 7-year-olds made approximately 50 per cent phonetic and 50 per cent nonphonetic errors on one and two syllable words, but J. M.'s errors were 100 per cent nonphonetic. Furthermore, his attempts at three syllable words were extremely difficult to decipher. These included 'sikeoleg' for cigarette, 'afveorl' for adventure and 'unenprl' for umbrella. Although 7-year-olds could not yet manage phonetic versions of these items, their attempts were much closer to target than those of J. M. To illustrate, they wrote 'sigret' for cigarette, 'atfench' for adventure and 'unberell' for umbrella.

To conclude, J. M. could without doubt be considered to be within the logographic phase of literacy development. In contrast to Reading Age-matched controls, his reading errors were primarly visual, he had difficulty in reading nonwords and his spelling errors were dysphonetic. Taken together with the problems he experienced on a range of segmentation tasks, these data suggest that J. M. was having difficulty in moving to the alphabetic phase. Whilst there is certainly heterogeneity amongst dyslexic readers, there is reason to believe that J. M.'s problems are characteristic of many of the group, especially those who are designated 'phonological' dyslexic (Temple and Marshall, 1983; Seymour, 1986). The development of these dyslexics appears to be arrested within the logographic phase. However if this is so, it falls to us to explain how, if at all, they in fact manage to learn to read and how their spelling can improve in the face of their obvious problems.

In principle, if literacy development is stemmed because of the nonavailability of phonological and segmentation skills, there are at least two ways in which it might proceed. First, with increasing age and maturity there may be an increase in phonological skill such that development can be resumed to continue along normal lines albeit slowly. Second, it may be possible for progress to be made along an alternative and compensatory pathway (Snowling, 1987). Here, consideration of the reading and spelling skills of dyslexics who have reached a higher level of attainment than J. M. is instructive. Four such dyslexics, all reading at the 10 years level or beyond, were tested by Snowling, Stackhouse and Rack (1986). While these dyslexics had reached a fairly high level of reading and spelling skill, their pattern of difficulty was remarkably similar to that of the dyslexics of lower Reading Age. Thus, they were worse at reading aloud complex nonwords, such as 'otbemp' and 'stipnoc' than Reading Age controls (in this case normal 10-year-olds), and their spelling errors, at least on lists of two and four syllable words, were less phonetic than those of their comparison group. Recently, we have had the opportunity of following-up J. M.'s case some four years later (Snowling and Hulme, 1989). His case represents a remarkably similar picture; he has learned to read in spite of a stable deficiency in phonological skill, presumably by relying on alternative strategies to those used by normal readers.

Progress following developmental arrest

J. M. was retested when aged 12 years, four years after the initial assessment. In the intervening time he had been educated in two specialist dyslexic schools, one at primary, one at secondary level. He was felt by his teachers to have progressed well although, according to standardized tests, his progress was moderate; his Reading and Spelling Ages had increased by only two years in the four which had elapsed.

Nevertheless, J. M. had learned to read. An important question for present purposes was how he had done so. To investigate this we administered the tests given on the previous occasion. First, J. M. was asked to read the matched regular and irregular words. He read 26/31 regular and 27/31 irregular items correctly, a similar level of performance to that of normal Reading Age-matched controls, in this instance 10-year-old readers (Snowling, Stackhouse and Rack, 1986). It is difficult to make any valid comment about the lack of a regularity effect in his data as he performed close to ceiling on the test but it might be considered relevant that, of the nine errors he made, three were visual in nature (shin/skin, cask/task, lever/level), two were lexicalizations following sound analysis (siege/sileage, suede/sewage) and four were unsuccessful sound attempts resulting in neologisms (beat/brit, shove/s-love, lobster/losper, marine/mEdIn). None of his errors were regularizations suggesting that he was still having difficulty in applying the basic grapheme-phoneme conversion rules which are characteristic of the alphabetic phase of development.

To explore J. M.'s reading strategies further, he was asked to read Coltheart's (1980) lists of regular and irregular words aloud. He read 75.5 per cent of the regular words and 59 per cent of the irregular words correctly. Thus, there was a suggestion of a regularity effect. However, analysis of the error data suggested that the use of grapheme-phoneme rules was an unlikely explanation for the regular word advantage. First, J. M. made very few regularization errors. He misread sixteen irregular words altogether but only four of his mistakes reflected the use of phonological rules, viz., shove/shoave, circuit/sir-cute, gross/gros, subtle/sˆ btl. By far the majority of his reading errors, some 54 per cent, were visual, sharing more than half their letters with target-words e.g. pint/paint, trough/thought, borough/brought, spend/spent, slate/state, sort/short. The remaining errors, some 23 per cent, were all unsuccessful sound attempts, e.g. debt/dit,tit,tab, gauge/kanjul, cough/coch.

Thus, as when previously tested, J. M.'s reading performance reflected the use of a direct reading route. It seemed that, although his Reading Age had increased, his reading development remained arrested within the logographic phase. To test whether or not this was the case, he was asked to read aloud the thirty-one nonwords compiled by changing the first phoneme of the irregular words he had read previously. On this occasion he read approximately 25 per cent of nonwords correctly. Although this was an improvement over his previous performance, he was inordinately slow and his performance was outside of normal limits: he did significantly less well than Reading Age-matched controls and his performance still fell one standard deviation below that of 7-year-old normal readers.

So, J. M.'s persisting inability to read nonwords adds weight to the evidence that his development has remained within the logographic phase. Although there had been some marginal improvement in his use of letter-sound corespondences, he remained unable to use phonological strategies with automaticity. We hypothesized, therefore, that he would have persisting spelling difficulties.

To test changes in spelling performance, he was given the test of one, two, three and four syllable spellings. This time he spelled one- and two-syllable words as well as Reading Age-matched controls but performance fell more than two standard deviations below the mean on three and four syllable items. Moreover, J. M.'s attempts to spell polysyllabic words were primarily nonphonetic; on the test as a whole, he made 78 per cent nonphonetic as compared with 22 per cent phonetic spelling errors and analysis of the errors he made in free writing presented a similar picture: 91 per cent of spelling errors were dysphonetic and only 9 per cent portrayed the correct sound sequence of the word he wished to write (see Figure 8.4). Taking the data as a whole, the argument is unequivocal; J. M., for the most part, is still functioning within the logographic phase of development.

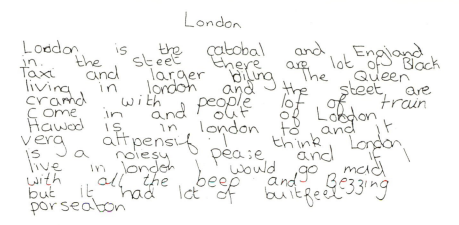

Figure 8.3 Seven minutes of free writing completed by J. M. at follow up

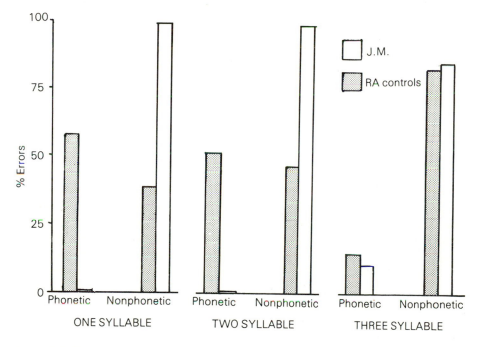

Figure 8.4 Phonetic and nonphonetic spelling errors on one, two, and three syllable words

But, it will be recalled that J.,M. has, nonetheless, learned to read. The progress which he has made with written language skills seems mainly attributable to an accumulation of word-specific knowledge (Ehri, 1985). What factors account for the particular course of development he has followed? First, we have seen that his auditory short-term memory has remained weak and since it is thought that this is required to support phonemic parsing, J. M. must have always been at a disadvantage. Further, his reduced memory span would surely have limited his potential for alphabetic processing operations, blending and spelling for example. On the other hand, J. M. has never, as far as we are aware, experienced visual perceptual or visual memory problems. When first assessed at 8 years 5 months, he copied the complex Rey Osterrieth figure perfectly and was able to reproduce it without difficulty after thirty minutes. When assessed at 10 years 10 months on the B.A.S. Test of Immediate Visual Recall, a pictorial memory task, he scored at the 70th centile. It is possible, therefore, that visual memory skills were able to support whole-word recognition to an extent accounting for the increase in sight vocabulary which was seen.

Moreover, it is important to bear in mind that, almost always, reading takes place in context. Since we have no reason to suspect that J. M. has a general language problem, the hypothesis that he has relied heavily upon contextual cues to compensate for his decoding difficulty was worth pursuing (Stanovich, 1980). To test the plausibility of this explanation, we administered two tests of text processing with the prediction that J. M. would do at least as well as normal Reading Age-matched controls, if not better than his decoding skill predicted.

Reading beyond single word level

J. M. was presented with two texts which had been devised by Snowling and Frith (1986) to investigate the reading comprehension of 'hyperlexic' children. The first, a story about beavers, used a modified cloze procedure. Subjects read the text aloud and, at intervals throughout it, chose one of three words to complete a 'gap'. The words were always of the same grammatical category but they differed according to plausibility within the sentence frame. One was always story-appropriate, another appropriate to the sentence in which it was placed but not to the story as a whole, and a third was implausible. The best choices were of story-appropriate words because these indicated proficient processing of story meaning; the worst were implausible choices which were associated with superficial 'barking at print'.

J. M. had no difficulty whatsoever with this task. He made only two errors. In both cases he chose sentence-appropriate rather than story-appropriate completions. His performance was within the range of normal readers of similar reading skill (Snowling and Frith, 1986). Next he read a text about hedgehogs in which his task was to detect anomalous words. These were of two types; implausible e.g. . . . . the scent of *electric* (spring) flowers and, more difficult to detect, plausible words e.g. . . . . all the time they were growing *cleverer* (stronger). J. M. detected 14/15 implausible words which was a similar number to normal readers. Significantly, he detected more of the plausible targets, some 12/15 than normal 10-year-old readers, revealing sophisticated 'metalinguistic' skill. Unlike normal readers, he made no false alarms.

Lastly, J. M. was asked twenty questions to tap his understanding and memory for the texts he had read. He answered 8/10 factual questions correctly and 9/10 questions which could be answered either by reference to the text or through the use of general knowledge. In both cases, his performance was better than that of normal controls who answered on average five to six Fact and seven to eight General Knowledge questions correctly. The results from these tests were therefore in line with our hypothesis that J. M. can use context proficiently during reading. He had no difficulty in processing written sentences, in following story-meaning or in understanding what he read. It is probable that he has used these intact abilities as a way of improving the automaticity of his reading. Furthermore, links between his cognitive and reading system, being intact, could have been used to facilitate decoding of unfamiliar words. We would speculate that these words were then memorized visually, accounting for sight vocabulary expansion.

To conclude, J. M.'s case illustrates a number of points which are relevant not only to our current understanding of dyslexia, but also for future research. His case indicates that dyslexia is certainly not just a reading problem and further, it is more than a problem with written language skills. Data presented from groups of dyslexics and from single case studies confirm that retarded readers are subject to a range of phonological deficits. The experiments described here have focused on segmentation deficits and problems with auditory lexical decision. Recent evidence also implicates memory and naming difficulties. It seems likely that it is individual differences in these basic processes which predispose certain individuals but not others to reading failure; in J. M.'s case, the deficits have caused arrest at the logographic phase of literacy development. However, not all children will have problems here. A reasonable hypothesis is that a number whose deficits are less severe may be able to proceed to the alphabetic phase although those who are subject to visual processing deficits will fail to make the transition to the orthographic phase.

So, in order to understand the precise reason for a child's reading difficulty, it is important to look to the interaction of his or her cognitive strengths and weaknesses with the demands of learning to read and spell, and the teaching to which he or she is exposed. Moreover, these factors will also have a bearing on how literacy development proceeds following arrest. J. M. evidently learned to read and spell by gradually accumulating word-specific knowledge. He did not do so by improving his phonological skills, despite four years of intensive teaching using a structured phonetic approach. This forces us to examine critically some current approaches to remediation. A question for the future is to examine, using a cognitive-neuropsychological framework, how individuals respond to specific interventions. Only when we know this will we truly be in a position to provide for a child's specific educational needs with regard to reading and spelling. It is unlikely that there will be a simple panacea for childhood dyslexia.

References

Baddeley, A., Ellis, N., Miles, T. and Lewis, V. (1982) 'Developmental and acquired dyslexia: a comparison', *Cognition*, 11, pp. 185–199.

Bradley, L. and Bryant, P. (1978) 'Difficulties in auditory organisation as a possible cause of reading backwardness', *Nature*, 271, pp. 746–747.

Brady, S., Shankweiler, D. and Mann, V. (1983) 'Speech perception and memory coding in relation to reading ability', *Journal of Experimental Child Psychology*, 35, pp. 345–367.

Brandt, J. and Rosen, J.J. (1980) 'Auditory-phonemic perception in dyslexia: categorised identification and discrimination of stop consonants', *Brain and Language*, 9, pp. 324–337.

Bryant, P. and Bradley, L. (1985) *Children's Reading Problems: Psychology and Education*, Oxford, Blackwell.

Coltheart, M. (1978) 'Lexical access in simple reading tasks', in Underwood, G. (Ed) *Strategies of Information Processing*, London, Academic Press.

Coltheart, M. (1980) *Analyzing Reading Disorders*. Unpublished manuscript.

Coltheart, M., Patterson, K. and Marshall, J.C. (1980) *Deep Dyslexia*, London, Routledge and Kegan Paul.

Ehri, L. (1985) 'Sources of difficulty in learning to spell and read', in Wolraich, M.L. and Routh, D. (Eds) *Advances in Developmental and Behavioural Paediatrics*, Greenwich, Conn., JAI Press Inc.

Frith, U. (1985) 'Beneath the surface of developmental dyslexia', in Patterson, K.E., Marshall, J.C. and Coltheart, M. (Eds) *Surface Dyslexia*, London, Routledge and Kegan Paul.

Gleitman, L.R. and Rozin, P. (1977) 'The structure and acquisition of reading I: relations between orthographies and the structure of language', in Reber, A.S. and Scarborough, D.L. (Eds) *Toward a Psychology of Reading*, New York, Erlbaum.

Godfrey, J.J., Syrdal-Lasky, A.K., Millay, K.K. and Knox, C.M. (1981) 'Performance of dyslexic children on speech perception test', *Journal of Experimental Child Psychology*, 32, pp. 401–424.

Goswami, U. (1988) 'Orthographic analogies and reading development', *Quarterly Journal of Experimental Psychology*, 40A, pp. 239–268.

Katz, R.B. (1986) 'Phonological deficiences in children with reading disability: evidence from an object naming test', *Cognition*, 22, pp. 225–257.

LaBerge, D. and Samuels, S.J. (1974) 'Toward a theory of automatic information processing in reading', *Cognitive Psychology*, 6, pp. 293–323.

Liberman, I.Y., Shankweiler, D., Liberman, A., Fowler, C. and Fischer, F.W. (1977) 'Phonetic segmentation and recoding in the beginning reader', in Reber, A.S. and Scarborough, D.L. (Eds) *Towards a Psychology of Reading*, Hillsdale, N.J., Lawrence Erlbaum.

Marsh, G., Friedman, M., Welch, V. and Desberg, P. (1980) 'The development of strategies in spelling', in Frith, U. (Ed) *Cognitive Processes in Spelling*, London, Academic Press.

Seymour, P.H.K. (1986) *Cognitive Analysis of Dyslexia*, London, Routledge and Kegan Paul.

Seymour, P.H.K. and Elder, L. (1986) 'Beginning reading without phonology', *Cognitive Neuropsychology*, 1, pp. 43–82.

Seymour, P. H. K. and McGregor, C. J. (1984) 'Developmental dyslexia: a cognitive experimental analysis of phonological, morphemic and visual impairments', *Cognitive Neuropsychology*, 1, pp. 43–82.

Snowling, M. J. (1981) 'Phonemic deficits in developmental dyslexia', *Psychological Research*, 43, pp. 219–234.

Snowling, M. J. (1987) *Dyslexia: A Cognitive Developmental Perspective*, Oxford, Balckwell.

Snowling, M. J. and Frith, U. (1986) 'Comprehension in ''hyperlexic'' readers', *Journal of Experimental Child Psychology*, 42, pp. 392–415.

Snowling, M. J., Goulandris, N., Bowlby, M. and Howell, P. (1986) 'Segmentation and speech perception in relation to reading skill: a developmental analysis', *Journal of Experimental Child Psychology*, 41, pp. 489–507.

Snowling, M. J. and Hulme, C. (1989) 'A longitudinal case study of developmental phonological dyslexia. *Cognitive Neuropsychology*, 6, pp. 379–401.

Snowling, M. J., Stackhouse, J. and Rack, J. P. (1986) 'Phonological dyslexia and dysgraphia: a developmental analysis', *Cognitive Neuropsychology*, 3, pp. 309–339.

Snowling, M. J. Van Wagtendonk, B. and Stafford, C. (1988) 'Object-naming deficits in developmental dyslexia', *Journal of Research in Reading*, 11, pp. 67–85.

Stanovich, K. E. (1980) 'Toward an interactive-compensatory model of individual differences in the development of reading fluency', *Reading Research Quarterly*, 16, pp. 32–71.

Temple, C. and Marshall, J. C. (1983) 'A case study of developmental phonological dyslexia', *British Journal of Psychology*, 74, pp. 515–533.

Vellutino, F. (1979) *Dyslexia: Theory and Research*, Cambridge, MA, M.I.T. Press.

Vellutino, F. and Scanlon, D. (1985) 'Free recall of concrete and abstract words in poor and normal readers', *Journal of Experimental Child Psychology*, 39, pp. 369–80.

Young, D. (1976) *The SPAR Reading Test*, London, Hodder and Stoughton.

Yule, W., Lansdown, R. and Urbanowicz, M. A. (1982) 'Predicting educational attainment from WISC-R in a primary school sample', *British Journal of Clinical Psychology*, 21, pp. 43–46.

9
Intervention Strategies for Backward Readers in the Primary School Classroom

Asher Cashdan and Judith Wright

Why do some children have difficulty in learning to read?

Considering the complexity of the task, it sometimes seems quite surprising that so many children learn to read without apparent difficulty. They almost seem to teach themselves. Indeed, as shall see later, this is probably exactly what they do. Nevertheless, a substantial minority of children do not have such an easy passage. They seem to find the task difficult, make poor progress and many of them do not become proficient readers for many years, if at all. Meanwhile, they fall further and further behind at school in a whole variety of reading-dependent areas. Knowing the reasons for a child's difficulties has often been considered an essential preliminary to doing something to help. Although this is not logically necessary, as some difficulties might be insuperable, it often seems a profitable first step. Let us therefore quickly survey the main reasons given for reading backwardness and see where they take us.

Low intelligence is often mentioned as a major causal factor in reading backwardness. The implication is that children of lower than average intelligence will not be able to read at the same age as average or brighter children, and that some of them may not learn to read at all. However, this traditional analysis is flawed: over twenty years ago Curr and Hallworth (1965) showed that at any score point on a standardized intelligence test as many children 'over-achieved' in reading as 'under-achieved'. In other words, although there *is* a correlation between intelligence level and reading attainment, this is only a rough and ready indicator and intelligence level is not a firm prerequisite of any particular reading attainment. It seems unwise, therefore, for Bryant and Bradley (1985) to return to this point twenty years later, the more so as the rag-bag of questions and answers involved in administering a standardized intelligence test and then scoring it to produce an IQ, yields no precise information on either specific skills or developmental level.

Similarly, referring childrens' reading backwardness/retardation to their position on the social class ladder gives very little help. Again, there will be correlations, but they will tell us little of the history of the individual child or of his/her strengths or weaknesses. Not only that, but stereotypes concerning social class (as in Bernstein's earlier work on 'restricted' and 'elaborated' codes) may positively lead us astray and unnecessarily lower our expectations.

Motivation and skills

Let us then leave such distant variables and focus on more proximal ones which should give us more usable help. We will approach these under three headings: attitudes, skills and knowledge.

It will be the contention of this paper that by far the best way to tackle negative attitudes is by providing children with the skills they need to solve educational tasks, whether in the reading field or elsewhere, together with the tools to acquire, monitor, develop and control them. So we will not discuss attitudes in any detail at this point, but merely note that many children are not so much inherently hostile to school and learning, but rather that they may be unaware of what is expected of them as well as of the purpose of school tasks and the advantages to be gained from succeeding at them — and repeated failure can easily develop into hostility. If at the same time demands are made upon pupils which they find incomprehensible and difficult it is not surprising that progress may be slow or non-existent.

Skill deficiencies

There are many obvious prerequisites to acquiring reading skill. The child (or adult) needs adequate vision, hearing, knowledge of language, memory and a number of more specific skills. Bryant and Bradley (1985) have reviewed this field very well and we intend merely to highlight some of their points and add one or two observations.

Without the skills just listed, it is clear that no one would learn to read at all. The question, however, is one of thresholds: how well developed do each of these prerequisite skills need to be? With the exception of a tiny percentage of really handicapped children, for instance, no one will have any difficulty in seeing well enough to discriminate different word or letter shapes. A couple of ten minute sessions with the average 2-year-old would be enough to bring this point home to any interested teacher or parent. What we therefore have to ask is how advanced are the demands which reading makes on each of our specific skills, over and above what may reasonably be expected of any 'uninstructed' child entering the learning process? We may also at some point need to ask questions about combinations of skills.

More detailed studies (and they are well reported in Bryant and Bradley) show that memory and visual skills are not likely to be the major problems. Where we seem to need to focus down much more is on phonological skills. In a very helpful paper, Wagner and Torgesen (1987) review the whole of this area. They divide phonological skills into three categories: phonological awareness, phonological recoding in lexical access and phonetic recoding in working memory.

Phonological awareness (also known as linguistic awareness and phonemic awareness) essentially means understanding the way sounds make up our spoken language. As Wagner and Torgesen put it: 'to an individual with well-developed phonological awareness our alphabetic system . . . is a reasonable approach to visually representing our spoken language. Conversely, an individual lacking such awareness will find the correspondence between symbol and sound capricious at best' (p. 192).

Phonological recoding in lexical access means moving from the written word to the spoken one. In other words, the reader turns the symbols on the page into the spoken words of the language. When reading has become automatic, particularly with common words, little of this recoding seems to take place. But as Wagner and Torgesen point out, it is an essential component in the early stages of learning to read.

Phonetic recoding to maintain information in working memory is Wagner and Torgesen's term for the process that needs to go on in working out what the words or phrases are that are made by the symbols on the page. It is no use recoding the individual sounds, however accurately, if some of them are lost before they can be integrated meaningfully.

Wagner and Torgesen's review makes it clear that all of the above three processes are important but that the first is by far the most significant. In other words, once the learner understands the system, the rest can follow relatively easily. This is a highly significant point to which we will be returning later. Within the development of phonological awareness, the ability to isolate syllables precedes the ability to break down words into phonemes; but it is phoneme skill that is most predictive of reading success. In passing, however, we must note the problem of direction of causation. It could be that effective readers get their understanding of phonemes within words by virtue of their knowledge gained through being effective readers rather than such knowledge leading to reading skill. This question is addressed by Bryant and by Bradley in Chapters 5 and 6.

Teaching methods

Teachers and academics have disputed hotly over many years concerning the relative merits of skills teaching as opposed to wholistic approaches. Frank Smith would have us believe that breaking down reading attainment into a series of sequential skills and teaching them is positively wicked and others, such as the Goodmans, often seem to have supported him. If only teachers would keep out of the way, the argument runs, children would get on with the job of teaching themselves reading, essentially by intelligent use of context. This is rather like telling a learner driver to get into the car and practise and everything will come right on its own. Apart from the physical danger involved, this approach looks at the beginner from the standpoint of the experienced practitioner. Those who have automatized a complex series of subskills such as are involved in driving, are often unable to disentangle the components any more; but that is not evidence of the way in which they originally learnt the skills. On the other hand, to pursue the analogy a little further, the contextual support of having been driven around a busy town as a passenger, having observed motor car behaviour as a pedestrian and having a general knowledge of roads, climatic effects on moving bodies and other such matters are all of inestimable value to the beginner before s/he sits down in the car to learn about the clutch, the brakes and the accelerator and their operation, both separately and in combination. It would be ludicrous to say to the learner driver, 'just try pushing the different foot pedals up and down until you get a good combination' and refusing to explain the functions of each of them.

We would argue that exactly the same principles apply to learning to read. Context is extremely important, both the general context of literacy behaviour and the specific context of, say, the sentence in which a difficult word is embedded. Nevertheless, it is access to, and understanding of, the specific components that make the whole skill possible right up to the point when the skill becomes so practised and automatic that the learner can afford to despise the atoms out of which it has been built up.

What then, of specific teaching methods? We feel it is essential for learners to know the nature of the task and to be given appropriate help in mastering it, particularly where there are potential problem areas. In general terms, this leads us to endorse strongly the two well-tried approaches currently advocated by Bryant and Bradley and explained clearly in their 1985 book. As a quick reminder, there are two main emphases. One is the use of plastic letters in the composition and decomposition of words, paying particular attention to letter patterns and sequences. Bryant and Bradley particularly stress the need to learn the connection between the written word's sounds and its visual appearance.

The second method employs 'simultaneous oral spelling' in which the child moves from the visual information of seeing the word, to the auditory/orthographic stage of spelling out its component letters, to the movements involved in writing it out.

We have no doubt that these are good methods and that they have been well developed by Bryant and Bradley. Our own experience, particularly recent experimental teaching by Wright, confirms the success of these approaches. Bryant and Bradley ally them with other techniques which heighten children's awareness of the basis of our written system, as well as adding to their interest and enjoyment. These include attention to rhymes and alliteration, together with other games and techniques which bring to open consciousness the essential nature of the English writing system: sound-letter and letter-sound correspondence (with all the historically-based irregularities and exceptions!).

Is this then the end of the story? If we teach the right skills and do this well, will all, or even most, backward readers catch up with their peers? And will *any* methods that concentrate on sound/letter relationships have equal success? Certainly Bryant and Bradley found that *all* the components in their scheme were needed to achieve good results and their programme has worked well. They consider that one particular reason why all the elements are needed is to get over the 'pronounced separation between reading and spelling' that seems to be a particular problem in backward readers' understanding.

Having agreed that the methods work, we still have to ask *why* they work. We can dismiss the suggestion that is made in considering many remedial programmes: that the children's improvement may be put down to individual attention, a carefully structured programme and initial success breeding greater confidence and thus continued success. If that were all, then Bryant and Bradley would not have found that dropping any particular element in their programme made a significant difference. Nevertheless, there are further questions to be asked. Do the methods work because they support weak skills or foster understanding of specific aspects of the reading process, or are there more general reasons for the programme's success?

The learner's knowledge — a *tertium quid*?

Good methods for teaching reading skills, particularly those involving the phonology of language and its relationship to the marks on the page, seem to be strongly related to backward readers' progress. Is the relationship a straightforward causal one or is it possible that some other factor contributes to both the phonological improvement and the reading skill? We think that this may indeed be the case and that the third factor is children's understanding of the reading/writing/spelling process together with their increasing control over their own learning. This is a multi-level understanding, moving from grasp of the specific skills involved at any moment to a very general grasp of the learning process and of how to monitor and improve it for oneself.

Why do we make this claim? Recent developments in both research and teaching have increasingly highlighted the value of ideas which, though not new in themselves, have been greatly developed in the last few years. They centre around what are now called meta-skills, sometimes with specific reference to language as in meta-linguistic skills or more generally as in meta-cognitive processes. In all cases, of course, we are talking about the learner's understanding of his/her own learning and thinking processes. These are sets of skills which some children, fortunately for them, seem to develop without much specific support. They soon become independent learners who can analyze a new task or problem, decide what learning/knowledge they bring to it, what its demands are, what resources they possess with which to tackle these demands, and so on to the final stage of solving the problem in question. It seems clear that this complex set of skills is not in fact inherently built in to the learner's system, except in the general sense that human beings have certain positive predispositions, along the lines for instance of Chomsky's language acquisition device. But the fortunate children learn these skills, approaches, techniques more or less incidentally from adults (including teachers) who model the skills. Other learners, for a whole host of reasons, many of them individual, do not become independent learners in the sense in which we are defining this. They need more specifically designed programmes.

What, then, do 'failing' learners need? First, to have their attention drawn to the nature of the task in which they are being asked to engage; then, to acquire a set of analytic and planning skills which will progressively lead them to full independence. This approach to studying and helping the learning process has been developed in considerable detail over the last few years and specific analyses have been made of the application of the approach to children who are not learning well. We propose therefore to give two or three examples of analysis and prescription in rather more detail.

Brown and Palincsar (1982) distinguished between skills training, self-regulation and awareness training. In skills training the focus is on the specific strategies that need to be practised for the skill in question; self-regulation training means 'instruction in the orchestration, overseeing, and monitoring of those skills'; while awareness training involves understanding the significance of the techniques used and the context in which they are appropriate.

Gelzheiser *et al*. (1986) take the same analysis and set it out very clearly, as in Figure 9.1.

Specific skill content

Explicitly teach the skill

Provide sufficient practice for mastery and automaticity

Begin with easy materials

Introduce difficult materials when students are proficient

General, self-regulatory skills

Free capacity for regulation, by reducing other demands

Explicitly teach self-monitoring, or

Support students as they ascertain the skill's effect

Have students graph their progress

Concept of appropriate skill application

Teach characteristics of task where the skill helps

Teach students to discriminate tasks where the skill helps

Use a variety of materials for practice

Source: Gelzeiser, Shepherd and Wozniak (1986)

Figure 9.1   A model for instruction to induce skill transfer

Gaskins and Baron (1986) have specifically applied this type of approach to readers with what they call 'maladaptive cognitive styles' — in other words, to children who are not fully in control of their own learning. They stress the need to bring the processes involved in successful thinking to the conscious awareness of poor readers. Their rationale is built around four factors:

Factors affecting thinking — students need to become aware of their particular learning characteristics and make a commitment to improve them.

Reasons for using strategies — students were told why a strategy was being taught and given examples of its use so as to assist generalization.

Methods of self-direction — students who do not intuitively employ methods of self-direction need direct instruction about how to organize their thinking, including active involvement in, control over, and monitoring of the tasks set them.

Cognitive strategies — these include learning devices, problem solving techniques, hypothesis formation and imaging.

The important point stressed by these researchers is that whenever the focus is on one aspect of these learning strategies, it is essential to lessen the load on other aspects of the task, so that the learner is enabled to concentrate on the particular need. Thus, when general self-regulatory skills are being advanced, the specific skill content must be made very easy. Again, there has to be considerable teacher support in the early stages. But the essence of the strategy — and this needs to be made quite explicit to the student — is that teacher support will be progressively withdrawn as the student learns to carry out the strategies for her/himself. The whole process is about teaching students to be *self-running*. An example of how this is achieved in dialogue work with preschool children is given in Meadows and Cashdan (1988) where we used Marion Blank's (1973) dialogue strategies. These concentrate not just on teaching the children specific knowledge or skills but on reorienting them towards control of their own learning.

How, more precisely, does this approach relate to the teaching of backward readers as advocated by Bryant and Bradley? We would suggest that much of the teaching of reading, particularly in the case of backward readers, is far too teacher-controlled and that this applies especially to skills teaching. In the teacher's anxiety to lessen the load on the child there is a great danger that s/he will not only teach specific skills in isolation from the main task but that the pupil may lose sight in the process (if they ever had it) of the purpose and nature of the whole activity. To quote from a much earlier paper by one of us (Cashdan 1973), 'the letter code can be explained quite explicitly to a five or six year old. He needs (and is entitled) to know that there are twenty-six letters, the functions they have and their relationships in forming words ...'. These and other items of knowledge (and associated skills) are often mistakenly denied to children. They need examples of adult reading models as well as detailed knowledge of what the whole reading activity is about at all its levels.

We are suggesting that the Bryant and Bradley approach is most successful where it offers most explicit help to the child in understanding such things as the letter basis of the alphabet (and their names), the nature of the forty-three (or, in some regional speech, forty-four) phonemes we use in English speech and writing, the nature of alphabetic translation from sound to sight and so on. Similarly with the practice of rhyming, segmentation of words and their synthesis. All combine to develop and enhance the child's understanding of the nature of reading, writing and spelling and of their relationships to each other.

The Litherland Moss project

In the summer of 1988 we decided to mount a small-scale pilot (or pre-pilot) study to see whether we could combine the Bryant and Bradley prescription with the systematic enhancement of backward readers' metacognitive skills. One of us (Wright) was already working with small groups of children at Litherland Moss Primary School in Sefton. She selected two mixed groups of five or six children, eleven in total and worked with each group for on average an hour and a half per week throughout the autumn term of 1988 and into the first term of 1989. The maximum number of sessions for each child was nineteen and there were in fact few absences. The children were all of average intelligence and each was retarded in reading by at least two years by comparison with their chronological ages of 8 to 9. The lessons were held either in a corridor space just outside the children's classroom where they were used to working, or in their 'activity' room.

Initially, the teaching sessions consisted of three distinct phases:

1. Metacognitive aspects of reading (and writing and spelling) were introduced and discussed with the children;
2. a direct teaching model was used to develop the children's understanding and analysis of word structure and the recognition that different words share common sound/letter sequences and spelling patterns. Words were constructed from 'chunks' (e.g. 'and') using alphabetic plastic letters;
3. a brief review of rules/concepts/principles learnt during the session.

After the eighth session we decided that the separation of stages one and two had become artificial and integrated them. All the subsequent sessions involved discussion of metacognitive aspects of written language with application of the direct teaching model at the same time. Verbal rationales were developed together with demonstrations of practical applications. In addition, the children were required to construct their own verbal rationales and to apply these practically through the use of plastic letters and/or in writing words. Additionally, in the final five sessions the children were introduced to bilingual texts in English/Urdu and English/Bengali. The children were all monolingual, but the purpose of introducing the bilingual texts was to extend their ability to generalize by demonstrating the conventional character of English orthography and print direction. Finally, cognitive modelling (see Meichenbaum, 1977) was used in some of the sessions to provide children with self-monitoring/self-regulating strategies when they were confronted with a word they thought they were unable to spell/construct/write. Fuller details of the teaching procedures are available from Wright.

At an intuitive level, we became quite convinced that the sessions were succeeding. Children's motivation was high — they obviously enjoyed the work and their spontaneous comments were often penetrating and illuminating.

Tom was asked to spell happiness and responded as follows:

'You need your chunk *ap* — then you need *h* because *h* is the first sound you say so it's the first letter you find. You need two *p*'s. I first thought it was *y* next, on Friday but it isn't, it's *i*. Then you need *ness*. N-E-S-S.'

A moment later, Tom suddenly called out excitedly: 'Loch — Ness — Monster!'

Discussing why it is that letters function as sounds written down, Josephine said:

'How did we start to write, Miss? How did we know to make lines and to make letters?'

One of the best remarks, when the Babylonian cuneiform was being explained as an example of early writing, again came from Josephine: 'Why — couldn't they speak?'

Finally, when confronted with the bilingual text the children began to attempt to match word and symbol formations of the non-English text with the English text with no prompting from the teacher.

With a short pilot study of this kind, designed essentially to show us whether the method seemed feasible and acceptable to the student, we did not expect significant results on psychometric tests. Nevertheless we thought it worth using them. The children had already been tested in the summer on the NFER *Primary Reading Test* (France, 1981). The school staff obligingly retested them for us after the nineteenth session. They showed small improvements; so did a comparable group of children in the school with whom we had not worked. We also did a 'before and after' test with the Downing *et al.* (1983) *Linguistic Awareness in Reading Readiness (LARR) Test*. Our experimental children showed small improvements in Part One (Recognising Literacy Behaviour) and Part Two (Understanding Literacy Functions). On Part Three (Technical Language of Literacy) their average scores went up from 70 per cent to 90 per cent correct. Part Three tests concepts such as letter, printing, writing, top line, bottom line, word and sentence and Downing and his colleagues suggest that 'such concepts are essential for logical thinking about the skills of reading and writing'. On the other hand, a handful of unselected children who had not been worked with also produced fairly high scores at this point on Downing Part Three.

To be honest, not only were the results of the formal tests inconclusive, but they told us far more about the tests than about the children. For intance, the Norman France reading test is in multiple-choice form and gives no guidance on whether children should be encouraged to guess. In fact, unsystematic guessing will lead on average to a higher score by more than two years of reading age! Again, in the LARR, children who decided that you cannot 'read' a clock or a number attracted much lower scores than those who were willing to extend their mother tongue in this way!

To return to more serious matters, we now feel convinced that children are interested in understanding their own language both in its spoken and written forms, that drawing their attention to the links between sounds, spelling, reading and writing is helpful, and that the Bryant and Bradley programme is essentially well-designed.

Certainly, teacher reaction to our work has been very positive. The children's teachers (they came from three different classes) reported substantial increases in motivation and in school success and Wright is continuing to work with the group and monitoring further developments.

We are clear, however, that we have only focused on *some* aspects of the skill transfer model. We have certainly worked on explicit skill teaching, practice and grading of difficulty of materials. But we have not gone far enough to satisfy ourselves in the area of self-monitoring and of generally freeing the student from the need for the teacher. We also need to do much more on helping students to see what skills they have and how to apply them and, most importantly, to be in charge of their own generalization processes. Generalization of learning is an important issue throughout education, whether in behavioural training, such as we have recently been exploring in language work with severely handicapped children (see Wright and Cashdan, 1988, 1989), or in more open learning situations. We hope to expand our study of backward readers in both scale and depth and to have more to report as it progresses.

In conclusion

We thought — and our pilot work has confirmed this for us — that an extra reason for the success of Bryant and Bradley's programme would prove to be the awareness it creates in pupils of what is involved in learning to read, particularly in terms of the 'translation' of sight to sound and vice versa. We see considerable scope in carrying the process further, in heightening awarenesses and teaching pupils to devise and control their own strategies and exploit their skills for themselves. Essentially, we want to 'democratise' the learning process, handing over more of it to the pupil and retaining less for ourselves as teachers. Such a process will not lessen either the amount or the complexity of the teacher's work. A recent book by Ashman and Conway (1989) explores the foundations in cognitive psychology for what the writers call *process-based instruction*. Their whole thrust is on lines very similar to what we are advocating in this paper. The book is to be highly recommended to all teachers of children with special needs.

Finally, let us return to a point we made at the beginning of this paper. We argued that if children had both skills and the knowledge to deploy these and control them, then attitude problems would not need to be tackled directly. Our experience at Litherland Moss has confirmed this prejudice. The children with whom Wright worked moved from apathy and low self-esteem to hard work and involvement. And while we are not fully able to rule out halo/Hawthorne effects, we have the courage to prophesy that more formal investigation will not refute our present convictions.

References

Ashman, A. F. and Conway, R. N. F. (1989) *Cognitive Strategies for Special Education: Process-based Instruction*, London, Routledge.

Blank, M. (1973) *Teaching Learning in the Preschool: A Dialogue Approach*, Colombus, Ohio, Charles Merrill.

Brown, A. L. and Palincsar, A. S. (1982) 'Inducing strategic learning from texts by means of informed, self-control training', *Topics in Learning and Learning Disabilities*, **2**, pp. 1–17.

Bryant, P. and Bradley, L. (1985) *Children's Reading Problems: Psychology and Education*, Oxford, Basil Blackwell.

Cashdan, A. (1973) 'Reflections on the beginning reading program', *The Reading Teacher*, **26**, pp. 384–388.

Curr, W. and Hallworth, H. J. (1965) 'A empirical study of the concept of retardation', *Educational Review*, **18**, pp. 5–15.

Downing, J., Ayers, D. and Schaefer, B. (1983) *Linguistic Awareness in Reading Readiness (LARR) Test (Administrative Manual)*, Windsor, NFER-Nelson.

France, N. (1981) *The Primary Reading Test (Teacher's Guide)* (Revised Edition), Windsor, NFER-Nelson.

Gaskins, I. W. and Baron, J. (1986) 'Teaching poor readers to cope with maladaptive cognitive styles: a training program', *Journal of Reading Disabilities*, **18**, pp. 390–394.

Gelzheiser L. M., Shepherd, M. J. and Wozniak, R. H. (1986) 'The development of instruction to induce skill transfer', *Exceptional Children*, **53**, pp. 125–129.

Meadows, S. and Cashdan, A. (1988) *Helping Children Learn: Contributions to a Cognitive Curriculum*, London, David Fulton.

Meichenbaum, D. (1977) *Cognitive Behavior Modification: An Integrative Approach*, New York, Plenum Press.

Wagner, R. K. and Torgesen, J. K. (1987) 'The nature of phonological processing and its causal role in the acquisition of reading skills', *Psychological Bulletin*, **101**, pp. 192–212.

Wright, J. and Cashdan, A. (1988) 'Teaching language in the classroom to children with severe learning difficulties: a case study', *Child Language Teaching and Therapy*, **4**, pp. 154–169.

Wright, J. and Cashdan, A. (1989) 'Teaching expressive language to a non-speaking child with Down's syndrome: classroom applications', *Child Language Teaching and Therapy*, **5**, pp. 33–48.

10
Evaluating Teaching Programmes for Children with Specific Learning Difficulties

Michael Thomson

Introduction

While there has been a good deal of recent research into the aetiology of children with specific learning difficulties (dyslexia), very little of this has been related to teaching methodology, or has evaluated specific teaching methods (see Gittleman and Feingold, 1983, for review). This paper addresses the issues of teaching methodology, and its relation to developmental perspectives. Three short studies will be outlined, giving further data in evaluating the progress of samples of children attending a special school for dyslexics. This adds to data already presented (Thomson, 1986, 1988).

Before reviewing aspects of teaching programmes that are typically used for the dyslexic, a review of the problems facing the dyslexic is helpful.

The comments made below present a generalized picture of the dyslexic. Of course, there are individual variations, and some evidence for sub-types of dyslexia (e.g. Boder, 1973: Thomson, 1982; Elliott and Tyler, 1987; Tyler and Elliott, 1988; see also Tyler in Chapter 3 of this volume).

Written language difficulties facing the dyslexic child

A major difficulty facing the dyslexic child is in reading. Such children's reading accuracy will be very poor, often two or more years behind their chronological age. In children who are very intelligent, and those whose reading might be expected to be above their chronological age, the discrepancy between actual and expected reading attainment is particularly marked. The child will be struggling in reading in relation to his or her peer group. As well as poor reading accuracy, dyslexic children often have a slow rate or fluency in reading. Reading is hesitant, uncertain and errors can be made in confusing basic sound/symbol correspondences. Other errors may involve similarity of letter patterns in words e.g. horse for house. Even when dyslexic children have been helped in the basics of phonics, difficulties continue in multi-syllable words and irregular letter combinations. However, the dyslexic's comprehension of the content of text is often better; the problem for the dyslexic is not in understanding, but in de-coding.

Spelling is also retarded in dyslexic children. Children taught to read fluently may still have serious problems in spelling and these are more difficult to remediate. Spelling errors can include so called 'bizarre attempts', e.g. kss/snake, tars/trumpet, as well as basic confusions and omissions of sound, e.g. grid for grind, side for slide and so on. Again, difficulties are often in multi-syllable words as well as in shorter words with irregular spelling patterns. This very weak spelling can often result in a child's written work being undervalued.

As well as spelling affecting written work, the actual writing process itself often presents difficulties for dyslexic children. In many cases this may be because of poor writing style and difficulty in the formation of letters. This could be due to a grapho-motor problem, or lack of confidence in spelling. As well as writing difficulties, dyslexic children have problems in expressing their ideas in written form. This reflects the gap between fluent ideas and poor written expression. In addition, problems are found in organizing ideas and sequencing. Punctuation and paragraph divisions are also weak areas. This will make written work difficult to read for somebody who is not familiar with dyslexic children's productions.

The relationship between written language difficulties and cognitive abilities

Dyslexic children are no more or less intelligent than children who do not have dyslexic difficulties. In other words, one will discover children with dyslexic problems who are below average intelligence, in the average range, or in the above average and gifted range. It is obviously much easier to spot a dyslexic child who is of well above intelligence. There will be a glaring discrepancy between their verbal understanding and their ability to express this in reading and spelling skills. The discrepancy between the child's *expected* and *actual* attainments is often very great. There are some areas in which some intelligence tests do provide some interesting profiles which relate to dyslexic children. For example, dyslexics tend to do less well on items involving information or general knowledge, as we might expect, and also items relating to simple arithmetic skills and those involving speed of writing, coding or aspects of short-term memory (see below). This contrasts with good ability in tests which are more associated with conceptual thinking, such as reasoning, comprehension, and sometimes good three dimensional/spatial skills. There may be high scores in one area and low scores in others. Nevertheless, the important aspect is that low intelligence, *per se*, in dyslexic children is not the major difficulty.

Research on memory and dyslexia indicates that, in the case of long term memory, and in the very brief sensory store, there does not seem to be a major problem amongst dyslexic children, although there may be some difficulty in accessing names correctly (Snowling, 1987; Thomson, 1989). It is in the short-term memory areas that there is evidence of weakness, where dyslexics have difficulties in remembering letter patterns, and basic sound/symbol correspondences. Here the problems appear to be in remembering series, in remembering sounds long enough to blend them together to form words in spelling, or in basic letter patterns for reading. A letter combination taught one day will be forgotten the next day by the child. This can be very frustrating for both the teacher and the child. This short-term memory difficulty shades into another area of weakness — that of being unaware of the sound structure of the written language, particularly in phonological coding. Phonemic awareness, that is the knowledge a person has that a word like 'cat' can be split into three phoneme sound units, viz. (k) (ă) (t), is limited. This phonemic awareness, or knowledge of the sound structure, is an important area of weakness in dyslexics. Another area links phonological coding with short-term memory, in translating visual symbols into their sound equivalents.

Basically, it is argued that there are two ways to read. One is to go directly from the visual input to meaning — this is the way we read if a text is very easy; we are reading fluently, or reading for meaning without any difficulty. An alternative way to read is to read in a so called 'mediated' way. This includes going from the visual symbol through sound coding or memory systems and then accessing meaning. This is when we read aloud, use speech to read, when the text is difficult, or we read something that contains letter patterns where we are actually de-coding as we are reading. This can, of course, be a sub-vocal process. It is here, in this early stage of reading, that research finds difficulties in the dyslexic pupil not only in terms of rhyme but also in terms of translating the visual symbols into sounds and in the short-term memory encoding systems that one needs for reading. This becomes clearer by recourse to a model of the written language process. Figure 10.1 illustrates a model of the reading process. Route A would be the direct route to reading. This links the visual input to the semantic system, followed by immediate spoken response. Route B involves the grapheme-phoneme translation system, as well as the memorial processes involved in phonemic segmentation and blending systems. This is the 'mediated' route.

Teaching programmes

The above generalized picture of the dyslexic child has given rise to a number of accepted 'truths' about the appropriate teaching (Hornsby and Shear, 1974; Hickey, 1977; British Dyslexia Association, 1982; Miles, 1983; Thomson, 1989). The following important principles form a consensus from these and other writers.

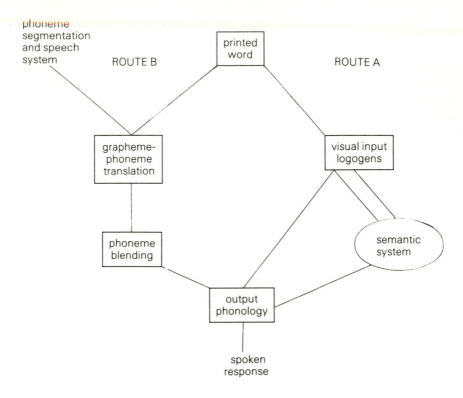

Figure 10.1   Model of written language processing showing 'visual' and 'grapheme-phoneme' routes to reading (after Snowling, 1987)

First principle: phonetic teaching

A major accepted approach is that the teaching should be 'phonetic'. This is rather different to current education fashion, where children are encouraged to read for meaning, as in the 'linguistic' approach. A phonetic approach here implies that one is explicitly teaching the phonology, sound/symbol association, orthography, spelling rules and other aspects of the written language system. This means that one takes specific components and teaches them in a structured fashion. For example, with a child having little reading attainment one starts with basic sound symbol correspondence in the alphabet, moving through into teaching consonant digraphs and blends, particular spelling or letter patterns and on through vowel combinations, suffix rules and the formal reading and spelling structure of English. These structured systems are well documented (see previous authors cited). The major point here is that one is explicitly teaching phonemic awareness, syllabification, and the relationship between sounds and their written equivalents.

The techniques for teaching this written language structure, which is extremely complex, do vary somewhat. Most approaches include sorting words into some form of 'word family'. This can be done aurally, by visual inspection, by using tactile sense or kinesthetic skills, by producing a dictionary or books, or in rhyming or other exercises. The approaches used can be a point of difference between learning centres. Of course, reading for meaning, cloze procedures and developing comprehension skills cannot be ignored; but these seem to be skills that arise out of the teaching of the written language system. We shall be examining later ways in which the teaching and learning of phonetically regular versus irregular words may have implications for theoretical points of view as well as teaching.

Second principle: overlearning

Due to the short-term memory and attentional problems outlined previously, another important element is that there must be some form of 'over-learning'. This implies that the same material should be presented again and again. In addition, a particular letter pattern or sound unit is taught separately and not with others that are similar.

Interference between different sounds can create greater difficulties in memory and organization for the child. Implicit in this notion of over-learning is the assumption that the teachers should recognize that some days dyslexics will perform at a higher level in their written language, whereas on other days they may perform less well. This variation in performance is most marked and requires a good deal of understanding.

Third principle: multi-sensory teaching

A third assumption made in many of the teaching approaches is that teaching should be multi-sensory. It is perceived that dyslexics have a particular weakness in the auditory or phonetic area, against rather better visual skills (although this does not always follow). It is proposed by most researchers and teachers of dyslexic pupils that teaching therefore ought to be multi-sensory. One can teach to the weakness, but one should also circumvent the major problem by presenting written language in alternative forms, namely visual and kinesthetic. The notion of multi-sensory teaching also refers to making links between the sound, the symbol and the written form. This may be using a specific technique, such as 'simultaneous oral spelling', where words are said aloud, spelt individually, the word then repeated, then written down, each letter being said as it is written individually, then read and covered up and spelt again. This reinforces hearing the word, organizing the sounds in it, feeling the structure of the word through the pen and fingers, hearing the sound patterns again, seeing the word on the page, and re-visualizing it. There are modifications of this technique and some teaching approaches are much more directive about how these should operate.

As well as the specific techniques of teaching, it is recommended that teaching be therapeutic. This means accepting the children's errors and difficulties, as briefly outlined above, as well as providing the opportunity for development in areas where the child may achieve success. This implies starting at a level just below current attainments and working up in the written language, but also recognition that the child will have problems in the emotional area in relation to the reaction to his or her learning difficulties. The reader is referred to Thomson and Watkins (in press) for more detail on teaching methods.

Some studies on teaching methods

It would be impossible in a relatively short article to examine all aspects of the teaching programme, but we shall be focusing on a number of specific areas in the ensuing presentation of data.

A previous study examined the development of attainments as one way of evaluating progress (Thomson, 1988). Further data in this area are presented below. In addition, Thomson (*op. cit.*) looked at the spelling of non-words in an attempt to evaluate phonological and orthographic skills appertaining to sound/symbol associations. Non-words can only be read by a phonetic, as opposed to a look-and-say strategy. The development of these skills in groups of children who had received remediation over a two year period was compared to children who had not received remediation. It was found that the non-treatment goup had greater difficulty in using phonological skills to de-code non-words. Those who had received remediation as outlined above had much better phonological skills. However, these skills were still weak when compared to a control group of younger children with similar reading ages.

Thomson (*op. cit.*) also examined the use of simultaneous oral spelling, a multi-sensory technique in the teaching of spelling (see above). This was compared to the visual inspection of words and it was found that the use of a simultaneous oral spelling technique was significantly advantageous.

It was concluded that some cognitive deficits could be overcome in dyslexics; particularly phonological coding, phonemic awareness and alphabetical skills could be helped. However, non-lexical phonological spelling was particularly resistant, whereas lexical, alphabetic skills could be improved considerably. In addition, it was found that help in phonemic awareness and kinesthetic coding can considerably improve spelling. Researchers should take care in their interpretation of data when examining children, as the effects of remediation may affect their data a great deal.

There now follow three studies examining the teaching approaches which have been outlined above. All the children involved have been attending East Court, a school with a modified curriculum specializing in helping dyslexic children. It should be noted that all the children are of at least average intelligence as measured by either the Wechsler Intelligence Scale for Children (WISC) or the British Ability Scales (BAS) (range 105–140). The data will be presented for each study, followed by a general discussion relating to all the studies.

Study 1 — Reading and spelling attainments of children following a remedial programme

This study outlines the results of children's attainments in a general way. The aim here is not to examine one detailed and specific teaching methodology or technique but indicate the levels of improvement that can arrive if one takes into account the teaching principles and approaches outlined previously.

Subjects

All the children who have left East Court up to July 1987 are included in the study — sixty-eight children in total. The chronological age at the time of entry to East Court was taken, along with reading and spelling attainments. These were compared to the chronological and attainment ages at the time of leaving East Court (July of the leaving year). The results are shown in Table 10.1. Achievement ratios were also calculated.

The achievement ratios look at the improvement in attainment against expected improvement in 12 months; thus (12/12) gives an improvement ratio of 1.00. Anything over 1.00 is 'better than expected' improvement and would begin the 'catching up' process in the dyslexic.

Thomson (1986, 1989) presented data from the University of Aston Clinic that dyslexics not given help have improvement ratios in the order of 0.40 in reading (5 months in 12) and 0.27 in spelling (3 months in 12) indicating a relatively worsening retardation.

There are statistical and developmental problems in using achievement ratios. One is that being a year behind in reading at 8 years is a greater retardation than being one year behind at 12 years. Similar improvement ratios may reflect somewhat different degrees of achievement. In addition, children may often develop rapidly, followed by a plateau. However, with these caveats in mind, improvement ratios are presented here particularly as they have the advantage of comparison with a 'control' group of untreated dyslexics.

Results

The results are shown in Table 10.1.

The results show that the children are not only doing better than dyslexics not given help, but are bettering the 'norm', and appearing to be catching up.

In Word Reading, (recognizing individual words), the children are almost up to their age level. In reading from a story (Neale Accuracy) the level is well above everyday competence and nearing the top of the norms for the test. The same applies to reading comprehension, although that is always less of a difficulty for dyslexics — their problem is in general concerned with de-coding, rather than in not understanding what is read.

Table 10.1 Mean Reading and Spelling attainment at entry and on leaving East Court

		Entering East Court	Leaving East Court	Improvement Ratio
Chronological Age		10y 11m	12y 10m	—
	Range	(8.7–11.7)	(11.9–13.6)	
British Ability Scales				
Word Reading Age		8y 9m	12y 3m	1.82
	Range	(6.1–9.11)	(9.2–14.5)	
Neale				
Reading Accuracy Age		8y 10m	11y 6m	1.39
	Range	(6.6–10.0)	(8.10–13.0)	
Neale				
Reading Comprehension Age		9y 8m	12y 0m	1.21
	Range	(6.8–11.2)	(11.1–13.0)	
Vernon				
Spelling Age		8y 0m	11y 0m	1.56
	Range	(6.0–9.2)	(8.2–14.2)	

Study 2 — The development of spelling regular and irregular words in dyslexics

This study focused on some theoretical issues. Many theories of reading and spelling development argue for the development of different stages in the reading and spelling process. For example, it is suggested that the initial stages of reading involve, firstly, looking at visual features and secondly, a visual–verbal paired associated learning. In spelling Ehri (1985) describes early processes as 'semi-phonetic', followed by the development of segmentation and phonemic awareness and finally the orthographic or morphemic approaches.

Frith (1985) proposed a more formal theory. In it, written language skills develop through logographic, alphabetic and orthographic stages. The logographic stage is essentially visual processing. Alphabetic skills require understanding the relationship between sound and symbols, as well as segmentation/phonological de-coding skills whereas the orthographic stage requires abstract representation of the printed word. She proposes that dyslexics fail to deal with the alphabetic stage. Ehri (*op. cit.*) describes this stage as recognition of spelling units. A summary of this work is also provided by Snowling in Chapter 8 of this volume.

The relevance of regular versus irregular word spelling and reading is that it is proposed that regular words may be read via two alternative routes (see Figure 10.1). The first is a direct 'look and say' approach and the second is by the application of grapheme to phoneme rules i.e. alphabetic skills. However, irregular words cannot be read by application of grapheme/phoneme rules and are read by the direct or visual route and would reflect the development of sight vocabulary. It has been found that dyslexics had difficulties in the phonological area, and the major development in written language skills seemed largely to be due to the development of sight vocabulary (Snowling, 1980).

As far as spelling is concerned, Ellis (1982) lists two contrasting routes in spelling. If the word is familiar, there is an automatic graphemic output. This is a direct spelling where the individual phoneme segmentation of a word is not necessarily required. The second, requires a phonemic buffer, that is a memory system which will hold sounds that are then passed through a phoneme to grapheme translation or alphabetic skills conversion route before they are spelt. This route is used in spelling unfamiliar words and also in non-word spelling.

Thomson (1988) found partial support for the notion that dyslexics have failed to reach the alphabetic stage in their written language skills. However, it was found that dyslexics did not meet predictions in respect of reading regular and irregular words. Both treatment and non-treatment dyslexics showed an advantage in favour of regular word reading. The prediction here was that, if dyslexics are failing to acquire alphabetical skills, there should be little difference in their reading of regular and irregular words, both would be read equally poorly or well. This is because the children will not have access to the grapheme-phoneme conversion skills required to read regular words and therefore will have to apply 'look and say' or immediate visual recognition skills to read them. The same would apply in spelling, except they would not have the so-called indirect skills of compiling spelling using phonology and phoneme to grapheme conversion skills.

It was decided to examine this issue in more detail, using both reading and spelling, and to employ a developmental strategy rather than using treatment versus non-treatment groups. This is because the effect of learning to read or spell may affect the strategies which children use. Examining the results of developing reading and spelling age enables an investigation of this issue (see also Chapter 7 by Cataldo and Ellis).

Subjects

Fifty-eight children attending East Court School for Dyslexic Children, age range 8 years to 13 years.

Method

All the children were given regular and irregular words to read and spell. The complete list may be obtained from the author. The regular words included one syllable words such as 'Ash, Blot, Swim' and two syllable words such as 'Bagpipe, Unjust, Punish'. Irregular words included one syllable words such as 'Ache, Said, They' and two syllable words such as 'Trouble, Answer, Sugar'. Familiarity was controlled by taking the words from current reading schemes used by the children. The children were divided into groups based on their reading and spelling ages. These attainment ages, ranged from 6 years through to 12 years.

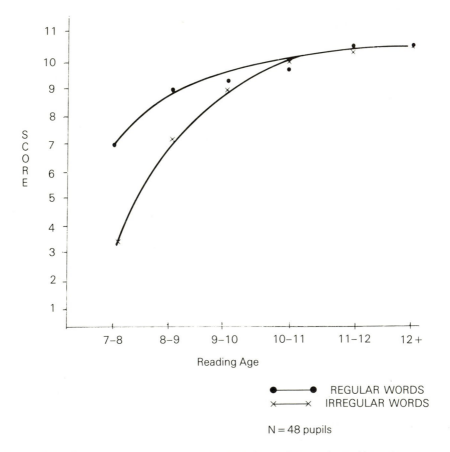

Figure 10.2 Graph of reading age against scores for reading regular and irregular words

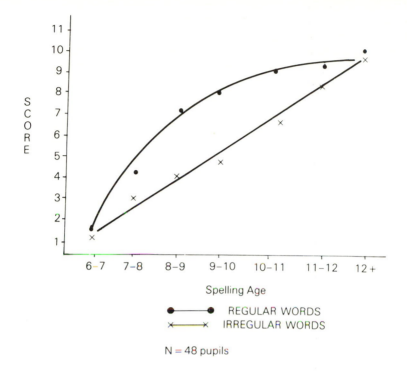

S
C
O
R
E

6-7   7-8   8-9   9-10   10-11   11-12   12+

Spelling Age

●————● REGULAR WORDS
×————× IRREGULAR WORDS

N = 48 pupils

Figure 10.3 Graph of spelling age against scores for spelling regular and irregular words

Figures 10.2 and 10.3 show the results of the childrens' reading and spelling performance in reading and spelling regular and irregular words. In reading the children are better at regular words at the lower reading ages, but then performance on regular and irregular becomes similar, until a ceiling is reached. In spelling, performance starts off at a similar level then diverges until a ceiling level is reached. The results show the effects of acquiring these reading and spelling skills through attainment ages. The issue is discussed later in more detail.

Study 3 — Syllabification skills

A number of researchers have shown that dyslexics have difficulties with phonological structure and segmentation of words in reading and spelling. For example Snowling (1987) found that dyslexics have particular difficulty with two syllable words and in relating phonological sequences and letter sound correspondences in multi-syllabic words. Thomson (1988) found that although treatment groups scored higher than non-treatment groups in their ability to spell multi-syllable words, both groups showed a clear syllable length effect.

They spelt less well as the number of syllables in the words increased. This weak performance with multi-syllable words related to the retention of phoneme sequences in short-term memory or in phonological re-coding skills. Phoneme segmentation is therefore a well established difficulty for dyslexics and clinical observations confirm this.

The aim of this study was to examine a technique of teaching of syllables to see whether this had any effect on the dyslexics' ability to read and spell words of more than one syllable.

Subjects

Twenty children — Mean CA 9 years 4 months; mean BAS Word Reading Age 7 years 1 month; mean Vernon Graded Word Spelling Age 6 years 9 months. The children were divided randomly into 'control' and 'experimental' groups.

Method

All the children were given regular one, two and three syllable words to spell, e.g. 'fresh, grin, spade, inside, nutmeg, lemonade, astonish'. Ten words from each category were given as a pre-test, and the same test given after a training period of two weeks. The words were taken from current reading schemes used by the children. The procedure for the training was to teach by 'syllable analysis'. This involves teaching the children that words in English can be divided into six basic syllable types. Children are encouraged to tap out words into their beats or units, and to recognize how many beats there are in a given word. They are then taught how to divide the words up into syllables and to assign them to one of the above six categories of classification. Particular attention is paid to the pronounciation of vowels and consequent syllable units. The syllables can be grouped as open, closed, vowel consonant 'e', vowel digraph, consonant 'le', and 'r' combination syllables.

At the early stages the first three categories, open, closed and vowel consonant 'e' (VCE) syllables are taught and it is these that the study focused on. An 'open' syllable is where the vowel is not 'shut in' by any consonants, and is open at the end of the syllable. The vowel is usually long, or says its own name. 'Me', 'no' and 'I' are all open syllables. The 'o' in open, the 'la' in lady, the 'du' in duet are all open syllables. A closed syllable is where one or more consonants 'shuts in' the vowel. Here the vowel is usually short or says its sound. 'In', 'must', and 'bin' are all closed syllables, as is 'pen' in open, or the 'et' in duet. A VCE syllable is the so called magic 'e' pattern, where the vowel is made to say its name by adding an 'e'. 'Made' and 'ice', are VCE syllables. The 'side' in inside, the 'pipe' in bagpipe are also VCE syllables. To analyze the syllables, the children are required to mark in the syllable divisions and to write over the top the particular syllable category. Thus open becomes o'pen, duet becomes du'et, lemonade becomes lem'on'ade, and lady becomes la'dy, (here the 'y' is acting as a vowel).

In the study children were given words on 'flash cards' and on the board to

Table 10.2 Mean Scores for spelling multi-syllable words by a training group taught syllable analysis and a control group

Syllable length	Training Group (n = 10)		Controls (n = 10)	
	Pre-test	Post-test	Pre-test	Post-test
		(Maximum Score = 10)		
1.	8.8	9.1	9.1	8.9
2.	6.2	8.7*	5.9	6.3
3.	2.9	6.8**	3.2	2.8

*   difference between pre and post significant at $p < 05$
** difference between pre and post significant at $p < 01$
    other differences n.s.

look at. The children were taught how to beat out the sounds in the words into their syllable components, and how to recognize the component syllable classifications by analyzing the words into their syllable types, and then writing them down. This was done by comparing possible pronunciations to real words, and feeling for the downward movement of the chin, as reflecting a syllable. It was also stressed that each syllable, in English, must have a vowel. Children were taught to decide if the vowel in the syllable was long or short, and then to analyze the syllable into its sub-type.

The control group were given the same words but asked to look at them and then simply copy them and read them, (with prompting if necessary), as opposed to writing them down in syllable types and reading that.

Table 10.2 shows the result of the tests before and after the two weeks training period.

The results show that both groups are more or less at the ceiling level for one syllable words, but that the syllable analysis training significantly helped the treatment group for two and three syllable words.

Discussion

The results in general show that it is possible to improve the dyslexics' written language skills in various areas by particular teaching programmes. The general attainment studies reflect the generalized programme. In all cases the children have made a great deal of progress in their written language and are almost certainly better off than would have been the case if they had been left without any form of remedial help. It should be noted that children's attainments are not, as a group, up to their chronological age level. Individual word reading skills are almost at age expected levels, but reading from text, as far as inaccuracies are concerned, is not up to age level. This is because children tend to read for meaning, understandably, as they have been encouraged to do this and can make a few errors and mispronunciations. These, of course, count as errors on the Neale Analysis of Reading Ability. It is also noticeable that spelling remains quite a major difficulty. Spelling problems often remain with the dyslexic throughout his or her life. The aim of teaching is to help them achieve a level of reasonable everyday competence so that their written language can be read and accepted as a fair representation of the ideas being presented.

It should also be pointed out that these are mean scores. Some children had reading and spelling ages well in excess of their chronological age and others who have not made as much progress as one would have hoped will still be rather retarded in their reading (see ranges in Table 10.1). In general, of about twenty children leaving East Court School every year, around one or two remain severely handicapped. Of course, this will pull down means reported in the tables. These particular children do not appear to have any common patterns to their difficulties, although they are profound.

Such general attainment results do not indicate what particular aspect of the teaching programme is important, merely that attending a particular school has some beneficial effects on attainments and progress in reading and spelling. Teachers can be convinced of the efficacy of a teaching programme but there may be no direct evidence for this. This is the aim of these more specific developmental studies.

Study 2, the development of regular and irregular word readings gives us further information in relation to particular mechanisms that may be in operation. There is some, but not unequivocal, support for Frith's notion that dyslexic children have problems with the alphabetic or phonological stage in the written language process. One source of evidence for this, it will be recalled, is that reading regular and irregular words might be at the same level in the dyslexic due to the lack of alphabetic skills. As far as reading is concerned, dyslexics do show a regularity effect. Their ability to read regular words was much better that their ability to read irregular words, at the lower reading ages. This suggests that they have some sound/symbol correspondence or alphabetic skills and are not still at the logographic stage as hypothesized by Frith. Perhaps the reason that irregular words are read less well is that in the early stages of reading the words are less familiar and, because a basic phonic skill has been acquired, children will tend to regularize irregular words. Typical errors show attempts at regularization, as well as guesses from one or two letters. As far as regular word errors are concerned, these seem mainly to occur due to incomplete grapheme to phoneme translation and consequent guesses as to what the word might be.

The 'growth' curve of the reading skills, shown in Figure 10.2 is also of interest. There is obviously a ceiling effect. As children's reading ages increased, they were able to read all the regular and irregular words quite accurately. This does not imply that they are losing alphabetical skills but merely that both sets of words are well within their normal capabilities! The shape of the curve matches quite closely the typical developmental curves that are shown for many abilities. In particular the rapid increase in early stages followed by a plateau is very similar to the growth in ability found in the Word Reading Scale of the British Ability Scales (Elliott *et al.*, 1983). This seems to suggest an early 'take off' at around the reading age of 8 to 9 years. This is matched by one's teaching experience where children suddenly seem to make sense of aspects of reading. What is clear here, possibly due to developmental factors or the emphasis on phonic skills at the school, is that irregular words show a similar development in their reading growth, but at a rather later stage. This suggests that the demands involved in reading regular and irregular words differ. Further work looking at control groups matched on reading and spelling ages would tease out whether these are features to be found in 'normal' children or are specific to dyslexics.

The spelling data show rather more support for Frith's position. It is noted that at the earlier levels of spelling, in terms of spelling age, spelling regular and irregular words is very similar. The children seem equally poor at regular and irregular words, there being no regularity effect here. The regular words then develop very rapidly, showing a similar growth curve to reading. Irregular word spelling progresses more slowly and makes a less dramatic jump. This matches one's teaching observation. The phonic skills can be improved greatly by appropriate teaching and this can lead to a sudden leap in performance in spelling regular words, be they one syllable, as in the early stages or multi-syllable, as in later stages. While some irregular words may be *read* quite early on by dyslexics, spelling of irregular words is the most difficult to remediate and is very often delayed.

Again, in the data presented in spelling, a ceiling effect comes in to play — the meeting of the performance at the top end of the spelling ages reflects that the particular words used are well within the capability of the children. Spelling errors at the early stages, in both irregular and regular word spelling, tend to show rather bizarre attempts as quoted in the literature (see Miles, 1983; Thomson, 1989). This indicates that there is a very little appreciation of the relationship between the sound and the symbol by the pupil. It is evidence of very weak alphabetic skills. In most cases these appear to be approximations to the sound, or application of inappropriate phonology. Later on during their performance one begins to see 'regularization' errors in irregular words as shown in the children's reading. This implies that the children are applying regular sound/symbol correspondence rules in their spelling, which is understandable.

The results of Study 3 are fairly clear cut. The particular approach to teaching syllables, by specific syllable analysis, significantly improves the performance of the treatment or training group. Whether this performance is stable over time is a moot point. Dyslexics' attainments characteristically are formed by spurts, plateaus and variations and it is difficult to make firm predictions. However, over the time tested and with the particular kinds of words used, syllable analysis does seem a helpful teaching method. This is not to imply that one is necessarily overcoming the basic segmentation and phonemic difficulties that may underlie the problems in multi-syllable spelling.

Here one is providing an alternative strategy to circumvent the difficulties dyslexics have.

The attainment data indicate that it is possible to remediate, very successfully, basic word reading, aspects of text reading and certainly reading comprehension difficulties. However, spelling is more resistant and requires continued remediation.

It also appears that a reading age of around 7 and a spelling age of around 6 are the most appropriate times to focus a major effort on the development of phonological skills and the acquisition or regular written language components at least. The notion that early identification and help is important is perhaps obvious but these data certainly underline this fact. They also indicate that there are many cases of older children (12 years and young teenagers) who are still reading and spelling at around the 7/8 year level and have not yet made this breakthrough. Therefore, one should be focusing on, or continuing the effort on phonological skills at this stage, as there may well be a very rapid gain in reading and spelling performance once the 'alphabetic barrier' has been breached. This emphasis on phonic skills is counter to current educational fashion. Perhaps the data presented here underline the importance of the 'bottom-up' approach to teaching the dyslexic.

It appears that the irregularities of our English Language system are somewhat more difficult to help, as reading and spelling irregular words are more delayed amongst the children in these studies. There does not appear to be a sudden insight into the spelling of irregular words by dyslexic pupils. Their progress will probably be long and slow. This matches one's clinical experience in attainment testing. Most spelling attainment tests start with regular simple words and then progress to rather more difficult irregular words. The final levels of spelling tests are often quite long multi-syllable words but are often amenable to pupils' understanding the regularities of sound/symbol correspondance, e.g. refrigerator or aggressive. Our experience has been that one gets a very quick 'take-off' in spelling age, then a plateau, followed by another 'take-off' once poly-syllabic skills are mastered.

Returning to the syllable work itself, it is clear that one particular technique of syllable teaching can help at least at the level of assessment that was reported. The teaching strategy may not be familiar to many teachers, but is well worth some study.

Conclusions

Curriculum and remedial teaching programmes based on those principles recommended by many authorities as helping dyslexic children can indeed help children with specific learning difficulties. Their progress and attainments can be boosted to compensate for the increased delay that otherwise besets dyslexic children as they get older. The gap that can widen between attainment and chronological age can be narrowed. Although spelling is more resistant, a good deal of progress can be made here also.

The present article suggests that there appears to be an 'alphabetic barrier' in the reading and spelling of *regular* words which can be overcome at around the 8 year reading age level. This seems to provide a platform for a relative 'take off' in aspects of written language learning. However, dyslexic children's problems in reading and spelling *irregular* words are much more difficult to remediate, progress being delayed somewhat in reading but showing a similar pattern to regular words. However, in spelling the break through of the 'alphabetic barrier', does not appear to speed up the slow development of the irregular word skills.

One specific technique, that of syllable analysis using the categorization of syllables based on the vowel sounds, can considerably help the spelling of regular words of two and three syllables. This seems to circumvent some of the dyslexics' problems in phonemic awareness and phonemic segmentation.

References

Boder, E. (1973) 'Developmental dyslexia: a diagnostic approach based on three atypical reading-spelling patterns' *Developmental Medicine and Child Neurology*, 15, pp. 663–667.

British Dyslexia Association (1982) *Booklets on Dyslexia*, Reading, BDA.

Ehri, L. C. (1985) 'Sources of difficulty in learning to spell and read', in Woolraich, M. L. and Routh, D. (Eds) *Advances in Developmental and Behavioural Paediatrics*, Greenwich, Conn. Jai Press.

Elliott, C. D., Murray, D. J. and Pearson, L. S. (1983) *The British Ability Scales*, Windsor, NFER-Nelson.

Elliott, C. D. and Tyler, S. (1987) 'Learning disabilities and intelligence test results: a principal components analysis of the British Ability Scales', *British Journal of Psychology*, 78, pp. 325–333.

Ellis, A. (1982) 'Spelling and writing (and reading and speaking)', in Ellis, A. W. (Ed) *Normality and Pathology in Cognitive Functions*, London, Academic Press.

Frith, U. (1985) 'Beneath the surface of developmental dyslexia', in Marshall, J. C., Patterson, K. E. and Coltheart, M. (Eds) *Surface Dyslexia in Adults and Children*, London, Routledge and Kegan Paul.

Gittleman, R. and Feingold, I. (1983) 'Children with reading disorders 1. Efficacy of reading remediation', *Journal of Child Psychology and Psychiatry*, 24, pp. 169–193.

Hickey, K. (1977) *The Dyslexia Teaching Programme*, Staines, Dyslexia Institute.

Hornsby, B. and Shear, F. (1974) *Alpha to Omega*, London, Heineman.

Miles, T. (1983) *Dyslexia: The Pattern of Difficulties*, London, Granada.

Snowling, M. J. (1980) 'The development of grapheme-phoneme correspondences in normal and dyslexic readers', *Journal of Experimental Child Psychology*, 29, pp. 294–305.

Snowling, M. J. (1987) *Dyslexia: A Cognitive Developmental Perspective*, Oxford, Blackwell.

Thomson, M. E. (1982) 'The assessment of children with specific reading difficulties (dyslexia) using the British Ability Scales', *British Journal of Psychology*, 73, pp. 461–478.

Thomson, M. E. (1986) *Attainment Follow Up Studies*. Unpublished papers. Ramsgate, East Court School.

Thomson, M. E. (1988) 'Preliminary findings concerning the effects of specialised teaching on dyslexic children', *Applied Cognitive Psychology*, 2, pp. 19–31.

Thomson, M. E. (1989) *Developmental Dyslexia: Its Nature, Assessment and Remediation*, London, Cole and Whurr.

Thomson, M. E. and Watkins, E. J. (in press) *Teaching the Dyslexic Child*, London, Whurr.

Tyler, S. and Elliott, C. D. (1988) 'Cognitive profiles of poor readers and dyslexic children on the British Ability Scales', *British Journal of Psychology*, 79, pp. 493–508.

11
Some Effects of a Dyslexia Centred Teaching Programme

Beve Hornsby and Maria Farrer

Over the last few decades, the teaching of children with dyslexia has become increasingly sophisticated. This is partly as a result of advances in theoretical formulations of dyslexia (Miles, 1978; Ellis and Miles, 1981; Miles and Ellis, 1981) and partly to the advances in teaching practice. It is still widely accepted that the most effective method of teaching these children is the multisensory approach (e.g. Hornsby and Shear, 1980; Miles, 1981; Miles and Miles, 1975; Hickey, 1977) and that this must be 'structured, sequential, cumulative and thorough' (Rawson, 1970). The multisensory methods have had their critics (Johnson and Mycklebust, 1967; Kirk and Kirk, 1971) who suggest that it is rather like throwing everything at a child in the hope that something will get through. However, if one considers the nature of written language skills there can be no doubt that they are multisensory. Combine this consideration with the fact that, in most children who are failing at these skills, one finds a pattern of strengths and weaknesses in the different sensory modalities, it would seem common sense to use a multisensory method in order to work through strengths and remediate weaknesses.

Hornsby and Miles (1980) set out to investigate the efficacy of such methods (described as a dyslexia centred teaching programme) with a group of 107 children who had been diagnosed as dyslexic. These children were taught at three centres. At centre A (a hospital clinic) the book that formed the basis of the teaching was Hornsby and Shear (1974). At centre B (a university centre) a syllabus was used which involved extensions and adaptations of Miles (1970) and Miles and Miles (1975), while at Centre C (a private centre) the teaching was based primarily on Hickey (1977). Also in use were the Gill Cotterill Checklist and the Edith Norrie Letter Case. The pioneer work of Gillingham and Stillman (latest edition 1969) has, of course, had considerable influence on the teaching of dyslexic children in many parts of the world. (For a recent survey of dyslexia centred methods see Naidoo, 1988.)

The Study

Method

Although the methods used in the study were all slightly different, they shared a common basis. They were all multisensory and were all structured, sequential, cumulative and thorough. It is also important to emphasize that the training given involved not simply remedial reading but a whole range of language skills of a more diverse kind, tailor-made to the child's individual needs.

A *structured* programme is one which has a specific organization: the different parts cohere and contribute to a planned whole. *Sequential* teaching means that there is a progressive disclosure by the teacher of the correspondence between sounds and letters (or groups of letters) of the English spelling system. Teaching is *cumulative* in the sense that each stage follows from what went before and cannot be studied in isolation. Furthermore, each stage in the programme must be fully understood before the pupil passes on to the next one i.e. the teaching must be *thorough*.

Whilst it is essential that studies of this nature are carried out, it is necessary to digress for a moment to discuss procedural difficulties. The major difficulty, both from a practical and ethical point of view, was that of obtaining a matched control group of untreated pupils. Firstly, one of the selection criteria for this study was that the child had to be diagnosed as dyslexic. The mere fact of diagnosis inevitably changes the climate for all the children so that the control group can no longer be considered as untreated. Not only will it change the attitude of parent, child and school to his or her problems but it is unlikely, given the diagnosis, that no specialist help will be sought; and this could not be monitored.

In addition one must consider the very real difficulties of the teaching situation: for example, teacher-pupil relationship, motivation of pupil, motivation of teacher and duration of lessons. Some of these difficulties will be highlighted when we come to look at the follow-up study.

It was decided, therefore, to use each child as his own control by comparing the rate of gain in both reading and spelling before teaching began with the rate of gain following a period of dyslexia centred teaching.

Before enlarging on this, it is worth pointing out some weaknesses in using rate of gain as a measure. Perhaps the most important of these is that it takes no account of the correlation between reading performance and intelligence. There is also the problem that a rate of gain of one year in reading between the ages of 5 and 6 is not equivalent to a rate of gain of one year in reading between the ages of, say, 9 and 10. With these considerations in mind, an alternative method that might have been used is a statistical procedure known as regression which allows a prediction of expected reading age according to both chronological age and intelligence, or any other pertinent variables. However, at the time of this experiment, the rate of gain measure was considered by the researchers to be the most useful and workable measure in the clinical situation. Rate of gain is calculated by assuming that a child's formal education begins at the age of 5 years. This assumption is mirrored in the standard tests of reading and spelling, many of which begin at the base level of 5 years. It is thereby possible to calculate a child's reading and spelling gain as from the age of 5 years by looking at the difference between his tested reading and spelling scores at the beginning of treatment and his expected reading and spelling scores given his chronological age. Thus if a child on being tested before teaching was aged 10 years 3 months and had a reading age of 6 years 9 months, his reading gain would be only 1 year 9 months (21 months) in 5 years 3 months (63 months) of formal education. The rate of reading gain during this period would be 21/63 or 0.33. A rate of gain of more than unity indicates that the child was 'keeping up with the chronological clock'. Rate of spelling gain was calculated in the same way. In the case of both reading and spelling the difference between during teaching rate of gain and pre-teaching rate of gain is taken to be an indication of the effectiveness of the teaching. The null hypothesis ('that teaching is ineffective') predicts no difference between the two.

Tests of reading and spelling had been given at all three centres, in most cases the Neale Analysis of Reading Ability (accuracy score), the Schonell R1 Graded Word Reading Test and Schonell S Spelling Test. To ensure a standardized procedure, only those children were included whose IQ had been assessed as ninety-five or more and whose spelling age was less than 80 per cent of their chronological age.

It is necessary to make it absolutely clear that this was an unbiased sample of dyslexic children and all children treated during the research period were included in the analyses regardless of success or failure.

Results

The results of the dyslexia centred teaching programme are summarized in Table 11.1.

From the results it was possible to compare before-teaching rate of gain and during-teaching rate of gain. This was done by subtracting the 'reading before' gain (RB) from the 'reading during' gain (RD): (RD − RB). The rate of gain for spelling was calculated in the same way (SD − SB). See Table 11.2.

The basic facts speak for themselves. The null hypothesis ('that teaching is ineffective') was refuted in the case of both reading and spelling at a level of confidence which leaves no room for doubt in the authors' opinions.

Reading gains in the during-teaching period averaged 1.91 years per year and spelling gains 1.94 years per year, compared with averages in the pre-teaching period of 0.53 and 0.32 respectively. Put more simply, none of the 107 children had 'kept up with the clock' for spelling before the onset of the dyslexia centred teaching programme and only two of the 107 children had 'kept up with the clock' for reading. During the programme, 91 of the 107

Table 11.1   Basic Data

	Mean	SD	No. of children
Age at start of teaching (months)	127.39	25.08	107
Time between 1st and 2nd testing (months)	17.50	12.42	107
Duration of teaching (months)	20.29	9.61	107
Reading age at start of teaching (months)	94.66	16.69	107
Spelling age at start of teaching (months)	82.08	14.46	107
Reading age gain during teaching (months)	27.68	16.24	107
Spelling age gain during teaching (months)	27.67	14.96	107
Reading age rate of gain before teaching (years per year) (RB)	0.53	0.19	107
Spelling age rate of gain before teaching (years per year) (SB)	0.32	0.18	107
Reading age rate of gain during teaching (years per year) (RD)	1.91	1.11	107
Spelling age rate of gain during teaching (years per year) (SD)	1.94	1.07	107

Table 11.2   Comparison of before-teaching rates of gain and during-teaching rates of gain

	Mean	SD
Reading (RD–RB)	1.38	1.10 (t = 12.8, df 101, P < 0.001)
Spelling (SD–SB)	1.62	1.10 (t = 15.0, df 106, P < 0.001)

children had gains of more than unity (i.e. had more than kept up with the clock) in both reading and spelling.

Discussion of Results

It is sometimes said that any teaching method will work provided the teacher can study the child's individual needs, is kind to him and gives him confidence. But is one to assume that before the child was given dyslexia centred teaching no one else tried to study his needs, was kind to him, or tried to give him confidence? At Centre A (which forms the basis of the follow-up study) all the children in the sample had already received remedial help in school before they came to the clinic and had been seen by the LEA educational psychologist regarding either reading failure or behaviour problems. Moreover, since assessment at Centre A was possible only if referral was made through a doctor, one must assume that the problem seemed to the parents to be sufficiently pressing to justify the seeking of help through medical channels which scarcely reflects confidence in what was being done educationally. Although at all three centres the 'remedial help in school' may have varied in quality and extent between one child and another, it is hard to believe that total indifference was the norm. Indeed, the experience of the authors suggests that the conscientious class teacher is often bewildered by the dyslexic child and does not know what his needs are or how to begin the task of giving him confidence. In these circumstances kindness does not go far and if one tells a child that he *ought* to have more confidence in himself without, at the same time, showing him how to achieve success, one is merely adding to his difficulties by adverse criticism. It is important, of course, not to underestimate the influence of the so-called Hawthorne effect (see, e.g. Sprott, 1952, pp. 234–237) i.e. the improvement in performance resulting from some intervention, regardless of the nature of that intervention. But most of these children had come from a caring environment: their families were willing actively to seek help because their own efforts had not helped their child's reading or spelling. In these conditions it is hard to believe that the Hawthorne effect on its own was the decisive factor. On the contrary, the most likely explanation of the results is the straightforward one, viz., that the reading and spelling of dyslexic children can be improved if the right kind of teaching programme is used.

The data do not, of course, establish that no other programme would have been successful, but the onus now rests with those whose programmes are different and/or not dyslexia centred to demonstrate their effectiveness.

Evidence from this initial study certainly showed that children with seemingly obstinate reading and spelling problems could be helped. It seemed an interesting proposition to do a follow-up study to look at the way in which these results translated into the real-life situation; what happens to dyslexic children later? (Hornsby, Farrer and Tylor, 1988) Did they feel they had benefited from knowing that they were 'dyslexic'? Did they find special tuition helpful and did their academic achievements live up to their expectations? Finally, how has being 'dyslexic' affected their employment?

A follow-up of young dyslexic adults

To this end, a sample group of fifty subjects was questioned, all of whom had been seen at the hospital clinic between the years of 1970 and 1980. Similar criteria were adopted as were used in the earlier study. All the subjects had to have been diagnosed as dyslexic and have an IQ of ninety-five or above. The major difference is that the sample was random and therefore included any subjects regardless of their age when they came to the clinic. Some interesting results emerged.

One of the most important facts that arose from the study was that relating to the value of diagnosis. Every subject said that they found diagnosis useful and comments suggested that the value was not only in practical terms but also emotional. From the practical angle, the value of diagnosis was that it led to specialist help being sought and that concessions could be obtained for examinations. As one subject commented,

> I was given a letter from the clinic certifying that I was dyslexic. This was offered to my 'O' level board. I don't know what difference this made but it certainly gave me confidence.

Indeed, the problem of confidence is one that cropped up repeatedly in answers in terms of the emotional difficulties associated with dyslexia. The following comments help to illustrate the importance and value of diagnosis:

> My son was not diagnosed until he was 12 years old. By this time the feeling of inadequacy had set in and he had no confidence.

> I was so frustrated at being called a dunce. (The) diagnosis and help opened up a new world that I could not otherwise have entered.

> Rather than thinking I was just a bad speller, it gave me an understanding of why I couldn't spell.

It would seem that the value of diagnosis cannot be underestimated but, even more important, it is crucial that this diagnosis is made as early as possible. However, one has to be aware of the fact that the earlier a 'diagnosis' is made, the greater is the possibility of identifying either false positives or false negatives, i.e. falsely diagnosing or not diagnosing a child as dyslexic.

Following diagnosis, all the subjects went on to receive dyslexia centred teaching. This was not necessarily at the clinic and so precise details of remediation are not available. As mentioned in the earlier study, it is impossible to control for all the extrinsic factors associated with the method of teaching, such as motivation, teacher-pupil relationship. Nevertheless, thirty-three of the fifty subjects said they found the teaching very helpful, sixteen found it fairly helpful and one subject did not find it helpful at all. The following are a selection of positive and negative comments:

> The help has given me confidence to work with and around my dyslexia.

> I found that although some of the help was very useful, all the hundreds of different rules of spelling were almost as hard to remember as the words themselves.

> He remains virtually illiterate despite an IQ in the bright average range. He progressed best while receiving weekly private lessons with one teacher but slowed considerably when allocated a different teacher.

> I found it of enormous help as specialist teaching was geared to *all* subjects, not just English.

There must be some interesting lessons to be learned from these comments in terms of the specific needs of each student. Dyslexia centred teaching tends to take place in a one-to-one or small group situation and this has both advantages and disadvantages. It means that the teacher has the opportunity to tailor-make the lesson for one specific pupil so that the pupil should obtain maximum advantage. However, the nature of the situation means that there is a great deal of pressure on the teacher-pupil relationship so that if rapport deteriorates, or never develops in the first place, the teaching will suffer as will the confidence and motivation of teacher and pupil.

Two further comments warrant special consideration:

The help received was not adequate as in forty minutes a week not much can be achieved.

Specialist tuition did not help me because two hours a week isn't hardly enough.

Here we see one of the major pitfalls that may be encountered in this kind of teaching. So often it is a matter of 'fitting it in' amongst all the other demands made on a child's time e.g. school, homework and leisure. This, of course, is far from ideal and may result in the child receiving only one session per week of maybe one hour. If this constituted the entire intervention programme, it would be unlikely to succeed. It is for this reason that the dyslexia centred teaching programmes place a great deal of emphasis on parental guidance, involvement and intervention. It is only in this way that continuity of learning can be maintained.

It is possible that, for a number of reasons, parental co-operation is highly variable in both quantity and quality and cannot be relied upon in every teaching situation. However, evidence from Hannon, Jackson and Weinberger (1986) suggested that parents' performance in hearing their children reading was in many ways similar to the teachers' performance and there was little to suggest that parental performance was adequate. Furthermore, it has been found that, given encouragement, specific suggestions for helping children with reading, and collaboration between parents and teachers, parental co-operation was very positive (Hannon, 1987).

It may be hoped that the interest and enthusiasm now being shown by many mainstream primary and secondary teachers will help with the continuity and carry-over into the school situation. Carry-over into the *school* situation is another problem with individual dyslexia centred teaching. In order to get some idea of how the dyslexic subjects fared in the school situation, we looked at their academic achievements in terms of public examination results. Table 11.3 shows the number of subjects passing a given number of exams.

At first glance the figures for the number of subjects who did not pass any examination in the various categories seems alarmingly high. However these figures include pupils who presumably did not even attempt those examinations. For example, most children whose work was considered to be of

Table 11.3 Number of passes achieved by subjects in public examinations

No. of passes achieved	No. of subjects gaining		
	CSE	'O' Level	'A' Level
0	23	23	33
1	3	2	4
2	5	1	6
3	3	4	7
4	3	1	—
5	1	4	—
6	4	5	—
7	4	4	—
8	2	2	—
9	—	3	—
10	—	1	—

an 'O' level standard would not have bothered to take CSE and *vice versa*. (This distinction will no longer be applicable with the advent of the GCSE examination.) To illustrate this point more clearly, the average number of 'O' levels passes per subject across the whole group was 3.02 per person. However, this includes those subjects who did not actually sit the exams. A second average can therefore be calculated for those subjects who passed one or more 'O' levels. This adjusted average comes out at 5.59.

It is difficult to make a direct comparison between the dyslexic group averages and the national averages (DES 1986) as the DES figures are calculated over a given year and the subjects in this study took their exams over a time span of nearly ten years. Bearing this in mind, it was felt that the comparison may be of interest (see Table 11.4)

Table 11.4 Number of examinations passed: National Average vs. Dyslexic Group Average

	Overall National Average	Overall Dyslexic Group Average	N	National Average for those attempted exam	Dyslexic Group Average for those who attempted exam	N
'O' Level	0.25	3.02	50	3.21	5.59	27
'A' Level	0.44	0.62	50	2.34	1.80	16

Source: DES (1986) Statistics on School Leavers.

It will be seen that two sets of figures have been given. The first are the averages across the whole population regardless of whether the examinations were attempted or not and the second is the average for those who attempted the examinations. There is a general indication that the overall performance of the dyslexic group was at least as good as the performance of the general population of school leavers at 'O' level although it must be remembered that the dyslexic subjects in this study all had an IQ score of greater than ninety-five.

From this, one might be led to assume that, to some extent, the problem of dyslexia 'just goes away'. However, this appears to be far from the truth as results of this study found that 46 per cent still find that their dyslexia causes them frequent difficulty. 55 per cent said that they occasionally had difficulties and only 2 per cent said that thay never had any difficulties. It is not so much that the difficulties go away but ways are found of overcoming, and working round them.

The results for further education and employment were equally encouraging. 62 per cent of the subjects went on, or are planning to go on, to take some form of higher education. (30 per cent degrees, 14 per cent diplomas and 18 per cent other e.g., City and Guilds.) Furthermore, subjects indicated that, in general, less emphasis was put on the quality of their literacy skills than was the case when they were at school, as the following comment illustrates:

> When I was doing my degree, nobody ever asked or seemed bothered about my spelling. This enabled me to write with a greater degree of freedom and concentrate on the arguments.

Only two of the subjects in the study are currently unemployed. Six are in further education. Table 11.5 shows the percentage of subjects in various classes of jobs.

Table 11.5 Breakdown of employment

		N
Professional High Status	8%	4
Professional Middle Status	20%	10
Skilled Technical	12%	6
Skilled Clerical and Office	10%	5
Skilled Manual	28%	14
Unskilled Manual	6%	3
In Education or Unemployed	16%	8
		50

Breakdown is based loosely on that used in market research.

The breakdown of employment shows that the subjects are engaged in a wide range of jobs reflecting a wide range of skills, interests and capabilities. Most felt that their dyslexia had not overtly influenced their choice of jobs but commented that, having lived with their difficulties for so long, it is really impossible to know, for example, what they would have done if they had not had those reading and spelling difficulties in the first place.

This follow-up study does much to enhance the results of the initial study. It suggests that, given the right sort of teaching, it is possible largely to overcome difficulties caused by being dyslexic. This is not to say that there is not enormous variation across the population of children who have this difficulty. Obviously some are going to be more severely affected than others and some may respond to teaching better than others. It is important that we do not get so involved with the child's dyslexic problems that we forget (or excuse) those factors that affect every child i.e., motivation, application and diligence, particularly in the area of examinations.

> I feel that my abysmal 'O' level results were not caused by dyslexia, but by laziness.

Conclusions

The authors feel that the most important message to come out of the two studies is that it is vital to diagnose, or certainly to be alert to, the problem of dyslexia as early as possible (taking into consideration the dangers of trying to diagnose too young) and to begin dyslexia centred teaching as quickly as possible. If this can be done in the everyday school situation, so much the better. It is only in that way that maximum co-operation and carry-over between individual and class teaching can be obtained.

Finally, there is a more important issue that should be considered. If all children were given the structured, sequential, cumulative and thorough multisensory teaching specified earlier right from the start, as a matter of course, would it be possible, in some degree, to prevent the problem of dyslexia arising in the first place? (For a recent review of the question of prevention see Bryant, 1985 and also Chapter 5 in the current book.) As knowledge of the practical and theoretical aspects of dyslexia continues to increase in sophistication and as teachers from all spheres become increasingly knowledgeable about the subject, it may be hoped that some of the dyslexia centred methods discussed here will be automatically combined with other teaching methods in the mainstream classroom and will thus give the dyslexic child a better chance of developing to his or her full potential.

References

Bryant, P. (1985) In Snowling, M.J., *Children's Written Language Difficulties: Assessment and Management*, Windsor, NFER-Nelson.

Department of Education and Science (1986) *Statistics on School Leavers*, London, HMSO.

Ellis, N.C. and Miles, T.R. (1981) 'A lexical encoding deficiency', in Pavlidis, G. Th. and Miles, T.R. (Eds) *Dyslexia Research and Its Application to Education*, Chichester, John Wiley.

Gillingham, A. and Stillman, B.E. (1969) *Remedial Training for Children with Specific Disability in Reading, Spelling and Penmanship*, Cambridge, Mass., Educators Publishing Service.

Hannon, P. (1987) 'A study of the effects of parental involvement in the teaching of reading on children's reading test performance', *British Journal of Educational Psychology*, 57, pp. 56–72.

Hannon, P., Jackson, A. and Weinberger, J. (1986) 'Parents' and teachers' strategies in hearing young children read', *Research Papers in Education*, 1, pp. 6–25.

Hickey, K. (1977) *Dyslexia. A Language Training Course for Teachers and Learners*, 3 Montague Road, London SW19.

Hornsby, B., Farrer, M. and Tylor, A. (1988) *The Effects of a Dyslexia Centred Teaching Programme: A Follow-up Study*, The Hornsby Centre, 71 Wandsworth Common Westside, London SW18.

Hornsby, B. and Miles, T.R. (1980) 'The effects of a dyslexia centred teaching programme', *British Journal of Educational Psychology*, 50, pp. 236–242.

Hornsby, B. and Shear, F. (1980) *Alpha to Omega*, 3rd ed., London, Heinemann Educational.

Johnson, D.J. and Mycklebust, H.R. (1967) *Learning Disabilities, Educational Principles and Practice*, New York, Grune and Stratton.

Kirk, S.A. and Kirk, W.D. (1971) *Psycholinguistic Learning Disabilities: Diagnosis and Remediation*, Urbana, Ill., University of Illinois Press.

Miles, E. (1981) 'A Study of dyslexic weaknesses and the consequences for teaching', in Pavlidis, G. Th. and Miles, T.R. (Eds) *Dyslexia Research and Its Application to Education*, Chichester, John Wiley.

Miles, T.R. (1970) *On Helping the Dyslexic Child*, London, Methuen Educational.

Miles, T.R. (1978) *Understanding Dyslexia*, London, Hodder and Stoughton.

Miles, T.R. and Ellis, N.C. (1981) 'Dyslexia as a lexical encoding deficiency, II', in Pavlidis, G. Th. and Miles, T.R. (Eds) *Dyslexia Research and Its Application to Education*, Chichester, John Wiley.

Miles, T.R. and Miles, E. (1975) *More Help for Dyslexic Children*, London, Methuen Educational.

Naidoo, S. (Ed.) (1988) *Assessment and Teaching of Dyslexic Children*, London, Invalid Children's Aid Nationwide.

Rawson, M.B. (1970) 'The structure of English: the language to be learned', *Bulletin of the Orton Society*, XX, pp. 103–123.

Sprott, W.J.H. (1952) *Social Psychology*, London, Methuen Educational.

Part Two: Responses
(B) Growth Points in Classroom Practice

12
Testing and Teaching Pupils with Reading Difficulties

Peter D. Pumfrey

Introduction

The English language comprises four distinct yet related aspects of communication. These are the two receptive skills of listening and reading and the two expressive ones of speaking and writing (including spelling). For the purposes of this paper, attention is deliberately focused on the testing and teaching of reading.

Aims

The main purpose is to consider issues bearing on the uses and limitations of reading tests and assessment techniques. To this end this chapter is in three sections.

   (i) To consider the relationships between the teaching and testing of reading.
  (ii) To outline a system for classifying and locating reading tests and assessment techniques (RTATs) for specific purposes.
 (iii) To describe examples of promising developments integrating the testing and teaching of reading.

With reference to the learning and teaching of reading, the continuing purpose of the teaching profession is more adequately to describe, to predict and to control children's reading development to the advantage of our pupils (Hoffman, 1986). It is not enough that teachers be effective in helping children learn to read. We must be able to discuss the basis of our successes and failures. We need to be able to say why we have adopted a given strategy, to predict an outcome and to evaluate the efficacy of our intervention (teaching). In any profession, all three activities must be carried out publicly and explicitly. It can be argued that the informed use by teachers of a variety of reading tests and assessment techniques is one essential ingredient in such an endeavour.

Currently RTATs are widely used in our schools. Increasingly, LEAs and schools are expected to demonstrate their accountability to the society that funds the state education service. The expenditure by the state on education during 1988–1989 was some 18.41 billion pounds; for 1989–1990 it is estimated to be 19.57 billion pounds. The cost per pupil per year in the Primary school is approximately 1,100 pounds. Literacy matters. Scores on RTATs provide a wide range of means whereby accountability can be demonstrated in this key aspect of the curriculum. As indicators they have both strengths and weaknesses.

The number of LEAs undertaking authority-wide testing of children's reading attainments at one or more age levels continues to increase. In 1973 the Bullock Committee circulated the then 146 LEAs in England and Wales prior to Local Authority reorganization. Ninety-three out of 146 (63.7 per cent) responded. Fifty of the 93 (53.8 per cent) reported that they carried out such testing of reading. In 1980 the SSRC (Social Science Research Council) funded the Evaluation of Testing in Schools Project. Of the then 104 LEAs in England and Wales who were circulated, replies were received from nine-six (92.3 per cent), eighty-eight (84.6 per cent) of whom completed the questionnaire. Seventy-one out of the eighty-eight (80 per cent) reported carrying out '... regular authority-wide testing programmes for reading covering at least one age group (plus a further four who tested ''English'')' (Gipps and Wood, 1981; Gipps *et al.*, 1983). A more recent survey obtained responses from all 104 LEAs in England and Wales. The findings showed that eighty-one LEAs out of 104 (77.9 per cent) organized the testing of children's reading attainments across the authority at one or more age levels. Metropolitan District LEAs, thirty out of thirty-six (83.3 per cent), responded positively more often than did the ILEA plus the Outer London Boroughs with sixteen out of twenty-one (76.2 per cent) and the Non-Metropolitan Counties thirty-five out of forty-seven (74.5 per cent) (Pumfrey, 1988).

How adequately is the teaching profession prepared concerning the use of reading tests? This is a topic of considerable importance (Sumner, 1987). Knowledge of both test theory and language development is a necessary, but not sufficient, condition for the effective use of reading tests. An appreciation of the pedagogy of reading is also essential. Insofar as the majority of Primary school teachers are concerned, test theory has all the appeal of a succulent fillet steak – to a vegetarian. This is almost certainly not because of the complexity of the ideas involved, but because of the genre in which they are symbolized. The danger in this situation is that responsibility for the development, use, interpretation and technical criticism of reading tests moves away from teachers and then rests largely with outside 'experts' in measurement. As long as the teaching profession remains unaware and uninformed of developments in the theory and uses of RTATs — for example, Rasch scaling and measuring attitudes towards reading — the distancing of teachers from test development will continue (Pumfrey, 1986, 1987; Vincent, Pugh and Brooks, 1986).

A recent series of in-service courses on the uses and limitations of a range of RTATs involved 188 qualified and experienced teachers. Course members completed a questionnaire concerning their training to use, and knowledge of, reading tests. When the teachers were asked whether they could recall studying the uses and limitations of reading tests during their initial training, sixty-one (32 per cent) said 'Yes' and the remaining 127 said 'No' (68 per cent). Those who had answered 'Yes' were asked how substantial was the component. The majority, fifty-five (90 per cent), indicated that it was minimal. Their typical comments were as follows.

'. . . a couple of lectures'.
'. . . scant — far too rushed'.
'. . . minute'.
'One lecture in a three-year course'.

All too few reported otherwise; but their comments indicate that there is hope.

'It was of major importance'.
'Very good, as I did a special needs course'.
'Uses of reading tests, YES; theory, NO'.

In order to get a crude indication of the number and variety of RTATs with which they were familiar, course members were also asked to name reading tests and assessment techniques that were being used in their schools or in their service. The distribution is shown below.

There was a tendency for those who had been trained more recently to have had a more substantial component of their course devoted to RTATs. A minority had subsequently taken brief non-examined courses in the general field of mental measurement, but only one had taken an examined course. Of the reading tests listed, the vast majority were covered by only eight tests. What was available and used by this particular group was a very restricted selection

Use of RTATs in school and services.

(N = 188 teachers)

No. of RTATs	No. of Teachers	% of Teachers	
0	21	11	
1	32	17	
2	30	16	
3	33	18	
4	37	20	
5	18	9	
6	8	4	
7	6	3	
8 +	3	2	(Pumfrey, 1989)

189

from the wide range of RTATs available. According to the same sample of 188 teachers, the manner in which most of them had been inducted into the use of RTATs was to be handed a reading test by a senior colleague on the staff of the school and asked to administer it to a group of pupils. For many valid reasons, most felt that this was far from satisfactory.

It is NOT claimed that the results from the above convenience sample are typical. The issue is one that merits further investigation. If the pattern is not unusual, then a considerable programme of in-service training would be required if RTATs are to be used effectively. It is already recognized that a massive INSET programme will be required to ensure that the evaluation of the National Curriculum English Programmes of Study starting shortly, are adequately carried out. At present, the Standard Assessment Tasks are still being developed and piloted (October, 1989).

The scientific and technological advances of which we are all material beneficiaries, electricity, transport and communications, for example, are all dependent on theories, on experiments and on measurement. Quantification is of the essence. The efficient identification and alleviation of reading difficulties requires the use of quantitative methods of assessment.

In connection with the learning and teaching of reading, opponents of testing sometimes claim that the complexities of the processes involved are such that these cannot be measured. There are too many intangibles involved. Of such critics, in relation to RTATs, it can be said that the perfect is the enemy of the better. Advocates of the informed use of RTATs are aware of the strengths and weaknesses of such instruments. For them, the development of increasingly effective instruments is a continuing professional challenge. They are heirs to the principle stated by Thorndike that 'Whatever exists, exists in some quantity and can, *in principle*, be measured'. Of even greater importance is the point that the refinement of mental measurement in general and of RTATs in particular, has many benefits to both teachers and learners (Schwartz, 1984; Johnston, 1985; Farr and Carey, 1986).

Lord Kelvin once remarked 'When you can measure what you are speaking about and express it in numbers, you know something about it; but when you cannot measure it, when you cannot express it in numbers, your knowledge is of a meagre and unsatisfactory kind'. This observation is as valid in relation to describing, predicting and understanding children's reading development in all its complexities, as in Lord Kelvin's field. Turning from a nineteenth century physicist to a twentieth century psychologist, some thirty-seven years ago Guilford underlined the importance of test theory and its applications at that time, 'No other contribution of psychology has had the social impact equal to that created by the psychological test. No other technique and no other body of theory in psychology has been so fully rationalized from the mathematical point of view' (Guilford, 1952). RTATs represent one of many fields in which test theory has been developed, applied and extended.

This is not to believe that quantification alone is sufficient. Figures can be used as a smoke screen to hide our lack of understanding and control of the reading process from ourselves and others, wittingly or otherwise. As teachers we need to be aware of the wide range of reading tests and assessment techniques available to help in our work (Vincent *et al.*, 1983; Levy and Goldstein, 1984; Mitchell, 1985; Pumfrey, 1985a, 1985b; Gorman *et al.*, 1988; Glazer *et al.*, 1988). We must also understand the limitations both of mental measurement and of our conceptualizations of the reading process.

Putting the teaching and testing of reading in the Primary school into its contemporary context requires that current initiatives by central government be considered (See Chapter 1).

The teaching and testing of reading

The educational programme in all Primary schools integrates three notions. First, the programme has a number of objectives. Second, it specifies a range of curricular methods, materials and teaching expertise whereby pupils are presented with experiences that will enable them to achieve the objectives. Third, a system for evaluating the success of the programme is required. Using the language of the 1988 Education Act, these ideas are re-labelled 'Attainment Targets', 'Programmes of Study' and 'Standard Assessment Tasks' respectively (Department of Education and Science, 1989). The relationships are shown in Figure 12.1.

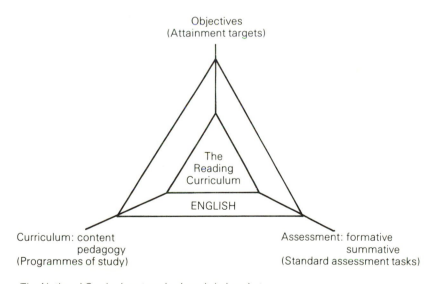

Objectives
(Attainment targets)

The Reading Curriculum

ENGLISH

Curriculum: content
pedagogy
(Programmes of study)

Assessment: formative
summative
(Standard assessment tasks)

The National Curriculum terminology is in brackets.

Figure 12.1   The reading programme and the National Curriculum in English: current terminology

A central component of the overall Primary school programme is that dealing with Communication. Within this is the Language programme. Reading is but one aspect of that Language programme. It is helpful to distinguish between the receptive and expressive aspects of language (see Figure 12.2). An appreciation of their respective developments and interrelationships is essential to understanding their normal development (See Chapters 5, 6, 7 and 8). This provides the basis against which anomalous developments of reading abilities can be better understood.

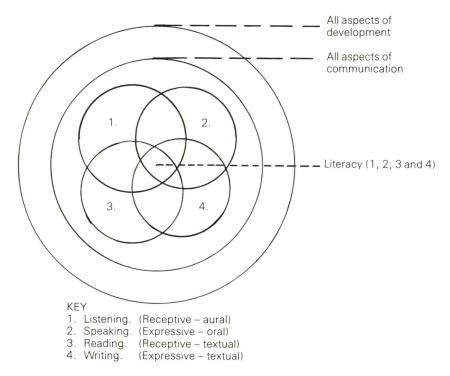

KEY
1. Listening. (Receptive – aural)
2. Speaking. (Expressive – oral)
3. Reading. (Receptive – textual)
4. Writing. (Expressive – textual)

Figure 12.2 Schematic representation of the place of reading in a Primary school curriculum

What is reading?

Effective reading can be defined as the ability to comprehend the thoughts and feelings of another mind via the medium of text. Such a definition includes both the cognitive and affective aspects of reading. Different genres make different demands on the reader. A manual on car repair and a poem can each be read. The interpretation of the former is more restricted than of the latter.

The means whereby non-readers become increasingly proficient involves the use of three cue systems: grapho-phonic, semantic and syntactic. For the skilled reader, grapho-phonic and syntactic textual cues are dealt with virtually at an automated, overlearned and subconscious level. The reader's attention is focused on the meaning of the text. Only when an unfamiliar word is met will recourse to the other cue systems be made. In contrast, the child learning to read is much more likely to utilize all three cue systems. Whether the reader is a beginner or highly competent, the semantic cues play a key role The change from being a non-reader to becoming a competent reader is schematically represented in Figure 12.3.

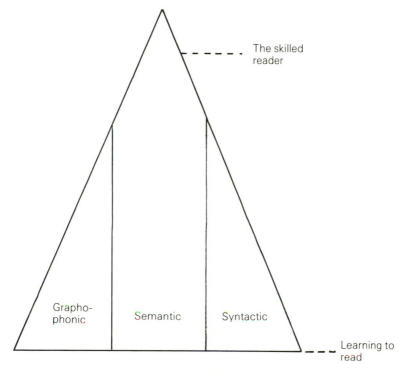

Figure 12.3 Cue systems and reader-text interactions

Learning to read is analogous to climbing a mountain. Children have differing abilities. They do not all learn to read by following the same path towards the summit represented by proficient reading. RTATs can help in plotting the pupil's attainments and progress. They can also assist in 'fine-grain' analyses of pupil's reading difficulties and suggest ways of overcoming these. To assume that the automated and subconscious reading processes of the competent reader are necessarily available to all children learning to read is suspect. The issue of whether *some* of the inter-individual differences in children's abilities underpinning their reading performances are quantitative and not qualitative, is an ongoing controversy. It is one in which reading tests and assessment techniques can help make explicit the nature of the cue systems used in a variety of reader-text interactions.

Reading tests and assessment techniques: their characteristics classification and selection

A RTAT should be an efficient means of eliciting valid information concerning cognitive or affective aspects of children's reading. The information elicited should improve decision-making related to children's reading programmes. Such information can be used for many purposes. Some of these are shown in the following Table 12.1.

Table 12.1   Some uses of reading tests and assessment techniques.

1. To provide public information (Accountability).
2. To improve communication by minimizing ambiguities.
3. To maintain and improve standards in reading at local, regional and national levels.
4. To compare the reading skills and attitudes of pupils within a class.
5. To measure the progress of individuals and groups.
6. To find starting points for instruction.
7. To evaluate various approaches to the teaching of reading.
8. To identify the pattern of an individual pupil's strengths and weaknesses (Diagnosis).
9. To help in matching reading materials and methods to the child.
10. To increase the teacher's understanding of the processes involved in reading.
11. To help in the early identification of later reading difficulties (Screening & Prevention).
12. Research.

N.B. The above uses are neither exhaustive nor mutually exclusive.

RTATs must never be judged by their titles alone. It is possible to find RTATs with virtually identical titles but having markedly different contents. There also exist RTATs with very similar content but dissimilar names. An inspection of the content and form of the RTAT is an essential pre-requisite to its adoption. There are also more technical issues that a potential user must consider.

The usefulness of RTATs as sources of information from which to make decisions about a child's reading skills depends on the RTATs' validities. Validity has two aspects: relevance and reliability. The former refers to the precision with which the text measures what it is intended to measure. Reliability refers to the accuracy and consistency of the instrument. Users of RTATs should expect to find evidence concerning the validities of any RTAT in the test manual. An understanding of the various types of validity and reliability is essential to judicious selection.

If a reading test is used for different purposes, it will have different validities. For example, children's scores on a word-recognition test such as Carver's Word Reading Test are highly related to children's ability to recognize a wide range of untimed flash-card presented words. In this instance, the Carver test would be a valid one for testing untimed word-recognition attainments. It would not necessarily be as valid for assessing reading comprehension. The validity of a reading test can be defined as the degree to which a test measures what it purports to measure. The importance of using

RTATs that are valid in terms of instructional objectives in the reading programme should be quite clear.

Types of RTAT

A vast range of RTATs exists. A classificatory system is essential if the teacher is to select judiciously. RTATs can be grouped into three broad categories. These are informal, normative and criterion-referenced RTATs. Each type has distinct characteristics.

Informal RTATs

The competent teacher of reading is continually observing the reading-related behaviours of her pupils. Her instructional objectives, methods of teaching and record-keeping tend to determine the behaviours to which her attention is directed. The day-to-day work in the classroom gives opportunities for systematic and extended sampling of children's reading attainments, progress, difficulties and attitudes towards reading. Because they can also be based on almost any textual material used in the classroom, Informal Reading Inventories (IRIs) and the associated analyses of oral reading miscues, are also included in this category (Arnold, 1984; Pumfrey, 1985a; Johnson, Kress and Pikulski, 1987; Pavlack, 1987; Goodman, Watson and Burke, 1987).

Normative RTATs

Often, when teachers think of reading tests they think of the many published ones that enable children to be ranked according to their performance and that performance related to the performance of, for example, all children of a given age group. The concern is with inter-individual differences and with standards. Such tests can also provide profiles of the intra-individual differences, the pattern of a child's relative strengths and weaknesses. An analysis of the major characteristics of such tests is given in Table 12.2.

Criterion-referenced RTAT

This refers to an assessment based on the quality of the pupil's performance irrespective of the performance of other pupils. Criterion-referenced tests are so constructed that they provide scores showing how adequately a child copes with specific reading tasks. The content of the test is clearly defined. The characteristics of criterion-referenced RTATs are shown in Table 12.3

Classifying and locating RTATs suitable for specific purposes

Classifying RTATs.

Three aspects of PURPOSE that have been used in classifying RTATs are:

- Goals of instruction;
- Sources of information; and
- Levels of interpretation.

Table 12.2 Normative and criterion-referenced reading tests contrasted:
(a) Norm-referenced tests

Issue	Norm-referenced
Purpose	To assess inter- and intra-individual differences in reading attainments and attitudes to reading in a specified group of pupils.
Focus	1 Generalized skills and reading abilities and attitudes. 2 Latent traits inferred from pupils' performances.
Construction	1 Based on conventional test theory using item analyses with given limits to Facility and Discrimination indices of items. 2 Specification of the group to which the test is to be applied is of the essence. 3 Mathematical basis of measurement well developed and articulated.
Standards	Test results usually compared with children of the same age and from the same population.
Reporting results	Standard scores (e.g. deviation quotients, 'z' scores, T scores, stens, stanines), percentiles, and reading ages.
Teaching implications	1 Items must *not* be taught as doing so would invalidate the norms that have been obtained. It would also be impossible to interpret the scores of pupils after such teaching. 2 Does not provide a clear guide to required instructional content but can suggest *method*. 3 Focuses attention on normative standards.

Table 12.3 *Normative and criterion-referenced reading tests contrasted:*
(b) Crtiterion-referenced tests

Issue	Criterion-referenced
Purpose	To assess the extent to which specified operationally defined reading objectives have been achieved.
Focus	1 Specific and narrow reading skills and behaviours. 2 Detailed task-analysis.
Construction	1 Tests are based on items developed from an analysis of the objective to be mastered. 2 Explicit normative considerations are irrelevant because the successful mastery of the criterion by all pupils is the objective. 3 Mathematical basis of criterion-referenced measurement is still in the early stages of development.
Standards	Test results compared to an explicit criterion of mastery, e.g. number of items correct for a given objective.
Reporting results	Percentage scores on number of items correct for a given objective.
Teaching implications	1 The items have been selected as both desirable and able to be mastered by pupils. The content of the test *must* be taught. 2 Provides guidance concerning instructional materials. Tests can be directly linked to such resources. 3 Narrowness of objectives can restrict curriculum adversely.

Goals of instruction concern whether the RTAT is concerned with children's ATTAINMENTS in, or ATTITUDES towards, reading.

Sources of information distinguishes between three different but complementary modes or sources of RTAT information. These are the three forms of RTAT described earlier, namely Informal, Normative and Criterion-referenced.

Levels of interpretation can be considered in two ways. The first level indicates that the information presented is intended only for DESCRIPTION. The second level is more complex. The information obtained is required for DIAGNOSING reading difficulties. Diagnostic RTATs provide detailed information having implications for interventions aimed at alleviating reading difficulties.

The above analysis of purpose provides a 2 (Goals) × 3 (Sources) × 2 (Levels) classificatory system. It has been used to classify a selection of 199 RTATs (Pumfrey, 1985a).

The classification is further broken down by Country of origin (British or other) and by five Age levels: Pre-reading; Infant; Junior; Secondary and Tertiary. Using this classificatory system, the teacher is able to identify a group of RTATs that may meet her specific purpose. To do this the questions in Table 12.4 have to be answered.

Table 12.4 Selecting a RTAT: 6 steps.

1. What goal of instruction is important to my purpose (Attainments or attitudes)?
2. What source of information is best suited to my purpose (Informal, normative or criterion-referenced)?
3. What level of interpretation do I need? (Descriptive or diagnostic)?
4. Does the RTAT have to British?
5. For which age range is it required (Pre-school, Infant, Junior, Secondary or Tertiary)?
6. Do I require an individual or a group test?

Having answered these questions, a set of potentially suitable RTATs can be identified. For each of these the following twelve items of information are provided:

> name of RTAT; author; country of origin; publisher; date of publication; type of RTAT; user classification (availability); number and designation of parallel forms; chronological age range of subjects; skills and/or attitudes observed, assessed or tested; average administration time; and a description of the RTAT with evaluative comments.

It is then up to the teacher to compare the respective strengths and weaknesses of each of the instruments that she has identified, and to make a decision. The important practical issues of cost and re-usability of materials must also be considered.

At a more general level, RTAT users are recommended to follow the guidelines in Table 12.5 when selecting any RTAT and interpreting its results.

Table 12.5 General guidelines for selecting and interpreting RTATs.

(a) Selection

1. Define the purpose for which information is required.
2. Select a RTAT suited to that purpose and population after reviewing available RTATs.
3. Check that the content and mode of administration meets your pedagogic requirements.
4. Work out the costs of using the RTAT both in your relation to your instructional purpose and also to the demands it will make on teacher and pupil time. It is essential that the cost/benefit ratio of using the RTAT should be acceptably low.
5. Consider how other sources of information additional to the RTAT results could corroborate and enrich the RTAT information.
6. Read the RTAT manual critically and ensure that full information on the development of the RTAT is provided.
7. Read independent evaluations of any RTAT that you are considering using.
8. Obtain specimen sets of the RTAT materials and pilot the RTAT to see whether it meets your requirements.
9. Select and use only RTATs for which you have the required expertise. If necessary, undertake further training to extend the range of RTATs that you can use.
10. Discuss the strengths and weaknesses of any RTAT you intend using with colleagues who have used it recently in their work.

(b) Interpreting data from RTATs

1. Be certain that you are familiar with the scale used in reporting scores.
2. Be aware of the validities and reliabilities of the RTAT results.
3. Be sensitive to possible differences between the group on which the test was normed, or the domain specified, and the characteristics of the individual or group with whom the RTAT is being used.
4. Be confident that the information to be elicited by the RTAT will improve curricular decision-making.
5   Insofar as possible, check that this proves to be the case.

Teaching and testing: promising practices

A selection of ideas and practices integrating the teaching and testing of reading is presented.

Diagnostic-prescriptive use of RTAT

For the teacher, the theory and practice of the teaching and learning of reading are inextricably linked. Whilst this is crucial to the promising practices outlined below, the pupil's viewpoint is less complex. To the child with reading difficulties, what matters is much simpler. Can the teacher (or anyone) help the pupil overcome difficulties, enjoy some success, and experience reading as both useful and enjoyable?

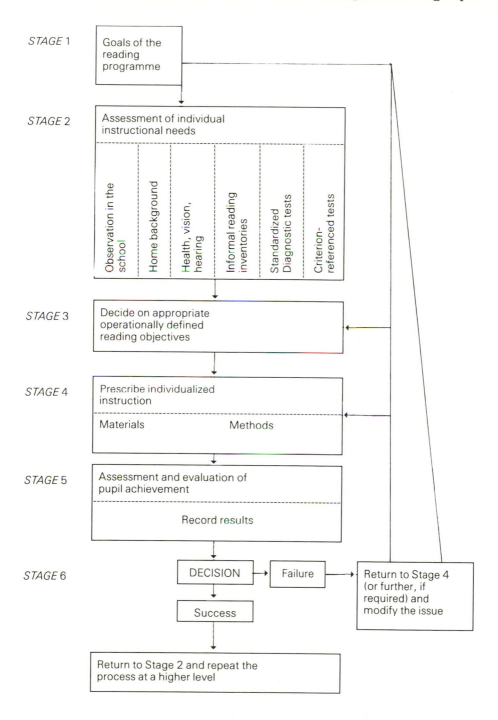

STAGE 1 — Goals of the reading programme

STAGE 2 — Assessment of individual instructional needs
- Observation in the school
- Home background
- Health, vision, hearing
- Informal reading inventories
- Standardized Diagnostic tests
- Criterion-referenced tests

STAGE 3 — Decide on appropriate operationally defined reading objectives

STAGE 4 — Prescribe individualized instruction
- Materials
- Methods

STAGE 5 — Assessment and evaluation of pupil achievement
- Record results

STAGE 6 — DECISION → Failure → Return to Stage 4 (or further, if required) and modify the issue

DECISION → Success → Return to Stage 2 and repeat the process at a higher level

Figure 12.4 Model of diagnostic-prescriptive teaching of reading

The diagram above (Figure 12.4) illustrates the six stages involved in the diagnostic-prescriptive teaching of reading. The adoption of such an approach integrates teaching and testing.

Individual educational programmes

One of the major consequences of the 1981 Education Act has been an increasing emphasis on identifying and helping individual pupils. Those experiencing learning difficulties in general and specific learning difficulties (dyslexia) in particular, may be made the subject of a Statement. An individual educational programme (IEP) may be prescribed. For such an IEP to be effective the above diagnostic-prescriptive approach will almost certainly have to be adopted. The strategy is of use with all pupils, but is time consuming. Detailed case studies of children with reading difficulties in which diagnosis and interventions are described and evaluated are available (Spache, McIlroy and Berg, 1981; Wilson and Cleland, 1985).

Aptitude × Instruction Interactions (AII)

In medicine, there is scepticism of panaceas. The history of 'snake-oil' charlatans provides a salutory signal to citizens. In view of the massive inter- and intra-individual differences in children's reading and reading-related characteristics, it is extremely unlikely that any one method will ever be the 'Royal Road' to literacy.

The reasons for children experiencing difficulties in learning to read are multitudinous. Some causes of reading difficulties are 'within-child'; others are environmental. A majority of children's reading difficulties involve both 'within-child' and environmental factors. The teacher's skill lies in modifying the child's educational environment in the light of the child's abilities. The eclecticism of the teaching profession, concerning the teaching and learning of reading to children experiencing reading difficulties, provides further testimony to the absence of a pedagogic panacea for reading difficulties. If there was one, it would almost certainly have been found by now.

Children differ greatly in their abilities, attitudes and motivations. Each child is unique. Despite this, it is possible to find groups of children with reading difficulties who share certain attributes (Tyler and Elliott, 1988). Identifying instructional programmes and methods that are most effective with groups of pupils having common characteristics, represents the search for AIIs. It is a continuing professional challenge. The road is not an easy one to explore, but is nonetheless important and holds promise (Arter and Jenkins, 1979; Naylor and Pumfrey, 1983; Freebody and Tyre, 1985; National Dissemination Study Group, 1988; Tyler and Elliott, 1988).

Uses of 'cloze' procedure

The deletion of words from a passage of text, coupled with the challenge to the reader to identify the missing words, is a valuable educational procedure. It integrates teaching and testing. The reader is required to utilize grapho-phonic, syntactic and semantic contextual cues. Cloze technique encourages reader-text interactions. Try the following passage.

> When cloze procedure is . . . . . . to reading tasks, the . . . . . . is asked to fill . . the gap, usually a . . . . . . word, which has been left . . . of the text. To . . this successfully the word . . . . conform to the rules of . . . . . . , have the correct meaning . . . be consistent with the . . . . and language patterns of . . . author' (Adapted from Walker, 1974).

One of the earliest uses of cloze procedure was by the German psychologist Ebbinghaus in the late nineteenth century. He deleted words from one of Aesop's fables to produce a test that was intended to sample aspects of the 'higher mental processes'. Subsequent re-discovery of the technique in the USA led to its use in assessing the readability of texts. More recently, a considerable number of reading tests and assessment techniques have been based on it. In addition, it has been increasingly used in the teaching of reading to pupils of all abilities (Rye, 1982; Mulholland, 1986; Beard, 1987).

There are many ways in which deletions can be made. The deletion strategies adopted can make the task of identifying the missing words either easier or more difficult for the reader. It follows that in preparing work for children experiencing reading difficulties, the choice of deletion policy can be used to match the task to the child's abilities and instructional needs. Deletion strategies include the following:

1. Delete every 'N'th word. The higher that 'N' is made, in general, the easier is the task of reconstruction. More cues are available to the reader when the proportion of deleted text falls. Common deletion policies are one in either five or ten words.
2. Overall, delete one word in 'N', but randomly vary the point in the text at which the deletion is made. If a one in ten deletion policy is adopted, the deletion of a word could be at any position in a sequence of ten words.
3. Delete particular types of words; for example, structure words such as articles, auxiliary verbs, prepositions and conjunctions or content words such as nouns, verbs, adverbs and adjectives. Some types of deleted words are easier to reconstruct than others. The order given indicates the relative difficulty of prediction. The frequency with which words of different types are used in text follows a somewhat similar, but not identical, pattern.

4. Delete by position in sentence. It is usually easier to regenerate words when their meaning is increasingly bound by their context.

Each of these deletion policies can be supplemented by providing the reader with additional information.

(a) Provide in the text one or more of the letters making up the missing word. Clearly, with only one letter missing, the identity of the missing word is more readily generated than if fewer letters are provided. The provision of initial and/or final letter in the deleted word are commonly used strategies.

(b) Indicate the number of letters in the deleted word. This can be done by using a number of dots.

(c) Provide an outline of the shape of the missing word.

(d) Present a combination of letter, length and word-shape cues.

Based on a deletion policy of one in five words, it has been suggested that cloze material is at 'Frustration level' for readers who can only fill in correctly up to 40 per cent of the gaps in the text. If they can reconstruct between 40 per cent and 60 per cent of the missing words, the material is at the 'Instructional level'. When more than 60 per cent of the gaps can be completed, the material is said to be at the 'Independent level' for the child. This last level indicates that the reader is likely to cope with the text without assistance (Rye, 1982).

The use of cloze materials with small groups of children experiencing reading difficulties has much to commend it. The task is for the group to agree on the missing words in a text. Working in small groups can benefit the social, language, cognitive and reading development of children of all abilities (Slavin *et al.*, 1985; Reason, Rooney and Roffe, 1987). Learning to read capitalizes on children's oral language development. Small group reading-related activities that require children to negotiate shared meanings can help improve their reading (Walker, 1974; Beard, 1987). These methods were seen as having the advantage that they redressed an over-emphasis on the individualization of instruction in reading, were efficient, motivational and effective. A subsequent major research funded by the Schools Council into ways of stimulating the effective use of reading used group discussion as a key strategy. This led to the development of Directed Activies Related to Texts (DARTS) (Lunzer and Gardner, 1979).

These group approaches include:

● Group cloze;
● Group sequencing; and
● Group prediction.

In 'Group cloze' the teacher presents the children with a passage of text from which certain words have been deleted. The group's task is to come to an agreement concerning the missing words. The activity typically leads to a lot of discussion, reading and re-reading of the text and the exploration and justification of alternatives. By increasing awareness of synonyms, and a heightened sensitivity to the constraints imposed by both the grammatical structure of the passage and of spelling, pupils' awareness of language is enhanced.

'Group sequencing', involves presenting children with the segments of a continuous sequence of either pictorial or textual material. The children's task is to order the materials in a manner acceptable to the group. They must also be able to justify the sequence they construct. An example of the former is the frames from a comic strip with (or without) 'bubble' speech from the characters involved. The difficulty of this task can easily be modified by changing the number of elements into which the sequence is divided. The fewer the divisions, the less challenging the task.

'Group prediction' can be carried out using, for example, an overhead projector. The beginning of a story can be presented. The group is asked a number of prepared questions such as 'What is happening?' and, more interestingly because they are more open-ended, 'What led up to this?' and 'What will happen next?'. (The technique is similar to that used by psychologists in some projective tests.) Children offering opinions are asked to support their suggestions by reference to evidence in the material on the screen. Frequently different interpretations and different predictions will be made. These differences may, or may not, be resolved. The presentation of subsequent material on the screen typically provides additional information that enables the validity of the earlier interpretations to be checked. The author has used this technique using pictures only, then pictures with 'Bubble' text and then text only with children of all abilities. Provided that the topic is one of interest to the group and the questions have been well-prepared, the technique leads to a great deal of reading, re-reading, thinking and discussion of the presented material.

Uses of word lists

Many lists have been made of the frequency with which particular words, and sequences of words, appear in textual materials of various types. Such lists provide valuable guidelines for teachers. The content of a list identifies commonly used words that the reader will have to master if he/she is to read effectively. The ability to recognize these words, decode to sound, comprehend, spell, write and use them in compositions are related aplications that also concern teachers.

Word lists define a domain-referenced corpus of material, mastery of which can provide a legitimate and operationally defined educational objective for all pupils. If it is found that certain individuals are having difficulty in reading important words in such a list, the teacher can select a methodology that will enable the child to master the words. The overlearning of a relatively small number of key words can have a considerable effect on the textual material accessible to the reader. Automatically in such activities is an essential pre-requisite of fluent reading.

A recent study involving 350 top infant school pupils analyzed the frequency of words encountered by these childen in their reading and writing. The main study was carried out in their last term of infant school education. Each child provided a piece of free writing. An equivalent sample of words was taken from their classroom reading material. The pupose of the study was to identify the corpus of words being encountered in their reading and writing by children at the end of the first of the four Key Stages (i.e. 7 years of age) specified in the Education Act, 1988.

This sample of the children's reading and writing yielded a total of 55,610 words. Within the total there were 2,477 different words. The striking point is that 216 words account for 75 per cent of the 2,447 different words in the combined corpus on the basis of the sampling procedures used (Laskier, 1986).

A mere eight words comprise 25 per cent of the specified corpus of writing and reading materials. Forty-five words account for 50 per cent and 216 words account for 75 per cent of the words (excluding four proper nouns) encountered and used by our sample of children. The importance of the mastery of this core of words can hardly be overemphasized if the child is to become competent in reading and spelling.

The words can be used as a domain-referenced word recognition text. When this was tried with a sample of seventy-one 7-year-old pupils, a mean score of 161 was obtained. There were significant sex differences in the scores obtained. Of more educational significance, the range of scores was from 31/216 to 215/216 correctly read. Massive individual differences between pupils exist in their word reading attainments at this quite young age. The explicit identification of such marked differences is of considerable pedagogic importance.

Currently a domain-referenced battery of reading and spelling tests is being developed based on the 216 words identified. The battery will be called the Early Words Test Battery (EWTB) (Pumfrey and Laskier, in preparation). Our aim will be to show that the group of 216 very frequently occurring words can be used in different ways for different purposes by the teacher. In part, the format and mode of administration of a particular sub-test in the EWTB will determine the purpose for which it can be used. It will also open up avenues for teacher ingenuity in teaching specific reading and spelling skills.

In the current work there is a significant positive correlation between the frequency with which these words are encountered by children and the children's ability to read them ($r = 0.53$; $N = 71$). It must be remembered that listing words in order of the frequency of their use does NOT necessarily list them in order of the ease with which they can be read or spelled.

Some recently developed materials linking the testing and teaching of reading

There are many reading kits and programmes linking the teaching and testing of reading. Four of the most widely used are the Reading Laboratory Series and Distar Reading I & II (Science Research Associates), Reading Workshop Series (Ward Lock) and Reading Routes (Longmans). The well-known National Association for Remedial Education publication 'An A–Z of Reading Books' gives full details of these and many others (Atkinson, Gains and Edwards, 1985). The following short selection of materials and methods have also been developed in order to help the teacher integrate the testing and teaching of reading (and other skills).

1. Barking Reading Project (Barking and Dagenham LEA, 1981/2).
2. Children's Observation Procedure (ILEA, 1982).
3. The Primary Language Record (Barrs *et al.*, 1988).
4. The Aston Index (Revised) and Portfolio (Newton and Thomson, 1982; Aubrey *et al.*, 1982).
5. QUEST Screening, Diagnosis and Remediation Kit (Robertson *et al.*, 1983).
6. Assessment and Teaching of Dyslexic Children (Naidoo, 1988).
7. Specific Learning Difficulties (Edwards, 1988).
8. 'Touchstones' (NFER, 1989).

Recently developed British RTATs include 'The New Macmillan Reading Analysis' (Vincent and de la Mare, 1985), and the 'The Macmillan Individual Reading Analysis' (Vincent and de la Mare, 1988). The NFER-Nelson Publishing Company has just published the 'Reading Ability Series' and the 'Test of Initial Literacy' (NFER-Nelson, 1989). The promise of these and many other RTATs has yet to be exploited.

Conclusion

The following questions merit the attention of ALL Primary school teachers. How would you answer them?

1. Am I sufficiently aware of the variety of RTATs that are available?
2. Am I using RTATs effectively?
3. Can I identify RTATs likely to meet my explicit pedagogic purposes?
4. Should I extend my knowledge of methods of testing reading?
5. Can the use of a wider range of RTATs improve my ability to help pupils with reading difficulites?
6. Can I better integrate the teaching and testing of reading?

The evidence available to the author suggests that, for many teachers, the answers to questions 1–3 is 'NO'. In contrast, to questions 4–6 it is highly likely to be a resounding 'YES'.

References

Arnold, H. (1984) *Making Sense of It*, Sevenoaks, Hodder and Stoughton.

Arter, J. A. and Jenkins, J. R. (1979) 'Differential diagnosis-prescriptive teaching: a critical appraisal', *Review of Educational Research*, 49, 4, pp. 517–556.

Atkinson, E. J., Gains, C. W. and Edwards, R. (1985) *An A–Z List of Reading Books*, Lichfield, National Association for Remedial Education.

Aubrey, C., Eaves, J., Hicks, C. and Newton, M. (1982) *The Aston Portfolio Assessment Checklist*, Wishbech, Learning Development Aids.

Barking and Dagenham LEA (1981/2) *Barking Reading Project*, London, Barking and Dagenham LEA.

Barrs, M., Ellis, S., Hester, H. and Thomas, A. (1988) *The Primary Language Record*, London, ILEA.

Beard, R. (1987) *Developing Reading 3–13*, London, Hodder and Stoughton.

Department of Education and Science (1989) *National Curriculum: From Policy to Practice*, London, Department of Education and Science.

Edwards, R. (Ed) (1988) *Specific Learning Difficulties*, Stafford, National Association for Remedial Education.

Farr, R. and Carey, R. F. (1986) *Reading: What Can Be Measured?*, 2nd ed., Newark, Delaware, International Reading Association.

Freebody, P. and Tyre, W. C. (1985) 'Achievement outcomes of two reading programmes: an instance of an aptitude-treatment interaction', *British Journal of Educational Psychology*, 55, 1, pp. 53–60.

Gipps, C., Steadman, S., Blackstone, T. and Stierer, B. (1983) *Testing Children*, London, Heinemann Educational.

Gipps, C. and Wood, R. (1981) 'The testing of reading in LEAs: the Bullock Report seven years on', *Educational Studies*, 7, 2, pp. 133–143.

Glazer, S. M., Searfoss, L. W. and Gentile, L. M. (Eds) (1988) *Re-examining Reading Diagnosis: New Trends and Procedures*, Newark, Delaware, International Reading Association.

Goodman, Y., Watson, D. J. and Burke, C. L. (1987) *Reading Miscue Inventory: Alternative Procedures*, London, Heinemann Educational.

Gorman, T. P., White, J., Brooks, G., Maclure, M. and Kispal, A. (1988) *Language Performance in Schools: Review of A.P.U. Language Monitoring 1979–1983*, London, HMSO.

Guilford, J. P. (1952) *Psychometric Methods*, New York, McGraw-Hill.

Hoffman, J. V. (Ed) (1986) *Effective Teaching of Reading: Research and Practice*, Newark, Delaware, International Reading Association.

Inner London Education Authority (1982) *Children's Observation Procedure*, London, ILEA.

Johnson, M. S., Kress, R. A. and Pikulski, J. J. (1987) *Informal Reading Inventories*, 2nd ed., Newark, Delaware, International Reading Association.

Johnston, P. H. (1985) *Reading Comprehension Assessment: A Cognitive Basis*, Newark, Delaware, International Reading Assocation.

Laskier, M. (1986) 'Word-recognition attainments of Infant school pupils: identification and modification', Unpublished M.Ed. thesis, Department of Education, University of Manchester.

Levy, P. and Goldstein, H. (Eds) (1984) *Tests in Education*, London, Academic Press.

Lunzer. E. A. and Gardner, K. (Eds) (1979) *The Effective Use of Reading*, London, Heinemann Educational for the Schools Council.

Mitchell, J. V. (Ed) (1985) *The Ninth Mental Measurement Yearbook*, Lincoln, New England, Buros Institute of Mental Measurements.

Mulholland, H. (1986) 'Cloze procedure in the diagnostic assessment of silent reading', in Vincent, D., Pugh, A. K. and Brooks, G. (Eds) *Assessing Reading*, London, Macmillan Education, pp. 81–97.

Naidoo, S. (Ed) (1988) *Assessment and Teaching of Dyslexic Children*, London, Invalid Children's Aid Nationwide.

National Dissemination Study Group (1988) *Educational Programs That Work*, 14th ed., Longmont, Colorado, Sopris West Inc.

National Foundation for Educational Research (1989) *Touchstones*, Windsor, NFER-Nelson.

Naylor, J. G., and Pumfrey, P. D. (1983) 'The alleviation of psycholinguistic deficits and some effects on the reading attainments of poor readers: a sequel', *Journal of Research in Reading*, 6, 2, pp. 129–153.

Newton, M. and Thomson, M. (1982) *The Aston Index*, Wisbech, Learning Development Aids.

NFER-Nelson (1989a) *Reading Ability Series*, Windsor, NFER-Nelson.

NFER-Nelson (1989b) *Test of Initial Literacy*, Windsor, NFER-Nelson.

Pavlack, S. A. (1987) *Informal Tests for Diagnosing Specific Reading Problems*, New York, Parker.

Pumfrey, P. D. (1985a) *Reading: Tests and Assessment Techniques*, 2nd ed., London, Hodder & Stoughton in association with the United Kingdom Reading Association.

Pumfrey, P. D. (1985b) 'Testing reading: recent developments', in Ewing, J. M. (Ed) *Reading and the New Technologies*, London, Heinemann, pp. 70–79.

Pumfrey, P. D. (1986) 'Measuring attitudes towards reading', in Vincent, D., Pugh, A. K. and Brooks, G. (Eds) *Assessing Reading*, London, Macmillan Education, pp. 115–135.

Pumfrey, P. D. (1987) 'Rasch scaling and reading tests', *Journal of Research in Reading*, 10, 1, pp. 75–86.

Pumfrey, P. D. (1988) 'Monitoring the reading attainments of children from minority ethnic groups: LEA practices', in Verma, G. and Pumfrey, P. D. (Eds) *Educational Attainments: Issues and Outcomes in Multicultural Education*, Basingstoke, Falmer Press.

Pumfrey, P. D. (1989) 'Teachers and the use of reading tests and assessment techniques', Unpublished research, Department of Education, University of Manchester.

Pumfrey, P. D. and Laskier, M. (in preparation) *The Early Words Test Battery*.

Reason, R., Rooney, S. and Roffe, M. (1987) 'Co-operative learning in an infant school', *Educational and Child Psychology*, 4, 3/4, pp. 40–48.

Robertson, A. H., Henderson, A., Robertson, A., Fisher, J. and Gibson, M. (1983) *QUEST Screening, Diagnosis and Remediation Kit*, London, Arnold-Wheaton.

Rye, J. (1982) *Cloze Procedure and the Teaching of Reading*, London, Heinemann Educational.

Schwartz, S. (1984) *Measuring Reading Competence: A Theoretical-Prescriptive Approach*, New York, Plenum Press.

Slavin, R., Sharan, S., Kagan, S., Hertz-Lazarowitz, C., Webb, C. and Schmuck, R. (Eds) (1985) *Learning to Co-operate: Co-operating to Learn*, New York, Plenum Press.

Spache, G. D., McIlroy, K. and Berg, P. C. (1981) *Case Studies in Reading Disability*, New York, Allyn & Bacon.

Sumner, R. (1987) *The Role of Testing in Schools*, Windsor, NFER-Nelson.

Tyler, S. and Elliott, C. D. (1988) 'Cognitive profiles of poor readers and dyslexic children on the British Ability Scales', *British Journal of Psychology*, 79, pp. 493–508.

Vincent, D. and De La Mare, M. (1985) *The New Macmillan Reading Analysis*, Basingstoke, Macmillan Education.

Vincent, D. and De La Mare, M. (1988) *The Macmillan Individual Reading Analysis*, Basingstoke, Macmillan Education.

Vincent D., Green, L., Francis, J. and Powney, J. (1983) *A Review of Reading Tests*, Windsor, NFER-Nelson.

Vincent, D., Pugh, A. K. and Brooks, G. (Eds) (1986) *Assessing Reading*, London, Macmillan Education.

Walker, C. (1974) *Reading Development and Extension*, London, Ward Lock Educational.

Wilson, R. M. and Cleland, C. J. (1985) *Diagnostic and Remedial Reading for Classroom and Clinic*, Columbus, Merrill.

13
Making Reading Real

Helen Arnold

The problem in public life is learning to overcome terror, the problem in married life is learning to overcome boredom .... Life in the world was nothing more than a system of atavistic contracts, banal ceremonies, preordained words (Garcia Marquez, *Love in the Time of Cholera*).

Perhaps less dramatically, though equally poignantly, for some children reading may be a similarly unhappy experience. The mastery of the alphabetic system may be threatening, and subsequent reading, when not fluent, will carry a sense of enervating boredom. The difficulties encountered in mastering reading will be compounded by the lack of relevance which the child finds in the text, which is likely to be less immediately rewarding than his more successful life elsewhere. Some aspects of reading instruction include 'atavistic contracts, banal ceremonies and preordained words'.

Martin (1986) shows how Leslie at nine could remember his early difficulties. His first day at school was 'horrible — I was really scared - and - and - the teacher asked me a question and I couldn't answer it'. The fear was later compounded with the boredom of reading and re-reading the scheme. The whole activity of reading became irrelevant and unreal.

Miscue analysis shows clearly how such attitudes are reflected in the strategies used. Hannah, reading a simple passage, exhibits them (note that correct words are in brackets).

I like chips. I have egg and chips for my tea. My dog, Sam, likes them too. He sits by the table. I drop a chip. He eats it. Mum does not see him. She is *dotting* (drinking) her tea. I *work* (wink) at Sam. He *knocks* (knows) it is all *round* (right).

Mum gives me milk. I don't like milk. The cat does, though. She runs into the *kitten* (kitchen) from the back garden. She looks for her milk. If the dish is empty she puts her tail up in the air. She looks very *curring* (cross). So we give her some milk. She *likes* (laps) it up first. Then she walks across the *kitten* (kitchen).

Hannah can decode, and starts off fairly successfully. But the impetus goes, and she begins to use the strategy of applying phonics to the first phoneme only. The sense goes. She makes other miscues to keep in line with her overriding strategy. Such children sacrifice meaning and reality on the altar of faith in a word-attack system which they have not mastered (see also Arnold, 1984).

Lack of short-term memory may have affected her reading; however, 'an alternative explanation for the short-term memory problems of retarded readers is that they are a consequence and not a cause of the reading problem' (Beech and Colley, 1987). Bryant and Bradley (1985) came to the conclusion that short-term memory scores may be influenced by success in reading, and not vice-versa. Whether or not this is finally proven, it seems clear that Hannah's reading strategies resulted in her inability to make suitable conceptual associations or to hold them in her memory. Very little internalization of the text was occurring.

Philip, 9 years old, typifies the 'boredom' cited above. He has a reading age of 8.3 and is, therefore, hardly classified as a retarded reader. Philip, however, chose to read a passage two years below this level, and made a number of both positive and negative miscues. Nine negative miscues showed that he was not reading for meaning on even a simple passage. He avowed, quite aggressively, that reading was boring. He thought that he was not a good reader, but could give no reason for this. The interviewer stated, 'I felt that during the reading of "A Fat Cat" that he knew how good reading should sound, but that he could not achieve it himself and was conscious of this'. He expected his self-chosen book to be difficult because the words were 'cramped up'. He thought that children should learn to read in order to pass exams. He did not enjoy school reading nor did he read at home. Like Hannah, he used the grapho-phonemic cueing system on the first phoneme only of a word. 'I felt that Philip should slow down a little and not panic so much.'

At the beginning of the next session a week later Philip showed the interviewer another self-chosen book, Helen Cresswell's 'Absolute Zero'. He had not yet started to read it, however, and quickly stalled on the words 'disbelief' and 'annoyance' in the first few lines. He put the book down, deciding it was too difficult. He appeared to choose books by looking at the cover only. 'He did not seem to think that it was actually necessary to read — he could get away with choosing new books.'

None of the children quoted above saw reading as real. For something to be real it must relate dynamically to an existing framework of cognitive and/or emotional experience; for reading to be real there must be linkage with already existing conceptual frameworks in two main spheres. The child must be aware of the content of the print and the message of the text (which may include affective response). He must also be aware of the relationship between print and the physical entity of the spoken word. In other words the arbitrary nature of the alphabetic system must become a reality.

The characteristics of mildly retarded learners

Although Reid (1966) and Downing (1970), among others, have shown that metacognition is lacking in children with reading difficulties, it seems that these children may develop reading skills in the same sequence as other children with no problems, but that the development may be slower (Blanton and Semmel, 1987, p. 72).

It does not appear that such children are unable to develop awareness, but it is possible that their cognitive development may be at an earlier stage than 'normal' readers. It seems useful here to think of them in relation to Bruner's stages of cognitive development, namely, the enactive, iconic and symbolic functions. Bruner uses a spiral analogy (Stones, 1970): 'any idea or problem or body of knowledge can be presented in a form simple enough so that any particular learner can understand it'. His theory suggests that the same problem can be approached with increasing complexity. The popular application of this theory to reading instruction has resulted in children learning to read being given very simple material. Unfortunately the retarded reader often remains stuck on the simple material, which becomes increasingly tedious and loses any reality which it once had. Perhaps one should look at Bruner more carefully and apply his model of development to reading in a slightly different way.

The following three sections of this chapter provide teaching suggestions for children at each of Bruner's three levels of development — enactive, iconic and symbolic.

Teaching suggestions for children at three developmental levels

A. Enactive level of development

If we accept that mild retardation may be evidence of slow development rather than lack of development, many older retarded readers may still be operating on an 'enactive' level. They still need to involve themselves actively, indeed physically, in their learning. Reading, as behaviour, seems singularly abstract to them; silent reading is almost synonymous with non-action, unlike all other behaviour except sleeping and thinking! This may be one of the underlying reasons why oral reading is so predominant in early instruction. Oral reading does involve overt 'behaviour', but one of its unresolved difficulties is that we do not know how far exactly oral reading mirrors the processes of silent reading. In oral reading, too, the child's difficulties are magnified by the need to reproduce sounds through the mouth. Negative feedback is inevitable either from the teacher or the child himself.

There are other ways in which physical action on a text might help mildly retarded learners who appear to be at an enactive level — new ways, because the methods they have already encountered seem to have failed. One or two of these somewhat unconventional approaches are suggested. The first emphasizes the nature of the word itself, not in its phonological components, but in the elements which govern its constitution. We become aware of what makes it possible to speak a word at all — the relationship between vowels and consonants. Vowels (open sounds) are necessary in speech to enable us to move from one consonant (closed sound) to another. Vowels, being little more than breath, become difficult to identify in written form and therefore a large and confusing number of ways of recording them have developed. The method is as follows.

Present a couple of sentences and remind the readers that there are five vowels in the alphabet, not defining them but simply naming them as A E I O U. Children can work in pairs. Each member of the pair has a different text. They are asked to rewrite their sentences, omitting all the vowels, a mechanical exercise. At first they can put dashes for the omitted letters, although it is quite possible to work without leaving gaps at all.

For example:

-nc- -p-n – t-m- th-r- w-s – sm-ll b-y c-ll-d N-ch-l-s. H- h-d – d-g c-ll-d J-ck -nd – gr--t fr--nd c-ll-d P-t-r P-rk-ns wh- l-v-d -t R-s- C-tt-g- n--r th- r--lw-y l-n- (Reeves, 1984).

The children then exchange their text with their friend, and try to read it out to each other (not to write in the vowels). There will be difficulties with some words, but it is surprisingly easy to read without the vowels. (Note that Pitman's Shorthand uses no vowels, and the written forms of Arabic and Hebrew omit vowels.)

When the children read the texts back, they will automatically supply appropriate vowel sounds. It is almost impossible to read the words as they stand, and this will quickly become apparent. We then begin to discuss the function of vowels and experiment with making closed and open sounds, noticing how different organs of speech are used in producing consonants. The children begin to see words in a new light while focusing on their physical identity in speech. Syllabification can follow; the fact that every vowel has its cluster of consonants may help children to split words into syllables. They could be shown an old primer in which the long words are physically broken down into syllables, and invited to rewrite a story from a modern text in the same way. Note also Thomson's method of teaching syllabification in Chapter 10.

The same sort of physical awareness can be applied at paragraph and discourse level. The principle of many of the Directed Activities Related to Text (DARTS) which were suggested by the Effective Use of Reading Project (Lunzer and Gardner, 1979) was similar. They said that physical manipulation of an existing text would motivate readers to look at it more carefully. Cloze Procedure has now become somewhat overused, but it can, for instance, help children to understand the difference between the way 'function' and 'content' words work. Sequencing cards which have been physically jumbled into a coherent order again involves physical manipulation which is motivating at the enactive stage.

Philip was given a set of instructions to sequence in the right order. At first he put the cards in a haphazard sequence and said he could not do it. We talked about one and then he did the others himself. He was not willing to say why he had chosen a certain order — he just said 'Because they fit'. His initial reaction was so often 'I can't do this or I'll look silly', but when he saw he was capable he tackled it quite enthusiastically.

A variation on sequencing which uses the techniques of 'Breakthrough to Literacy' often works well. A very short poem or rhyme is split up into single words, each of which is put on a separate piece of card and presented in jumbled form. The child then makes a poem from the words. He may leave out up to about five words so that the problem does not become too mechanistic. He is shuffling the words about physically, and later copies out the finished poem. Then he can compare it with the original (which may not be all that superior!).

Too many retarded readers struggle with text on their own. Reading has become a cut-off activity which separates them from the group. It need not be. One of the most fruitful ways of bringing what is read to life is to let a group work on a tape-recorded interpretation of a picture book, using sound effects only. The unity of the story is conveyed through the series of sounds, which can be made with anything which comes to hand, other than musical instruments. When the tape is completed, one member of the group turns over the pages of the story as the sound-track is played back. The audience may not get the details of the plot, but moods and climaxes emerge clearly.

B. Iconic level of development

Bruner sees the next stage of development as 'iconic representation', in which children may appreciate knowledge as 'a set of summary images or graphics that stand for a concept without defining it fully' (Stones, 1970). Many retarded readers continue to use the pictures of a text without decoding the words. This, of course, is not reading, and it may indicate that these children are still at an iconic stage. Imaging should continue to be an important element of mature reading, however. Shirley Hughes, who writes and illustrates excellent children's books, argues that very young children have better visual memories than adults. 'I suspect that it [visualization] may fall off a little when the thrilling and prestigious skill of reading is achieved' (Hughes, 1987). She recommends the presentation of a variety of pictures to train appreciation of style and the retention of visual imagery. Retarded readers should be encouraged to look into pictures carefully and to pick out their distinctive features. Puzzle pictures with hidden elements could be particularly helpful here. This may help them to discern the distinctive features of words. The ability to dwell and reflect upon what is on the page, either in picture or word form, seems to be lacking in many children. Focusing, not flitting, is necessary. Adult literacy students often exhibit the same type of behaviour as young children failing with reading; they fidget rather than focus. Their eyes dart all over the room, anywhere but on the page, they shift and tap nervously — all classic signs of loss of concentration because the text is unwelcome and fearful.

A slightly bizarre activity is suggested which attempts to break down such barriers, and to turn words themselves into visual entities. A few examples will set most children off devising their own visuals. They may incidentally become aware of spelling patterns. Many words can be made into pictures, signifying their meaning visually, as in Figure 13.1.

It is sometimes a positive drawback to have a large number of illustrations in a story. When there are few illustrations there can be extensive discussion — even argument — about the images of the characters which can be created in the mind.

Diagrammatic and representational outcomes are particularly appropriate at this stage. Children can make a strip cartoon of a story they have read, allowing a specific number of pictures, which will necessitate summarizing and selecting important events. They are allowed to devise speech bubbles and one caption for each picture, thus using different modes of writing. If several children illustrate the same story, comparisons can be made of the selections for illustration.

C. Symbolic level of development

Bruner's third level is that of 'symbolic representation'. It is likely that older children with reading difficulties may not be performing on this level. This does not mean that they are not able to, and there may be ways to help such children. They must be able to systematize their strategies so that they can apply rules that work. In reading this involves the appropriate and economical use of all cueing systems. Children have been used to plodding through text word by word. With the help of the teacher they can become more flexible in their mode of reading. This may involve going away from the type of familiar text with which the children have been struggling. To become real the learner must translate instruction into his own ways of solving a problem.

Learning new material is possible only within some knowledge distance of the learner's present knowledge (Rosenberg, 1987). In practical terms, it is suggested that setting advance organizers is one of the best ways of harnessing existing knowledge and of creating awareness before a text is approached.

Infant teachers often familiarize their pupils with the words that they are going to meet when they start reading, by introducing words and characters

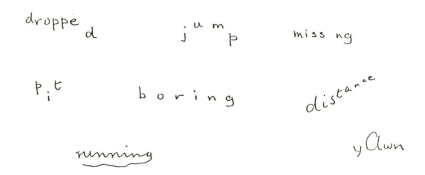

Figure 13.1 Making words into pictures

first, and discussing them. This technique can be used with effect with older readers.

Select a number of isolated words from a story or article. Present them on cards spread out on a page, jumbled, as in Figure 13.2. Ask each individual to cluster the words into small groups in any way she or he likes, intuitively and quickly. Compare with a partner to see how far the groupings are similar. By this time a 'story' will be emerging. General discussion follows on what the story might be about, and where the words will fit. Some words will be more difficult than others; 'sail' may be a noun or a verb, for instance. The children become intrigued to know what the original story says:

Figure 13.2 Random layout of words (on cards)

They made little rafts out of twigs, and they paddled away over the water to Owl Island to gather nuts. Each squirrel had a little sack and a large oar, and spread out his tail for a sail.

Few will have the originality of Beatrix Potter, who thought of each squirrel's tail as a sail! (*The Tale of Squirrel Nutkin*).

It is equally possible to use information passages. This activity was tried with three 7-year-olds who were presented with words from a geography text which seemed on the face of it far too difficult. The teacher finally read the passage to the children. What followed was unexpected. The children listened to the reading with their eyes glued to their jumbled words. As they heard one of the words, their fingers darted towards it. It was an added bonus to the original experience.

Teaching scanning

Very few adults remember being taught to skim and scan, and these skills are often classed as study skills, suitable only for advanced readers. The realization for the slow reader, however, that it is not always necessary to wade through every word on a page, may come as a release. Such readers will often need convincing of this, as they think of accurate reading as the only 'right' way to read. Purposes for reading need to be planned carefully in advance, and the idea of 'letting words jump out from the page' to be demonstrated. Even virtual non-readers can look down a page and find proper names or the names of places. Eventually they will be able to collate two or three pieces of information from different paragraphs.

Scanning, (looking for specific predetermined items), means that one does not have to assimilate the whole passage. Speed is important, because slowing up tends to make one forget the original goal and to be waylaid by irrelevant information. Two activities will now be presented.

A. *The scanning game*

Duplicate a short passage at an appropriate readability level. Distribute, warning readers not to look at the text until a signal is given. The teacher asks questions without giving time for the passage to be read fully. Answers can be oral or written, but should be one word or short phrase. Questions should start with easily discernible words, and increase in difficulty as the readers become familiar with the text through constant scanning. Here is an example from Dineen (1987a).

The age of a tree

Each year a tree grows more branches. The roots grow deeper. A thin layer, or ring, of new sapwood grows around the trunk. These rings are called GROWTH RINGS. If the trunk of a tree is cut right across, the rings can be seen. Each ring counts for one year. So it is possible to tell how old a tree is. Some trees live to a great age. The oldest trees in the world are the bristlecone pine trees in North America. One of these trees is more than 4000 years old. It is the oldest living thing known on earth.

Questions:

What are the age rings on a tree called?
How long does each ring count for?
How old is the oldest living thing on earth?
How can you see the rings on a tree?
Where are the bristlecone pine trees found?

Another useful activity helps children to focus on the text in advance, and then to skim and scan to check whether their assumptions are correct.

B. *True or false*

Present some statements relevant to a short passage of information text. The children tick whether they think the statements are true or false before they read the text. They may be guessing, or using prior experience. They then read the text in order to check whether they were right or wrong, filling in their results in a third column. Here is an example.

A double page spread from Dineen's (1987b) 'Living by the Water' (pp. 12–13) was used. The teacher presented the following statements:

	TRUE	FALSE	WAS I RIGHT?
1. Thousands of years ago, people used logs to travel by water.			
2. No one makes dug-out canoes today.			
3. Some barges can carry heavy goods.			

4. Barges need deep water to sail.
5. Some people make their homes on barges.
6. The River Thames is crowded with pleasure boats today.

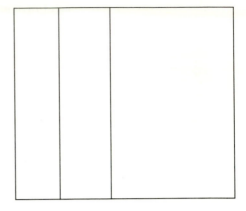

Subsequently, the children themselves made up statements from another page of the book, for their friends to answer:

Sports and Holidays (Dineen, *op. cit*, p. 20).

1. Most people have holidays in the Summer.
2. Surf boards are always fast.
3. Some holiday towns close down in the winter.
4. Sailing boats are no longer than 2 or 3 metres.

An activity-centred teaching approach

It is clear that setting varied purposes for reading will necessitate flexible strategies. It is also clear, in practice, that some of the most rewarding activities are those which the children concoct for others to carry out.

Most of the suggestions made already use books as a focus for reading. It is equally important that other kinds of text are used, particularly those which are already 'real' for children. 'English for Ages 5 to 11', the proposals of the Cox Committee for Implementation of the National Curriculum, emphasizes awareness of 'labels and notices' (Department of Education and Science and the Welsh Office, 1988). The first objective of Attainment Target II:[1] Reading, Level 2, is: 'Read accurately straightforward signs, labels and notices'. All children, however handicapped in formal reading, have been exposed to labels since babyhood, but not many of them consider these as perfectly legitimate reading material. Activities centred round labels can be applied at the enactive, iconic and symbolic levels. Labels incorporate visual and lexical items in a meaningful context, though not necessarily simply. Because information, notably on food labels, tends to contain more factual details than ever before, the reading skills employed may be complex. A language project could be devised round labels. The overall purpose would be to help children to use a variety of clues in examining real containers. Possible development would include:

1. RECOGNITION

(Linking experience of contents with description.)
From a selection of containers, choose one to look at in detail, asking, for example,

What do you think is inside this?
Are there any other boxes here which have the same sort of thing inside?
How do we know what's inside, without opening it?
What do we do with what's inside?

2. DIAGNOSIS THROUGH LINGUISTIC AND PERCEPTUAL DISCRIMINATION

Look carefully at one of the labels.

Where is the name of the product?
Does the label tell you anywhere what the product is for?
Read out the part which tells you what is inside.
Can you tell me in your own words?
Does the label tell you how much is inside?

Children can start collecting lists of the different terms used on labels to denote weight, capacity, quantity etc.

Does the label tell you who made the product?
Can you find where it came from?
Is there anything else written on the label? What? Why?
Compare the visual with the text. Do they match each other? Do you get some information from the pictures that you don't get from the text? Vice versa?

3. CLASSIFICATION

Give a group of children a collection of containers with different types of contents (food, medicine, cleaning materials, games). Ask them to group them in any way they choose, giving reasons for their decisions.

The classification will, of course, depend on what has been presented. One group might work with nothing but, for example, cleaning materials. They could then classify them according to different cleaning jobs, or the composition of the contents — liquid, solid, powder, cream, etc., or those that carry danger notices and those which are non-toxic.

4. EVALUATION

Find all the words which say how good the product is. Which words do you think are best? Which words sound like the product (onomatopoeic words are plentiful on labels, often including the name of the product itself). Can you guess what a product is from its name only? What would you add to a label to make it better, clearer? Would you buy this product? Why?

Consumer questionnaires and surveys can be devised to find out how far people are influenced by labels.

5. CREATIVE USE OF LABELS
Create new names, slogans, rhymes etc., for selected products. Devise complete labels for invented products.

Conclusions

'English from 5 to 16' (Department of Education and Science, 1984) and 'English in the National Curriculum' (Department of Education and Science and the Welsh Office, 1989), suggest that the objectives for learning language can best be attained by setting tasks which require communication for real or realistic purposes. Many of the suggestions above set up 'realistic' rather than 'real' situations, but in carrying them out children may be encouraged to see reading as a 'real' necessity for life. The activities suggested in this chapter have the following implications:

1. We should not give undue emphasis to the artificial structures and irrational content of many conventional reading schemes.
2. Narrative is not the only way into reading.
3. We should encourage children to vary the way they read for different purposes at all stages of learning, and we should encourage interruption of the 'straight read'.
4. We should make use of the familiar material which surrounds children in everyday life.
5. We should help failing readers towards cognitive clarity by involving them in game-like analyses of textual features.
6. We should encourage the sharing of reading for real purposes and audiences, which will include talking and writing as well as reading.

Note

1. The subsequent modification of the Attainment Targets does not substantially affect the argument we presented. The final list of Attainment Targets in English was published in May, 1989 (Department of Education and Science and the Welsh Office, 1989).

References

Arnold, H. (1984) *Making Sense of It*, Sevenoaks, Hodder and Stoughton.
Beech, J. and Colley, A. (1987) *Cognitive Approaches to Reading*, London, Wiley.
Blanton, L. P. and Semmel, M. I. (1987) in Rosenberg, S. (Ed) *Advances in Applied Psycholinguistics*, Volume 2, London, Cambridge University Press.
Bryant, P. and Bradley, L. (1985) *Children's Reading Problems*, Oxford, Blackwell.
Department of Education and Science (1984) *English from 5 to 16*, London, HMSO.
Department of Education and Science and the Welsh Office (1988) *English for Ages 5-11: Proposals of the Secretaries of State* (The Cox Report), London, HMSO.
Department of Education and Science and the Welsh Office (1989) *English in the National Curriculum*, London, HMSO.
Downing, J. (1970) 'Children's concepts of language in learning to read', *Educational Research*, 12, 2, p. 106.
Hughes, S. (1987) 'The art of looking', *Times Educational Supplement*, 16 November, 1987.
Lunzer, E. A. and Gardner, K. (Eds) (1979) *The Effective Use of Reading*, London, Heinemann.
Martin, A. (1986) 'Leslie: a reading failure talks about failing', *Reading*, 20, 1, pp. 43–52.
Reid, J. F. (1966) 'Children's concepts of language in learning to read', *Educational Research*, 12, p. 106.
Rosenberg, S. (Ed) (1987) *Advances in Applied Psycholinguistics*, Volume 2, London, Cambridge University Press.
Stones, E. (1970) *Readings in Educational Psychology*, London, Heinemann.

Texts used as examples of activities

Dineen, J. (1987a) *Trees and Forests*, London, Macmillan World Library.
Dineen, J. (1987b) *Living by the Water*, London, Macmillan World Library.
Potter, B. (1903) *The Tale of Squirrel Nutkin*, London, Warne.
Reeves, J. (Ed) (1984) *A Golden Land*, Harmondsworth, Puffin.

14
Learning Strategies for Pupils with Literacy Difficulties: Motivation, Meaning and Imagery

Morag Hunter-Carsch

Introduction

The introduction of the new National Curriculum in England and Wales requires that teachers demonstrate a range of professional skills. Of particular importance are those related to keeping track of the progress and problems of *all* of their pupils including those with learning difficulties which affect reading, writing and spelling across the curriculum.

To do this successfully will require access to a wider perspective on literacy and methods of teaching than may have been generally available in the past. It will have to take account of issues which are not 'subject-specific' (e.g. how spelling difficulties affect progress in science) and others which are not solely the concern of the class teacher for the particular year group (e.g. recording of attainment cumulatively through the levels).

Thus the introduction of the new curriculum could be very helpful for pupils with literacy difficulties to the extent that their teachers are assisted with the daunting task they face. The assistance is needed firstly in the disseminating of information and the sharing of a wide enough frame of reference to take into account, in the educational context, the value of both macrostrategies and microstrategies for supporting such pupils' learning. This must be done in such a way as to maintain their *motivation*, willingness to seek *meaning* and to find ways of making their own *imagery* (pictures or ways of processing learning) to assist them to overcome their learning difficulties.

This chapter attempts to provide a framework for meeting special educational needs in the normal classroom. It includes insights gained from relating the three major theoretical perspectives, the psychoneurological, psychodynamic and psycho-educational (Hunter, 1982). However their practical applications have been extended to adapt and develop what was previously a somewhat static view of 'the structured approach' (Cruickshank, 1963).

The 'new dynamism' should also involve parents as partners with teachers in finding suitable microstrategies to assist their pupils' learning. It should also take account of the expansion in knowledge from a multidisciplinary perspective, drawing on advice and collaboratively working with colleagues from speech therapy, physiotherapy and linguistics as well as developmental, cognitive and educational psychology.

Figure 14.1 illustrates the centrality of the questions, 'WHAT has to be learned?' and 'HOW is it to be learned?' These questions point the way to devising *primary strategies* (Dansereau, 1978) which Leong (1987) reports as relating to identifying important portions of materials, techniques to comprehend, to retain or recall. Questions concerning the pupil's attitude and motivation would lead to devising *support strategies* which would also include techniques for monitoring and correcting primary strategies (Dansereau, 1978).

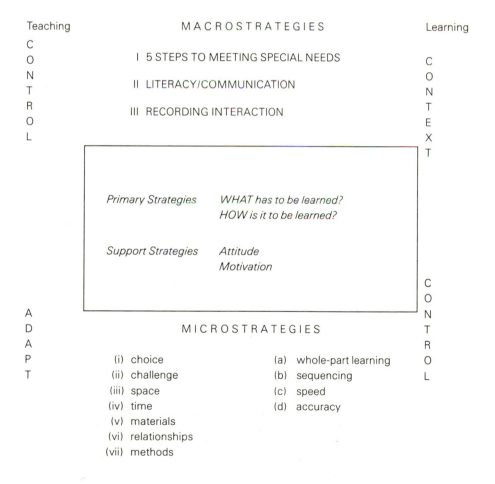

Figure 14.1 Strategies for Assisting Learning

Figure 14.1 differentiates between *macrostrategies* for learning (philosophies of instruction and general themes) and *microstrategies*. The latter include procedural considerations such as whole/part learning, sequencing, emphasis on speed, accuracy or both, and other aspects. By integrating the two frames of reference, the relationship between teaching and learning might helpfully be reconsidered in terms of their reciprocity in bringing about 'control from *within*' the learner. This can be achieved by adapting or 'structuring' or controlling the context i.e. *outside* the learner by using e.g. microstrategies (i) to (vii) inclusive.

It is only possible in one chapter to outline briefly the framework. This, it is proposed, would include three 'macrostrategies'. These are:

I   a five step approach to meeting special needs within the ordinary classroom,

II a wider perspective on literacy, and

III a method for recording teacher–pupil interaction to assist reading, writing and spelling incidentally in the course of classroom work.

This chapter will also provide examples of literacy difficulties and microstrategies. Information on primary strategies for selecting, preparing and presenting texts for learning is provided elsewhere, for example, in the approach known as ERICA, 'Effective Reading in the Content Areas', (Morris and Stewart-Doré, 1987) and in 'Reading for Learning' (Lunzer and Gardner, 1984).

Characteristics of children with literacy difficulties

A number of generalizations is made concerning the characteristics of children with literacy difficulties. Each generalization is based on classroom experience and on research evidence. As this chapter is oriented towards classroom practice, the research evidence is deliberately not presented. Some references are included in the bibliography. Other contributers have covered the relevant research.

Some children who are otherwise fairly normal or above average in their school achievements in other areas of the curriculum, experience persistent difficulty in any learning which specifically concerns one or more of the following:

(i)   Handwriting (motor coordination/clumsiness)

(ii) Speech, listening, speaking and language (making sense of what is heard, experienced and planning what is to be communicated), and

(iii) Reading (decoding the words and the writer's message) and spelling (encoding a dictated or composed message).

The three categories are not exclusive but for educational purposes are helpful to differentiate as curricular work can be adapted for the purpose of developing the following:

    (i) Fluency in writing,

    (ii) Fluency in making mental associations, word finding and appropriately articulating sequences of sounds, words and ideas, and

    (iii) Competence in decoding and encoding the printed word.

Difficulties particularly in (ii) and (iii) above, may include (a) *object naming* — word finding, (b) *phonemic segmentation* — splitting the word, which can be heard as a whole, into phonemes in order to write down graphemes. This presupposes a firm grasp of phoneme-grapheme relationships and the alphabetical basis of our encoding system; and (c) *memory*. Memory difficulties may involve more than one mode of recall i.e. by reauditorizing, revisualizing, motor-memory (kinesthesis) or other associations of touch, taste or smell that may initially seem like memory difficulties. They may however involve selective and sustained attention, rather than either working-memory, or the 'laying down of a trace' into longer term memory. Thus some of the behaviour regarded as lack of application, laziness and carelessness may in fact reflect difficulties or even disabilities in a number of processes. These include sustaining attention, particularly in certain classroom situations and at certain times when the child's '*energy level*' and '*mood*' are variable. Paradoxically, a child may be described as 'lacking stickability' because his concentration is intense. He may be described as 'unable to get something out of his mind and go onto what has to be done next', if he is over-intensely attending.

Such children may also be anxious. This may sometimes relate to difficulties in predicting what will happen next, particularly in classrooms where there is not a regular routine attached to at least a part of every day. Pupils may be *disorganized*, possibly as a function of memory problems relating to the location of things in both time and place. They may also be *accident-prone* or *clumsy*. They are often inconsistent in their achievements in language-related school work. The inconsistencies may relate not only to moods and energy levels but to the nature, frequency and patterns of spelling errors and to reading which involves the recalling of words. They may devise socially acceptable ways of obscuring the extent of their learning difficulties e.g. excuses for not getting started, or not finishing a task in time. Similarly, adults with learning difficulties often make excuses such as not having their glasses with them. In school, pupils may, or may not, initially show behavioural or emotional stress or disturbances but they usually experience extreme frustration in the face of failure to learn what seems to be 'automatic' and easy for others. They are likely to be easily tired in school yet some may sleep less (stay up late) and get up earlier than other children.

Quick tempers and hyperactivity may be a resultant as well as a causal factor affecting attention, memory and learning in the busy normal classroom.

The emphasis in teaching must therefore be on *de-toning anxiety*, *building confidence through self-awareness*, teaching for *relaxation* as well as

I am rieting to show you my haedrieting is bater then befor. I my goting on at school uery well. but dust I have head a akcdent in P.E. I (yo) was playing hokey and I got hit in the mawth by a Hokey boll It hut one of my font teeth. It brok in herf. my mawth is sowr. I had to go to the nentis becorse I had to have a nerve out and lots of work done. I had a soper brthday I got a personal radio and lots of beoks and more. I hop to Meat you soon

Figure 14.2 Excerpt from a letter by David aged 13 years

sustained attention. The generation of a capacity to create a condition for learning, as well as the mechanisms or *strategies for coping* with the learning problems as such, are also essential.

The excerpt from David's letter (Figure 14.2) shows persistent difficulty with spelling. There are additions and omissions of letters and words as well as substitutions of words and of letters within words. However the message he conveys is clear and coherent. David had received individual tutoring at home and support at school. He learned to sustain his attention, to become capable of writing in a fairly fluent hand with clear well-formed letters and good word spacing. His interest and attitude became more positive as his self control and achievement increased. It is possible that his tutoring has contributed to some over-generalization of phonics in his spelling but at least he acquired a successful strategy for getting down a fairly good approximation to the words he wished to use. Much of his later 'success' in spelling relied on mastery of the use of the ACE Dictionary (Moseley and Nichols, 1986) which he greatly appreciates and for the use of which, his earlier training in alphabetical order, syllabification and phonics was crucial.

Parents and teachers often ask about whether there is realistically a chance of an individual child with specific learning difficulties overcoming spelling difficulties. It is neither wise nor helpful to make sweeping generalizations particularly as there are so many factors which could be involved. What is clear is that many children with such difficulties have succeeded in getting around their difficulties, if not in overcoming them. Some continue to rely on special dictionaries and checking programmes as well as a review of their personalized lists of 'hard words'. It is particularly helpful to monitor from the beginning, the extent to which the child can identify in a passage of his own composition those words which he is unsure about and those which he knows to be spelled correctly. The use of brackets in systematic drafting and redrafting is helpful not only for spelling but for many aspects of developing written language (Binns, 1989).

Before discussing what might become more detailed and special strategies for use in dealing with children's literacy difficulties, the following section outlines, at the 'macro level' an approach which provides the framework for describing and meeting special educational needs. It could be used with reference to a range of special needs, not only those concerning writing, reading and spelling. Trials of the approach have borne out the importance of checking the child's awareness of his or her positive abilities and interests. Too often it is the difficulties which dominate in the teacher's recall. Thus efforts should be made to discover pointers towards ways of adapting teaching by approaching the child's learning through 'strengths', not only trying to identify and improve 'weak' areas.

Macrostrategies I: a framework for describing and meeting special educational needs

The approach involves taking the following five steps:

1. DESCRIBE the child's difficulties
2. ANALYZE the notes
3. STATE the child's special needs
4. ADAPT teaching
5. RECORD findings.

To use this framework (first introduced in Dawson, 1985) requires no detailed specialist knowledge. It is designed to capitalize on the teacher's existing and considerable expertise.

1. *Describe* your impressions of the individual pupil's difficulties. Do so away from the classroom, if possible, in cooperation with a colleague. Record your comments about the child in one of four quadrants of a page divided into (i) learning difficulties, (ii) learning disabilities, (iii) behavioural difficulties, and (iv) social development (see Figure 14.3). These comments (enumerated to record the sequence in which they were spoken) can then be summarized in terms of the perceived major areas of difficulty (the 'minuses' [–]) and

contrasted with any recognized areas of relative interest or ability (the 'pluses' [+]). The analysis identifies gaps in your knowledge of the child. It also helps identify and prioritize the issues that the teacher wishes to address (the questions [?]). Since these are generally 'impressions', it is essential to go beyond your awareness of your own opinions to check what is actually observable in the classroom. To do this adopt the following simple strategy. Take two minutes to observe what the child actually does and discuss with him or her the way in which the work is being 'learned'. Make notes using the 'Teacher Interaction with Child' (TIC) approach. This involves compiling a dated record of your observations of the way the child listens, speaks, reads and writes and attempts to cope with difficulties in using any one or more of these modes. The system is illustrated on p. 233. It has been demonstrated in Thames Television 'Seeing and Doing' (Hunter-Carsch, 1989b).

2. *Analyze* the observed difficulties in order to try to differentiate between problems which occur as a result of

a developmental gaps (changes of schools or teachers, or absence due to illness)
b mild learning difficulty (not 'catching on', slower learner across most of the curriculum)
c 'crisis' situations or sudden severe problems which are uncharacteristic of the child (emotional or physical)
d specific learning difficulties.

3. *State* the child's special needs and how you think these might be met. Include advice and support from colleagues, parents and, where relevant, specialists in the field.

4. *Adapt* your teaching to permit you to give some individual support. How is a class teacher to do this? It can take as little as one minute to introduce a three minute task for which the child can use an egg timer. The teacher then observes and tries to 'mark' i.e. review immediately *with* the child. This requires about five minutes daily, or at least every two days.

5. *Record* your findings with reference to the child's skills of learning. Make notes about the nature of any difficulty.

The procedures described above will be illustrated by a case study of James, a primary school child with learning difficulties (Hunter, 1982).

Step 1. Describe the child's difficulties

Firstly, his difficulties are summarized, as in Figure 14.3. The 'checklist' records the following information: James has difficulty with concentration, produces only limited work unless 'anchored', can be silly and day-dreams. He has cooperative parents and a brother with major communication problems. The picture is one of a child with learning difficulties (concentration, work patterns) and behavioural difficulties in the sense of being 'silly' and 'day-dreaming'. There is no immediate note of any specific learning disabilities. These notes are then analyzed, as in Figure 14.4.

```
Name:  James
Age:   10 years
Date:
```

LEARNING DIFFICULTIES	BEHAVIOUR DIFFICULTIES
3. work limited 4. no concentration 5. when anchored will work within limits	1. can be silly 2. daydreams
LEARNING DISABILITY	SOCIAL DEVELOPMENT
	6. cooperative parents 7. older brother with major communication difficulties

The above format for Step 1 was devised by C. Skilling, Adviser, Leicestershire Local Education Authority.

Figure 14.3 Description of James' difficulties

+	−	?
can work under clear directions	produces little without help	1. How long has he had concentration difficulties? 2. How well can he cope with basic skills of reading, writing and counting? 3. Has he a history of good health? Physical problems?

Figure 14.4 Analysis of James' notes

Step 2. Analyze the notes

Questions arise as to why James behaved differently in various situations.

1. What behavioural difficulties did he show and what was he meant to be doing at the time?
2. To what extent was his 'silly' behaviour and lack of concentration reflective of his behaviour at home? (Does he have behavioural problems at home?)
3. What are the differences in the work that James does when 'anchored' and when not concentrating? (Are these differences in interest level or in difficulty?)

4. Might he fear that he cannot cope in the large class situation, or that he cannot do his work at all?
5. Is he exploiting the teacher's goodwill, and seeking constant attention?
6. Might he be modelling his behaviour on the 'silly behaviour' of any other people in the class, or out of school?
7. Is the 'silly behaviour' a nervous reaction? (Does it really interfere with anyone else, or himself?)

It is tempting to focus on behavioural aspects since they draw attention to themselves more obviously in the classroom. However, it is possible that the problem in James' case may be related to underlying learning, memory or attentional factors. The issues may more constructively concern the ways in which James' apparently successful learning in the tutorial situation can be carried over into the classroom situation. The following suggestions for further exploration are made tentatively:

1. Discover by use of Informal Reading Inventories what James can do and where there may be 'gaps' or specific difficulties.
2. Describe precisely what James does in particular situations in which his behaviour is considered problematic.
   a) What was the class/group/child asked to do?
   b) What did James do/say/throw!?
   c) How is this different from the behaviour of other children and what was intended?
   This will necessitate keeping systematic notes which are *dated* and indicate details of the context (e.g. time of day, subject area and any special circumstances). It may sound a difficult additional task for the class teacher to keep detailed records. However, noting just one or two situations as soon after they occur as possible can help to throw some light on what is happening. Such observations lead to the formulation of questions aimed at understanding the child's difficulties.
3. What is the child's state of health and attendance?
4. What, if any, specific factors seem to affect James' concentration, e.g. what kinds of noises distract him? Do changes in particular sights or situations affect him in similar ways to particular noises?

These suggestions are tailored to fit James' situation. Some of them may, however, prove useful in general for work with other children.

Questions might also include the following:

5. What causes James' 'silly' and 'daydreaming' behaviour?
6. To what extent is it a cause of learning problems or the result of having difficulty in learning?
7. What is James' attitude to school in general and to books and reading in particular?
8. What are James' interests in school and out of school?
9. In what ways might further information about how James learns at

home, his parents' views and their ways of relating to James and his
brother, be of help to James' teacher?

10. Since James seems to respond well to 'limit setting' in the classroom ,
    what kinds of limits are effective? (Space — where he works; times;
    materials/resources he uses).

Step 3. State the child's difficulties and special educational needs

Tentative hypotheses as to James' problems and special needs:

1. James has difficulty in learning. His behavioural problems are probably
   the result of lack of successful or rewarding learning in the classroom
   context.
2. James will learn more effectively in a small group or individual tutoring
   situation for part of the time. This would possibly also make it easier to
   study how he learns and what he already knows and can do. Where
   there is no chance of working along with a colleague to free one of
   them to work more individually with James, try to adapt work in the
   classroom so that you can spend at least five minute sessions two or
   three times a week on concentrated study of how James learns.

Step 4. Adapting teaching

Try out individualized teaching within a tutoring situation out of the classroom
for regular short times over several weeks. Try working with materials or topics
that are not immediately connected with 'hard school work' (if possible in a
'games' context using basic literacy skills so that James' skills in this area can be
informally assessed).

Step 5. Recording of findings

In a very small group situation, making and using board games, James
appeared to be enthusiastic, careful, accurate in copy writing, able to pick out
key words in his reading book and had 'original ideas'. There was no evidence
of silly behaviour or daydreaming in this situation.

James did experience some difficulty in writing words from phonics and
expressed some anxiety with this task. He may have difficulty with visual recall
of letters. He also appeared to be distracted by noise.

His teacher reported that on returning to the classroom he reverted to
showing behavioural difficulties. Continued special tutoring was required,
linked with classwork and systematic evaluation of the programme.

Macrostrategies II: teach 'literacy' in a communication context
(a wider view, re-connecting reading and writing)

In teaching children with reading and writing difficulties it readily becomes apparent that many of them have become bogged-down with their feelings of failure. Many are confused by what must seem to them, a plethora of details of signs and symbols that have to be memorized and applied automatically. In the first instance it may be necessary to stand back from the scene and together, teacher and child, possibly along with the whole class or a group, check that there is real enjoyment and evidence of the will to communicate in a context which involves 'reading' (decoding) or 'writing' (encoding) *other kinds of symbols and messages* e.g. art, drama, dance, music. The need is to be able to grasp the underlying idea of the exchange of messages, and that communication is 'about something', not just a task in itself. The re-connecting with the wider, larger purposes of communication in life is essential. Then a sufficiently strong, shared interest and learning/teaching bond can be established and maintained in order constructively to address literacy-related learning difficulties together. It is only when this understanding (grasp) of reading and writing as decoding and encoding messages is kept in mind that the task of coping with the alphabetical system becomes conceptually manageable. To make it practically achievable, requires systematic work. This can begin with the handling of cut-out letters (wooden, magnetic, plastic or card) and the acquisition of the feeling of being able to 'grasp' the letters (and the whole alphabet), as well as the intellectual understanding of the idea of phoneme-grapheme match (see Morris, 1984). Her system, integral to 'Phonics 44', involves grasping sequences of letters, at once (automatically). Certain letter strings (more than blends; e.g. -ing, -ed) are basic to spelling and important to consider in terms of *morphemes* or basic meaning units. Then the jump from single letters to words, both in 'unlocking' (decoding/reading) them and in 'constructing' (writing/spelling) them, is based on the meaningful ways in which our language is constructed. We had the words for 'cat' and 'dog', 'eat' and 'run' before the printed symbols of our alphabetic system. In this Macrostrategy, remembering the breadth of the educational aims of developing 'communication', assists in keeping 'literacy' in its place as a lively element in the teacher-learner exchange.

For further information on teaching reading and writing within a broader perspective on literacy see also 'The Art of Reading' (Hunter-Carsch 1989a). For children with literacy difficulties there is a particular need to see that the 'bottom-up' approach (letters→words→stories) is firmly linked with the 'top-down' approach (emphasis on story approach→words→letters) otherwise the idea of using context cues ('guessing' words and filling in from general understanding of the story) may otherwise go on well beyond the usual time at which word recognition should be developing. Explicitly taught strategies for making bonds between each letter shape and sequence will then be necessary along with valuing the spirit of enquiry which is encouraged via a story approach. The value of, for example, making phonemic awareness explicit is clearly described by Cataldo and Ellis (Chapter 7).

Macrostrategies III: monitoring language development

Keeping track of the child's progress and problems in the classroom need not be tiresome and complex. The following 'macrostrategy' involves noting Teacher-Interaction with Child (TIC) in a two minute chat about the task being carried out at the time. Most work in the classroom involves listening and speaking; some of it involves reading and writing. It is relatively easy, in talking over what the child is reading or writing about, to note comments on his listening and speaking ability as well as his reading and writing ability. However, comments simply on listening and speaking can be noted quickly on the suggested format (using the quadrant for listening, speaking, reading and writing as in Figure 14.5). This can be done in the context of discussing, for example, artwork, craft or design, practical mathematics or science.

Anna 8 yrs		2/2/89
L ② attentitive in discussion — responded well when her ideas were discussed		R ① page 8 Dragon II obviously enjoying story — grasped main ideas/events — can read 'sn' blends (snakes)
S ③ fluent but some trouble with pronouncing 'S' (like 'th' in 'snake' → thnake) Lisp? developmental?		W ④ can re-read her notes under her illustration of the snake and dragon. Can find her own spelling problems.
	[Does she share stories/read aloud at home?]	

Figure 14.5 TIC informal record-keeping approach (Teacher Interaction with Child)

Observe and discuss work with one child in the course of routine classwork. On any piece of paper, make a quick note of your observations using the 'Language Cross' quadrant for each area — listening, reading, speaking, writing. Be sure to note the child's name, age and the date. It is helpful for later reference if you also note any reading material disscussed; interests and abilities as well as difficulties. Children are usually interested in helping with the process, like to see your notes and learn to keep their own records. Normally, two minutes is sufficient to carry out a short 'conference' and to make brief notes. They can be added to later and transferred, where relevant, to more formal records, perhaps with examples of the child's work.

A TIC record for the whole class can be completed in a month if only one child is observed and has a brief intereaction each day. It becomes easier to extend the discussion times when all the children know that their turn will come and they enjoy the short conferences. With experience, the class will 'tolerate' TICs of more than five minutes, more than twice per day. See also Southgate *et al.*, regarding the need to discuss what is done by the pupil (1981).

Microstrategies I: support strategies

The structured approach (CCSTMRM)*

In the past some of the support strategies generally considered as part of 'the structured approach' were employed by teachers who may not have had a sufficient understanding of the whole philosophy of that approach. To that extent their use of a single support strategy without the relevant background knowledge of how it fits into a way of thinking and relating, was rather like a child's use of a 'splinter-skill' such as being able to copy a letter of the alphabet but not to recognize its meaning in a word or another style of writing (Kephart, 1963).

What is required is familiarity with the underlying rationale. This provides the basis from which to make informed judgments about how and when to adapt an aspect of the approach and what might be added, omitted or altered with reference to the basis or rationale itself to improve the strength of its theoretical underpinning. It is in that sense that Valtin's (1984) suggested critique of the structured approach as possibly 'boring' and with 'no room for individuality' misses the point, since the approach is intended to be designed precisely for the individual. Thus the criticism can only be valid if the teacher lacks imagination and fails to devise effectively engaging material. This could arise because of lack of knowledge of the child and/or lack of clarity of communication verbally and non-verbally with the child concerning the overriding principles (macrostrategies). What is required by the teacher is an appreciation of the principles of the structured approach and its adaptation and extension to include, centrally, the previously overlooked but essential focus on *'shared meaning'*. This along with a range of variables which can be adapted to suit the instructional needs of pupils, constitutes the seven support strategies. These are as follows:

* (i) Choice (greater or lesser)
  (ii) Challenge (greater or lesser)
  (iii) Space and places for working/resting
  (iv) Time allocated for tasks and whole timetable
  (v) Materials used e.g. for writing, reading, spelling help
  (vi) Relationships e.g. with the teacher
  (vii) Methods of teaching and learning.

To be successful, teaching of children with learning difficulties needs to be in part *incidental*, not recognized by the pupil as direct teaching but just part of what is expected, i.e. 'the rules', or what is usual in the classroom situation.

The delineation and discussion of the seven support strategies must be provided elsewhere due to the limits of space within this chapter and the deliberate choice to provide a few illustrations of microstrategies in the remaining space. Details of the support strategies can be obtained from the author.

Microstrategies II: ways of remembering

Examples of microstrategies for assisting memory and recall can be provided by trying to explore how you as a reader would set about the task of recalling what might be regarded as the main ideas in this chapter. They might be recalled by use of 'keywords' (e.g. the subtitle). These words should bring to mind the importance which the writer attributes to consideration of (i) the *learner's motivation*, (ii) the *meaning* of the content, concept, skill or material to be covered and (iii) the *imagery* through which it is to be rendered memorable.

It is generally the case that a sufficient level of intensity of motivation and sense of purpose is necessary to bring about a state of readiness to 'register' the experience as 'memorable' or worthy of recalling (e.g. because it felt 'good' or 'right').

To assist with recall, particularly in word recognition and spelling which must be learned to the level of automaticity, it is also necessary to have a route to forming what are essentially idiosyncratic *images* employing both imagination and reasoning. This can be undertaken in group or class teaching. It requires an underlying structured approach for 'routines' for learning and a steady small increment in the amount to be learned. What has been learned should be reviewed each day. More usually the pupil requires individual tutoring either in the normal classroom (a few minutes, even two to three minutes) with one child or by a special tutor at school or home or both. This may be required until a basic vocabulary is built up and a successful 'word bank' or 'morpheme bank' developed. It can then be drawn upon by the pupil at will and across a range of contexts.

If you set out to learn the three 'keywords', do you use a spelling strategy such as LOOK, COVER, WRITE AND CHECK? (Peters, 1985). Which features of the words do you try to highlight as you are 'learning' them? What strategies do you employ? Do you 'picture' them in terms of ideographs or envisage the written forms of the words? Do you find yourself mentally or actually tracing (writing) the words and/or 'learning' the words or do you work on a reasoned associative pattern such as might employ mnemonics? Here are two associative recall patterns which can provide routes to recall of '*m*otivation, *m*eaning and *i*magery' for the person with literacy difficulties.

(i) mnemonic MM1 (Motorway M1)
(ii) a synthesized 'word' *motimeanim* (because its rhythm is 'catchy' and could involve 4 beats or 4 parts of 1 beat).

There are many other possibilities for helping children capitalize on their own idiosyncratic associative patterns as aids to remembering and recall. Do you have another way of recalling that you can reveal to yourself? If you think these are extraordinary associative patterns you may not yet have had sufficient experience of working on this topic with children (or adults) with literacy difficulties. Frequently they can learn more readily once 'freed' to regard encoding and decoding as employing delightfully personal 'language pictures' in the communication process. *Idiosyncratic imagery is something to explore in a way which generates easy recall for the individual.* Self-awareness as a learner and self-confidence must be developed.

Most children, with (or without) literacy difficulties, delight in this kind of exploration of their own learning. It helps them appreciate how they acquire and develop facility with language, including reading, writing and spelling.

References

Binns, R. (1989) 'Re-creation through writing', in Hunter-Carsch, C. M. (Ed) *The Art of Reading*, Oxford, Blackwell Education and UKRA.

Cruickshank, W. (1963) *A Teaching Method for Brain-Injured Hyperactive Children*, New York, Syracuse University Press.

Dansereau, D. (1978), in Leong, C. K. (Ed) (1987) *Children with Specific Reading Disabilities*, Amsterdam, Swets & Zeitlinger, pp. 269–270.

Dawson, R. (1985) *A Teacher's Guide to TIPS*, London, Macmillan.

Hunter, C. M. (1982) 'Reading and learning difficulties: relationships and responsibilities', in Hendry, A. (Ed) *Reading: The Key Issues*, London, Heinemann.

Hunter, C. M. (1985) 'Exploring reading problems', unit 17 in Dawson, R. (Ed) *The MacMillan Teacher Information Pack*, London, MacMillan Education.

Hunter-Carsch, C. M. (1989a) (Ed) *The Art of Reading*, Oxford, Blackwell Education and UKRA.

Hunter-Carsch, C. M. (1989b) in *Teachers' Notes for 'Seeing and Doing'*, London, Independent Television Publications, p. 19.

Kephart, N. C. (1963) *The Slow Learner in the Classroom* , New York, Merrill.

Lunzer, E. and Gardner, K. (1984) *Reading for Learning*, London, Heinemann.

Morris, A. and Stewart-Doré, N. (1987) *Effective Reading in the Content Areas*, Melbourne, Addison-Wesley.

Morris, J. M. (1984) 'Phonics 44 for initial literacy in English', *Reading*, 18, pp. 13–24.

Moseley, D. and Nichols, C. (1986) *Aurally Coded English Dictionary*, Cambridge, Learning Difficulty Aids.

Peters, M. (1985) *Spelling caught or taught?* London, Routledge and Kegan Paul.

Southgate, V., Arnold, H. and Johnson, S. (1981) *Extending Beginning Reading* London, Heinemann for the Schools Council.

Valtin, R. (1984) 'German studies of dyslexia: implications for education; *Journal of Research in Reading*, 7, 2, pp. 79–102.

15
ARROW: Alleviating Children's Reading and Spelling Difficulties

Colin H. Lane

Introduction

The problems surrounding the pupil with reading and/or spelling difficulties can be based on one or more factors derived from physiological, environmental or psychological roots. 'Aural-Read-Respond-Oral-Written' (ARROW) is a multi-sensory teaching/learning approach which uses and strengthens elements from all three of these roots.

The use of a multi-sensory approach in helping alleviate reading/spelling problems has long been advocated (Hornsby, 1984; Hulme, 1981; Peters, 1967). ARROW therefore has its origins in accepted practice and is essentially based on traditional infant teaching/learning methods. Most recently the importance to literacy skills of speaking and listening has been emphasized by the National Curriculum proposals and it will be seen that ARROW closely follows the suggestions given (Department of Education and Science and the Welsh Office, 1988). Several independently conducted studies provide evidence of the efficiency of ARROW with reference to these skills (Jones, 1986; Lane, 1981; Rowe, 1987).

ARROW does bring to current thinking one vital additional component: the child's own voice replayed through high fidelity recording equipment. The relationship between a child and his own voice (the self-voice) forms the core of ARROW training for reading/spelling.

ARROW training and equipment

ARROW training can be supervised by teachers, welfare assistants or volunteer helpers. Training is given on a one-to-one basis between teacher and child and usually takes only fifteen minutes per day for three to five sessions per week.

Many mainstream children undertake ARROW training on their own. ARROW is also used in the home by children, under parental supervision.

Although several of the ARROW techniques can be achieved on a standard tape recorder, unfortunately not all can be followed. The ARROW equipment is a specially designed two-track machine which does not erase any pre-recorded material, but allows many children to record their own voices if a gap is allowed on tape after the permanent pre-recordings. The pre-recorded material can be prepared by a teacher or is available commercially from the suppliers of the ARROW recorder (The Cambridge System Ltd, 63 High Street, Buckden, Huntingdon, PE18 9TA). Several other features of the recorder are important. The rapid rewind is not common to standard recorders, whilst the headset boom microphone configuration on ARROW recorders gives a much higher fidelity voice recording than normal machines, and may well be an important factor contributing to its success. A pause control used on ARROW is instrumental in effecting a high standard of edited recording and is necessary for some techniques followed in the teaching of reading and spelling. A lesson indicator on the tape machine makes referencing relatively simple between the location of text and its approximate position on a tape. This feature is essential to the commercially produced Level III Word Family Spelling Book and tapes in the ARROW system.

ARROW: A definition

ARROW is an acronym for Aural-Read-Respond-Oral-Written, and all children utilizing the ARROW method for reading and/or spelling will use at least one, if not all of these components. The use of the self-voice is, however, the key to the ARROW approach.

The requisite components of ARROW are as follows:

AURAL: The child listens to speech on headsets, which can range from a single word to complex sentences. The speech can be from a 'live' or recorded voice and is usually produced by a teacher, assistant, parent or volunteer helper.

READ: Whilst listening to the voice the child refers to written material or, if a non-reader, looks at visual support material.

RESPOND: After listening and reading the child usually responds by imitating the words given on tape (or live) by the teacher.

ORAL: The child repeats the utterance given by the teacher and listens to his own recorded speech on replay. Often children elect to turn off the teacher voice when undertaking this part of the sequence.

WRITTEN: When his own voice is being replayed the child may be asked to write down what he has heard, whilst non-readers may be required to rearrange visual support material such as individual pictures and cartoon sequences.

The basic ARROW method for improved reading and spelling lends itself to many variations dependent upon the needs and ability of the child. The techniques have evolved through trial and error and are based on the author's work as a mainstream Infant/Junior teacher and clinical experience with Special Needs children. A detailed explanation of these techniques is given in the ARROW manual (Lane, 1986).

A discussion on the use of ARROW for reading and spelling will be divided into four main sections: reading, spelling, research and classroom organization.

ARROW Reading

The application of ARROW to children's reading problems will be discussed in seven sections, as follows:

(i) The pre-reader
(ii) Child centred language
(iii) Structured reading schemes
(iv) Sight vocabulary practice
(v) Reading for meaning
(vi) Curriculum based reading
(vii) Poetry.

The headings given are for purposes of organization but there are many areas of overlap between the various classifications.

(i) The pre-reader

At present ARROW is being used for children who are: (a) late in developing the pre-reading skills, or (b) at risk of not attaining the requisite skills.

In essence the approach for the pre-reader requires one-to-one teaching in which the child and teacher sit together wearing headsets, and the teacher records the child's voice speaking appropriate text ranging from a single word to several sentences. The recordings are usually obtained after the teacher has discussed the text with the child and practised manageable portions for the child to repeat. The child then listens back to his own recording whilst following the short sequence of text with his finger.

After the child has listened to himself reading the text, he is asked to read the text again 'live' as confirmation of learning.

Should a child fail to remember a word or series of words the relevant part of the child's recording is replayed two or three times in rapid succession. This process is known as 'echoing' and has proven itself invaluable in sustaining an item of information within the child's auditory short-term memory (Cooper, 1987; Lane, 1985).

If a child cannot, in the teacher's opinion, adequately repeat a required sentence or phrase, a technique known as 'split-tape' can be employed. Using 'split-tape' the teacher and child practise one section of text at a time and, by using a pause control, record each section separately with only a minimal gap apparent between each recording on replay. When listening to the split-tape recording the child is asked to follow the text with his finger, then to read the text again 'live', without recourse to his replayed voice. The split-tape approach has the advantage that it lets a poor reader hear himself 'reading' fluently with the appropriate rhythm, stress and intonation patterns normally associated with the use of inner language in reading (Beggs and Howarth, 1985).

(ii) Child centred language

The importance of child centred language in the acquisition of reading skills is well documented in the literature (Hendry, 1982; Smith, 1978; Stauffer, 1980). The use of ARROW in forming banks of reading material based on the child's personal linguistic experience is reported by the author (Lane, 1978).

The approach is one in which the child and teacher first discuss the reading interest material, picture (s), objects, or item of news brought in by the child. The teacher elicits a response from the child which is then written down by the teacher as originally given by the child or is amended into an acceptable structure. By operating a special switch on the ARROW recorder the teacher permanently records a sentence or phrase for the child to copy orally, allowing, of course, a gap on the tape for the child's utterance. A second and third response from the child can be treated in a similar fashion.

Once the appropriate amount of material has been written and recorded by the teacher, the child undertakes the ARROW process of Listen, Read, Speak before following the text from the self-voice. The child is then required to read the material 'live' and identify words or items from the text. ARROW practice sessions can follow at a later point to help consolidate learning.

(iii) Structured reading schemes

If a child is able adequately to repeat text following a teacher's 'live' model, then he can be introduced to pre-recorded material, using teacher-designed or commercially available reading books.

Prior to the child meeting the material, the teacher or assistant can record early reading books for ARROW by pressing down the pre-recording switch, recording a sentence from the text, allowing a space on tape for the child to copy, then recording another sentence. The teacher introduces the poor reader to text from each page, following which the child listens to the teacher track on the recorder and repeats each line. The teacher plays back the recordings and the child follows, whilst listening to his replayed voice. The child then reads the page 'live' and can practise the same material afterwards. ARROW can also help reading reinforcement. In such cases the child makes his reponse in the space *before* the teacher track recording is played. The teacher track recording thus provides confirmation of his efforts.

ARROW can be used in conjunction with commercially produced or teacher-designed pre-reading schemes which do not allow a space on tape for the child to record. The approach is usually one in which the child follows the text of a reading book whilst listening to continuous non-spaced recordings of the text on tape. If the pause control is used, the child can temporarily stop the recorder, repeat the text aloud then progress to the next part of the text. It is stressed that the approach does not involve the replayed voice but relies on the 'simultaneous' monitoring of the self-voice. The author has often found a difference in effect from the two forms of monitoring (Lane, 1985). In the early stages of reading or spelling the use of the replayed voice has many advantages, in particular that of allowing the child to hear himself repeating information without the need to articulate it again.

An ARROW technique known as 'over-recording' allows a child to listen to his voice on a continuous piece of taped text (Lane, 1986). Over-recording requires the child to read and record at the same time as the teacher voice is being played on tape. The child thus tries to reproduce not only the text but the same prosodic features as the teacher voice. The teacher and child recordings can then be replayed simultaneously or in isolation as necessary. The over-recording approach does require close supervision with the poor reader but nevertheless appears to hold considerable promise for children with telegraphic staccato-type reading skills.

(iv) Sight vocabulary practice

It is widely acknowledged that direct visual access is important to reading performance (Barron, 1980; Coltheart *et al.*, 1986) and thus all children should aim to maximize their sight vocabulary, particularly of frequently used words. ARROW can be used for this purpose and requires the child to meet flash cards or word list presentation of words to be learnt, through direct visual presentation.

If a child consistently fails to identify words presented visually through normal 'look-say' methods, then the words can be recorded by the child on tape, with the teacher allowing a slight delay between each child recording. The child's voice is then replayed and the child required to identify each word from his own voice. Should a word from the list still cause identification problems, then the 'echoing' process can be followed to reinforce learning. Extra practice can be given if the teacher records key words on the teacher track for the child to repeat and identify. Further experience in the use of the 'look-say' words can be given by including the words within short phrases or sentences for the child to listen, read, repeat, follow the self-voice.

(v) Reading for meaning

ARROW can help the child's understanding of language by explaining and extending vocabulary and involving the child in comprehension tasks (see Table 15.1).

Table 15.1 A reading comprehension passage.

SPRING – IN THE TOWN

In a town spring can be very good. The shops may have new things to sell. The shopkeepers have all been busy. A boy called John is in town. John could do with new shoes. He has an old pair. He looks at the shoe shops. He also looks at his money. John has about ten pounds.

1. Can spring be good in a town?
2. Do the shops have new things to sell?
3. Who have been busy?
4. Does John need new shoes?
5. Where does John look?
6. What also does John look at?
7. How much money does John have?

The approach is one in which the child listens to a pre-recorded tape linked to the text, and reads and records each sentence or part of a sentence separately. The child then listens to his recording again whilst following the text. Questions are presented in written form for the child to answer. Questions can also be recorded on the teacher track allowing a space for the child to answer with the option of either (a) proceeding to the next question or (b) providing the answer on the teacher track to the initial question posed. In the latter (b) option, the child therefore records an answer to a question then hears the appropriate answer given on the teacher track.

In some passages a long sentence can be divided into two or three sections for recording purposes. In such cases however, the natural pause and flow of the sentence should still be maintained.

Cloze procedures are being used with ARROW in which the child speaks the required word in a blank space allowed between words on the teacher track. The child thus listens to the teacher voice whilst reading the text, and speaks the missing item, then progresses further along the sentence/passage.

(vi) Curriculum based reading

Curriculum based material, e.g., from History, Geography and Science, has been used as an ARROW platform for helping improve reading skills. The approach follows the usual ARROW format. An example is given in Table 15.2 of a passage used for History.

Table 15.2 A history passage.

(Each section requiring a response from the student is marked for purposes of clarification with an asterisk.)

*The Romans first came to Britain in 55 BC. *They did not stay in Britain in 55 BC. *They came on a raid. *The Romans were led by a general called Julius Caesar. *Julius Caesar led the Romans to Britain across the sea. *The Romans came to Britain from France. *When Julius Caesar was alive, *France was called Gaul. *Gaul was part of the Roman Empire in 55 BC. *Britain was not part of the Roman Empire until much later.

1. When did the Romans come to Britain?
2. Did the Romans stay in Britain in 55 BC?
3. Who led the Romans in 55 BC?

Joint (1988) has observed that more able readers will readily assimilate the material presented in this fashion, yet will form their answers using their own linguistic patterns. The children do not simply 'parrot' the answers but will provide correct written and spoken structures of their own. The author has consistently observed poor readers branching from the text when providing oral answers to a passage although lifting from the text when initially beginning to give written answers.

(vii) Poetry

ARROW techniques can be used for poetry. The system allows the child to copy the teacher voice, as in the standard approach, to speak at the same time as the teacher track (over-recording), or to revise sequences by responding before the teacher track item is played. It has been found useful for children to hear a complete poem (if short enough) before beginning the 'follow my leader' approach. In such cases the entire poem is recorded on the teacher track immediately before the sections to be practised using ARROW. There is a collection of pre-recorded poems already available, and the author has found

ARROW treatment of poetry and prose compiled by local schools a particularly appropriate platform. A child's own collection of poems can, of course, be used for ARROW.

ARROW spellings

This second section deals with ARROW spelling and will be dealt with under seven separate headings:

  (i) ARROW — an eclectic approach
 (ii) Pre-recorded material
(iii) Child centred spellings
 (iv) Curriculum-based spellings
  (v) Self-pacing
 (vi) Corrective procedures
(vii) Progresssion from ARROW.

Note that these headings are for purposes of organization and that many areas of overlap exist.

(i) ARROW: an eclectic approach

There is some debate as to the relative importance of the auditory and/or visual channels in helping poor spellers, but it is stressed that ARROW is an eclectic approach which uses auditory, visual and kinesthetic modalities. ARROW embraces both 'bottom-up' and 'top-down' philosphies to spelling and reading (see Reason's discussion in Chapter 4). The commercially available software uses a 'bottom-up' structured approach. A 'top-down' philosophy is followed when using individual child-centred programmes, prepared by a teacher and based on the linguistic experience and needs of a child.

It is important to note that ARROW can be used in conjunction with existing spelling schemes and can support both holistic and structured learning processes currently being used by teachers. In addition, therefore, to look-say-write the teacher can help the child in the use of phonic rules and their exceptions and should if necessary explain these to the child before the ARROW approach is used.

(ii) Pre-recorded material

ARROW and requisite pre-recorded material is used with children at various stages of spelling development. These stages are accommodated within three levels of software (Lane, 1988).

Level I (sounds)

At present within the Level 1 book and tapes there are three sections. The first involves the child in auditory/visual training of initial sounds, the second introduces all short vowels, whilst the third gives experience in the use of consonant blends linked to short vowels.

Level II (key words)

This part of the overall programme is also split into three sections involving the use of frequently used 'key' words presented in isolation, presented within phrases and sentences, and presented within passages.

Level III (word families)

The third level of the ARROW spelling scheme introduces the child to visual and phonic patterns presented as 'word families'. The Word Family book and associated tapes contain nearly 300 examples of letter/sound combinations used in the English language. Within this format can also be found 100 of the most frequently occurring words in English, plus all the sounds of speech in English when given in their initial position. The presentation of each letter/sound combination follows the basic ARROW formula in that the student learns from listening to his own voice whilst following a multi-sensory approach involving listening, reading, speaking and writing.

The flexibility of the ARROW system means that a teacher can embrace the 'top-down' philosophy and prepare lists of words lying outside those provided in stages I to III, viz. child-centred and curriculum-based spellings.

(iii) Child-centred spellings

In this approach the child meets lists of words based upon his errors. The lists will not, therefore, be based upon a specific sound or letter pattern but upon a child's faults. For example a word list may contain 'across', 'carry', 'feeling', 'through', 'winter'. The format follows the usual ARROW procedures with pre-recorded samples on the teacher track and adequate space allowed on the student track for the child to record. The word may be given first in its 'look-say' form, followed by the naming of each letter.

(iv) Curriculum-based spellings

In addition to child-centred words, ARROW can be used for material based directly upon vocabulary the child meets as part of the general school curriculum. Children therefore practise spelling specific to a subject area. For example, in mathematics, the words 'area', 'circular', 'diagonal', 'estimate', 'plan', may be practised. Normal ARROW recording and playback techniques are followed.

(v) Self-pacing

One of the benefits of ARROW is that children can be self-pacing and are encouraged to operate the recorder themselves, receiving only the minimum of supervision once the basic approach has been mastered. It is, however, most important that children do not attempt too much within a session. With reference to the Level III Word Families Scheme, some children only complete one section within a fifteen minute session, whilst others complete an entire page. In the early stages it is recommended that each section is treated separately and the full ARROW process is undertaken before the next section is attempted.

(vi) Corrective Procedures

If a child cannot learn words in a lesson and/or at home, then additional help is given by the teacher in terms of echoing and split-tape procedures. The use of appropriate cues for a spelling, e.g. whether phonic rules can be applied or not, are pointed out to the child as additional help. Spellings which are very difficult to acquire are reintroduced at a later date. Revision of spellings is very necessary and can be undertaken on ARROW. The child listens to the teacher voice giving a word then writes it down and checks his spelling from the book. In Levels II and III the checking is further supported by the naming of letters on the recorder. Levels II and III use revision sheets containing all their respective words. Children can take these home for practice purposes.

(vii) Progression from ARROW

Once the child has learnt 'how-to-learn' the spelling of a word, then the acquisition of spellings for the entire key word or word family scheme may be possible without using the recorder, provided sufficient stimulation and revision is undertaken. Some children, however, will not be able to undertake the required learning unless using ARROW because of various factors including ability, motivation and support from home. There is no rigid rule concerning children's need to pursue ARROW, but the use of a teacher's discretion is deemed most important. As a 'half-way' measure, some schools allow children to take home ARROW pre-recorded spellings to use on an ordinary tape player as part of a general revision process. The children can only hear the teacher voice using this method.

Short-term memory has a most important role to play in the acquisition of spellings. A child may know precisely what is required to learn a spelling, but may not have the short-term memory capacity to do so. The child may therefore be able to learn the spelling of the word 'hand' but be unable to learn the spelling of the word 'advance' because the short-term memory of the child is incapable of holding seven letters in sequence. In such cases it is suggested that the child progress to the next lengthy series of words and continues along the requisite scheme. The teacher should return to the learning of any words causing problems the following day (or within the session if there is time) and the appropriate corrective procedures for spelling followed.

Research into ARROW

The ARROW approach has been the subject of research in several interrelated areas involved in reading and spelling. These are classified as follows:

(i) Subskills relating to reading and spelling
(ii) The use of internal speech
(iii) The learning and retention of ARROW spellings
(iv) A one year study
(v) The psychology of the self-voice.

(i) Subskills relating to reading and spelling

The first of the classifications relating to reading and spelling covers the improvement of listening skills, short- and long-term memory, and speech.

Listening Skill Improvement

Johansen (1988) and Sticht and James (1984) stress the importance of auditory perception for good and poor readers. The author had noticed that, in clinical practice, listening standards of hearing-impaired children improved after ARROW training, and hence further investigated the use of the approach with twenty-three special needs children (Lane, 1981). The children aged between 6 and 13 years were given a battery of listening and speech tests including identification of environmental sounds, consonant discrimination, sentence understanding, short-term memory for digit and word recall, and a vocalization test. A decision was made to use each child as his/her own control in an AB design spread across two consecutive five-week periods. During period 'A' all children received their normal educational provision; during period 'B' all children received ARROW training. The children were tested at the commencement of period 'A'. They were then retested again at the close of the five-week period.

Five weeks ARROW training (period 'B') was then given each day for up to fifteen minutes by a teacher or welfare assistant. Children practised simple couplets, poems, Christmas carols, and so on. At the end of the ARROW five-week period ('B'), the identical test battery was again administered. Results showed that ARROW training made significant improvements at the .005 level of confidence for the six previously described tests. No significant movement of performance in these tests was apparent in the preceding five-week control period despite most of the children receiving listening and/or speech training as part of their normal educational provision.

Rowe (1987) conducted an investigation into the use of ARROW with eight hearing-impaired children and noted an improvement in listening skills reflected in a lowering of amplitude at which children preferred to listen. Rowe observed two other points of interest: the faint smile on the child's face when the self-voice was being played, and the silent mouthing of words in synchrony with the sound of the self-voice.

Short-term memory improvement

Short-term memory has been found to be an influential factor in the development of reading and spelling skills (Cohen, 1980; Ellis and Large, 1987; Hulme, 1981).

The children used in the author's study (Lane, 1981) made statistically significant improvements in short-term memory for strings of digits or known words after ARROW training, on couplets and poems.

In a separate study, an investigation was conducted into the short and long term learning of multiplication table items by male dyslexic adolescents (Lane and Chinn, 1986). Five groups of five randomly selected students were used. Each group undertook different tasks in order to learn the test items. Students were tested after training at intervals of one day, one week, and one month. Results showed that self-voice echoing through the ARROW recorder was the most effective way of learning items, followed by read-and-say methods, and self-voice from a commercial tape recorder. The authors concluded that the three most effective methods entailed large self-voice content.

Speech improvements

The association between speech development and reading/spelling skills is well documented in the literature (Marcel, 1980; Goodman and Goodman, 1980). The relationship is recognized within the National Curriculum proposals. Three studies exist which reveal that the speech of children can be improved given ARROW training.

Lane (1981) undertook a vocalization count made by children when watching the actions of puppets. It was found that there was a significant improvement in vocalization skills after five weeks ARROW training of non-test material. Jones (1986) investigated the effects of ARROW training upon the intelligibility of hearing-impaired children's speech and concluded that the approach was instrumental in effecting more acceptable speech patterns. Cooper (1987), a speech therapist, advocates the use of ARROW techniques to help improve the speech skills of children with speech and/or language disorders and describes the effectiveness of the echoing and split-tape procedures for alleviating articulatory/short-term memory deficits.

(ii) The use of internal speech

There is a close relationship between internal speech (talking to oneself silently), subvocalization (the silent movement of the articulators), and reading skills. Edfelt (1960) established amongst proficient readers that there was an increasing use of internal speech in relationship to the difficulty of the material being read, i.e., the more difficult the material, the more the use of subvocalization. Conrad (1979) found a direct correspondence between the use of internal speech and reading ability amongst deaf school leavers, i.e., the more able the reader, the greater the use of subvocalization; the less able the reader, the less use. Beggs and Howarth (1985) applied Conrad's test to normally hearing children aged between 8 and 11 years and established that internal speech develops at a different rate according to the ability of the reader — the slower reader acquiring the skill later than his more proficient peers. Beggs and Howarth make the suggestion that a primary role of inner speech is to allow the reader to restructure written language by adding prosodic features (rhythm, stress, intonation) to text in order to add meaning.

Whilst there is evidence concerning the role of internal speech and reading ability, there is far less information on the relationship between internal speech and spelling ability. Peters (1967) does, however, make the point that the more able speller articulates subvocally a word as it is being written and also makes slight hand or finger movements apparently in rhythm with the production.

It has been found that children and adults when using ARROW will silently 'mouth' the material being replayed to them in their own voice, and yet are apparently unaware that this effect is taking place. Rowe (1987) in her research with hearing-impaired children also observed this effect.

As a direct result of these observations of subvocalizing ARROW, the author decided to conduct an experiment at the Hugh Sexey Middle School in Somerset. The aim of the study was twofold. The first aim was to establish whether there was any relationship between the use of internal speech and spelling ability. The second aim was to establish whether the use of internal speech could be encouraged within these children.

The subjects were 105 children from the first year, age range 9–10 years with a mean age of 9 years 5 months. The children were given Conrad's Internal Speech Test. In essence this test indicates whether a child tries to remember a word sound or word shape when trying to recall a series of similarly shaped words or similar sounding words (true, who, blue). Experiments showed that homophonous (similar sounding) words confuse on recall more readily than similarly shaped words having dissimilar sounds. From these and earlier experiments it has been shown that in the series recall tasks used within the tests, subjects used an auditory code more than a visual code for storing information.

Lists of eight similarly shaped or eight similar sounding words were permanently displayed in each classroom. Children were familiarized with these prior to testing. Three cards from one of the lists were shown in succession to the children, who were then required to write down the words. Results revealed that thirteen out of the 105 children were not auditorily but visually dominant when attempting the recall tasks. Further inspection of scores from class teachers' records showed most interestingly that twelve of these thirteen children were ranked in the lowest third of the class according to spelling ability.

The thirteen visually dominant children were given ARROW training on twenty commonly misspelt words. Normal training times were followed for a two-week period and children were supervised by volunteer helpers or a welfare assistant.

After two weeks the internal speech test was again administered. Results showed that twelve out of the original thirteen visually dominant children had shifted their coding strategies to the more 'normal' auditory code, whilst the control group of sixty auditorily dominant children retained their original form of processing.

Examination of scores also revealed a marked improvement in the short-term memory scores for those children who received ARROW training. In effecting a shift to the auditory code, the thirteen children on average improved their short-term memory recall of non-rhyming words by 35 per cent. The experimental group's means of words correctly remembered in sequence rose from 23.69 to 32.15 from a possible thirty-six correct, whilst the control group rose from 32.7 to 34.4.

It should be emphasized that the improvements for the experimental group were realized from the children attempting to learn spellings using ARROW and were not the result of a direct attempt to shift coding practice using the test material.

From the study it can be argued that reliance on a visual form of coding without recourse to some form of verbalization is questionable in terms of children's spelling progress. It is, however, clear that given ARROW training, an appropriate coding strategy can be employed by children within a short period of time.

The author feels that the children concerned had not suddenly become proficient spellers, but had in fact actualized their ability to use subvocalizing skills in order to learn how to learn a spelling, provided it lay within their short-term memory span.

(iii) The learning and retention of ARROW spellings

The author conducted a series of experiments investigating the short- and long-term retention of spellings learnt through ARROW (Lane, 1987).

Twenty-four children aged 9–14 years were selected from three mainstream schools on the basis of their poor spelling ability. Before ARROW training the children were given a spelling test of twenty words of six letters, proven to be commonly misspelt by 9 year old children at a parallel middle school. The group obtained a mean pre-training score of 7.7 out of 20. The children trained on ARROW for fifteen minutes per day for ten days. Training words were first presented on tape holistically and then had their letters named. The children practised ARROW under adult supervision. At the close of the ten-day period their mean score had risen to 18.2. The shift in scores is significant at the .005 level of confidence.

Fourteen children from the twenty-four were able to take the test again one month after training was completed and results showed that the mean scores realized 13.8; that is, there was a 76 per cent retention of post training improvement. The spellings were acquired by rote learning without recourse to phonics and it is interesting to note that the long term retention reflects that of dyslexic adolescents learning their multiplication tables (Lane and Chinn, 1986).

(iv) A one year study

Ten children attending the author's Unit with severe literacy problems were introduced to ARROW reading and spelling techniques, and measurements were taken across a one year period. The children, who had a mean age of 11 years 1 month (11:1; range 9:9 to 12:11), practised ARROW for fifteen minutes each day, and met at least one of four procedures. These are:

(a) ARROW spellings — All children, dependent upon their ability, met either keywords or word families.
(b) ARROW curriculum material — History, Geography, etc.
(c) Commercial reading scheme material. This material was appropriate to all ability levels, was mainly directed to the poorest readers, and had been pre-recorded by ancillary staff.
(d) Factual informative readers with comprehension cards using cloze procedures for the less able child and open-ended questions for the more able child.

Reference to the children's initial, pre-ARROW, scores in Table 15.3 reflects the extent of the literacy problem for the children concerned. The children were given a Schonell sight recognition test, Daniels and Diack contextual reading test, and Schonell spelling age test before beginning ARROW. Results after one year show a marked and statistically significant increase in performance across all three tests, despite a ceiling effect caused by a 9-year maximum score on the Daniels and Diack test. Unfortunately there are no long term data available from this recent study, as some of the children were unable to follow the ARROW technique consistently after this period.

Table 15.3 *Reading and spelling age scores of ten children before and after the one-year ARROW study.*

	Sight Recognition: Schonell		Contextual Reading: Daniels & Diack		Spelling: Schonell	
	Before	After	Before	After	Before	After
Mean	7.88	9.02	8.04	8.75	7.26	8.21
Range	6.1 to 9.5	8.1 to 9.9	6.0 to 9.0	8.0 to 9.0	6.1 to 8.3	6.7 to 9.6
t	4.87		3.22		7.40	
df	9		9		9	
p	<.01		<.01		<.01	

The standard of the children prior to meeting ARROW allowed for marked improvements to take place, but nevertheless the results are encouraging considering that the children often worked unsupervised.

(v) The psychology of the self-voice

The author suggests that an important cognitive relationship exists between the self-voice as replayed back to the child using ARROW and internal speech. Research also suggests that, by using the self-voice, a highly motivating influence is being brought to bear insofar as children like to hear their own voices on tape (Lane, 1985). For example, Lane (1985) reports on studies conducted with 216 normally-hearing and 19 hearing-impaired children aged 9–13 years. The children were asked to rank on a like/dislike continuum a selection of ten voices, one of which was their own. The voices repeated an identical sentence, list of words, or vowel. Results showed that the child's own voice was placed highest in terms of liking. The self-voice in fact achieved a seven times greater maximum ranking than any other voice.

In a separate investigation the author looked at self-voice recognition. The same sample of children were used and it was found 80–90 per cent correct self-voice identification was achieved from amongst ten peer group voices.

The use of prosodic features (rhythm, stress, intonation) greatly aided self-voice recognition for those children with hearing problems and this finding influenced the use of prosodic features in the production of spellings on taped samples. Children have since confirmed that the use of rhythmic patterns when naming the letters in spellings aided their later recall.

Organization within the classroom

A key issue is how best to organize ARROW. Fortunately the system is very flexible. Its application to a wide range of children means that ARROW can be organized in many different ways according to the needs of a child and the availability of school staffing.

It should be remembered that ARROW can be supervised not only by teachers but by welfare assistants or volunteer helpers, and that training times are short, often not exceeding five to ten minutes per session. Many mainstream children can undertake ARROW training on their own. The author has described how ARROW is organized in several sites in Somerset, but feels a discussion concerning the relative merits of its use either within a classroom or on an extraction basis will be useful (Lane, 1987).

ARROW began initially within a mainstream classroom with children listening to a pre-recorded tape whilst undertaking dictation processes. It is therefore largely a question of classroom management, the degree of the spelling/reading problem and the ability and experience of the child in operating the ARROW recorder. Many children, if familiar with the equipment, can undertake ARROW within a quiet area of a classroom. Ideally the recorder should be placed in a well-lit screened corner of a room with the child facing away from the other children. A succession of children can thus use the equipment for practice with a minimum of disruption to the class timetable.

In ARROW practice sessions the teacher or assistant should overview the organization but intervene only if necessary. In many cases children should be able to find and load the appropriate software then begin training within two minutes. The use of a headset boom microphone configuration helps minimize background noise when a child is listening or recording; this allows children to practise within a normal classroom working environment, a strategy not usually possible with a standard tape recorder.

ARROW 'therapy' in a one-to-one session can be undertaken in a classroom providing staffing allows, but is perhaps best achieved on an extraction basis within a vacant room. When undertaking one-to-one ARROW training the child should be able to see clearly the teacher's face and care should be taken by the teacher not to dominate the child too much within a session. Whenever possible the child should be encouraged to operate the equipment, the adult again assuming the role of supervisor.

References

Barron, R. W. (1980) 'Visual and phonological strategies in reading and spelling', in Frith, U. (Ed) *Cognitive Processes in Spelling*, London, Academic Press.

Beggs, W. D. A. and Howarth, P. N. (1985) 'Reading and verbal behavior', *Journal of Experimental Child Psychology*, 39, pp. 396–411.

Cohen, G. (1980) 'Reading and searching for spelling errors', in Frith, U. (Ed) *Cognitive Processes in Spelling*, London, Academic Press.

Coltheart, V., Laxton, V.J., Keating, G.C. and Pool, M.M. (1986) 'Direct access to phonological encoding processes in children's reading: effects of words characteristics', *British Journal of Educational Psychology*, 56, pp. 255–270.

Conrad, R. (1979) *The Deaf School Child*, London, Harper Row.

Cooper, J. (1987) 'The use of the patient's own voice in therapy', *Bulletin of College of Speech Therapists*, 418, pp. 8–9.

Department of Education and Science and the Welsh Office (1988) *English for Ages 5–11*, London, HMSO.

Edfelt, A.W. (1960) *Silent Speech and Silent Reading*, Chicago, University Press.

Ellis, N. and Large, B. (1987) 'The development of reading', *British Journal of Psychology*, 78, pp. 1–28.

Goodman, K.S. and Goodman, Y.M. (1980) 'Learning about psycholinguistic processes by analyzing oral reading', in McCullough, M. (Ed) *Inchworm, Inchworm*, Newark, International Reading Association.

Hendry, A. (1982) *Teaching Reading: The Key Issues*, London, Heinemann.

Hornsby, B. (1984) *Overcoming Dyslexia*, London, Dunitz.

Hornsby, B. and Shear, F. (1974) *Alpha to Omega*, London, Heinemann.

Hulme, C. (1981) *Reading Retardation and Multi-sensory Teaching*, London, Routledge and Kegan Paul.

Johansen, K. (1988) 'Hearing, an overlooked factor in dyslexia', paper presented at *21 Nordisk Kongress I Spesialpedagogikk Storefjell*, Norway.

Joint, H. (1988) Headmaster, Catcott Primary School, Somerset, *Personal Communication*.

Jones, R. (1986) Follow the arrow, *Unpublished M. Ed., Thesis*, Exeter, Exeter University.

Lane, C.H. (1978) 'The ARROW approach for aural rehabilitation', *The Volta Review*, 80, pp. 149–154.

Lane, C.H. (1981) 'ARROW', *Links*, 6, 3, pp. 10–12.

Lane, C.H. (1985) 'Various aspects of voice self-concept amongst normally-hearing and hearing-impaired children', *Unpublished Ph.D. Thesis*, Exeter, Exeter University.

Lane, C.H. (1986) *The ARROW Manual*, Buckden, The Cambridge System Ltd.

Lane, C.H. (1987) 'Aiming ARROW at learning targets', *British Journal of Special Education*, 14, 3, pp. 99–101.

Lane, C.H. (1988) *ARROW Software*, Buckden, The Cambridge System Ltd.

Lane, C.H. and Chinn, S.J. (1986) 'Learning by self-voice echo', *Academic Therapy*, 21, 4 pp. 477–482.

Marcel, T. (1980) 'Phonological awareness and phonological representation', in Frith, U. (Ed) *Cognitive Processes in Spelling*, London, Academic Press.

Peters, M.L. (1967) *Spelling Caught or Taught*, London, Routledge and Kegan Paul.

Rowe, M. (1987) 'ARROW in free flight', *Teacher of the Deaf*, 11, 2, pp. 42–54.

Smith, F. (1978) *Reading*, Cambridge, Cambridge University Press.

Stauffer, R.F. (1980) 'Reverence for remedial reading instruction', in McCullough, M. (Ed) *Inchworm, Inchworm*, Newark, International Reading Association.

Sticht, T.G. and James, H.J. (1984) Listening and reading', in Pearson, P.D. (Ed) *Handbook of Reading Research*, New York, Longman.

16
Suggestions for Helping Children with Spelling Problems

David Moseley

The nature and scale of the problem

For more than a century, educationalists, employers and politicians have argued about standards of spelling. In an attempt to improve matters, programmes of study for spelling and a proposed weighting of 20 per cent for spelling in the assessment of primary children's writing have recently been put forward by the Secretary of State as part of the National Curriculum proposals (Department of Education and Science and the Welsh Office, 1988). It is, however, far from certain that better spelling will result from the ways in which these proposals are likely to be implemented. There is, indeed a danger that some teachers will pay too much attention to spelling mistakes and that the quality of written expression will suffer. English spelling is difficult and at least half of the population have problems with it. In a typical class of thirty pupils, five will misspell more than 10 per cent of the words they write and another ten will misspell between 5–10 per cent (Moseley, 1989b). Present methods (copying out misspelt words and learning lists at home for tests) clearly do not work. 'Look, cover, write, check' is little more than a superstitious chant (as well as being rather boring).

Difficulty with spelling is manifest both in what is written and what is not written (for fear of error). Effective writing requires thought and prior organization, and can be spoilt if the flow of ideas is interrupted by problems in spelling the words or in finding alternatives. The writer has recently shown that, unlike the best 25 per cent of spellers, 75 per cent of a nationally representative sample of 15-year-olds tend to avoid using high-frequency commonly-misspelt words (Moseley, 1989b). He has also shown that, in the attempt to avoid making errors, it is common for less confident spellers to use a higher proportion of regularly-spelt words, not to use long words, to use fewer words outside a basic vocabulary, and to repeat words rather than to introduce variety.

On the basis of national studies carried out in New Zealand (Croft, 1987) and by the APU in this country (Department of Education and Science, 1983) it appears that there is a progressive reduction in spelling error rate from an average of 6 per cent to 2 per cent between the ages of 7 and 15. Nevertheless, in normal classroom and homework conditions, higher error rates may prevail. In one such sample of narrative writing which was made available to the author for study, a class of top-band 13–14-year-olds misspelt 208 different words. Three pupils accounted for 78 (38 per cent) of these, but half of the class made ten or more errors. If this can happen after seven years' apprenticeship in 'creative' writing and with normal access to dictionaries, new approaches are surely needed.

Providing help for children with spelling difficulties is, therefore, a matter of trying to find effective methods for a broad range of pupils, as well as considering the special needs of a smaller proportion for whom spelling is a major disaster area. A priority goal must be to remove as far as possible the inhibitions about poor spelling that lead so many to limit their written language both in quantity and quality.

The ideas put forward in this chapter have not all been tested out on a large scale, but all have been applied either in classrooms or in pilot programmes. Some are at present labour-intensive, but will become increasingly practicable as computer technology gains acceptance.

Questions with answers

Does experience with rhyme and listening for sounds in words help in learning to spell?

The work of Bradley and Bryant (1985) demonstrates a causal connection here, but most teachers have neither the training nor the time to work intensively in the ways recommended. It is difficult to sustain silence and attention to the spoken word when working with whole classes, and this kind of instruction is likely to be more effective when children can be more actively involved at an appropriate level in small groups. A reading and spelling scheme which emphasized listening for sounds in words was published some years ago, but was more often used with tape-recorded instructions rather than in interaction with the teacher (Moseley, 1971). The Aurally Coded English (ACE) Spelling Dictionary is a more recent resource for developing awareness of the sound-structure of words (Moseley and Nicol, 1986). This dictionary is intended for use in the explicit study of spelling, not only as a means of accessing words. It can be introduced to 7-year-olds who have mastered the following pre-requisite skills:

tap out the number of spoken syllables after hearing and pronouncing a word identify the probable first letter of any word on the ACE index page after hearing a one-syllable word, isolate and repeat the vowel sound.

In an unpublished study of forty secondary pupils with severe reading and spelling problems, the writer found that auditory confusions were more common than other types of error. Perin (1983) reported that good readers who were poor spellers resembled poor readers in having problems with phonetic segmentation. Research suggests that this kind of difficulty is preventable. However, teachers require a basic knowledge of the auditory characteristics of speech and of phonology if they are to help effectively.

Is synchronous visual and auditory presentation of word, phrase, and sentence elements helpful in reducing confusion about the conventions of spelling?

It does not take most young children long to realize that letters are important elements within words. Even though one-to-one correspondence between letters and sounds applies only to about one third of the words encountered in early reading, Bradley and Bryant (1979) showed that 5- and 6-year-olds apply a phonetic strategy when attempting to spell unfamiliar words. Bradley (1985) drew the further conclusion that children make better progress if they are shown how to relate sounds within words to the letters which represent them. This is consistent with the writer's finding that twenty-nine backward readers made rapid gains (mean gain 21 months in 6 months) after being provided with plastic grapheme tiles for word-building (Moseley, 1972). In the context of a language-experience approach the teacher supplied the appropriate tiles for the more difficult words. For example, if the pupil wanted to write the word 'noise', the teacher would supply the following symbols: oi se n. The pupil would work out the correct order and copy the word.

The method described above is labour-intensive, but it does enable children to see for themselves how sound elements correspond with visual elements within words. They can then more realistically appreciate the complexity of the learning task facing them, and begin to be selective in directing their attention at visual elements (graphemes). 'Look, cover, write, check' is not going to work unless you have some idea of the linguistic function of particular letters and letter strings. Spelling of words longer than three or four letters are not learned as wholes. Only one or two elements need be studied in a word like 'dinosaur' — the 'o' (because, being a neutral vowel, it could just be easily be 'a' or 'er') and the 'saur' (which includes an uncommon spelling for the 'or' sound).

Computer technology now makes it possible to present (simultaneously or sequentially) intelligible speech together with corresponding written symbols. This can be done with phonemes, syllables, words, phrases or larger units of meaning. Flexibility of timing and of visual display format, the amount of elaboration and repetition and facilities for self-monitoring are available to a degree to which few teachers can aspire without using a computer. Pilot work suggests that children with specific learning difficulties respond very positively to such an expert system. Even without speech, computers can be of great value in improving spelling, if words are split up visually into no more than four pronounceable chunks. This is done in 'The Complete Speller' (Nicol, Bennington and Moseley, 1989). In a recent independent evaluation of this program, eleven poor spellers improved in spelling by an average of eight months after six weekly sessions.

Is word recognition speed an important pre-requisite for telling whether a word 'looks right'?

Lesgold (1983) produced evidence to show that instruction which emphasizes spelling-to-sound correspondence leads to faster word recognition than does a conventional whole-word approach. He also reported that word recognition speed is the key to comprehension, not the reverse. Underwood and Underwood (1986) have also summarized research which supports this conclusion.

Children with specific reading difficulties are likely to have problems in telling whether a word they have written looks right, since they are slower both in matching and in reading non-words than younger children at the same reading level (Seymour and Porpodas, 1980). When few words are recognized instantly in reading, either on the basis of whole-word access or by means of within-word symbol/sound correspondence, children will often try to apply different strategies in succession, making increased use of context and then guessing on the basis of reliable cues. Tension builds up during these periods of uncertainty, as the child knows that the longer he/she delays, the greater is the chance of forgetting relevant information and failing to comprehend. Directing the gaze away from a word and on to the next is constantly reinforced negatively (removal of an aversive stimulus), and no positive reinforcement is associated with the kind of looking at words which helps to build up knowledge of what is regular and predictable. This is perhaps why Seymour and Porpodis found that dyslexics with spelling ages around 7.5 years showed no orthographic regularity effect when matching non-words.

When reading is slow and inefficient it unlikely that spelling skills will be developed as a spin-off from reading. In the desperate search for meaning, a slow reader will make greater use of content than of function words and may even skip over or misread short high-frequency function words. Many such words are irregularly spelt, and they tend to be used by poor spellers as little as possible. As a consequence of the pattern of negative reinforcement outlined above, when they are put on paper, suspect spellings are more often not looked at again rather than studied to see if they look right. So if they are not instantly recognized as right or wrong, the writer may not even notice that they need checking at a later stage.

This is not to say that rapid reading is always associated with good spelling, since some poor spellers are so linguistically competent that they can read with a minimum of attention to orthographic detail. However, rapid automatic decoding of isolated words or of function words in short phrases may well be a valuable skill for slow readers and poor spellers to acquire. It seems likely that accuracy in proof-checking depends heavily on word recognition speed.

Although some children with specific reading and spelling difficulties are very slow in reading and in scanning text for target words, the teaching methods used in schools and centres specializing in work with dyslexic children place little emphasis on speed of word recognition. The writer has recently completed a follow-up study of twenty-seven dyslexic boys, in which measures of reading and scanning speed were repeated after a period of twenty months. Although these boys had received special tuition in seven different places, the two sets of reading speed scores were remarkably consistent (r = 0.85) and the mean increase in fluency of oral reading was only 11 per cent. A greater instructional emphasis on the development of word recognition speed, using techniques like RSVP (rapid serial visual presentation) and precision teaching to increase fluency is clearly indicated. As a result of designing and piloting a short 'Precision Spelling' course on these principles the writer is able to report a mean gain on the Vernon spelling test of 16 months in five weeks (Moseley, 1988).

How can errors in high-frequency words be reduced?

One method of dealing with this problem is through 'Precision Spelling'. A student taking the 'Precision Spelling' course creates a personal list of words he or she wishes to spell correctly. The words are then read out one at a time by a helper and the student locates as many as possible in the ACE Dictionary in a daily five-minute practice period. Alternatively, a good starting point for such work is a list of forty words which are among the most commonly used 300 words in children's writing. The chances are greater than 1 in 10 that each will be misspelt (except for the word 'were', which accounts for 1 per cent of all misspellings, but which is spelled correctly fifteen times out of sixteen). Altogether, these words accounted for 20 per cent of all misspellings made by a representative sample of New Zealand children aged 8–13. Source data were provided by Croft of the New Zealand Council for Educational Research.

The 40 words are given below in order of spelling difficulty (reading across the page):

too	their	bought	knew
until	right	stopped	caught
lot	through	an	kept
sometimes	know	where	off
another	myself	outside	heard
suddenly	inside	it's	always
running	friend	police	hour
turned	want	again	tried
decided	might	still	opened
thought	there	into	were

The sources of difficulty in these words can be classified under six main headings and some of the words have as many as three problematic features. The student is made aware of these characteristics and undertakes word searches for words with similar features. The headings are: unusual sound-spellings, silent letters, neutral vowels, doublings, homonyms, and splits (? one word or two).

It is important to notice that the student is not required to learn lists of this kind. Motivation and success rate are likely to be low if the child is asked to memorize commonly misspelt words (Moseley, 1987). Instead, students need to be aware of their difficult features and of the reason why the use of particular words should be closely monitored (confusion is likely to persist when there is a long history of misspelling). The monitoring can be done at the point of production if the student has a short list (up to twenty of those given above) printed on a card. Monitoring of other words is best done later at the proof-checking stage.

Is there a need for an instructional system in which spelling patterns are progressively mastered alongside one in which no limits are placed on the choice of words written?

One of the claims made for Pitman's Initial Teaching Alphabet was that it made it possible for young children to write with confidence, since even long and unfamiliar words could be rendered phonetically. Given the complexities of English orthography, it is not clear what the long-term effects will be if (as is sometimes suggested) young children are encouraged to write without checking spelling beyond making sure that it conforms broadly to graphemic patterns and to phonetic structure.

Traditional practice has certainly diminished pupil confidence by its emphasis on copied work and on children queuing to ask the teacher for spellings. This simply wastes time, as does trying and failing to find a word in a dictionary. Nothing could be more effective in training children to restrict themselves to words they think they can manage.

It was in order to overcome these problems that the ACE Spelling Dictionary was designed. If the use of the index system is carefully taught, even top infants can quickly find words they want to use, since search time is reduced by a factor of sixty-four and fail-safe multiple entries cover cases where the first letter is not known or the vowel sound is not clear. Children can thus take on responsibility for correct spellings and in the process will learn a great deal about spelling-related aspects of language.

It is therefore quite unnecessary, even for individuals with severe difficulties, to limit children's writing to words which include previously studied patterns. However, a structured programme of this kind can be of value if used alongside a language-experience approach. For children who have failed a great deal in the past, it can provide a progressive series of performance objectives, with clear evidence of success at each small step.

The Precision Spelling approach (referred to above) provides another structured programme which makes use of a set of objectives which are based on an empirically-determined order of difficulty. Examples of these objectives are given below:

(a) After reading a sentence containing one of the target words and without the sentence in view, the child writes the target word correctly (criterion: 8 out of 10)

> target words: a am an as at be by do go he I if
> in is it me my no of on or so the to up us we

(b) After reading a sentence containing one or more of the target words and without the sentence in view, the child writes a target word correctly (criterion: 8 out of 10)

> target words: words like 'baby' and 'sister' — i.e. two-syllable words ending in -er -ing -ly -y

(c) Working with lists of twenty (or ten) words, the child responds to the instruction, 'Put a line under the letters which stand for the vowel sound in each word' (criterion: 8 out of 10)

> been each eat feed field green keep leave piece please
> queen read see she sleep sweet tea three tree week

(d) After hearing a one-syllable word containing up to four consonant sounds, the child says (or writes down) the appropriate number of consonant sounds

(e) In proof-checking, the child identifies words with either or both of the following characteristics: (e.g. three or more syllables and containing a neutral vowel spelling).

From these examples it can be seen that the emphasis is on generalizable features of words rather than on one spelling pattern at a time. Although sets of words of the same pattern are also presented for study, the weakness of this approach seems to be that it is unrealistic to expect pupils to remember which patterns apply to which words.

How can accuracy in proof-checking be improved?

A baseline measure can be obtained if the number of errors in a passage is known and the student is asked to underline words he or she thinks are spelt incorrectly. In the case of poor spellers, initial detection rate is often in the range of 25–50 per cent, with several false positives (i.e. words falsely identified as incorrect) occurring as well. It is important to address this problem in a systematic way, but in the past this has not formed part of normal classroom activity. A table or graph should be kept of progress over time and individuals should be directed to check specific kinds of word, depending on their personal error profiles. It sometimes happens that if the teacher places emphasis on proof-reading, the quality of writing deteriorates, as the pupil 'plays safe' with words. This can be picked up by an observant teacher, but is more easily detectable if samples of writing are entered onto a word processor and scanned with a program like 'Watchword' (Moseley and Muxworthy, 1987).

Table 16.1 List of words in 'Mem' by word length.

Length Number	1–2 13	3–4 44	5–6 16	7–8 6	9+ 1
	A	ago	around	becorus	somethink
	as	all	coluer	Birthday	
	at	and	friend	looking	
	be	away	happnd	nothink	
	I	bey	haurs	presund	
	in	Book	money	wrapped	
	It	But	pukit		
	me	come	saiing		
	my	day	sethv		
	no	did	sister		
	of	down	stars		
	to	draw	street		
	up	for	there		
		got	thing		
		had	trown		
		hand	window		
		her			
		home			
		just			
		land			
		look			
		ment			
		mum			
		next			
		not			
		oat			
		one			
		payd			
		pen			
		put			
		said			
		same			
		shop			
		the			
		then			
		they			
		this			
		time			
		uway			
		was			
		went			
		whet			
		wish			
		won			

Proof-checking is an area where computers have a lot to offer. The 'Watchword' program prints out all the words used in a text file in columns, as shown in Table 16.1. This kind of layout makes it much easier to focus on orthography without being tempted to scan without looking and without being distracted by other linguistic features. As each word is printed only once, checking can be accomplished more quickly and without visual fatigue. A further advantage of the columnar layout is that short words and long words can be examined separately. Niemi and Virjamo (1986) found that errors in proof reading are most likely to occur with short function words and with long content words.

Most, but not all errors can be identified from a printout like that shown in Table 16.1. Morphemic errors are best dealt with in a separate scan, and may only be detectable if the passage is read aloud (by a person or by computer).

There is as yet no computer program which will carry out a full analysis of proof-checking skills and provide individually tailored practice. This would mean that immediate and objective feedback would be available. If the program also had a built-in spelling checker, teachers would be almost completely freed from the chore of marking spellings.

Do electronic spelling checkers help to improve spelling?

Both hand-held and computer-driven spelling checkers are available which are fast in operation, contain very large vocabularies and display a list of possible words if a misspelt word is typed in. In the writer's experience some students with spelling problems have found these easier to use than a dictionary, although for a sample of errors taken from the writing of nine dyslexic children, the average success rate proved to be only 80 per cent. Spelling checkers cannot, of course, distinguish between homonyms, and they are not yet cheap enough for general use. Nevertheless they do offer hope and support to those with severe problems.

Interactive checkers which require selection or correction during the initial process of typing are probably best used after an initial draft has been produced on paper. One possibility which has not yet been tried in schools is for an interactive checker to give an immediate signal which can later (during proof-checking) be reactivated in visual form (perhaps by a colour change). One can even envisage a spelling checker which can distinguish between orthographic legality and illegality. The reader will be able to detect six examples of this kind in the 'Watchword' printout to which reference has already been made.

Further development and evaluation is clearly needed before firm answers can be given to this question. It seems likely, however, that checkers which demand some discrimination and thought are likely to be more beneficial than those which work more automatically.

Is is desirable that both teachers and pupils should work towards clearly-defined spelling performance targets?

Little research has been carried out in this area, but current practice appears to be based on global aims rather than on objectively defined targets. There are, of course exceptions to this, in the case of direct instruction programmes and structured multisensory techniques. Nevertheless it is likely that most children think of writing as a type of test-taking in which they know they will fail when matched against the teacher's adult standards (Raphael *et al.*, 1986). The message most commonly conveyed to pupils (whether explicitly or implicitly) is: if you do these things (learn your list of twenty spellings/write out your corrections five times/look, cover, write and check every word you get wrong and write in in your personal spelling error book) you will be able to improve your spelling. This message has an unstated corollary: if despite all this you still need me to correct your work with a red pen, you are either lazy or stupid.

Most of the spelling targets put forward by Kingman (Department of Education and Science, 1988) and by Cox (Department of Education and Science and the Welsh Office, 1988) are also global and imprecise as the following examples show:

spell correctly (Kingman)
attempt to spell less frequent words with increasing confidence (Cox)
show a growing awareness of word families and their relationships (Cox).

Graeme is eighteen. He took 'O' Level and G.C.S.E. examinations in 1986, without seeking a concession for his severe specific difficulties in spelling and in written sentence construction. He is currently employed and taking a building and construction course. He was interviewed about the teaching and learning of spelling.

'All I can remember is big red circles. . . . I had to write every word out five times in the back of my book . . . It ended up reaching the front!'

'Everyone should have a chance to correct drafts . . . You need quick feedback — a week later is no good. You should go through looking for one thing at a time, like looking for the grammar, changing bits to improve the flow and correcting your spelling.'

'You need to be shown what is wrong and how to learn spellings . . . You need to know what progress you're making.'

'I think you should get marks for spelling — maybe 20 per cent otherwise people would spell any kind of way. But the marks for spelling should be separate from the rest . . . '

The fact is that most teachers do not enter into dialogue with pupils in order to negotiate and evaluate learning strategies for spelling or for other aspects of literacy. If they did, pupils might produce (under guidance) checklists for use in self-monitoring as well as advisory 'think and learn' sheets. These could be applied in proof-checking, in using dictionaries and thesauri and in the active and purposeful study of spelling.

While writing and spelling conventions are only one part of the writing process, they have been played down by 'process-writing' advocates. Perhaps as a consequence of this, Bos (1988) was able to report that in a resource-room setting fourteen students aged 9–11 years gained in thematic maturity, vocabulary and coherence of writing, but found that they made only minimal gains in spelling over a two-year period. In this study, four fifty-minute periods per week were devoted to writing, using the process-oriented framework suggested by Graves (1983). Personal spelling dictionaries were compiled and peer 'experts' were consulted, one of them for spelling. However, no direct instruction in spelling was given and the major emphasis was on planning, drafting, conferencing and sharing of content.

The idea that teaching points about spelling (and other aspects of language) should arise naturally out of activities in which there is a genuine communicative purpose, is a justifiable reaction to the over-use of isolated and ineffective drills. It is, nevertheless, a counsel of perfection, and makes the assumption that the enabling teacher or other competent person is always at hand when needed in thirty different places at once. Similar problems arise once an attempt is made to implement individual programmes based on a large number of precisely-defined steps. If this kind of approach is to work, self-monitoring and/or assistance from peers, aides or parents must be built into it if the teacher is not to be reduced to a clerical assistant, keeping checklists up-to-date.

It is more realistic to devise written performance targets which can be understood both by children and parents and to work towards them by means of a combination of whole-class activities, group work and individual programming. There is a place for direct instruction as well as for discovery and process-oriented approaches, and there are purposeful ways of relating the two kinds of activity.

An outline of age-appropriate activities and levels of competence in spelling which are directed towards the Kingman targets has been prepared and is obtainable from the author. The ACE Spelling Dictionary is seen as the most comprehensive, but not as the only relevant source. The intention is to provide a framework for skill-development with an emphasis on precision and practicability.

What benefits can be expected if children are given greater individual and collective responsibility in attempting to improve their spelling?

The study by Bos (1988) shows that spelling does not improve as a natural consequence of establishing a supportive writing community, even when teacher-pupil ratios are favourable and when pupil independence and sense of ownership of the writing product is encouraged. What is probably needed is the explicit extension of these principles to the area of spelling, combined with the introduction of techniques that really work. Gettinger (1985) found that children with specific spelling problems made better progress when they were actively involved in a learning strategy than when the same routines were imposed by teachers. It was better, for example, for children to identify for themselves the 'tricky' parts in words than to have teachers point out such elements (even through the parts focused on by children were not always linguistically impeccable).

On two occasions the writer has worked with teachers who already used a process-writing approach, in order to see what difference would result from the introduction of specific techniques for improving spelling. The first teacher worked in a school for children with emotional and behavioural disorders and introduced a structured spelling programme using hand-held electronic machines. The second taught a mainstream class of twenty-six children aged 10–11 years and introduced the ACE dictionary for checking spelling whenever written work was undertaken (Moseley, 1989a). In both cases there was not only a substantial gain in spelling (as measured by standardized tests) but marked increase in the amount of writing produced in a given time.

The second study indicated that the improvement in fluency (measured over a six-month period) resulted from increased efficiency in the use of the time available. The gain in fluency was significantly less in the groups which had been trained to use the dictionary twice (during the production of the first draft and in subsequent proof-checking), than in groups where it was used once (at the proof-checking stage). The teacher found that 'the fact that children no longer needed to ask for spellings made it easier to concentrate on the individual child's written expression'. At the same time 'the dictionary had the added bonus of encouraging children to think about the spoken word and to notice when sound and written symbol did not correspond as expected. This proved to be intriguing and stimulating in that children often made connections with other words with the same root or suffix'.

The teacher made greater use of conferencing, as there was time for children to read their work aloud and to discuss it with her while it was still fresh in their minds. She recorded an average gain in reading of 14 months over a six-month period and the five poorest readers in the class improved by an average of 21 months. Over the first three months, the five children whose spelling test scores were more than a year behind their reading scores made an average spelling gain of 11.4 months on the Vernon Graded Word Spelling Test. The children themselves made the following comments:

'I have found a lot more confidence which gives me a feeling to write longer stories.' Gareth, 11.

'When you put it into your book you are worrying about getting everything wrong — when you do a draft you know you can correct it and you can check your spellings.' John, 11

'I use the word that first comes into my head instead of thinking, "Oh no, I can't spell that".' Jane, 10.

References

Bos, C. S. (1988) 'Process-oriented writing', *Exceptional Children*, 54, 6, pp. 521–527.

Bradley, L. (1985) *Poor Spellers, Poor Readers: Undertaking the Problem*, Reading, Reading University Centre for the Teaching of Reading.

Bradley, L. and Bryant, P. E. (1979) 'The independence of reading and spelling in backward and in normal readers', *Developmental Medicine and Child Neurology*, 21, pp. 504–514.

Bradley, L. and Bryant, P. E. (1985) *Children's Reading Problems: Psychology and Education*, Oxford, Blackwell.

Croft, C. (1987) 'Word use and spelling mistakes in a national sample of primary writing', *New Zealand Journal of Educational Studies*, 22, 2, pp. 215–220.

Department of Education and Science (1983) *How Well Do 15 Year-Olds Write?*, London, HMSO.

Department of Education and Science (1988) *Report of the Committee of Inquiry into the Teaching of English Language*, London, HMSO.

Department of Education and Science and the Welsh Office (1988) *English for Ages 5 to 11*, London, HMSO.

Gettinger, M. (1985) 'Effects of teacher-directed versus student-directed instruction and cues versus no cues for improving spelling performance', *Journal of Applied Behaviour Analysis*, 18, pp. 167–171.

Graves, D. H. (1983) *Writing: Teachers and Children at Work*, Exeter, NH, Heinemann.

Lesgold, A. M. (1983) 'A rationale for computer-based reading instruction', in Wilkinson, A. C. (Ed) *Classroom Computers and Cognitive Science*, New York, Academic Press.

Moseley, D. V. (1971) *English Colour Code Programmed Reading Course*, London, NSMHC.

Moseley, D. V. (1972) 'The English Colour Code Programmed Reading Course', in Southgate, V. (Ed) *Literacy at All Levels*, London, Ward Lock.

Moseley, D. V. (1987) 'Words you want to learn', *British Journal of Special Education*, 14, 2, pp. 59–62.

Moseley, D. V. (1988) 'New approaches to helping children with spelling difficulties', *Educational and Child Psychology*, 5, 4, pp. 54–58.

Moseley, D. V. (1989a) 'Building fluency in word recognition and spelling through the use of an aurally coded dictionary: a classroom study', *Glossa* (in press).

Moseley, D. V. (1989b) 'How lack of confidence in spelling affects children's written expression', *Educational Psychology in Practice* (in press).

Moseley, D. V. and Muxworthy, A. (1987) *Watch Word* (computer program and documentation), Newcastle-upon-Tyne, NORICC.

Moseley, D. V. and Nicol, C. M. (1986) *Aurally Coded English Spelling Dictionary*, Wisbech, Learning Development Aids.

Nicol, C. M., Bennington, P. and Moseley, D. V. (1989) *The Complete Speller*, Newcastle-upon-Tyne, NORICC.

Niemi, P. and Virjamo, M. (1986) 'Proofreading: visual, syntactic or all of these?', *Journal of Research in Reading*, 9, 1, pp. 31–38.

Perin, D. (1983) 'Phonemic segmentation and spelling', *British Journal of Psychology*, 74, pp. 129–144.

Raphael, T.E., Englert, C.S. and Kirschner, B.W. (1986) *The Impact of Text Structure Instruction and Social Context on Students' Comprehension and Production of Expository Text*, East Lansing, Michigan State University Institute for Research on Teaching.

Seymour, P.H.K. and Porpodas, C.D. (1980) 'Lexical and non-lexical processing of spelling in dyslexia', in Frith, U. (Ed) *Cognitive Processes in Spelling*, London, Academic Press.

Underwood, G. and Underwood, J. (1986) 'Cognitive processes in reading and spelling', in Cashdan, A. (Ed) *Literacy*, Oxford, Blackwell.

17
Meeting the Challenges of Specific Learning Difficulties

Harry T. Chasty

Introduction

Aim of the Paper

The fascinating process of learning does not occur only in crowded classrooms or sterile experimental or laboratory conditions. It is maintained throughout everyday life in more or less conducive social conditions by people who feel and think, and who may bring to the learning process less than fluent skills, and who may have preferences in the way the materials to be learned are presented. Learning is often a less than efficient skill which must be delivered through working memory. *Specific learning difficulties are defined as organizing or learning difficulties affecting hand skills and working memory skills, causing significant limitations in the development of aspects of some or all of speech, reading, spelling, writing, numeracy, and behavioural skills in the student.*

Teachers working with children who experience specific learning difficulties must be interested in how these children learn and all the circumstances which influence their inefficiencies in learning. There is a circular relationship between the child's difficulties in learning and how teachers teach, which shapes the nature and extent of the child's special needs and influences how wide-ranging special needs can be met in the classroom.

This paper examines how children learn, the effect of teachers' presentation to them of the information to be learned and the range of circumstances in which children learn, so that the fundamental issue in teaching students with specific learning difficulties (SpLD) may be addressed. *'If this child doesn't learn the way we teach, can we teach him the way he learns, and, can we then extend his range of learning options?'*.

The spectrum of difficulties in learning

Before we consider the narrow problems of SpLD children, we must look broadly at how children learn in schools, the circumstances in which they learn, and what they learn. Learning is defined as the ability to store, recall and use facts, knowledge and skills. The abilities to 'recall and use' are the essential delivery factors which determine success in learning. We teach facts and knowledge in our classrooms, but we also teach skills. For children who have difficulty in recalling, which is more important? Is it facts leading to knowledge, or skills in handling knowledge?

Recently, when moving house, I cleared out a room I used as a study for a number of years. I found on a shelf a textbook which I had used many years ago when I was studying A level physics. Further along the shelf was the textbook my son had used for his physics A level a few years ago. I opened both the books and compared the contents, assessing facts in physics and how these had changed over a significant period of time. I came to the conclusion that those facts I had worked so hard on all those years ago were now more or less redundant. But the facts in themselves were not important. What was important was the ability to organize, manipulate and handle them in a particular way. The ability to make use of them in developing information handling procedures leading to a range of thinking skills was much more important than the facts.

The facts taught in a whole range of subjects will change alarmingly quickly over the next twenty years. Is it important for children with specific learning difficulties, who have difficulty in recalling, to struggle to handle a mass of facts, or to develop skills in handling whatever factual information is important? We must think carefully about that choice, and what we mean by 'learning' in our classrooms, so that we can understand the problems of these children who learn differently.

What kinds of learning difficulty are 'specific'

In children, different kinds of failure are evident in learning. Failure to learn may be very severe and broadly based for some children. For them progress is the slow but steady development of the simple skills of everyday living such as sitting up, walking, looking and paying attention, skills in establishing eye contact, skills in making and saying simple words.

Failure to learn may be moderate. A child with a moderate learning difficulty will learn to walk, and talk. He will eventually read, write and spell at a basic level, but all these skills will develop at a slower pace and to a lesser extent than normal. All his skills in learning will be retarded.

Failure to learn which is specific is limited only to certain skills, particularly those in information processing. These children have deficiencies in narrow aspects which particularly relate to the delivery of learning. Some things they will do well, other things they will do rather badly. It is this group of enigmatic learners which must now engage our attention.

How are such specific difficulties affected by the curriculum?

While such children may have special needs in class, it must be considered whether those special needs are determined by (i) the child's individual differences in learning and how he learns, (ii) the nature, complexity and style of presentation of the material taught, or (iii) a mixture of both.

What causes these problems in learning? Is it the child's individual difficulties in specific areas such as hand skills, working memory skills, and speech skills? Are the child's problems solely in reading? Mothers of children with specific learning difficulties will often respond with a categorical 'No' to that question because they know that their child has as many problems outside school, in their home environment in aspects of everyday living skills, as are observed in their development of literacy skills in school. All the SpLD child's learning is, to a very considerable extent, different. In accepting that this child's learning is different, we must then consider how that child is affected by his school curriculum, and what balance should be maintained between facts to be remembered, or skills. It is in the evaluation of this individual equation that the special needs of the child with SpLD will be met.

Individual differences in learning

Individual differences in learning style are evident in the child's early development. In those important formative years before the child attends school, his learning is not subject to the bias of the formal prestige presentation of the material to be learned, in a specific way by teachers. The child himself relates to, surveys and learns in his own environment, in his own way. There are clearly evident characteristics in that unbiased early learning which give indications of his later learning preferences which we must consider if we are to understand how the child learns. Generally, children with SpLD seem to show difficulty in building 'little skills' into 'bigger skills'. Little things they can do very well. Bigger, more complex skills they handle much less effectively.

Three major areas of preschool experience, which are of considerable relevance to later language learning, will be considered: (1) fine motor skills in the preferred hand; (2) working memory skills; and (3) speech skills.

Hand skills

The development of appropriate hand skills in children is a much too neglected area in our education system. In a lecture, the vast majority of teachers use hand skills to write notes turning the ideas discussed into motor movement patterns on paper which will be reconsidered and interpreted at leisure. That skill in expressing ideas as words recorded through movement patterns is an essential part of our existing education system. Ultimately success or failure is determined by fine manipulations made from left to right across a page in response to a complex question such as 'Sterling M3 is a useful indicator of inflationary trends within the British Economy. Discuss'. Rightly or wrongly the hieroglyphics produced are considered to be fully representative of the student's thinking, and the examiner may make only very marginal allowances for the hand skill deficiencies underlying his failure to express his ideas fully and comprehensively in the permitted time.

Teachers must therefore be interested in the development of hand skills, and their eventual automatic control and integration into a complex process of written expression of ideas. We must also be concerned for the special needs of children with difficulties in fine motor manipulation in our classrooms for whom this writing process is different.

Groden (1969) quoted incidence figures which have been substantiated by later research. He indicated that 81 per cent of the child population in school are right-handed and 6 per cent left-handed. Teachers should be aware of these figures and must consider the special needs of the remaining 13 per cent of the child population in schools who are uncertain about which is their preferred hand. (This is not to say that all such pupils will experience literacy difficulties — Editors' comment.)

If the child has no sense of left or right, how does he know where 'begin' or 'end' is? How can he sequence or organise activities? These children show problems in hand skills at the preschool stage, and later sequencing difficulties which alter the structure of their learning and experience, and must be considered from enrolment in school. The ability to use fine motor skills is one of the major channels for registering information leading to long term storage and recall. This is very important and must be available to all children.

Working memory

Baddeley (1976) and others have argued that short-term or primary memory is more appropriately labelled working memory to emphasize the fact that it is used as work space while operating a skill, or thinking about something. Baddeley argues that we should regard working memory as a system involving constituent skills which are employed on some occasions, but not on others, depending upon the subject's strategies and the particular task being undertaken.

Baddeley and his co-workers have presented evidence for the existence of several constituent systems within working memory. A *central executive* has been postulated (Baddeley, 1982), linked to a range of 'slave systems' which function as information holds. The major sub-systems are a *primary acoustic memory* (Colle and Welsh, 1976; Colle, 1980; Salame and Baddeley, 1982), an *articulatory rehearsal loop*, (Baddeley and Hitch, 1974; Baddeley, 1978; Salame and Baddeley, 1982), and *a visuospatial scratch pad* (Baddeley *et al.*, 1974; Kolers and Smythe, 1979; Baddeley and Lieberman, 1980).

This work is discussed by Reisberg, Rappaport and O'Shaugnessy (1984), who argue that the properties of the working memory system are extremely flexible and strategy-dependent. They consider that the constituents of working memory are activity-based strategic processes or skills and suggest there are no limits in principle to the constellation of constituent skills comprising working memory, and thus on the extent to which it can be expanded.

Working memory has also been regarded as a process, rather than a structure; (Craik and Lockhart, 1972; Craik and Levy, 1976; Cermak and Craik, 1979; Crowder, 1982; Reisberg, Rappaport and O'Shaugnessy, 1984). This process has four major functions:

i to provide short-term storage in strategy-dependent systems related to the five major sense areas, but particularly auditory, motor, and visual information processing.

ii to facilitate encoding of incoming material for effective storage and retrieval in long-term memory.

iii to enable recall of already learned material stored in long-term memory back to the executive to facilitate perception and problem solving using past experience.

iv to enable the automatic control of a previously learned skill, while other incoming information is processed in the sub-systems.

Working memory competences in students with SpLD

The child with specific learning difficulties has not acquired the skills and strategies referred to by Reisberg, Rappaport and O'Shaugnessy (1984), and has difficulty in developing working memory competences, and using them in the development of literacy.

Often, the child's parents will have gained some knowledge of his difficulty from his fluctuating skills in recalling. They know that if you ask him about events which happened last year, such as the Christmas party at Grandma's house, the location of the Christmas tree, where people sat in the lounge, the presents they received from under the tree, he will tell you all about it, recalling it accurately in great detail. But, if you say to him, 'Johnny go upstairs, switch on the immersion heater, put this towel in the airing cupboard, put this shirt on your bed, and put this parcel in the spare room', he will find it difficult to retain the lengthy aurally coded instructions long enough to enable him to carry out the sequence. His parents are making a nice distinction between Johnny's competence in long-term remembering, and immediate short-term remembering of orally presented information. Mum knows he is forgetful, and if she sends him to the shop, he will return with some of her requirements missing. There are differences in his skills of remembering, which have practical implications and must be taken account of.

Although SpLD children show difficulties in the peripheral aspects of working memory such as auditory and visual short-term recall, the most significant difficulty they experience is in the fourth area of working memory described above, that is, the automatic control of the subskills in a major schema such as reading, when the peripheral sub-systems are heavily committed in contributory recall tasks (Perfetti and Lesgold, 1977; Daneman and Carpenter, 1980; and Chasty and Zdzienski, 1986). The argument advanced is that children with limited working memory capacity will experience a conflict in the use of working memory for temporary storage as well as for processing the skill, which will reduce the effectiveness of one or other of these functions. For example, in reading aloud the child may say the words correctly, but be unable to store and recall the sense effectively in comprehension. However when required to do so, he can switch priorities, using available memory capacity for retaining the sense, but in doing so, makes many more word recognition errors.

A practical example will enable further understanding of the functions of working memory in problem solving.

It's cold these evenings. Our gas fire is not working. We asked the gas board to come and fix it last week. They told us they would come on Thursday. They didn't turn up. We took the day off work so we are not pleased. How do we solve that problem? Clearly, we must communicate with the appropriate people at the gas board. The easiest way is by telephone. So we get out the 'Yellow Pages', find 'gas board' and locate the appropriate six figure string of digits: six, five, seven, eight, two, four.

This information is coded and relayed in chunks to the working memory for attention. The first skill is one of capacity. What is our capacity to handle that information? How many bits can we retain, store and use positively at one moment and how long do we take to do it (see Stanley and Hall, 1973a)? That will decide the size of the information package we can operate in that system. It will not determine how cleverly we think, but it will establish how much information can be processed in that channel at a given moment.

In our teaching we need to consider the special needs of children whose capacity to handle information in this way is limited.

Now that the number has been dialled and we have got through, another working memory strategy is required. What happens to those digits, when the girl at Reception says, 'Gas Board'? We cannot sort out the gas board, and retain 'six, five, seven, eight, two, four' as well. We delete the digits fast. The ability to delete unwanted information quickly to free capacity for the next stage of the problem is very important (see Stanley and Hall, 1973b). We must also be interested in the special needs of children who cannot delete information from auditory register fast.

At this stage we apply a previously determined recipe for the solution of the problem which requires us to present six linked questions sequentially:

Question One: Why didn't you come last week?
Question Two: When are you going to come?
Question Three: What will you do to my gas fire when you do come?
Question Four: How much will this cost me?
Question Five: Seeks information about the eventualities: Is this repair likely to last or do we need a new fire?
Question Six: Why is the gas board so difficult to deal with anyway?

This recipe for the solution of the problem is held in central executive of working memory and applied step by step. Some of the responses will be retained by the peripheral systems for later use. Like, 'The fitter will come next Wednesday at 4 o'clock. It's going to cost you £45. He will replace the burner elements. These are likely to last a few years then the whole fire must be replaced'.

The application of a range of strategies in working memory brings a solution to the problem. While the strategies used will differ from individual to individual, teachers must question how a six element recipe from the solution of a problem can be used, if it exceeds the capacity available in the child's working memory. The answer must be 'with difficulty', and here we touch on the specific difficulty in SpLD.

If it were only a two or a three element recipe which was required, this could be operated effectively, but because the loading placed on working memory exceeds capacity, difficulty is experienced either in overall control of the schema, or in the efficiency with which the related sub-skills are carried out. Little skills or schemas which have only a few sub-skills are handled well, but big skills or schemas are applied rather badly. This offers an explanation of why children with specific learning difficulty fail on bigger skills. How does working memory enable this level of automatic control or automaticity in the management of big skills?

Automaticity is important

The development of automaticity in driving provides a useful example of the role of working memory in skill control.

What do people think about as they drive to work each morning? It is apparent that they think about many things. Very little of their attention is directed towards the 'big' and complex skill of driving. But this was not always so. In the first driving lesson, working memory was operating beyond capacity in controlling the complex schema necessary. Where is the steering wheel? Where is the accelerator? Where is the brake? The action governing each control had to be thought about separately and the learner is often unsuccessful in coordinating the actions to manage the car. On occasions the driving instructor must take quick action to prevent an accident. There was no capacity available to allow the driver to think about anything but driving. After some practice, the learner manages to control the complex skill of driving but it still occupies all the available capacity of the learner's working memory. With even more practice, the learner can actually spare some attention to think about other things such as the route, or the infinite patience and charm of the driving instructor and engage in conversation with him. Eventually the learner becomes a skilful driver and welds all the sub-skills together into a single unitary big skill or schema which can be controlled so automatically in working memory that, when driving, he has the capacity available to think about a whole range of other problems.

The establishment of automaticity which compacts the skill to provide the capacity required to think about other things is easy for some, but others, who have more limited working memory, struggle much harder to achieve it. It is this factor which lies behind the SpLD child's slow acquisition of control over the basic literacy and numeracy skills which, in the author's opinion, are composed of complex sequential patterns of sub-skills. As practitioners working with SpLD children it must be our concern to develop in our learners this automatic skilled performance, where the sub-skills are managed effectively in working memory, so that these children develop the capacity simultaneously to control the skill and to manipulate and think about the ideas being expressed.

The reading schema

Every reader has a schema or recipe for reading. While no teacher would teach the activity in this rigid sequential way, all the listed sub-skills must be controlled effectively to ensure a successful performance. The major sub-skills in temporal order are as follows. Firstly move eyes from left to right, and take in shapes (which might be letters, words, phrases, or lines, depending on the individual's skills). This visual input must be recognized, the appropriate sounds linked to the visual input. In reading aloud, the sounds must be said. Then the sense of that chunk is extracted and stored temporarily. Finally, the whole meaning needs to be constructed and recalled for effective action.

Successful control of the performance of all ten of these sub-skills in sequential order places an immensely heavy load on working memory. The errors made by the SpLD child when handling such a complex processing problem within his limited working memory capacity are readily understandable. The teaching procedure followed should meet this difficulty.

Is 'real books' reading relevant to this problem?

There is a range of answers to the problem of working memory overload. The learner could group and organize the reading sub-skills into linked units so that they are manageable. Carefully structured multi-sensory learning is helpful because its teaching rationale links the sub-skills together in a way which facilitates the development of working memory competence so enabling control over the large skill of reading.

Alternatively, the teacher might do as the driving instructor did, and give lengthy intensive practice in the whole skill in the 'real books' approach. This raises a fundamental issue. If we are teaching a child whose problems in handling the reading skill are caused by working memory deficiencies, is it more constructive to say that he has a reading problem and teach him reading, or is it better to say he has a specific learning difficulty and extend and develop his skills in remembering and learning? This properly places the onus for the development of the learning skill on teacher, rather than relying on the child passively acquiring the necessary working memory competences from prolonged reading practice which he has already found to be difficult, disturbing and unhelpful.

In schools we teach facts, knowledge, subjects. We develop communication skills. We do 'real books' reading. By teaching skills like reading and spelling and writing, and factual subjects like history, geography and nature study, we expect children to derive a range of competences in remembering, in auditory, visual and motor terms, the facts and procedures we give them to remember. But we never actually teach them the skills of remembering. We have not analyzed the range of relevant strategies and we have not looked at the applications of these in learning. This leads to a limitation in our capability of meeting the special needs of children with difficulties in remembering, who do not develop memory competences easily from the haphazard curriculum practice we give them.

The writer looks forward to the day when teachers will take as much pride in developing the skills of remembering in their children, as they now take in developing skills of reading, or writing, and spelling. Memory is not a solid immutable organ like a concrete block. It is an extendable series of sub-systems contributing to a trainable skill (Reisberg, Rappaport and O'Shaugnessy, 1984). In this skill a range of abilities and difficulties will be evident in each class. How can we teachers meet the special needs of children with these difficulties in remembering, which is acknowledged to be one of the major learning skills they must acquire?

Speech difficulties

The child's inefficiencies in expressing skills in spoken language are often apparent, but major problems, which are much less evident, also occur in receptive language skills.

Expressive language problems

Initially, in expressive speech, the SpLD child may have problems making certain sounds. Usually, the high frequency sounds such as f/th, v/th, s/sh, are affected. These sounds are not well made in speaking, and are often poorly recognized, and badly spelt.

Difficulty is also evident in using sounds sequentially as parts of words. SpLD children may experience sequencing problems in speech, long after other children have overcome this difficulty. They may still be mispronouncing words, saying 'aminals' for 'animals' or 'suspectable' for 'susceptible'. They may report, 'My dad was pushing a ''mow lawner'' across the grass' or 'He left his car at the par cark'. They get sounds in the wrong places in words. This is often regarded by others as amusing, and when children are laughed at for producing such utterances they quickly learn not to expose themselves to ridicule by risking spontaneous communication in class.

An equally serious problem is often observed in expressive language skills where a child must formulate an idea as a spoken or written sentence. There is an idea implicit in Figure 17.1.

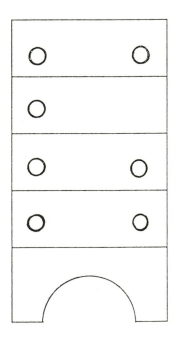

Figure 17.1 Anomalous Chest of Drawers

Something is missing and must be identified. If the problem is solved visually, it is easy. All the child has to do is point to the missing knob on the picture. This is a very direct solution and the loading it presents to working memory is consequently low. It only occupies one or two slots in memory if it is solved this way. However, if it is solved verbally, the problem is of a different calibre. It requires the coordination and control of systems in handling auditory, visual, linguistic and semantic information in working memory. Now try to analyze that picture, work out what is missing, and construct a good grammatically correct English sentence expressing all the information for others. It is quickly apparent how complex the problem is when solved verbally.

An acceptable sentence is something like, 'The right hand knob of the second drawer down is missing'. To construct this sentence requires a very high level of verbal skill. Children with SpLD can see the idea and understand it. They may solve the problem effectively in visual and motor terms, but putting the idea into an acceptable speech form is very difficult for them. The kind of speech they use in response is something like this: 'Yes! It's that thing there you hold on to if you want to open it'. Mother will understand, and friends in the playground may grasp the idea. As communication, the utterance may be effective in a limited way, but language such as this is not so useful in the classroom as a basis for thinking, reading, spelling and higher writing skills required in examinations.

Initially children use language for social communication. But the further the child progresses through school, the more teachers expect him to use language as a way of expressing and manipulating ideas. The question to be considered is how useful speech such as, 'It's that thing there you hold on to if you want to open it' is a step on the way to manipulating and discussing the complex questions requiring verbally mediated thinking, encountered in our examination orientated senior school system. Would the child who uses 'It's that thing there', develop his thinking in this specialized way? The answer is probably not, unless the teacher does a lot of work on the development of his spoken language competences.

The thrust of our present consideration must be that there are other ways of handling the ideas. The child has alternatives. What ought the implication of these individual differences in his use of language in learning be for us in schools?

Receptive language problems

The SpLD child's difficulties in receptive language are much less obvious, but no less serious. Teachers tend to build lengthy sentences, and give spoken instructions in long sequential lists which are incomprehensible to the dyslexic child. An instruction such as 'Before you go home, do your spelling corrections', is wrongly comprehended by many SpLD children who take in the key words 'go', 'home', 'do corrections', and dash immediately for the door.

A basic speech principle which is too often neglected by teachers is 'order of mention'. The teacher should give instructions to the child in the order they are to be done. If the teacher varies the order in the way illustrated above, she gives the child the additional problems of (i) recognizing the obliqueness of the form of communication, and (ii) holding the instructions in working memory, while resequencing to the required operational order. This is a totally unnecessary complication to teacher–child communication which reinforces the question posed at the beginning of this paper: 'If this child doesn't learn the way we teach, can we teach him the way he learns?'. The teacher's duty must be to give the child the information he requires in a way which is acceptable and usable by him at a rate which does not lead to overload.

Achievement Difficulties

Reading skills

While the reading skills of students with specific learning difficulties have already been discussed in this paper, further detailed consideration is necessary. Reading is not a single skill: it is multi-faceted and has a range of purposes. In the early stages of learning reading, word recognition difficulties are apparent.

There is a deficiency in our early teaching of reading skills, which stems from incorrect assumptions made about the child's working memory competences. Teachers should try to think as a cognitive psychologist would,

Figure 17.2 Associating symbols with sounds

about the processes of the early teaching of reading skills. We give the child visual information, usually on a flash card. This word says, 'Jane'. Simultaneously, we are also giving the child auditory information, the sound of 'Jane'. We are using two systems, or modes, or registers in working memory, an auditory store and a visual store. The teacher has given the child the word shape, and its sound. The child is required to link these two elements together and store them in long-term memory as a unit which is recallable and usable within very precise time limits in reading. What training have we given children to enable fast easy establishment and accessing of these linkages prior to the commencement of reading instruction? Knowledge of nursery–infant teaching suggests that often no training whatsoever is provided. We expect the child to develop that complex working memory process in learning for himself.

We could develop this skill prior to reading by playing games which encourage the child to recognize shapes, by attaching individual sounds to name them (see Figure 17.2). The child can recall and identify the shape by its sound, and equally important, the sound by its shape. By playing a game which links shapes with sounds and establishing working memory competences, we give the child with such memory deficiencies a chance of succeeding in developing reading skills which require fast accurate cross-modal representation of information.

While many SpLD students deal with the simpler aspects of reading adequately, difficulty is more frequently encountered when the stress of examination conditions, demands of speed, or pressures of work, place undue loading upon the established automaticity developed for this skill in working memory. The unpredictable breakdown of the skill under stress is even more inhibiting than consistent difficulty which is predictable.

Writing skills

The writing of Pearse (see Figure 17.3) indicates many of the difficulties encountered by dyslexic students. Pearse is writing about a history lesson which he obviously found fascinating. He finds the problems of sequencing the ideas, expressing them in sentences comprising words which must be spelt and represented by letters written from left to right across the page all too much for him. The task greatly exceeds his capacity to control it and despite his high ability, his work is laboured and subject to frequent errors which concern him, as is evidenced by his attempts at corrections. He is interested in history, concentrates upon the strategies of the battle, and has little working memory capacity left to handle the writing and spelling problems.

Pearse has written some fifty-six words. He has misspelled some twenty-three of these words and shows a very high spelling error rate of 41 per cent in writing. Because of his difficulties in establishing hand preference and fine motor skills his writing is extremely slow and laborious, much below the thirty-six letters per minute one might expect of a boy of Pearse's age. His spelling

WISC (R) Verbal Scale 136, Performance Scale 120

Dotting speed R 30.2 Slow times show motor difficulty. Similar times indicate
         L 31.4 ambidexterity

Vernon Graded Word Spelling Test: score 7y 6m.

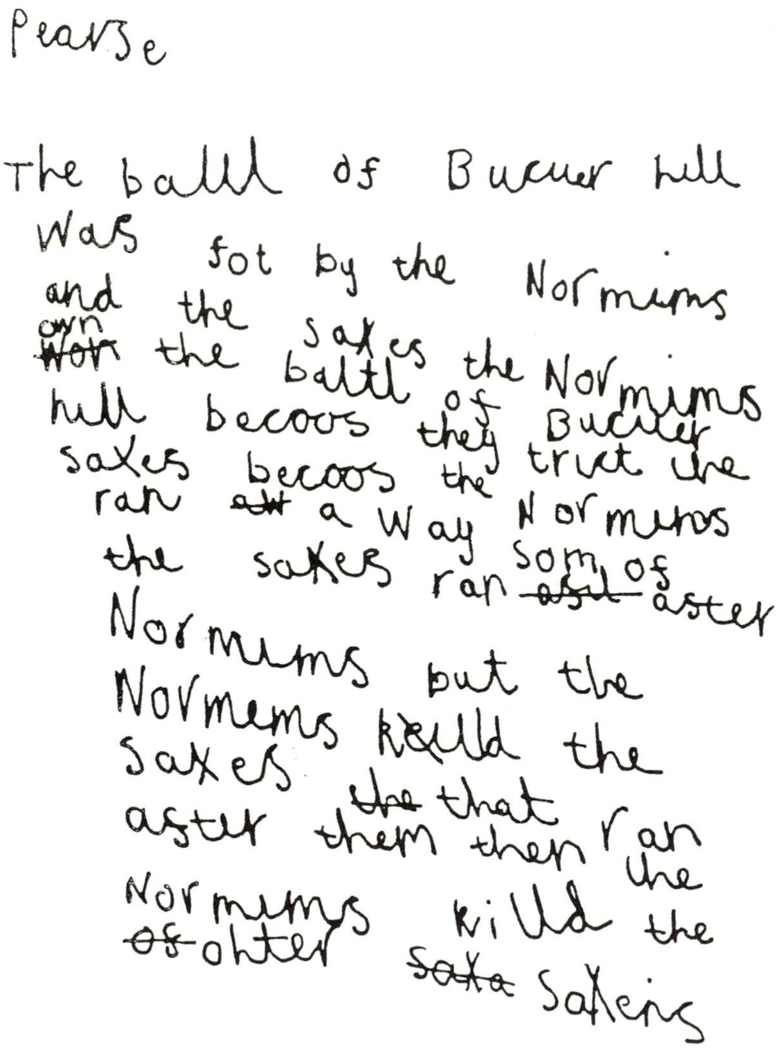

Pearse

The balll of Bucuer hill
was sot by the Normims
and the saxes
own the balll of the Normims
hill becoos they Bucuer
saxes becoos the trist the
ran a way Normuos
the sakes ran som of
Normums but the
Normems kould the
Saxes the that
aster them then ran the
Normums killd the
ohter sata Sakeis

Figure 17.3 History notes written by Pearse, aged 8y 0m

282

skills on the Vernon Graded Word Spelling Test are below expectation, but not seriously so, and his serious spelling weakness in writing reflects the reduced capacity available in working memory to control spelling in this condition. His ability to transfer and apply his knowledge of spelling in writing is impaired and he has not developed anything like the level of automaticity required to enable him to express his detailed knowledge of history with the precision required in class.

Pearse is a skilful artist. It is questionable whether he should have written his ideas or drawn a picture with a few verbal explanations. His difficulties in writing are all too evident. Even at the age of 8, Pearse should have been asking, 'Why am I doing this? What is the best way to do it? How can I apply my skills to the best advantage in handling this information?'.

Numeracy

Similar problems in the expression of ideas by written symbols are often observed in numeracy. From the psychological assessments carried out in the Dyslexia Institute it is evident that some 70 per cent of dyslexics also experience difficulties with the language of number. Some years ago the author observed a number skills lesson which illustrates the difficulties experienced by these children.

The SpLD child was working on a horizontal table, while the teacher used a vertical blackboard. The teacher said, 'Put down 5'. The child did this accurately. He was also able to put out his counters to represent 5 in a domino pattern. The teacher's next instruction was: 'Underneath 5 put 6'. The child was very confused and looked under his table. Most teachers would interpret that as provocative. Which of us would say, 'What an interesting receptive language problem he has'? The teacher's next instruction was, 'Draw a line and put down the add sign'. The child with specific learning difficulties acting on these teaching instructions produced a 'sum' which looked like that illustrated in Figure 17.4.

His numeracy difficulties were very similar to his written language difficulties. Problems in both literacy and numeracy reflected his specific difficulties in learning.

Pearse, whose writing has been shown earlier, had similar information-recording difficulty in number. He could count effectively in practical terms with fingers or counters. His trend to reversals resulted in his producing figures such as those in Figure 17.4, and confusions were evident between 2 and 5, 6 and 9. His directional problems caused difficulty in working out where to start. Sequencing right to left, down to up, up to down, as well as left to right, was too much for him. His short-term memory weakness affected his storage and retrieval of information from the question. Number facts, components and tables were not recalled with the efficiency necessary for accurate computation on paper. His difficulties in numeracy were similar to those he experienced in literacy and were clearly related to his identifiable learning difficulties.

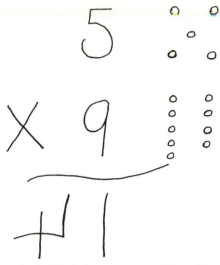

Note the competent practical skills, but poor representation of the numerical ideas on paper.

Figure 17.4 A SpLD child's representation of a dictated addition sum

Behaviour

Children with specific learning difficulties can also show some behavioural difficulties. They may lose the thread of long sequential activities such as dressing and can be found in the bedroom half dressed, playing with toys when they should be at breakfast. They may be very inefficient on times, places and dates, and are often classified as disobedient when the problem really stems from lack of understanding of instructions such as 'Come and see me on Tuesday at 2.30 p.m.'. In class, some SpLD children are clumsy, socially awkward to the point of belligerence, and do not establish effective working relationships with their teachers. They have been slow to establish an appropriate understanding of the rules of behaviour, which is also a learned skill. They show similar difficulties in the acquisition of skills of behaviour to those evident in their development of the skills of reading, spelling, writing and numeracy.

Teaching provisions

The range of teaching provisions to be made for SpLD students will be wide and varied. The provision made must be individual and relate to the abilities and difficulties in learning experienced by the student. The provision should cover (a) learning skills, (b) (i) language skills, (ii) numeracy skills, (c) study/thinking skills, (d) behavioural skills and (e) link effectively to the school curriculum.

The skills list to be covered is set out below:-

(A) *Learning Skills*

1. Fine motor skills development: (train the hand).
2. Laterality-sequencing training (where do I start).
3. Working memory training:
    develop deliberate control of available capacity;
    extend capacity;
    teach discarding of irrelevant information;
    choose time for learning;
    switch modalities frequently;
    multi-sensory is best.
4. Visual perceptual training:
    skill in recognizing shapes consistently.
5. Auditory perceptual training:
    skill in recognizing sounds consistently.

(B) (i) *Language Skills*

6. Language development through talk:
    (i)   getting sounds and words right;
    (ii) getting sentences right;
    (iii) concept/idea/labelling;
    (iv) creating an organization for talk.
7. Structured multi-sensory training to develop simultaneous skills in reading, spelling and writing and making most effective use of deficient memory skills.

(B) (ii) *Numeracy Skills*

8. Number language training: using structured multi-sensory methods.

(C) *Study/thinking Skills*

9. Extraction, representation, storage and recall of ideas.
10. Expression of ideas in writing.
11. Development of active control of the learning/thinking process in metacognition.

(D) *Behavioural Skills*

Developing the competences to enable the learner to operate effectively in a range of social and learning groups with varying purposes, structures, climates.

(E) *Relate to School Curriculum*

Local education authority staff responsible for planning individual programmes should note that, while two or three hours specialist teaching may be adequate at age 6, 7 or 8, for teenage students working on a much more literacy demanding curriculum, and experiencing serious difficulties, a provision of ten to fifteen hours each week may be required. When making a special provision under the Education Act 1981, authorities are required to take due account of efficient use of resources. Skilled teaching resources are used more efficiently when given early, and at a saturation level. The National Curriculum requirements will also bear on this issue (see Chapter 1).

Is skills development enough?

Even teaching the skills of learning as outlined above is not enough. The teacher of SpLD students should also teach control over the skill, related to analysis of the task, so that the skill may be used to maximum efficiency.

The ability to survey a task and apply the available strategies to maximum efficiency is the key to learning to learn. The term metacognition was coined by Flavell (1971) to refer to this process of developing awareness, monitoring, and regulation of one's cognitive processes (see also Nisbet and Shucksmith, 1984; Forrest-Pressley and Waller, 1984; Meichenbaum, 1985).

Experimental practical work in teaching metacognitive processes to students is currently appearing in the literature and shows interesting results. Haller, Child and Walberg (1988) report a very detailed research programme containing twenty studies comprising a total student population of 1,533 showing significant gains from metacognitive instructions on reading comprehension. Such an approach could have very beneficial effects on SpLD students.

However, the teaching of these processes should not be left to the early teenage stage. They should be taught in relation to the major teaching processes described earlier in this article. Metacognitions should be taught in parallel with all these skills from the earliest stage to enable each skill to be used with maximum efficiency, and transferred to other learning.

In this metacognitive learning, action standards in information processing and problem solving are developed:

(a) Purpose: Why am I doing this?
(b) Outcome: What is required at end?
(c) Strategy: What strategy should be used?
(d) Monitoring: Was it successful?
(e) Development: How can it be improved?
(f) Transfer: Can it be transferred to another skill? Thus we learn how to learn.

Future trends

Programmes currently devised to meet the special educational needs of SpLD students take a much too limited perspective. Teaching literacy skills to illiterate students is a laudable but limited aim. The aim should not be restricted to improving reading and writing to enable the student to read his textbook more effectively and write his assignments better.

Research in cognitive psychology is leading to much more detailed and effective work in cognitive skills development. Teachers of SpLD children should recognize the abilities and limitations in their students' learning and literacy competences, and identify and teach strategies which enable the development of these skills and their effective control in the range of circumstances relevant for life as it may be in 2005. In adopting this wider approach we make our students not just 'active interrogators of the text', but active interrogators of the learning/thinking process, and in full control of their skills, and options.

Do we still consider remedial reading teaching an adequate provision for students with specific difficulties in learning? If the child does not learn the way we teach, can we teach him the way he learns, and then extend and develop his competences in learning? That is the challenge of working with children with specific learning difficulties.

References

Baddeley, A. (1976) *The Psychology of Memory*, New York, Basic Books.

Baddeley, A. (1978) 'The trouble with levels: a re-examination of Craik and Lockhart's framework for memory research', *Psychological Review*, 85, pp. 139–152.

Baddeley, A. (1982) 'Reading and working memory', *Bulletin of the British Psychological Society*, 35, pp. 414–416.

Baddeley, A., Grant, S., Wight, E. and Thomson, N. (1974) 'Imagery and visual working memory', in Rabbit, P. and Dominic S. (Eds) *Attention and Performance, V*, New York, Academic Press.

Baddeley, A. and Hitch, G. (1974) 'Working memory', in Bower, G. (Ed) *The Psychology of Learning and Motivation, Volume 8*, New York, Academic Press.

Baddeley, A. and Lieberman, K. (1980) 'Spatial working memory', in Nicherson, R. (Ed) *Attention and Performance, VIII*, Hillsdale, N.J., Lawrence Erlbaum.

Cermak, L. and Craik, F. (Eds) (1979) *Levels of Processing in Human Memory*, Hillsdale, N.J., Lawrence Erlbaum.

Chasty, H. and Zdzienski, D. (1986) 'Working memory and comprehension', *Paper given to British Psychological Society, Cognitive Section*.

Colle, H. (1980) 'Auditory encoding in visual short term recall: effects of noise intensity and spatial location', *Journal of Verbal Learning and Verbal Behaviour*, 19, pp. 722–735.

Colle, H. and Welsh, A. (1976) 'Acoustic masking in primary memory', *Journal of Verbal Learning and Verbal Behaviour*, 15, pp. 17–32.

Craik, F. and Levy, B. (1976) 'The concept of primary memory', in Estes, W. K. (Ed) *Handbook of Learning and Cognitive Processes, Volume 4*, Hillsdale, N.J., Lawrence Erlbaum.

Craik, F. and Lockhart, R. (1972) 'Levels of processing: a framework for memory research', *Journal of Verbal Learning and Verbal Behaviour*, 11, pp. 671–684.

Crowder, R. (1982) 'The demise of short term memory', *Acta Psychologica*, 50, pp. 291–323.

Daneman, M. and Carpenter, M. (1980) 'Individual differences in working memory and reading', *Journal of Verbal Learning and Verbal Behaviour*, 19, pp. 450–466.

Flavell, J. H. (1971) 'First discussant's comments: What is memory development the development of?', *Human Development*, 14, pp. 272–278.

Forrest-Pressley, D. L. and Waller, T. G. (1984) *Cognition, Metacognition and Reading*, New York, Springer-Verlag.

Groden (1969) 'Lateral preferences in normal children', *Perceptual and Motor Skills*, 28, pp. 213–214.

Haller, E. P., Child, D. A. and Walberg, H. J. (1988) 'Can comprehension be taught? A quantitative synthesis of metacognitive studies', *Educational Researcher*, 17, pp. 5–8.

Kolers, P. and Smythe, I. (1979) 'Images, symbols and skills', *Canadian Journal of Psychology*, 33, pp. 158–184.

Meichenbaum, D. (1985) 'Teaching thinking: a cognitive behavioural perspective', in Segal, J. W., Chipman, S. F. and Glaser, R. (Eds) *Thinking and Learning Skills, Volume 2, Research and Open Questions*, Hillsdale, N.J., Lawrence Erlbaum.

Nisbet, J. and Shucksmith, J. (1984) *The Seventh Sense*, Edinburgh, Scottish Council for Research in Education.

Perfetti, C. A. and Lesgold, A. M. (1977) 'Discourse comprehension and individual differences', in Carpenter, P. and Just, M. (Eds) *Process in Comprehension*, Hillsdale, N.J., Lawrence Erlbaum.

Reisberg, D., Rappaport, I. and O'Shaugnessy, M. (1984) 'Limits of working memory: the digit digit span', *Journal of Experimental Psychology: Learning, Memory and Cognition*, 10, pp. 203–221.

Salame, P. and Baddeley, A. (1982) 'Disruption of short term memory by unattended speech: implications for the structure of working memory', *Journal of Verbal Learning and Verbal Behaviour*, 21, pp. 150–164.

Stanley, G. and Hall, R. (1973a) 'Short term visual information processing in dyslexics', *Child Development*, 44, pp. 841–844.

Stanley, G. and Hall, R. (1973b) 'A comparison of dyslexics and normals in recalling letter arrays after brief presentations', *British Journal of Educational Psychology*, 43, pp. 301–304.

18
Children with Spelling and Writing Difficulties:
An Alternative Approach

E. Neville Brown

This chapter suggests an alternative to the current dominant phonic-cum-multisensory approach to the remediation of spelling and writing difficulties. It is divided into three parts: firstly an account of the development of the notion of a unisensory principle in the context of learning to read and spell; secondly, a case study in which the unisensory principle is applied to the teaching of spelling and handwriting to a severely dyslexic and dysgraphic child; and thirdly, an account of the development of a handwriting and spelling policy within the context of a school, using the findings from the two preceding sections.

The unisensory principle and the treatment of literacy difficulties

Henry Ford is reputed to have informed his customers that they could have any colour automobile they wished, provided that it was black. Similarly, it appears, as far as those agencies that recommend treatment for dyslexic-type difficulties are concerned, a dyslexic child should follow 'the structured multisensory programme to meet...the precise nature of the learning difficulty e.g. Specific Learning Difficulties relating to the acquisition of literacy skills and mathematics' (Brereton, 1988), or, typically, from the report of an educational psychologist attached to a dyslexia institute: 'Because of his specific area of weakness he should be taught by multisensory methods. These methods focus on the links to be made between the way letters and words look, sound and feel as they are produced in speech and simultaneous writing'. The syllabuses for certain of the recently introduced diplomas in specific learning difficulties or dyslexia are biased by emphasis and exclusion towards multisensory and phonetic/phonic methods — 'Courses should include a critical evaluation of:

> the principles of multi-sensory teaching and the available methods,
> the English phonic system and a brief introduction to phonetics.'

(from the Course Content of the RSA Diploma for Teachers of Pupils with Specific Learning Difficulties, RSA 1987.) Hornsby (1984) recommends that a dyslexic child should follow:

> a structured phonetic/linguistic method (which) is the most effective
> system used in centres where dyslexics are taught . . . It is preferable to
> have a thorough knowledge of phonetics (the science of speech
> sounds) and linguistics (the science of language) in order to teach it.

It must be said, however, that most, if not all, those advanced diplomas introduced by universities do not appear to suffer in this way, e.g. the recently introduced Diploma in Specific Learning Difficulties at Manchester which began in 1987.

The assumption that phonetics is necessary and/or sufficient for reading and spelling may, however, be challenged. Hynds (1987) retorts that 'I have not so far been able to find anyone, amongst even the most accomplished of readers, who has more than the vaguest notion of the twenty or so pure vowel sounds in English'. Hynds deplores the widespread ignorance in dyslexia writings of multiplicity of cue systems and strategies used in reading and spelling by both apprentice and mature literati. Much useful work has been done since Goodman (1967) suggested that anyone who relied solely on phonic/phonetic strategies or cue-systems would take such an inordinate time to read a book that the thread of meaning would be lost. Goodman also suggested that miscue analysis could indicate which strategies an apprentice reader was using to produce a response in 'mechanical' reading. Consequent research concluded that poor readers tended to make significantly less use of semantic graphic information than did good readers, e.g. Clay, 1968, 1969; Murray and Maliphant 1984. It is very likely that poor readers, far from being deficient in language organization, have an instructional set which emphasizes phonic strategies to the detriment of others (Brown, 1980; Francis, 1984).

There is the possibility, however, that Goodman's linguistic cue systems, semantic and syntactic, are present at such a complex level of organization in the good reader *as a result* of gaining facility in the written language rather than a high level of language ability being a precondition for their development. When considering dyslexic children, diagnosis usually entails the exclusion of factors such as poor language ability. At-least-average scores on the Similarities, Vocabulary and Comprehension subtests of the WISC(R) [Wechsler Intelligence Scale for Children, Revised] may be taken as indicators of adequate language ability. It is important, too, not to infer that a child has a receptive or mediational language difficulty from the existence of a speech-articulation defect.

Most, if not all, researchers into acquired dyslexia (i.e. where the facility to read or to spell/write is lost through cerebral insult) now conclude that the phonological route from print to meaning is one of a number of routes that are, or may be used independently, though not necessarily simultaneously, in the reading process. Marshall's (1984) model is typical (Figure 18.1) in that it allows a phonic processing route, with meaning or 'barking at print', a whole word route ('look-and-say' or 'look-and-mean'), and also a morphographic or direct linguistic route such as that suggested by Brown (1980). A similar model is presented by Snowling in Chapter 8, Figure 8.2.

Brown further suggested that, although simultaneous processing, or rapid-switch processing as suggested by Senf (1969), might be possible in fluent readers, undue emphasis on the use of the phonological route in apprentice readers, especially those with obvious difficulties, might inhibit the development of other processing strategies. Brown suggested that this might even be so in the majority of poor readers who exhibited a strong visual-processing preference. Brown compared a phonic teaching regimen (letter sounds, phonic rules, syllabification etc.) with a morphographic regimen using visual mediators only ('icons') in a controlled experiment and found the latter approach significantly superior for teaching the recognition, comprehension and spelling of long words which were present in the oral vocabulary but not hitherto in the written.

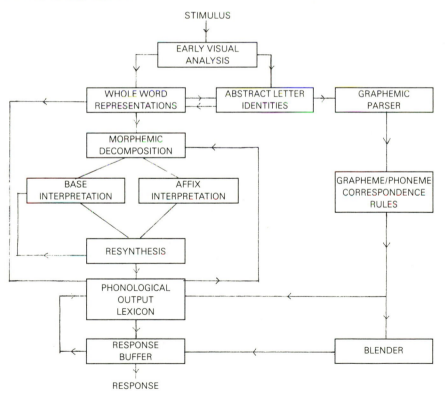

Figure 18.1 Architecture of the Normal Reading System (Marshall, 1984)

If the premise is accepted that 'human language is essentially a device for associating things with sounds, the link between which is arbitrary' and that 'written language depends upon an analysis of each (spoken) word into a succession of *separate* sounds' (Heaton and Winterson, 1986, p. 32), then the direct linguistic approach is not possible. It is, however, not only in Chinese and Japanese written languages where the ideographs have no necessary phonological associations, but in the English written language as described by the model. Thus a person who is unable to master the spelling of a semantically complex word such as '*corporation*' by segmenting the oral word into syllables — '*cor-por-ay-shun*' — and then into discrete sounds which are then tagged to letters, may possibly learn and retain its spelling when presented morphemically as '*corp-or-at(e)-ion*' with some clue as to the meaning of the particles presented. It is interesting to note that even children without reading difficulties tend to find such words, where there is a mismatch between syllable- and morpheme-boundaries, more difficult to read than other words of similar length and familiarity. This is perhaps because there is some indecision as to which processing strategy to use with long words that are not too familiar. The occurrence of this phenomenon, which the writer has not noticed in children who have been taught by a predominantly morphemic approach, suggests that morphemic analysis of words is undertaken by normal readers even when no such skill has been taught or when the reader cannot report that the strategy is being used.

In the profoundly deaf, where it must be accepted that the phonological route is impaired if not entirely absent physiologically, the writer has found it possible to teach individual words by the morphographic approach, using 'icons' as mediators, and subsequently to build sentences for reading and response in writing where no such facility was known to exist before. In dysarthric and anarthric children, it has recently been found that even the 'indirect' route which involves phoneme-grapheme conversion does not necessarily implicate phoneme sounding or subvocalization (Bishop and Robson, 1989).

If 'phonic' or phonological mediation is not a requisite for reading or for spelling/writing, then it cannot be argued that written language is *merely* a means of rendering speech sounds on paper, as many writers on dyslexia seem to suggest. Thus the requirement to make 'an analysis of the (spoken) word into a succession of *separate* sounds' is not necessary and, if inappropriately emphasized, might inhibit the development of other strategies, leading to what Hynds regards as the defining characteristic of the dyslexic, a 'muddle' 'caused by over-concentration on meaningless surface systems' (Hynds, 1987).

In the original research, reported in Brown (1979), letter-or syllable-sounding was found to inhibit the learning of vocabulary recognition and spelling by a morphographic approach which, proceeding directly from the visual stimulus to meaning without phonological mediation, can be regarded as unisensory at least in respect of input. In the next section, a case study is presented in which the principle is applied to spelling and writing problems.

Alex, A Case Study in the Treatment of Severe Literacy Difficulties

Alex, a lively 8-year-old, was typical in having the low WISC Digit Span and Coding scores often quoted as redolent of dyslexia. His test scores were:-

Alex — Chronological age 8:5
WISC(R)   Full Scale I.Q. 121
         Verbal I.Q.   122
         Performance I.Q. 115

WISC(R) Subtest scaled scores:

Information	7	Picture Completion	13
Similarities	16	Picture Arrangement	13
Arithmetic	10	Block Design	15
Vocabulary	16	Object Assembly	14
Comprehension	19	Coding	6
Digit Span	6	Mazes	17

Neale Analysis of Reading Ability:

Rate — Base level.   Accuracy — Base Level
Comprehension — 6:9
Schonell Spelling — 5:1 (*i.e.* one word correct)
Problems of Position Test (Mosely) Quotient 95
Age norms levels for WISC language subtests:-
Similarities — 12:10   Vocabulary — 11:10
Comprehension — 16:6 (lowest ratings from raw scores).

Alex had been referred to the schools' psychological service of his local education authority. He had had specialist remedial provision based on the psychologist's recommendations that letter-sound associations should be 'overlearnt' with multisensory reinforcement — letter tracing with sandpaper letters, blackboard writing, use of lower case plastic letters etc. — which also required liaison with the parents. However, on being tested, Alex could only spell one word on the Schonell spelling, 'in' (see Figure 18.2).

see   mat   in

Figure 18.2 Alex–Schonell Spelling Test

Alex was confused about letter sounds and names and even had difficulty printing letters, the 'n' in 'in' being produced from the line, working upwards for each stroke beginning with the righthand leg. On the Graphomotor Test (see Figure 18.3), Alex's performance was interesting in that every loop was reversed. Whilst some children with severe difficulties were found to form the loops separately under strong visual control, there was no occurrence of this phenomenon in Alex.

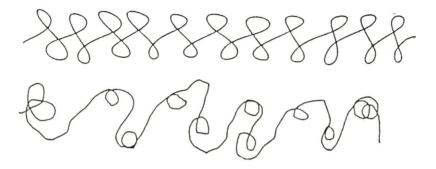

Figure 18.3   The Graphomotor Test and Alex's Response

Even when copying small words, Alex reversed letters such as 'b', 'd' and 'c'. Despite not knowing his letter sounds, Alex had succeeded in learning, in addition to 'in', the word 'look' which was the one word presented on every page of a picture book at school. This had been learnt holistically. After three years of formal schooling, Alex had made negligible progress in literacy whereas his peers seemed to have progressed normally. There had been few absences from school, no relevant medical condition(s), no lack of parental support and, in the early years at least, no lack of motivation, although at the time of referral Alex was thought by his teacher to be a fidget whose energy had to be diverted to classroom 'domestic' tasks to prevent his behaviour becoming tiresome. Alex was perhaps slightly clumsy but played football and other games quite robustly and with co-ordination that was estimated to be fairly normal. His self-image, understandably, was at a very low ebb.

In the Lichfield clinic, some success was obtained in reading by a holistic approach using rebuses, but progress was very slow and there was no noticeable effect on writing/spelling. Even with practice, the looped pattern of the Graphomotor Test could not be reproduced by Alex. The unisensory principle had been used with much success for improving reading and spelling in those (much more numerous) children who made phonic substitutions or attempts in spelling but who could reproduce visually-presented words/letter-strings without much difficulty. This was based on the assumption that they were using phonic strategies when visual strategies were appropriate. At that stage the principle had not been applied to spelling/writing difficulties such as those of Alex. The writer's attention was therefore focused on this problem, which was clearly not one of written language *per se*. Applying the unisensory principle, Alex was blindfolded and his hand (and 2B pencil) guided through the looped pattern several times without verbal accompaniment, the teacher's guidance being gradually withdrawn so that he could produce it on his own kinesthetically (see Figure 18.4).

With later subjects, it was found that if the blindfold were removed prematurely, there was a reversion which took further unisensory kinesthetic practice to put right. It was also found that asking a child to close his eyes was not satisfactory, presumably because he would have to attend to this action to the detriment of the task in hand.

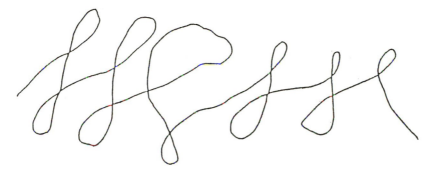

Figure 18.4 *Graphomotor Test, Unisensory Response*

Alex was delighted with the result and practised further, then being taught to write a range of small words such as 'man', 'is', 'on', 'cat', 'dog', either using rebuses or icons as stimuli. A rebus, useful for teaching the spelling or recognition of short words, is a pictorial representation of an example of the use of a word; an icon is a graphic representation of the meaning of a letter string.

Straightforward copying of the words or letter-strings was found to generate much confusion, so this was avoided. In teaching Alex kinesthetically, the whole word or letter-string was rehearsed as a whole with no verbal control or phonic accompaniment. Alex was then required to respond to the icon or rebus by writing in what was perforce a fully cursive script. By the sixth lesson, a small range of words, verbs, nouns, prepositions and articles, was learnt and Alex was required to write sentences (see Figure 18.5).

The stimulus pictures were drawn by the teacher during the course of the lesson with the aim of allowing some spontaneity of grammatical and syntactic structure. All the words, or in the cases of 'canal' and 'lady' the component morphograhs, were well-practised unisensorily before being used with the eyes open. In addition to writing sentences efficiently, that is with both fluency and accuracy, Alex had no difficulty in reading back the sentences even though there had been no rehearsal of this aspect. Neither Alex nor any subsequent pupil exhibited any difficulty in equating the printed form of a word with the fully cursive form.

Figure 18.5 Alex: Stimulus and Writing, Sixth Lesson

By the twelfth one-hour lesson, Alex had mastered about thirty words and 'bits' or morphographs and was able to produce more interesting sentences (see Figure 18.6), again from stimulus drawings and, of course, without copying.

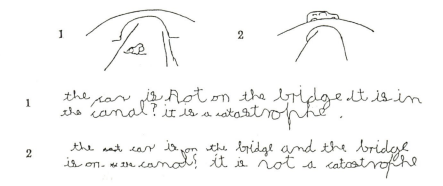

Figure 18.6 Alex: Stimulus and Writing. Twelfth Lesson

After a further period of tuition, Alex transferred to the then newly-opened specialist school where he continued to make progress in a small class of nine or ten children, pursuing a reasonably normal curriculum. His 'bread-and-butter' English work, for example, was quite adequate, although not near his intellectual level, before he passed into his local comprehensive school at 11 years (see Figure 18.7). Alex was the first case of such severe literacy difficulty to be treated according to the emergent unisensory principle. From the onset of teaching there was no recurrence of letter reversals, though there were occasions when the order of letters was reversed within the morphographs of long words. As he gained proficiency in spelling and writing Alex's reading improved without undue attention.

In the early teaching of Alex, the tactile input of sandpaper letters appeared to divert attention from the task of developing a trace of kinesthetic memory for the letters. Using a soft pencil or even guiding Alex's finger on a smooth surface produced results where none could be elicited before and Alex reported that he learnt better. Whilst critics may argue that in Alex's learning, the kinesthetic sense may have been dominant but not exclusive, the effect of strong tactile input suggests a contrary view. Certainly Alex was attending to the learning of a kinesthetic trace rather than to the minimized residual tactile potential of the soft pencil on paper. In activities such as learning skills with the hands where two or more sense mechanisms must be available or present, the appropriate instruction may be held to be unisensory if the subject is attending to the set modality and if distraction introduced into the supposedly

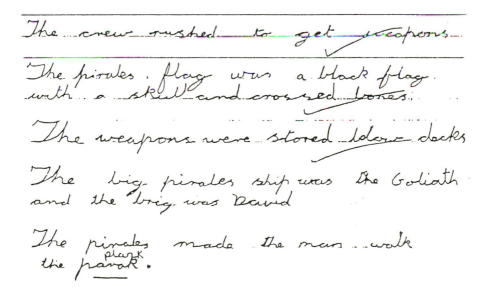

Figure 18.7 Alex: Written Work in English Lesson

unattended modality inhibits learning. The conclusion reached is that where a child has failed to learn to read, for meaning, despite adequate instruction, the restriction of the task to its essential component(s) has the highest probability of success; such an approach will be direct, that is to say from visual stimulus to meaning, and therefore unisensory. Similarly where a child has failed to spell the words that are available in a lexicon in any other modality, the approach with the highest probability of success will be initially by direct kinesthetic input leading to kinesthetic output with visual control introduced after the letter, word or morphograph trace has been learnt. Following this procedure has, in the writer's research and subsequent experience, resulted in the complete eradication of such phemomena as *b*/*d* reversals which suggests that they are induced by the instruction though there may be within-child factors which may favour such a tendency.

The development of a handwriting policy in the school context

From the work with Alex and others in a weekly clinic, a number of conclusions were drawn which subsequently guided the school's policy towards handwriting and certain aspects of spelling difficulties. The first is somewhat obvious:

1.   Where an apprentice writer has difficulty with the formation of letters, with letter-reversals and letter-order problems, emphasis on putting spelling patterns unisensorily into kinesthetic memory, excluding visual attention, is a promising way of proceeding. Having established the principle, the ingenuity of the teacher can be called upon to devise the best methods for the individual child. After the kinesthetic learning has occurred, visual integration can be attempted.

2.   Most, if not all, problems of the kind found in Alex can be avoided or at least ameliorated if fully cursive handwriting, with its heavy emphasis on kinesthetic learning, is employed from the outset of schooling. From the point of view of treatment, such problems are best regarded as artefacts of pedagogy rather than deficiencies in the child's neurophyschological make-up, even though there may be neurological or neuropsychological co-factors or predispositions to having particular kinds of difficulty.

3.   Alex had difficulties with reading and spelling that could be termed *'dyslexic'*, mainly phonic attempts at spelling for example. However, his difficulty with letter-formation, especially reversals, and with the looped pattern of the Graphomotor Test, suggests the use of another term, *'dysgraphic'*, to describe such difficulties. The writer has found that the incidence of such difficulties correlates highly with low scores on the WISC(R) Coding subtest but with no other subtest of the WISC(R).

4.   Aids for letter formation and writing practice in children with specific difficulty should be designed to take account of the possibility of intersensory confusion. Unlike the majority of the plastic letter shapes and other aids on the

market, they should be kinesthetic- rather than visual-oriented. They should not introduce distractors or interference such as the strong tactile stimulus from letter-shapes cut from sandpaper which inhibits kinesthetic learning.

5. The writer has not observed any significant confusion, even in children with quite severe literacy difficulties, of printed with cursive letter forms. Therefore there seems little point in teaching children first to print, converting to cursive when the child is able to spell adequately, as seems the almost universal practice in primary education. Even illiterates are taught cursive writing 'from scratch' at Maple Hayes School.

Letter- and letter-order reversals are commonly noted in 'normal' apprentice writers (though predominantly in boys) but tend to disappear after two or three years of schooling in the majority of cases. In the SpLD (specific learning difficulties) children referred to the writer's school, however, there is a high incidence of reversals which in the writer's opinion result from the use of printing. Almost all the referrals exhibit ill-formed, printed writing, very slowly executed which is regarded as immature by others. In order to improve the accuracy and fluency of handwriting, the teaching of a fully cursive style was indicated so that whole words, if small enough, the component morphographs of longer words could be written holistically in what, in output terms, might be the equivalent of Miller's 'chunking'. The aim of any aid to handwriting should be to allow maximum use of kinesthetic memory for words and letter strings with minimal visual control. It is often said of a skilled craftsman that he can do the job 'with his eyes shut' and this applies no less to handwriting. Visual control is, however, necessary to keep writing on the lines of exercise paper, to cross t's and to dot i's, to gauge the placement of words on the line so as to avoid descenders from the line above and avoid overshooting. Obviously, a writing style has to be legible to the pupil and teacher, but this aim is quite compatible with fluency if a suitable style is required of the pupil. Unfortunately, the multiplicity of habits acquired by SpLD children requires quite drastic action and there was a clear need in the school for hand-writing

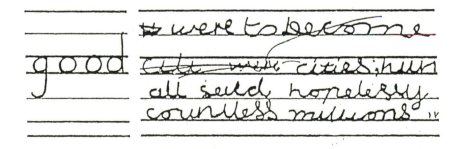

Figure 18.8 Printing on 4 mm/16 mm Guides and Writing Between the Lines

guides. These were designed to favour the development of a very efficient handwriting style which would transfer without further learning — or more importantly *un*learning! — to the standard 8mm blue-feint exercise paper. They would also permit recourse to unisensory learning of letter strings by blind-writing where a child had specific difficulty or wished to improve efficiency of response on vocabularly and spelling tests.

The conventional handwriting practice paper for infants and lower juniors, usually comprises double lines 5mm apart centred on red or blue guidelines 22mm apart (other variants noted — 4mm/16mm, 5mm/19mm). These had been found to be quite inappropriate, having been designed for large printing rather than the smaller-sized cursive writing (see Figure 18.8), and also because it invites children to write entirely between the guides in order to produce a more 'natural' or 'mature' size writing (also Figure 18.8).

An analysis of handwriting in older children in the school and also from school exercise books dating back as far as the early nineteenth century revealed a strong measure of agreement on the ratios between and sizes of letter-bodies (the c shape in d etc.), ascenders (from the line) and descenders (from the line), the standard wide feint of approximately 8mm being used throughout to the present day.

In comparison with adult fluent writers, it was noted that many of the SpLD (specific literacy difficulties) children foreshortened certain letters with ascenders or descenders, 't' for example which was also crossed very low. Incidentally, the occurrence of this phenomenon is regarded by many graphologists as indicative of a feeling of subordination (e.g. Singer, 1969, p. 189). The next stage was to devise a handwriting guide using a single hairline as base, with shading rather than line boundaries for the ascender and descender zones as is found in the infant printing guides. Trial guide papers in black on white suggested that 10 per cent shading provided an adequate guide which would be visible but unobtrusive (see Figure 18.9). From analysis of the boundary transgressions on a further trial printing of 9mm feint guide paper in Process Blue, two further scalings were produced, 8.7mm and 8.2mm, to accommodate preferences for large and small script.

Figure 18.9 Handwriting Guides, 8.7mm Feint

Instead of presenting the task as one requiring slow laborious calligraphy, the children were required to write quickly in order that the suitability of the guides, in terms of scale and proportions, could be ascertained. A range of conventional medium or fine nibbed fountain pens (including Fountain

Pentel) was used, writing with ballpoints and others being found to lack leadstroke-downstroke differentiation and neatness. All children gained in fluency using the guides, though the experiment was conducted in the school context and was not controlled. There was a further increase in fluency and also reported satisfaction when the 8.2mm format was printed in Reflex Blue on a good quality 100gm paper. In copying a well-known text, M, a 13-year-old new placement in school when the handwriting guides were introduced, increased his fluency from thirty-one characters per minute using a printed hand to seventy-six characters per minute in cursive hand (see Figure 18.10). A typical example of M's printed style a few months prior is given for comparison

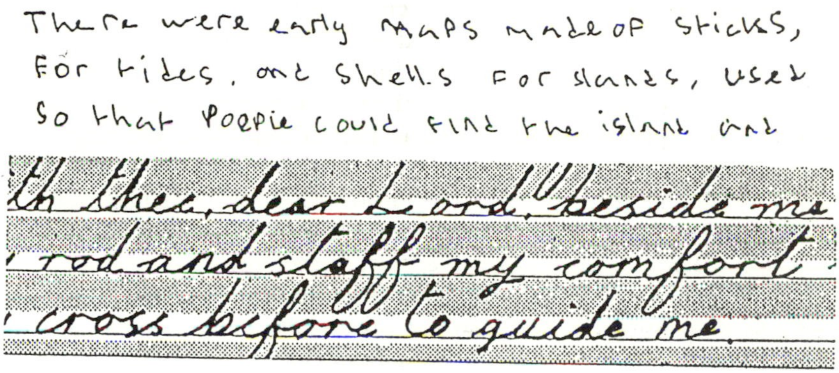

Figure 18.10   M: Copying onto 9.0mm Guides

Similarly, W, a left-hander noted for illegibility and slow production, increased his writing rate from thirty-two to sixty-eight cpm in copying (see Figure 18.11).

Figure 18.11   W: Copying onto 9.0mm Guides (Left-hand)

Using a professional publishing system of the production of 'hard copy' theoretically allows the production of exercise paper with different size guides to suit individuals, but the question arises as to how far one should go in designing individual guides for beginners when the aim is ultimately to standardize handwriting on the 8mm feint. So far, the consensus amongst teachers at the school is that two scales should be available, 9mm or 8.7mm for those whose initial attempts indicate a need for such and 8.2mm for those whose writing is naturally small enough to be directed towards the standard 8mm unguided feint. Most noticeable has been the effect of the handwriting initiative on the regularity of letter bodies (c, o, the c in the letter d or g etc.) and in the lengthening of the ascenders and descenders when the children are writing without the guides. There has also been an improvement towards uniformity of slope. Further work with more stringent recording is, however, necessary in these aspects. Experimentation is also taking place in the best writing load per page of the special exercise paper and also into the incorporation of handwriting practice into subject areas in the curriculum, using the specially printed handwriting books for short answer tests etc. where speed is important. Tachistoscopic presentation of words (from slides onto a screen) from subject vocabularies, followed by writing, seems to be quite an enjoyable activity, even amongst older pupils. The majority of SpLD children have low self-image, printed handwriting such as that of M (see Figure 18.10) being perceived by teachers, parents, peers and themselves as immature and inferior. Controlled cursive writing therefore not only enhances fluency of expression but is associated with enhanced self-image and confidence.

Whilst there is an obvious advantage in conducting such experiments in a school environment, a greater advantage accrues from children being in a closed environment of a specialist school with others who have failed and have perceived themselves to have failed in 'normal' education, there being an 'all in the same boat' attitude which favours trial of new ideas and methods. The work described above, however, would have been impossible even two years ago, before modern technology put near-professional printing quality at the behest of the teacher-researcher, with the ability to recast and redevelop materials very quickly in response to emergent or contingent demands.

Conclusion

The purpose of this paper has been to give a brief outline of the unisensory principle leading to an account of its application to an area of learning difficulty not originally envisaged, followed by its development from a clinical to an educational application. It is an account of some of the ways in which the different perception entailed by the acceptance or trial of an innovation restructures observation and intervention. The original research, conducted at the University of Aston from 1974 to 1978 is perhaps unusual not only in that two possible treatment regimes were compared with placebo and non-treatment controls, but also in that the principles underlying the treatment of the literacy difficulties described were derived from studies of the attentional styles of children with literacy difficulties and complexity of the written language they were required to master. Such a theoretically-based approach, the writer would maintain, is a promising one compared with the approach of evaluating techniques, for the most part eclectic, derived and refined from teaching experience.

In academic terms, an approach to the remediation of such controversial difficulties as dyslexia and dysgraphia in the educational context might and should be judged on its intellectual integrity and cohesiveness with other areas of psychology, especially attention and skill-learning, and other disciplines. There is much commercial investment and vested interest in conventional approaches and their attendant publications. The writer's unisensory principle and the 'icon' method were researched and presented at a time when state education was at its least receptive. At that time, proliferating dyslexia agencies were exclusively and effectively promoting the phonics-cum-multisensory approach to remediation despite considerable criticism from the many professional psychologists in the education service who were known to the writer. The writer took the unusual step of opening a specialist school combined with a research centre and subjecting the ideas and their application to the scrutiny of the Department of Education and Science under the 1981 Education Act. The value of the unisensory principle to the writer lies in prompting new perceptions of a wide variety of individual children's learning problems and their solutions, being applied successfully to children's specific difficulties in literacy with implications for and effects on the pupil's attainment in other subjects.

It is suggested that a radical shift of emphasis is needed in research so that the interaction between the child, task requirements and instructional set is investigated. The phonics-cum-multisensory approach to early instruction and to remediation of SpLD or (educational) dyslexia appears to have become the convention, but there is a dearth of objective research into its effectiveness. In education, the 'Hawthorne effect' is notoriously difficulty to control. The writer's view is that where the phonics-cum-multisensory approach is successful, it is so insofar as the intensive tuition imparts a clear *unisensory* instructional set to specific acts of learning. The suggested radical shift of emphasis entails a reappraisal of the effectiveness and underlying rationale of early literacy teaching in general.

References

Bishop, D. V. M. and Robson, J. (1989) 'Accurate non-word spelling despite congenital inability to speak: phoneme-grapheme conversion does not require subvocal articulation', *British Journal of Psychology*, 80, pp. 1–13.

Brereton, A. (1988) 'The Statement — a check list', in Millich, L. C. and Sheldon, E. *I'm edukationable*, London.

Brown, E. N. (1979) 'Coding strategies and reading comprehension', in Friedman, M. P., Das, J. P. and O'Connor, N. (Eds) *Intelligence and Learning*, Plenum, New York.

Brown, E. N. (1980) 'Attentional style, linguistic complexity and the treatment of reading difficulty', in Knights, R. M. and Bakker, D. (Eds) *Treatment of Hyperactive and Learning-Disordered Children*, Park Press, New York.

Clay, M. M. (1968) 'A syntactic analysis of reading errors', *Journal of Verbal Learning and Verbal Behaviour*, 7, pp. 434–438.

Clay, M. M. (1969) 'Reading errors and self-correction behaviour', *British Journal of Educational Psychology*, 39, pp. 47–56.

Francis, H. (1984) 'Children's knowledge of orthography in learning to read', *British Journal of Educational Psychology*, 54, pp. 8–23.

Goodman, K. S. (1967) 'Reading, a psycholinguistic guessing game', *Journal of the Reading Specialist*, May, pp. 126–135.

Heaton, P. and Winterson, P. (1986) *Dealing with Dyslexia*, Better Books, Bath.

Hornsby, B. (1984) *Overcoming Dyslexia*, Dunitz, London.

Hynds, J. (1987) 'Diagnosing dyslexia', *Gnosis*, 10, March, pp. 19–23.

Marshall, J. C. (1984) 'Towards a rational taxonomy of developmental dyslexia', in Malatesha, R. N. and Whitaker, H. A. (Eds) *Dyslexia: A Global Issue*, Nijhoff, The Hague.

Murray, L. A. and Maliphant, R. (1982) 'Developmental aspects of the use of linguistic and graphemic information during reading', *British Journal of Educational Psychology*, 52, pp. 155–169.

Senf, G. M. (1969) 'Development of immediate memory for bisensory stimuli in normal children with learning disorders', *Developmental Psychology Monograph*, 1, 6, p. 2.

Singer, E. (1969) *A Manual of Graphology*, London, Treasure Press.

Further Reading

LaBerge, D. and Samuels, S. J. (1974) 'Towards a theory of automatic information processing in reading', *Cognitive Psychology*, 6, pp. 293–323.

Kinsbourne, M. (1988) 'Developmental language and learning problems', *Journal of Neurolinguistics*, 3, 1, pp. 1–27.

Samuels, S. J. and LaBerge, D. (1983) 'Critique of a theory of automaticity in reading: looking back — a retrospective analysis of the LaBerge–Samuels reading model', in Gentile, L. M., Kamil, M. L. and Blanchard, J. S. (Eds) *Reading Research Revisited*, Columbus, Ohio, Charles E. Merrill.

Notes on Contributors

Helen Arnold is a consultant and lecturer. Her address is Flint Cottage, 55 Westley Waterless, Newmarket, Suffolk CB8 0RQ

Dr Lynette Bradley is Research Officer at the Department of Experimental Psychology, South Parks Road, Oxford OX1 3UD

Dr Neville Brown is Principal, Maple Hayes Dyslexia School and Research Centre, Abnalls Lane, Lichfield, Staffordshire WS13 8BL

Dr Peter Bryant is Watts Professor of Psychology, Department of Experimental Psychology, South Parks Road, Oxford OX1 3UD

Asher Cashdan is Professor of Communication Studies, Sheffield City Polytechnic, 36 Collegiate Crescent, Sheffield S10 2BP

Suzanne Cataldo is presently pursuing postgraduate research on reading and spelling at the Department of Psychology, University College of North Wales, Bangor, Gwynedd LL57 2DG

Dr Harry Chasty is Director of Studies, The Dyslexia Institute, 133 Gresham Road, Staines, Middlesex TW18 2AJ

Dr Colin Elliott is Senior Lecturer in Education, Centre for Educational Guidance and Special Needs, School of Education, University of Manchester, Manchester M13 9PL

Dr Nick Ellis is Lecturer in Cognitive Psychology, Department of Psychology, University College of North Wales, Bangor, Gwynedd LL57 2DG

Maria Farrer is London RSA Course Tutor in Specific Learning Difficulties. She can be contacted at the Hornsby Dyslexia Centre, 71 Wandsworth Common, Westside, London SW18 2ED

Dr Beve Hornsby is Director of the Hornsby Dyslexia Centre, 71 Wandsworth Common, Westside, London SW18 2ED

Morag Hunter-Carsch is Lecturer in Education, University of Leicester School of Education, 21 University Road, Leicester LE1 7RF

Dr Colin Lane is Head of the Special Unit, Hugh Sexey Middle School, Blackford, Wedmore, Somerset BS28 4ND

Dr David Moseley is Reader in Educational Psychology, Department of Psychology, 4th Floor, Claremont Place, Newcastle-upon-Tyne NE1 7RU

Peter Pumfrey is Reader in Education, Centre for Educational Guidance and Special Needs, School of Education, University of Manchester, Manchester M13 9PL

Rea Reason is Senior Educational Psychologist for Oldham LEA and Tutor for Professor Training in Educational Psychology, Centre for Educational Guidance and Special Needs, School of Education, University of Manchester, Manchester M13 9PL

Dr Margaret Snowling is Principal, National Hospitals College of Speech Sciences, Chandler House, 2 Wakefield Street, London WC1N 1PG

Dr Michael Thomson is Co-principal, East Court School, Victoria Parade, Ramsgate, Kent CT11 8ED

Dr Stephen Tyler is Educational Psychologist, Stockport Metropolitan Borough Education Department, Town Hall, Stockport SK1 3XE

Judith Wright is Senior Lecturer in Education, Edge Hill College of Higher Education, Ormskirk, Lancashire L39 4QP

Subject Index

activity-centred learning   218–20
Adult Literacy Basic Skills Unit   4
alliteration   65–7, 69
  reading skills   147
  tasks   87–8
alphabetic
  phase   126, 130, 135, 138
  rhymes   94, 98–9
  script   68–9
  stage   101–3, 110, 122
  system   64, 69, 84–5, 209, 226
anarthria   292
Aptitude × Instruction Interactions
  AII   200
articulation   101
articulatory
  -motor programmes   132
  rehearsal loop   103, 112, 273
Assessment of Performance Unit   10
assessment techniques   54–7, 187, 191–8
attitudes to learning   145
  see also motivation
auditory
  -lexical representation   132
  organization   106
  stage   147
  training   244–5
Aurally Coded English (ACE)
  Dictionary   256, 259, 265
Aural-Read-Respond-Oral-Written
  (ARROW)   237, 246–8
automaticity in learning   274–6, 283
awareness training   149

behavioural problems   4, 229–30, 284
British Ability Scales (BAS)   34, 161
British Dyslexia Association   23–4

child-centred language   240–1
children's
  individual ability   4
  learning   246
    difficulties   51, 85
    see also learning difficulties
    specific learning difficulties
  metacognition   148
  pre-school experience   63–4
  rhyming   83–4, 86, 88
classroom organization and ARROW   253
cloze procedures   201–3, 213, 243
cognitive psychology   43–5, 49–50,
  156–7, 160
  and development   126–7, 153
communication   45–6, 187, 192, 231–2
comprehension, reading   210–11
computer assisted learning   257–8
consonants   76–8, 212
  -Vowel-Consonant (C-V-C)   105, 107
content, meaning of   235
corrective procedures in ARROW   246
cue systems   290
culture and education   47–8
curriculum   84, 243
  Specific Learning Difficulties and   271,
  286–7

deaf children   249, 292
deciphering skills   102, 111
deletion strategies   201–2, 274
  see also cloze procedures
developmental arrest   137–40
dictionaries, personal spelling   265
Directed Activities Related to Text
  (DARTS)   212
dysarthria   292

Name Index